Free Will

Marco Hausmann • Jörg Noller
Editors

Free Will

Historical and Analytic Perspectives

Editors
Marco Hausmann
Philosophy
Ludwig Maximilian University of Munich
Munich, Germany

Jörg Noller
Philosophy
Ludwig Maximilian University of Munich
Munich, Germany

ISBN 978-3-030-61135-4   ISBN 978-3-030-61136-1   (eBook)
https://doi.org/10.1007/978-3-030-61136-1

This Palgrave Macmillan imprint is published by the registered company Springer Nature Switzerland AG.
The registered company address is: Gewerbestrasse 11, 6330 Cham, Switzerland

Contents

Notes on Contributors

Helen Beebee is Samuel Hall Professor of Philosophy at the University of Manchester, UK. She has published widely on Humean theories of causation and laws, and on free will. Her books include *Hume on Causation* (2006), *Free Will: An Introduction* (Palgrave 2013), and, with Michael Rush, *Philosophy: Why It Matters* (2019).

Claudia Blöser is a postdoctoral researcher at Goethe University Frankfurt. She has specialized in practical philosophy, broadly construed, including the history of ethics (mainly Kant), moral psychology (especially forgiveness, hope, and philosophy of the emotions in general), and practical rationality. She is the author of the book *Zurechnung bei Kant* (2014).

Thomas Buchheim is Professor of Metaphysics and Ontology at the Ludwig Maximilian University of Munich. He is the author of numerous contributions on freedom of the will from a historical and analytic point of view, including his book *Unser Verlangen nach Freiheit* (2006).

John Martin Fischer is Distinguished Professor of Philosophy at the University of California, Riverside, where he held a University of California President's Chair. He is University Professor in the University of California system. He is the author and co-author of several books on free will and moral responsibility, including *The Metaphysics of Free Will:*

An Essay on Control (1994), *Responsibility and Control: A Theory of Moral Responsibility* (1998), and *Four Views on Free Will* (2007). Many of his several articles on free will and moral responsibility can be found in a trilogy of collections of his essays: "My Way: Essays on Moral Responsibility" (2006), "Our Stories: Essays on Life, Death, and Free Will" (2009), and "Deep Control: Essays on Free Will and Values" (2012).

Dorothea Frede is Professor Emerita at the University of Hamburg and Honorary Professor at the Humboldt University at Berlin. She also taught as Mills Adjunct Professor at the University of California Berkeley from 2006 to 2011. Her main publications include *Aristoteles und die Seeschlacht* (1970); *Plato, Philebus*, translation with introduction and notes (1993); *Platon, Philebos*, translation and commentary (1997); *Platon, Phaidon* (1999); *Aristoteles, Nikomachische Ethik*, translation and commentary (2020); many articles and contributions to books on Plato, Aristotle, Hellenistic philosophy, and the philosophy of Martin Heidegger.

Marco Hausmann is Lecturer in Philosophy at the University of Munich, Germany. He is the author of the papers "The Consequence Argument Ungrounded" (*Synthese*, 2018), "Against Kripke's Solution to the Problem of Negative Existentials" (*Analysis*, 2019), and "The Consequence of the Consequence Argument" (*Kriterion*, forthcoming). His research interests include metaphysics, logic, and the philosophy of language, freedom, and religion.

Julia Jorati is Associate Professor of Philosophy at the University of Massachusetts Amherst and works mainly on the history of early modern philosophy. She has published several articles about Leibniz and is the author of the book *Leibniz on Causation and Agency* (2017).

Jörg Noller is Lecturer in Philosophy at the University of Munich, Germany. He is the author and editor of a number of books and articles on freedom from a historical and systematic perspective, including *Die Bestimmung des Willens* (2016), "Kant and Reinhold's Dilemma" (*EJP*, 2019), and "Schiller on Freedom of the Will" (*EJP*, 2020). His research interests include metaphysics, freedom, personhood, and German Idealism.

Thomas Pink is Professor of Philosophy at King's College London, London. He works on the philosophy of mind and action; on ethics, political, and legal philosophy; and on the history of these subjects. He is the author of the books *The Psychology of Freedom* (1996), *Free Will: A Very Short Introduction* (2004), as well as *Self-determination: The Ethics of Action* (2016).

Nicholas Rescher is Distinguished University Professor of Philosophy at the University of Pittsburgh and Chairman of the Center for Philosophy of Science. He is the author and editor of more than 100 books, including *Free Will. A Philosophical Reappraisal, 2nd ed.* (2009).

Carolina Sartorio is Professor of Philosophy at the University of Arizona. She works at the intersection of metaphysics, philosophy of action, and moral theory. She is the author of several articles on free will and moral responsibility, as well as of the books *Causation and Free Will* (2016) and (with Robert Kane) *Do We Have Free Will? A Debate* ("Little Debates About Big Questions" series, Routledge, forthcoming).

Helen Steward is Professor of Philosophy of Mind and Action at the University of Leeds. Before moving to Leeds, she was Fellow and Tutor in Philosophy at Balliol College, Oxford, for 14 years. Her interests lie mainly in the philosophy of action and free will, the philosophy of mind, and the metaphysical and ontological issues which bear on these areas (e.g., causation, supervenience, levels of explanation, the event/state distinction, the concepts of process and power). She has also worked on the category of animality and on understandings of the human being which take seriously our membership of the animal kingdom.

Peter van Inwagen is John Cardinal O'Hara Professor of Philosophy Emeritus at the University of Notre Dame and is Research Professor of Philosophy at Duke University. He works in many areas of philosophy, but much of his work has been in metaphysics, the philosophy of action, and the philosophy of religion. His books include *An Essay on Free Will* (1983), *Material Beings* (1990), and *The Problem of Evil* (2006). A collection of many of his essays on free will has recently appeared: *Thinking About Free Will* (2017). He was elected to the American Academy of Arts and Sciences in 2005.

1

Introduction

Marco Hausmann and Jörg Noller

1 Aims and Scope

There are few topics, if any, that have received more attention throughout the history of philosophy than the topic of free will. In the last years, the problem of free will has received special attention in the analytic debate. It is not surprising, therefore, that a significant number of anthologies about free will have recently been published. However, while there are anthologies that attempt to shed light on the free will problem from an analytic perspective (see, for example, Watson 2003, Kane 2002, 2011, Campbell et al. 2004) or from an interdisciplinary perspective (see, for example, Swinburne 2011, Mele 2014, McCann 2017), hardly any anthology takes historical perspectives on the problem into account (see Timpe et al. 2017 and McCann 2017 for an exception), and hardly any anthology tries to advance the debate by combining historical and analytic perspectives. This book attempts to fill this gap.

M. Hausmann (✉) • J. Noller
Philosophy, Ludwig Maximilian University of Munich, Munich, Germany
e-mail: joerg.noller@lrz.uni-muenchen.de

© The Author(s), under exclusive license to Springer Nature Switzerland AG 2021   1
M. Hausmann, J. Noller (eds.), *Free Will*,
https://doi.org/10.1007/978-3-030-61136-1_1

The aim of this book is not to give a survey on the history of the problem. Instead, this book aims to advance the current debate by bridging the divide between more analytically and more historically oriented approaches to the problem. It aims to initiate a philosophical discourse that profits from both areas of research. On the one hand, the analytical tools that are familiar from the current debate can be used to sharpen our understanding of classical philosophical positions. On the other hand, the rich philosophical tradition can be reconstructed so as to inspire new solutions to the problem and thereby advance the current debate. For this reason, this volume does not only comprise either purely analytic or purely historical contributions. For the most part, this volume comprises chapters that attempt to look at historical positions from the vantage point of recent discussions or, alternatively, chapters that build on ideas that can be found in the history of philosophy in order to contribute to the current debate.

2   The Problem(s) of Free Will

The debate about free will has been thought to be significant at least in part because moral responsibility has been thought to require free will. The idea is that, in order to be morally responsible for what one has done, what one has done has to be (or has to result from) an exercise of free will. The debate has mainly focused on two alleged necessary conditions for having free will: being the *ultimate cause* of one's own actions and having the *ability to act otherwise*.

In the discussion, many arguments have been put forward to cast doubt on the assumption that we are the *ultimate cause* of our own actions. It has been argued, in particular, that the assumption is in tension with the principle of the *causal closure of the physical*, with *causal determinism* (or, equivalently, with the principle of *universal causation*) as well as with *causal indeterminism*. According to the principle of the causal closure of the physical, every cause of something physical is itself something physical.[1] However, we are only the ultimate cause of our own actions, if we (or our beliefs, desires, and motives)[2] are the *cause* of our actions. Further, we (or our beliefs, desires, and motives) appear to be mental (and, therefore, *not* physical) while our actions appear to be physical. Therefore, if every cause of something physical is itself something physical, we (or our beliefs, desires, and motives) are not the cause and, a fortiori, not the ultimate cause of our actions.

The problem of causal determinism and causal indeterminism usually takes the form of a dilemma: if, as causal determinism has it, *everything* has a cause (including us and our beliefs, desires, and motives), then we (or our beliefs, desires, and motives) are not the *ultimate* cause of our actions. If, on the other hand, our actions have *no cause at all* and are, therefore, causally undetermined, then we (or our beliefs, desires, and motives) are not the cause and, a fortiori, not the ultimate cause of our own actions. Further, even if we (or our beliefs, desires, and motives) were the *uncaused cause* of our own actions, then, given that we (or our beliefs, desires, and motives) have *no cause at all*, our actions would still appear to be nothing but random and capricious "bolts from the blue"— surely not the kind of actions that should count as genuine exercises of free will.

Likewise, many arguments have been put forward to cast doubt on the assumption that we have the *ability to act otherwise*. It has been argued, in particular, that the assumption is in tension with *logical, theological, nomological, and ethical determinism* as well as with *nomological indeterminism*. According to logical determinism, if something is true, it has already been true in the past that it will be true. According to theological determinism, if something is true, God has already known in the past that it will be true. Thus, according to logical and theological determinism, our actions are *entailed by the past*. For, according to logical and theological determinism, if it is true that we act the way we do, the proposition that we act the way we do is entailed by a true proposition about the past (the proposition that it has already been true in the past that we will act the way we do, or the proposition that God already knew in the past that we will act the way we do). Therefore, if we were able to act otherwise, we would be able to falsify a true proposition about the past. This, however, appears to be impossible (intuitively, nobody is able to change the past). The assumption that we have the ability to act otherwise, therefore, is in tension with logical and theological determinism.

There is a similar argument when it comes to nomological determinism. According to nomological determinism, every truth is entailed by a past state of the universe together with the laws of nature. Thus, according to nomological determinism, our actions are *entailed by the past and the laws*. Consequently, if it is true that we act the way we do, the proposition that we act the way we do is entailed by a true proposition about the past (a proposition that describes a past state of the universe) together with a true proposition about the laws of nature. Therefore, if we were able to act otherwise, we would be able to falsify a true proposition about the past or a true proposition about the laws of nature. This, however, appears to be impossible (intuitively, nobody is able to change the past or able to break the laws). The assumption that we have the ability to act otherwise, therefore, is in tension with nomological determinism.

The assumption that we have the ability to act otherwise is, further, in tension with ethical determinism. According to ethical determinism, we act the way we do because of the way we are (because of our character). It seems, therefore, that we would only be able to act otherwise if we were able to change our character. This, however, might seem to be false (it might seem, intuitively, that nobody is able to change his or her own character). For it might seem that, in order to be able to change our character, we would have to be able to act "out of character," and it might seem that we are not able to act "out of character." For this reason, there is a tension between the assumption that we have the ability to act otherwise and ethical determinism.

Finally, the assumption that we have the ability to act or that we have the ability to act otherwise is in tension with *nomological indeterminism* (or, at any rate, with the assumption that our actions are nomologically undetermined). The idea is that having the ability to act (or having the ability to act otherwise) requires a certain amount of control over whether we act or whether we act otherwise—an amount of control that we do not have if our actions are nomologically undetermined. For if our actions are nomologically undetermined, then it is not entailed by a past state of the universe and the laws of nature that we act the way we do: given the past and the laws, we might act the way we do and we might as well act otherwise. It appears to be a pure matter of chance, therefore, whether we act the way we do, or whether we act otherwise. We, therefore, appear to have neither the ability to act, nor the ability to act otherwise. Thus, there is a tension between nomological indeterminism and the assumption that we have the ability to act or that we have the ability to act otherwise.

3 Proposed Solutions to the Problem(s) of Free Will

There are, of course, many solutions that have been proposed in order to solve these problems. In what follows, only a selection of the most prominent solutions will be presented.

When faced with the threat of causal determinism (or the principle of universal causation), some philosophers have distinguished between causes that necessitate their effects and causes that merely incline their effects—a distinction that goes back at least to Leibniz (Theodicy § 288)—and have claimed that free will is only incompatible with the view that everything has a *necessitating cause* but not with the view that everything has a *merely inclining cause.*

Still other philosophers, such as Thomas Aquinas (Summa Theologiae I q. 83 a. 1), have been prepared to deny that one has to be the *ultimate* cause of one's own actions in order to have free will (what is required, according to these philosophers, is only to be a cause, but not to be the *ultimate* cause, of one's own actions).

With respect to the dilemma of causal determinism and causal indeterminism, philosophers have sometimes distinguished between *two types of causation* (Chisholm 1964): the type of causation where an *event* causes an event to happen (e.g., where the motion of the first billiard ball causes the motion of the second billiard ball), and the type of causation where an *agent* causes an event to happen (e.g., where an agent causes the motion of the first billiard ball). These philosophers insist that, in order to be *ultimate* cause of one's own actions, an *agent* (as opposed to events that merely happen "inside" the agent) has to be the uncaused cause of his or her own actions and that this is all that is needed in order to genuinely exercise free will.

The threat of the causal closure of the physical, by contrast, has been met by questioning the assumption that something mental cannot be something physical (Davidson 1980; Kim 1993), as well as by questioning the assumption that a cause of something physical has always to be itself something physical (Yablo 1992).

When it comes to logical and theological determinism, philosophers have followed Ockham who distinguished between propositions that are about a time "as regards both their wording and their subject matter" and between propositions that are about a time "as regards their wording only" (Predestination, God's Foreknowledge, and Future Contingents, q. 1). The idea is that some propositions *really are* only about the past (such as the proposition that Leibniz was born in 1646) while other propositions *only appear to be* only about the past and are, instead, in part about the future as well (such as the proposition that Leibniz was born 400 years before traffic on earth will become completely climate neutral). According to these philosophers, propositions such as the proposition that it has already been true in the past (or that God already knew in the past) that we will act the way we do *appear* to be only about the past but are, instead, in part about the future as well. There is, therefore, no reason to assume that we are *not* able to falsify these propositions and, therefore, no reason to assume that there is a tension between logical or theological determinism and the assumption that we are able to act otherwise.

In response to the problem of nomological determinism, many philosophers have followed David Lewis (1981) in distinguishing between a weak and a strong sense in which we are able to falsify a law of nature: roughly, we are able to falsify a law of nature *in a strong sense* if and only if we are able to act in such a way that, if we did act that way, a law of nature would have been broken by our act (that is, if and only if we are able to *break* a law of nature) and we are able to falsify a law of nature *in a weak sense* if and only if we are able to act in such a way that, if we did act that way, a law of nature would have been broken (though not necessarily by our act). These philosophers claim that, if nomological determinism were true and we were able to act otherwise, then we would still *not* be able to falsify a law of nature in the strong sense (that is, we would still *not* be able to *break* a law of nature). We would, instead, only be able to falsify a law of nature in the weak sense (which, according to these philosophers, is unproblematic). There is, therefore, no reason to assume that there is a tension between nomological determinism and the assumption that we are able to act otherwise.

The problem of ethical determinism rests on two assumptions. First, that, in order to be able to change our character, we would have to be able to act "out of character." Second, that we are not able act "out of character." Philosophers have questioned both assumptions. Schelling, for example, has suggested that it might be part of our character not to refuse to accept external help when put in the right kind of situation and, then, part of our character to *change* our character with the help of others (Philosophical Inquiries into the Essence of Human Freedom I, 7 389). His suggestion is that, in such a situation, we might act in perfect accordance with our character *by changing our character*. Philosophers have denied, moreover, that we are not able to act "out of character." Sartre's dictum that existence precedes essence, and his assertion that, before defining oneself and before being what one has made of oneself, one is nothing (Existentialism is a Humanism), need not but may be read as the assertion that one *has* to act "out of character", in order to acquire one's character.

The reason why nomological indeterminism is thought to be problematic is that it is thought that, if our actions are nomologically undetermined, then, given the past and the laws, we *might* act the way we do, and we *might* as well act otherwise. Philosophers have denied this assumption. They have, perhaps inspired by Molina (Concordia IV disp. 52 par. 9), held that, even if our actions are nomologically undetermined, we *would* act the way we do given the particular situation in which we find ourselves (given the past and the laws). It is false, according to these philosophers, that we *might* as well act otherwise given the particular situation in which we find ourselves (given the past and the laws). There is, therefore, no reason to assume that it would be a pure matter of chance, whether we act the way we do or whether we act otherwise, and, therefore, no reason to assume that there is a tension between our having free will and nomological indeterminism.

Finally, in the debate about free will, it has often been tacitly assumed that we are only morally responsible for our actions if our actions are (or result from) an exercise of free will. This has recently and influentially been denied (at least on the assumption that having free will requires having the ability to act otherwise). Harry Frankfurt (1969) has argued that we might be responsible for our actions even if we have not been able to act otherwise (as long as we have acted "on our own"). Following Frankfurt, many philosophers have argued that we might still be morally responsible for what we have done, even if, for whatever reason, what we have done is not (and does not result from) an exercise of free will.

It goes without saying that all proposed solutions are still controversial and that the debate about free will is, therefore, far from having come to an end.

4   Overview of the Contributions

The contributions of this book aim, for the most part, to advance the debate about free will by drawing on ideas that can be found in the history of philosophy. The book is divided into three sections. The first section focuses on free will and determinism, the second on free will and indeterminism, and the third on free will and moral responsibility.

In the first section, problems concerning free will and various versions of determinism are addressed. Nowadays, many participants of the debate define determinism in terms of entailment. In her chapter "What Is Determinism? Why We Should Ditch the Entailment Definition," Helen Steward questions that assumption. Steward argues that what most participants of the debate have in mind when they talk about determinism ought *not* to be defined in terms of entailment, but rather in terms of metaphysical necessitation. According to Steward, the attempt to define determinism in terms of entailment (instead of necessitation) can be traced back to Hume's skepticism about necessitation as an objective relation between things (or state of affairs). However, as Steward points out, not only is Hume's skepticism coming more and more under attack (and getting more and more replaced by ideas that allow to make sense of necessitation), a definition of determinism in terms of necessitation would, for various reasons, allow to make much more sense of the current debate than a definition of determinism in terms of entailment.

According to Dorothea Frede's chapter "Aristotle and the Discovery of Determinism," Aristotle can not only be seen as the discoverer of three different variants of determinism—logical determinism, physical determinism, and ethical determinism—he can also be seen as an important proponent of the view that we can be responsible for our actions and that our actions, therefore, can be "up to us." As Frede explains, Aristotle is prepared to deny that what is true has already been true in the past (and, thereby, to deny logical determinism). He, further, rejects the view that every natural event is the *inevitable* result of prior events and the laws of nature (and, thereby, rejects physical determinism). For although Aristotle subscribes to the view that every natural event has a cause, he holds that something from outside of a causal chain can always interrupt a causal chain and, thereby, prevent the natural course of events from happening. Finally, Aristotle does not reject the view that our actions depend on our character (that is, he does not reject ethical determinism). What Aristotle rejects is, rather, the reasoning that our actions are not "up to us" because our actions depend on our character and our character is not "up to us." For, in Aristotle's view, we can, at least to a certain extent, change our character.

Many problems concerning free will rest on the assumption that having free will requires having the ability to act otherwise. Drawing on Locke's example of a person who, of his own free will, remains in a locked room, Nicholas Rescher ("Defending Free Will") argues against the assumption that having free will requires having the ability to act otherwise. In his view, exercising free will requires only acting in virtue of one's own, appropriately formed, motives. He argues, further, that having free will is not only compatible with our actions being causally determined (that is, with our action's having a cause) but also with our actions resulting from a causal chain with *infinitely many causes*. For, as Rescher argues based on Zeno's paradoxes, a causal chain with infinitely many causes need not trace back to the distant past (contrary to what is usually supposed)—as long as the temporal distance between the causal steps gets ever shorter.

As has already been pointed out, one might, inspired by Ockham, distinguish between propositions that *really are* only about the past and propositions that *only appear to be* only about the past. Further, nomological determinism (as well as theological determinism) appears to be only in tension with our having free will, if there are propositions that completely describe a past state of the universe (as well as propositions that describe God's knowledge) that *really are* only about the past. Marco Hausmann ("Some Free Thinking About 'Thinking About Free Will'") takes issue with the assumption that such propositions *really are* only about the past. He argues that many philosophical views (the view that necessarily equivalent propositions are identical, the view that proper names are abbreviations for definite descriptions, and the view that there is no such thing as the past) as well as independent arguments strongly suggest that propositions that completely describe a past state of the universe (as well as propositions that describe God's knowledge) *only appear to be* only about the past.

Following David Lewis, many philosophers have distinguished between a weak and a strong sense of having the ability to falsify a law of nature and have argued that there is no incompatibility between nomological determinism and having the ability to act otherwise, because, if nomological determinism is true, having the ability to act otherwise implies only to be able to falsify a law of nature in the weak sense (it implies *not* to be able to falsify a law of nature in the strong sense). John Martin Fischer questions this line of reasoning. In his chapter "Local-Miracle Compatibilism: A Critique," he points out, first, that one might still appeal to the principle of the fixity of the past and laws (PFPL) according to which one is only able to act otherwise, if there is a possible world with the same past as the actual past and the same laws as the actual laws in which one acts otherwise. For, if nomological determinism is true, there is no such possible world and one is, accordingly, *not* able to act otherwise. It is, therefore, still plausible to maintain that having the ability to act otherwise *is* incompatible with nomological determinism (quite apart from the distinction between a weak and a strong sense of having the ability to falsify a law of nature). He argues, second, that, if one would reject the principle of the fixity of the past and laws (PFPL), one might, in certain contexts, be committed to implausible attributions of rationality to certain decisions as well as to implausible attributions of abilities to certain agents.

Thus, Fischer argues that rejecting the principle of the fixity of the past and laws (PFPL) might turn out to be problematic. Helen Beebee ("Backtracking Counterfactuals and Agent's Abilities") questions Fischer's arguments. For, according to Beebee, there is a variant of Lewis's strategy to reconcile nomological determinism with our having the ability to act otherwise that can be defended despite of Fischer's arguments. According to this variant of Lewis's strategy, if nomological determinism were true and we were able to act otherwise, we would neither be able to *break* the laws nor able to *change* the past; we would, at most, be able to act in such a way that, if we did act that way, the past would have been different. Beebee argues that Fischer's arguments fail to undermine this variant of Lewis's strategy.

In her chapter "Moral Necessity, Agent Causation, and the Determination of Free Actions in Clarke and Leibniz," Julia Jorati challenges the standard interpretation, according to which Samuel Clarke holds a libertarian, indeterminist, and incompatibilist theory of free will, whereas Gottfried Wilhelm Leibniz proposes a compatibilist account. Jorati argues that this standard interpretation is wrong. She shows that both philosophers attempt to find a middle way between Spinoza's necessitarianism and Hobbes's weak compatibilism, and the Molinist account of indifferentism and voluntarism. Therefore, both Clarke and Leibniz can be regarded as compatibilists about free will and determinism.

The second section focuses on free will and indeterminism. Although, according to Carolina Sartorio ("Indeterministic Compatibilism"), we are only responsible for what we have done, if what we have done is *caused* in the right kind of way, our having free will and being responsible for what we have done is still compatible with indeterminism. For even given indeterminism, as Sartorio explains, what we have done might still be *caused*, roughly, by reasons as well as by the absence of reasons for acting otherwise—although, presumably, only *probabilistically caused*. There are specific problems that might arise once the notion of probabilistic causation comes into play. Sartorio argues, however, that the problems should not be seen as stemming from the view that, given indeterminism, what we have done might still be caused by reasons as well as by the absence of reasons for acting otherwise, but rather as stemming, presumably, from an overly simplistic explication of the notion of probabilistic causation.

In his chapter "The Culpability Problem and the Indeterminacy of Choice," Thomas Buchheim develops a solution to the dilemma of nomological determinism and nomological indeterminism that builds on Aquinas's account of a free human choice. He argues that, even if the past and the laws do not entail our actions, it need not be a pure matter chance whether we act the way we do or whether we act otherwise. For, as David Lewis has suggested, there might be possibilities that are "more possible" than other possibilities. Accordingly, it might, *because of our rational deliberation*, be "more possible" that we act the way we do than that we act otherwise and it would, then, be false that we *might as well* act otherwise (even if the past and the laws do not entail our actions). It would, instead, be true that we *would* act the way we do (even if the past and the laws do not entail our actions). Buchheim concludes, accordingly, that it is *not* a pure matter of chance whether we act the way we do or whether we act otherwise (even if our actions are nomologically undetermined).

Jörg Noller ("Ambivalent Freedom: The Problem of Willkür After Kant") discusses the notion of *Willkür* (the power of choice) from a historical and analytic point of view. Drawing on the history of the concept and Kant's philosophy, Noller argues that *Willkür* must not be understood in terms of mere chance or irrationality. Rather, *Willkür* involves reasons for actions and therefore constitutes what Harry Frankfurt has called "second-order volitions." Finally, Noller shows how the notion of *Willkür* has been revitalized in analytic philosophy, referring to Robert Kane's theory of volitional self-formation.

Thomas Pink ("Determination, Chance and David Hume: On Freedom as a Power") takes issue with Hume's contention that actions are either causally determined by prior events or happen by chance (and that actions can, therefore, never be free). Hume's failure, according to Pink, is the failure to recognize a difference in the way in which an outcome gets determined when there is *ordinary causation* (the outcome gets determined by excluding alternative outcomes) and the way in which an outcome gets determined when there is *freedom* (the outcome gets determined by making alternative outcomes available). For, once the distinction is appreciated, actions need not be seen as either causally determined by prior events, or as happening by chance. Instead, actions can be seen as determined by an agent who, by exercising a power, determines the action while making alternative actions available.

The third section is about free will and moral responsibility. Claudia Blöser ("Kant's Justification of Freedom as a Condition for Moral Imputation") considers Kant's account of moral imputation and its relationship to human freedom. For this purpose, she analyzes the interaction of theoretical and practical freedom in Kant and discusses the question of how we are really free. Finally, Blöser turns to the analytical debate. She discusses Derk Pereboom's objections to Kant's practical justification of freedom and argues that Kant's transcendental idealism is essential for Kant's notion of moral responsibility.

In his chapter "Does 'Ought' imply 'Can'?" Peter van Inwagen explores the connection between, on the one hand, the dilemma of nomological determinism and nomological indeterminism and, on the other hand, the principle that one only *ought* to act in a certain way if one is *able* to act in that way—a principle similar to principles that, as van Inwagen explains, are often ascribed to Kant and can already be found in the Pelagian controversy of the fifth century. It follows from this principle, together with the thesis that we never have been able not to act the way we did act, that we never ought not to have acted the way we did act (which, as van Inwagen remarks, is an unacceptable result). In the remainder of the chapter, van Inwagen critically examines and rejects a recent attempt to question the truth and the analyticity of the principle that one only *ought* to act in a certain way if one is *able* to act in that way on the basis of a survey conducted among non-philosophers.

Notes

1. This principle is often justified by appeal to the view that everything that is physical and has a cause has a *sufficient* physical cause and the view that everything that has a *sufficient* cause has no other cause than the sufficient cause itself. For it follows, then, that every cause of something physical is a sufficient physical cause, and, therefore, itself something physical.
2. It is a matter of controversy whether free will requires that *we* are a cause of our actions, or whether free will requires only that our *beliefs, desires, and motives* are a cause of our actions. This is not the place to go into the details of this debate.

References

Campbell, J.K., M. O'Rourke, and D. Shier. 2004. *Freedom and Determinism (Topics in Contemporary Philosophy)*. Cambridge, MA: MIT Press.

Chisholm, R. 1964. *Human Freedom and the Self*. The Lindley Lecture, Department of Philosophy, University of Kansas.

Davidson, D. 1980. Mental Events. In *Essays on Actions and Events*, 207–224. Oxford: Oxford University Press.

Frankfurt, H. 1969. Alternate Possibilities and Moral Responsibility. *Journal of Philosophy 66*: 829–839.

Kane, R. 2002. *The Oxford Handbook of Free Will*. Oxford: Oxford University Press.

———. 2011. *The Oxford Handbook of Free Will. Second Edition*. Oxford: Oxford University Press.

Kim, J. 1993. *Supervenience and Mind*. Cambridge: Cambridge University Press.

Lewis, D. 1981. Are We Free to Break the Laws? *Theoria 47*: 113–121.

McCann, H. 2017. *Free Will and Classical Theism*. Oxford: Oxford University Press.

Mele, A. 2014. *Surrounding Free Will*. Oxford: Oxford University Press.

Swinburne, R. 2011. *Free Will and Modern Science*. Oxford: Oxford University Press.

Timpe, K., M. Griffith, and N. Levy. 2017. *The Routledge Companion to Free Will*. New York: Routledge.

Watson, G. 2003. *Free Will. Second Edition*. Oxford: Oxford University Press.

Yablo, S. 1992. Mental Causation. *The Philosophical Review 101*: 245–280.

Part I

Free Will and Determinism

2

What Is Determinism? Why We Should Ditch the Entailment Definition

Helen Steward

What is the thesis of determinism? Since there are many possible theses which might warrant the label 'determinism' (amongst them, for example, sociological, economic, genetic and psychological determinisms), let me put my question somewhat more precisely: what is the *general* thesis of determinism, the thesis with which philosophers who worry about the free will problem mostly concern themselves—and which, perhaps more often than any of the other versions, tends simply to be given the general name, 'determinism'?[1] J.L. Austin once claimed that 'determinism' was "a name of nothing clear" (1970, 231). But I think someone might reasonably wonder whether this remains the case today. On the whole, philosophers working on the free will question tend to operate with a definition of determinism, the main components of which are now fairly standard, and that appears to be pretty well accepted on all hands. I call it the *entailment definition* and it will be helpful, in order to render later

H. Steward (✉)
University of Leeds, Leeds, UK
e-mail: h.steward@leeds.ac.uk

discussion clearer and easier, to spell out one representative version of it explicitly here:

> (ED) For any given time, a complete statement of the [non-relational] facts about that time, together with a complete statement of the laws of nature, entails every truth as to what happens after that time.[2]

Of course, there are concepts contained within ED which it has generally been realised need considerable unpacking and which raise myriad philosophical issues of their own. What, for instance, is a 'complete statement' of the facts about a time and is there any reason for supposing that such a thing could be formulated, even in principle? Which, exactly, are the 'non-relational' facts, and do we know how to distinguish them properly from the relational ones? What is a law of nature and how should such a law be stated? These are important questions to which it is not clear that we have satisfactory answers; and indeed I suspect satisfactory answers to some of them are not to be had. But for present purposes, I intend simply to allow the possibility that there may be ways of answering them which will permit (ED) at least to be considered a reasonably clear and coherent doctrine. My main focus here will be on a different question—namely, assuming for the sake of argument that (ED) is not objectionable for reasons to do with the unclarity of some of its main concepts, is the overall *form* of (ED) correct? By which I mean: is it right to think that the claim to which determinism centrally commits itself should be expressed as a thesis concerning the entailment of certain true statements by certain sets of others?

In this paper, I want to argue that the answer to this question is 'no' and that acceptance of the entailment definition of determinism has been a historically understandable, but now recognisable mistake. In a sense, of course, one is free to define technical terms as one will, and it might be argued that even for non-technical concepts, the only court of appeal for definitions is generally established usage. One might wonder, therefore, how an argument for the inappropriateness of a particular definition of a quasi-technical concept (one which, moreover, I have conceded already is certainly the market leader) can hope to get off the ground at all. What I shall try to show is that (ED) does not permit us to set up the free will problem in the best and most illuminating way. I shall offer two, closely related reasons for thinking this is the case: (i) (ED) is too weak to capture the deterministic thesis that troubles most incompatibilists; and (ii) (ED) does not sort compatibilists from incompatibilists in the way they ought really to be sorted, leaving many people who would account themselves *incompatibilists* on the wrong side of the compatibilist-incompatibilist divide, according to the letter of the definition. At the root of the problem, I shall suggest, is the fact that *entailment* is a logical concept; it is about what is *logically* compossible with what. Whereas determinism as it often figures in discussions of the free will problem—and more importantly still, in our thinking about it—is an inescapably *metaphysical* thesis whose import cannot be captured by (ED). The proper expression of determinism needs a metaphysical connection at its heart. Entailment will not do the job.

The paper falls into four sections. In the first, I ask the question what the thesis is that we are really worried about when we worry about free will, and offer what I call a *metaphysical* definition of determinism as a potential rival to (ED), an alternative I call (MD) (for 'metaphysical determinism', of course), as a means of stating the potentially worrisome thesis. In the second, I examine the relationship between (ED) and (MD), asking first whether (MD) entails (ED), to which my answer is a tentative 'probably'; and then whether (ED) entails (MD), to which it is a definite 'no'. (MD) is thus shown to be a stronger thesis than (ED). In the third section, I try to say something about how we have arrived historically at (ED), in order to encourage the thought that it is no more than a contingent product of the philosophical thinking of a very particular way of viewing the world, one from which philosophers today increasingly dissent, and so is something we need not feel is written in stone. Then, in the final section, I try to argue the case for thinking that it would be better, at any rate for the purposes of the free will debate, if ED were replaced by something much more like MD—and try to respond to what I think are likely to be the two main objections to my argument.

1   What Is the Thesis We Are Worried About When We Worry About Free Will?

Let me begin by asking: what is the thesis which worries us, when we are concerned that the world might not permit us free will because something called 'determinism' might be true? Here are some rough first shots at saying what seems worrying: it is the idea that things that have already happened (and which we cannot therefore alter) might *settle* or *fix* the future, or that the universe is so constrained by governing laws that *nothing can happen* other than what in fact does happen, or that the future is causally or physically *necessitated* by what has gone before it.[3] As William James puts it metaphorically, "[determinism] … professes that those parts of the universe already laid down absolutely appoint and decree what the other parts shall be" (James 1968, 40). Note that concepts of natural modality (such as physical possibility, causal necessity and what are plausibly derivative relatives of these such as the idea that the future might be 'settled' or 'fixed' by the past)[4] are central to these thoughts. If anything of the sort expressed by such claims were true, we might worry, there could be no such thing as free will, no such thing as the power to do otherwise than one in fact does. In order to have a handy label for this general conception of determinism, let us formulate the following definition (modelled on the same formal lines as (ED), for ease of comparison), and call it (MD), for 'metaphysical determinism':

> (MD): For any given time, the total set of [non-relational] facts[5] about that time, causally or physically or naturally necessitates every fact about what happens after that time.

In (MD), note, it is the relationships of causal, physical or natural necessitation, rather than that of entailment, which have pride of place.

A few clarificatory comments are immediately in order. First, I use the term 'metaphysical determinism', rather than, say, 'causal determinism' or 'physical determinism', and offer a disjunctive elucidation of what is meant by it, in an attempt to formulate a definition which will serve to include quite a wide variety of related doctrines. There may be those, for example, who do not suppose that everything is describable in physical terms, or who do not believe that the physical is fundamental, and so cannot be called *physical* determinists, but who nevertheless believe that everything that happens in the world is causally settled by past facts. And there may be those who are suspicious of the parochiality of the concept of 'cause', and so would not want to be accounted *causal* determinists, but nevertheless believe that determinism can be perfectly well expressed by means of the idea that the laws of nature, conceived of as metaphysical realities, are both all-encompassing and deterministic. I use the term 'metaphysical', therefore, in order to allow for views of both these kinds— and perhaps also for other possible variants of what I regard as the idea, centrally important to the formulation of determinism, that there are necessitating forces, powers or causes in the world that make it the case that certain things *must* follow upon certain others.[6] The crucial point is that metaphysical varieties of determinism, as I conceive of them, are doctrines according to which the determinative relation holds between *worldly states of affairs* and is owed to *a worldly variety of constraint*, though perhaps one of which we have very little real understanding. The crucial contrast class by means of which to understand what counts as a metaphysical conception of determinism, for my purposes, will be the *entailment* conception, which formulates determinism as essentially a matter of the holding of certain entailment relations, and does not explicitly mention any relationship of natural necessity.

A second point that deserves comment is the fact that there is, in (MD), no explicit mention of the laws of nature. We have grown very used to formulations of determinism which explicitly mention the laws, as well as past conditions. But this, I believe, may be a corollary, at least in part, of our penchant for definitions along the lines of (ED). If one is trying to formulate the thesis of determinism using entailment as one's central concept, it is arguable that one simply *must* mention the laws, on the grounds that at least some of the relevant statements about the future will fail, otherwise, to be entailed by the relevant sets of non-relational facts about previous times.[7] But if we are aiming at a *metaphysical* formulation of determinism, it is by no means clear that we must mention laws explicitly. The relation of natural necessitation itself, I suggest, when thought of as a metaphysical relation, might rather be thought of as something which can hold simply between past and future facts or states of affairs. The idea would be simply that past combinations of states of affairs are such as to draw future ones inevitably in their train. They may do so, of course, *according to* laws—but that is, I suggest, a different matter.

One thing which has perhaps made it hard to get clear about this is the fact that the idea that laws are, as it were, the ontological necessitators of the natural world is a powerful and very influential one[8] (though it has come under increasing pressure in recent years from alternative, more Aristotelian ideas).[9] There are those, therefore, who will be wont to insist that it is in fact the laws (in the form, for example, of necessary relations amongst universals) that provide the ontological *ground* for necessitation relations in general. I do not wish to take a view here on the question whether this idea about laws is in any sense correct; though it seems important to note that the view that the existence of laws is the inevitable corollary of belief in natural necessity is by no means universally held.[10] But I do want to argue that *even if* it were true that (something like) relations between universals provided the ontological ground for natural necessity, it would not follow that the determinist must include the relevant laws in her account of the facts which (according to her thesis) together naturally necessitate each given future one. Of course, if we accept the existence of laws of nature, it is going to matter to what happens, given any particular set of non-relational facts, what the relevant natural laws are—but even if the laws are contingent, it doesn't follow that those laws need to be *added* to the list of necessitating circumstances before we can say that a natural necessitation relation obtains between some set of facts holding at t1 and a fact or set of facts holding at t2. To say that these natural laws exist *implies* that the relevant relations of natural necessitation obtain simply amongst the particular facts in question; it is not to say instead that the relevant relations of necessitation obtain between the particular facts about a given time t1 *in combination with* the laws, on the one hand, and the particular facts about any given later time, t2, on the other. This is to suppose that everything that matters to the holding of a relation, R, must be specified when we specify its relata. It would be to make an analogous error to that that would be made by someone who thought that the rule of *modus ponens*, say, always needs adding to the *premises* of any argument which exploits that form if the argument is to be valid. Someone who thinks that the laws must be *added* to the particular facts before we can suppose that those particular facts necessitate certain future ones, indeed, invites the question whether *further* laws of nature are required which govern the necessitation relations between circumstances plus first-order laws, on the one hand, and, further, future circumstances, on the other—and whether those further laws then *also* need to be added to the account of the total list of necessitators ... and so on. The regress should be avoided (as is usually best with regresses) by refusing to take the first step and insisting that the natural necessitation relation itself always holds between particular facts or circumstances, even if we believe in laws.

Someone might say that (MD) is immediately problematic because we do not really know what natural necessitation is. I have some sympathy with this thought, but for the purposes of this paper, it will not be relevant to address the question whether we can, in the end, make sense of the idea of natural necessitation. If it turns out to be the case, in the end, that the concept of natural necessitation contains some unresolvable incoherence, I would then want to argue that no worrying conception of determinism of the secular and science-compatible kind I am attempting to characterise here will make sense either, and we will simply be home free on the free-will problem. It will be relevant for my purposes here, though, only to establish that we are not entitled to *assume* without argument when we set up our definition of determinism that natural necessitation is an illegitimate notion, something I shall aim to argue in Sect. 3. Moreover, there are things that can be said which might encourage us to think that we *do* understand the idea of natural necessitation. When one billiard ball rolls into another and the second moves off, for example, it is very natural to think that the precise way in which the second moves off is necessitated by a large set of facts, including the velocity of the ball which struck it, the position in which it was struck, the composition and topology of the surface and so forth—meaning that given all these facts together, the precise result which actually follows *must* follow, in virtue of the constitution of the natural world. It is plausible, to be sure, that if the relation between the obtaining of these facts and the facts about the way in which the second ball moves off is really to be *necessitation*, the set will, in addition, have to include facts which entail the *absence* of the huge range of things which might have interfered with the motion of the second ball, had they been present—for example, a person positioned so as to be able to stop the ball in its tracks and bent on doing so, a meteorite poised to land at the crucial moment on the table and so on. And perhaps there are insuperable obstacles, in the end, to the idea that any such definite set of facts exists, even in principle—but still, it is not *obvious* that this must be so. For now, anyway, we may remark that whatever one thinks about the coherence of the idea of natural necessitation, the entailment definition seems not to mention it explicitly at all. It says nothing about the future being necessitated, fixed or settled by facts about the past. It says nothing whatever about natural necessitation. Rather, it speaks merely of certain statements being *entailed* by certain other statements. The entailment definition, then, seems to be at one remove from the central worry which motivates the free will problem (assuming I have characterised that worry more or less correctly to begin with).

One might, of course, think that this is all to the good—and that in so far as we have moved away from the original worry with which we began, we have done so only to render it clearer and more perspicuous. We might hope that with the entailment definition, we are substituting clearly defined logical concepts which are tractable and relatively free from obscurity, for murky metaphysical notions out of which not much sense can be made. But there is not much point substituting clear notions for murky ones if we thereby lose the essence of the very idea we were originally trying to express, the core idea about a possible way our world might be whose compatibility with free will seemed doubtful. The question is: will we have lost our grip on that idea if we exchange (MD) for (ED)? I shall be arguing that the answer is 'yes'—for the purposes of which argument I now turn to ask the question how precisely (MD) and (ED) are related.

2   The Relationship Between (MD) and (ED)

Let us ask first, then, whether (ED) follows from (MD): that is, whether it would follow from the claim that the total set of non-relational facts about a given time causally or physically or naturally necessitates every fact about what happens after that time that a complete statement of the

non-relational facts about a given time, together with a complete statement of the laws of nature, entails every truth about what happens (or is
the case) after that time. I am happy to allow that given a suitably broad
conception of what is allowed to count as a statement of a law of nature,
it probably does follow—though perhaps only at the cost of robbing the
concept of a law of nature of some of its usual connotations. To see this,
consider a couple of imaginary possible worlds that might be thought, at
first glance, to represent possible obstacles to the entailment of (ED) by
(MD). First: one might wonder whether there could be a possible world
in which the sum-total of facts holding at a given time naturally necessitated all future matters, but in a way that was extraordinarily complex
and irregular, so that, for example, the facts at t1 necessitated the facts at
t2 according to one set of general principles, but that the facts at t2 necessitated the facts at t3 according to another, alternative set (and so on).
One might wonder whether there could, in such a world, be such things
as 'a statement of the laws of nature', and accordingly wonder whether
(ED) would be true. But of course, if determinism of the form encoded
by (MD) is to be true in such a world, the question which laws are operative at any given moment are going to have to be settled *somehow* by the
facts about previous times. And so we will always be able *somehow* to
express the 'laws' of this world—including, as it were, the 'meta-laws'—
the laws which will enable us to infer which laws will hold at each particular moment. These laws might be untidy and complex—perhaps too
complex to be readily usable by a human being to predict what will happen or to be recognised in the human world as the 'laws of nature'. But
they will still be in principle stateable. And if such laws as these are genuinely to count as laws, then determinism as characterised by the entailment definition will hold in this world—that is to say, it will be true of
this world that at any given time, a complete statement of the non-
relational facts about that time, together with a complete statement of
the laws of nature, will entail every truth about what happens after
that time.

Someone might think that this possible world fits the entailment definition only because we have not been sufficiently imaginative. We have
remained within a world in which there are laws, even though they are
laws which change moment-by-moment. But what about an entirely

lawless world? One might perhaps wonder whether the natural necessitation of the character of one temporal world-slice by another must be lawful at all—and if it were not, one might think one had imagined a world in which settling of future by past obtained, but in which no relevant entailments could be found. But this suggestion does not seem to be coherent. What the suggestion invites us to imagine is an entirely particularistic form of settling such that one particular time-slice of world just somehow determines the next temporal world-slice, but not in virtue of any *general character* it has, of the sort we could attempt to encode in something that would suffice at least to serve as a potential *candidate* for a statement of law. It is hard to make sense of what this could mean; it would perhaps demand turning time itself into a causal factor. But even here, one might say that if (MD) holds, there would still have to be statements of the form 'If $p_1 \ldots p_n$ at t1, then q_1 at t2'; 'if $q_1 \ldots q_n$ at t2 then r_1 at t3'; and so forth.—statements which simply describe, as it were, the particularistic, but deterministic, chaos. And one might simply say that in such a world, these are the laws, and so that the entailment definition continues to hold in a kind of 'limit' form.

This point, or something very like it, is considered by Bertrand Russell, in his classic and highly influential paper 'On the Notion of Cause' (Russell 1986/1912). Russell suggests that if we are to operate with a notion of determinism such that not every world turns out to be deterministic, it will be essential to insist that *time* must not enter explicitly into the formulae in terms of which the laws of nature are expressed (Russell 1986/1912, 196). This would prevent the intuitively lawless world just imagined from counting as a deterministic world according to (ED). But could such a world nevertheless be deterministic according to (MD), and thus be an obstacle to the entailment of (ED) by (MD)? I am not sure. It depends on whether there could, as it were, be *brute* causal necessitation—an entirely particularistic drawing on of the future by the past of a form which could not be encoded at all in any way—an idea which I confess I find difficult to make much sense of. Certainly it is hard to see how one could ever have any reason to believe in natural necessitation in such a world.[11] My tentative conclusion, then, is that (MD) probably does entail (ED), provided we are armed with a sufficiently generous conception of a statement of a law of nature, such that the statements in question are permitted to be very great in complexity or very great in number, or both.

It seems possible, then, to defend the claim that (MD) entails (ED). But what about the reverse implication? Does the holding of determinism as characterised by (ED) imply the holding of determinism as characterised by those who advert to the murky notions of settling and necessitation? Here, I think, it is much more obvious that the answer is 'no'. What makes it evident that the answer is 'no' is brought out rather beautifully by Helen Beebee in her paper, 'The Non-Governing Conception of Laws of Nature' (Beebee 2000). In that paper, Beebee contrasts the positions held by what she regards as two main camps in the debate about the metaphysics of laws. On the one hand, there is the realist view that laws are relations of necessity between universals, various versions of which are developed by Dretske (1977), Tooley (1977) and Armstrong (1983). On the other hand, there is what she calls the 'Ramsey-Lewis' view.[12,13] On the Ramsey-Lewis view, Beebee points out, laws do not *govern*. They are not that kind of thing. According to Lewis, for example, "a contingent generalization is a *law of nature* if and only if it appears as a theorem (or axiom) in each of the true deductive systems that achieves a best combination of simplicity and strength" (Lewis 1973: 73). Beebee's explanation of Lewis's idea is very neat and picturesque, and so I quote her here at length:

> [T]he idea is something like this. Suppose God wanted us to learn all the facts there are to be learned ... He decides to give us a book—God's Big Book of Facts—so that we might come to learn its contents and thereby learn every particular matter of fact there is. As a first draft, God just lists all the particular matters of fact there are. But the first draft turns out to be an impossibly long and unwieldy manuscript, and very hard to make any sense of—it's just a long list of everything that's ever happened and will ever happen ... Luckily, however ... God has a way of making the list rather more comprehensible ... he can write down some universal generalizations with the help of which we can derive some elements of the list from others ...
> ... God ... wants the list of particular matters of fact to be as short as possible—that is, he wants the axioms to be as strong as possible; but he also wants the list of *axioms* to be as short as possible—he wants the

deductive system—the axioms and theorems—to be as simple as possible. The virtues of strength and simplicity conflict with each other to some extent; God's job is to strike the best balance. And the contingent generalizations that figure in the deductive closure of the axiomatic system which strikes the best balance are the laws of nature. (Beebee 2000: 574)

On the Ramsey-Lewis conception, then, the laws are not rules written into the fabric of reality which the universe must follow. Rather, the universe just consists of "a vast mosaic of local matters of particular fact, just one little thing and then another" (Lewis 1986a, ix). Laws are fundamentally *descriptive* and fully knowable by us, as it were, only *post facto*—since of course the laws, on the Ramsey-Lewis conception, are to be the principles which achieve the best balance of simplicity and strength in an axiomatisation which fits the whole history of the world, not just the portion of that history which is past. Laws are not *constraints* on the forward flow of reality at all.

Suppose, then, that one held the Ramsey-Lewis view of laws. And imagine a world in which the only laws are Ramsey-Lewis laws and which is also deterministic according to (ED). Must this world also be deterministic in the sense that the past in any way naturally necessitates or settles the future? I think the answer to that question is fairly obviously 'no', as Beebee indeed argues in her paper. With the laws thought of only as descriptive and non-governing, and the world consisting merely of one little thing and then another, there is no necessitation, no settling of the sort that an incompatibilist defender of free will need worry about. As Beebee says, "the sense in which I am constrained … is a purely logical one. And this logical sense surely cannot be an obstacle to free will" (Beebee 2000, 579).[14]

I have argued thus far, then, that even if (MD) implies (ED), (ED) does not imply (MD). There could perfectly well be worlds in which the entailment definition was satisfied, though the metaphysical definition was not—worlds where the laws did not govern—provided only that Ramsey-Lewis laws are permitted to *count* as statements of the laws of nature—a proviso to which I shall return in Sect. 4. Those like Beebee and Vihvelin who have recognised this rather clearly have both suggested that this gives us a ready route to compatibilism about free will and determinism. Vihvelin, indeed, makes it clear at the outset of her book, *Causes, Laws and Free Will,* that she regards any embrace of a metaphysical style definition of determinism as confusing and misleading, insisting that "determinism should not be confused with the view of laws that has been called "the governing conception of laws", "the pushy explainer view" and most commonly "the necessitarian view" (Vihvelin 2013, 4). It is easy, she says, to get confused, "because determinism is often formulated in a loose and misleading way, e.g. as the thesis that the facts about the past 'metaphysically determine' or 'necessitate' or 'fix' all future facts" (Vihvelin 2013, 4). She recommends that these loose ways of talking be avoided. But my question is whether this is really the right response to what, I think, is agreed on all hands is an important distinction between different conceptions of what a law of nature might be. For having recognised that the entailment definition can be satisfied when the metaphysical definition is not (provided only that we are permitting "the contingent generalizations that figure in the deductive closure of the axiomatic system which strikes the best balance between simplicity and strength" to count as statements of laws of nature), ought we not to question whether the entailment definition really and truly captures what it was we thought we were worried about when we were worried, originally, about determinism? Does not the coming apart of the two definitions reveal, in fact, that the entailment definition is inadequate to capture the *worrying* doctrine of determinism? In the next section of the paper, I want to address this question.

3   Deciding on the Definition of Determinism

Vihvelin begins her discussion of determinism in *Causes, Laws and Free Will* by stating what she takes to be its definition—a definition which seems fairly clearly to be a version of the entailment definition: "determinism is the thesis that for every instant of time t there is a proposition that expresses the state of the world at that instant, and if P and Q are any propositions that express the state of the world at some instants, then the conjunction of P together with the laws of nature entails Q" (Vihvelin 2013, 3).[15] And then, on the basis of this definition, Vihvelin proceeds to argue that those who embrace metaphysical conceptions of determinism and use concepts such as necessitation are confused. But on what basis can she possibly justify this claim? Definitions in philosophy are negotiable. The particular definitions of the crucial concepts with which we operate have histories; and it may be instructive, sometimes, to reflect on why we have ended up with the ones we have, and in this particular case, why we have ended up with a definition of determinism that has the concept of entailment, rather than the concept of natural necessitation, at its heart.

It is an interesting historical question when precisely the doctrine of determinism understood by way of the entailment definition began to be substituted for the more metaphysical-sounding thesis that used to be called the 'doctrine of necessity', and why. Although Hume's (1975/1777, 1978/1740) views on the absence of any proper provenance for the idea of causal necessity must be a very important part of the story that needs to be told, the full adoption of the entailment definition of determinism does not seem to have occurred until rather later. Pierre-Simon Laplace's 'demon', who, knowing the location and momentum of every particle in the Universe at a given time, would also be able to know its entire future, that future being, in Laplace's view, a mere consequence of the laws of classical mechanics, was doubtless an important stepping stone towards the entailment definition.[16] But it was not until after various developments in logic and mathematics encouraged philosophers to begin to appreciate the usefulness of the concept of a function that the entailment definition really came into its own. I suspect Russell was very likely a very powerful voice in the shift made by philosophers to definitions of determinism resembling (ED). According to the highly influential paper, 'On the Notion of Cause', which I've already had occasion to mention, Russell claims:

A system is said to be 'deterministic' when, given certain data, $e_1, e_2, \ldots, e_n$, at times $t_1, t_2, \ldots, t_n$ respectively, concerning this system, if E_t is the state of the system at any time t, there is a functional relation of the form $E_t = f(e_1, t_1, e_2, t_2, \ldots, e_n, t_n, t)$. (Russell, 190)

On this conception of determinism, determinism holds wherever the way things are at a given time is a function of the way they are at another time—a function that will be encoded by some relevant law of nature. But there need be no implication at all that the law *constrains* anything; for all Russell's definition of determinism implies, the law which encodes the functional relation may just be a Ramsey-Lewis law. The functional relation is entirely descriptive, and merely expresses the fact that where such a relation exists, one can in principle infer the state of the world at one moment in time from the state of the world at another. Moreover, the relationship between past and future states is now completely symmetrical—one can infer past states from future ones, as well as the other way around. Determinism thus ceases to be merely a doctrine about the *development* of the world through time—and becomes instead a doctrine about the relationship between descriptions of the world at different times, a relationship which has no particular implications pertaining to *constraints* on the development of reality.

What motivated Russell to formulate the concept of determinism in this way? Earlier in the same paper, Russell expresses his suspicion of the idea that causes *compel* their effects—compulsion, he insists, is "a complex notion involving thwarted desire" (182)—a concept of psychology and not of metaphysics. One can see in this critique the influence of the Humean idea that we have no clear idea at all of necessitation, and that in so far as the idea has a source in our experience, that source is in the mind and not in external objects. Empiricism had no room for the unverifiable existence of necessary connections between states of affairs, and the concept of determinism developed by adherents of empiricism unsurprisingly followed suit. I believe, then, that we should see the entailment definition as the product of a long and important period of philosophical history in which realistic ideas about powers and causes faced an empiricism that refused to countenance them, and also at the same time, had to be encompassed within a mathematicisation of parts of metaphysics that promised new ways of thinking about the concept of law. The doctrine of necessity was effectively, then, declared dead owing to a bad case of unintelligibility: and the entailment definition entered in its place as the respectable expression of the doctrine of determinism.

However, unless I am much mistaken, I think it is fair to say that philosophy has now entered a new phase of development, in which that empiricism itself faces serious challenges. Those who believe in the reality of such things as powers and natures and objective laws which constrain reality have been once again admitted into the fold of philosophical respectability.[17] Of course, it cannot yet be said that they have won the day. There are still those who do not think that the idea that laws truly constrain the development of reality can ultimately be made sense of; regularity theories of causation and Ramsey-Lewis theories of law remain quite widely held. But there are now many adherents of more realistic conceptions of natural necessitation. We cannot, then, simply assume as perhaps Russell once did, that determinism, as defined by (MD), is the mere product of silly confusions of psychological concepts with metaphysical ones. There are plenty of philosophers these days who are absolutely happy to sign up to the existence of natural necessitation, either because they believe in constant objective forces, such as the fundamental forces postulated by physics, or in governing laws, or because they embrace the doctrine of intrinsic natures which dictate how objects and substances will behave with respect to one another. But if it is respectable once again to believe in real, producing causation and objective, metaphysical laws, it should be respectable once again to formulate determinism in ways closer to the ways in which the doctrine of 'necessity' used to be formulated—as a firmly metaphysical thesis about the natural necessitation of future facts or states of affairs, by past ones. And in that case, we are not entitled simply to *assume* that (ED) is the correct definition of determinism—as though that were written somewhere in an unchallengeable philosophical dictionary. We are entitled to ask whether (ED) might not itself be the outdated relic of a long-gone empiricist era and whether we do not have an obligation, as the custodians of a rather different philosophical period, to ask whether it is really any longer fit for all the purposes to which we might wish to put it.

4   Why (MD) Is to Be Preferred to (ED) as a Definition of Determinism

Thus far, then, I have argued that there is no clear reason that is agreed on all hands for regarding the thesis expressed by (MD) as illegitimate, and so that arguments such as Vihvelin's that those who adopt alternative definitions are obviously 'confused' should be rejected. In this final section of the paper, I want to suggest that, more than that, we should re-embrace (MD) as our preferred definition of determinism when it comes to the free will debate.

The main reason for thinking that (MD) offers a better definition of determinism than (ED) for the purposes of the free will debate is that it more exactly expresses the thesis we have reason to suppose might possibly be in tension with free will. Vihvelin points out that her own (ED)-like definition of determinism is strictly neutral concerning the concept of law and is consistent with the Ramsey-Lewis conception as well as what she calls the governing conception. She may even regard its neutrality as an advantage. But neutrality, I submit, is not what we should want from our definition of determinism, if we are seeking a definition suitable for formulating the free will problem. We should want a definition of determinism that makes determinism look, at least *prima facie*, as though it might present some sort of serious threat to the existence of free will. When we teach students to state problems in philosophy, we teach them to offer the best version of the problem that they can manage, even if— perhaps even *especially* if—their eventual intention is to argue that the problem can be solved. That is presumably because we think it is a methodological *desideratum* to do so. And it is this same methodological assumption on which I mean to rely here. For, I submit, there simply *is* no threat to free will from determinism as construed by the entailment definition, provided a 'complete statement of the laws of nature' is permitted to be a complete statement of the regularities which achieve the best combination of simplicity and strength in the axiomatic system that attempts to organise God's Big Book of Facts into a more digestible read. If laws are merely descriptive and have no constraining power, (ED) can be satisfied easily in a way which does not even begin to raise any worries about free will. The question should go away before we even have chance to raise it. And so to use (ED) to state the free will problem is to state it in a way which makes it much too easy to solve. To make the free will problem hard, to assure ourselves of a real issue, we need the metaphysical definition. We need to raise the spectre of the world as governed by real necessitating laws, or natures, in order to be confident we have described the problem in its most worrisome form.

A second, related reason for thinking that (ED) should be replaced by (MD) is that it would generate a more illuminating division of positions on the free will debate into compatibilist, on the one hand, and incompatibilist, on the other. If (ED) is the definition of determinism, indeed, I find it quite hard to see why *anyone* would remain an incompatibilist, once it had been pointed out to them how weak a thesis (ED) actually is. It is not very hard to see (as Beebee and Vihvelin argue) that Ramsey-Lewis laws do not constrain us—so provided these laws are permitted to count as the laws whose 'statement' figures in (ED), it should be clear that we ought all to be compatibilists. But do we really *want* a definition of determinism which leaves no one sensible in the incompatibilist camp? Surely we should prefer a definition which states a thesis which some, at least, believe creates problems for our belief in free will—at any rate, if a coherent statement of such a thesis exists. But if (MD) is coherent, as I have been assuming for the purposes of this discussion, then (MD) states such a thesis. (MD) ought therefore to be preferred to (ED) as the definition of determinism.

I want now to address two possible objections to the case I have made for replacing (ED) with (MD).

The first and I think most pressing objection is that my claim that the problem with (ED) is about its central use of the relation of *entailment* is mistaken—since we could perfectly well meet the desideratum I have proposed (that is, of ensuring that determinism remains a thesis strong enough to figure in the statement of a potential threat to free will) and yet retain (ED) as the definition of determinism, *provided* we are careful what we permit to count as a 'statement of a law of nature'. It might be conceded that mere Ramsey-Lewis descriptive generalisations might indeed need to be excluded if we are to represent determinism as a doctrine potentially threatening to free will. But provided law statements themselves somehow incorporate the idea of natural necessitation within them, it might be thought, it will not matter if we retain the entailment definition.

But the question I would like to ask is how exactly it is proposed to incorporate the idea of natural necessitation into the 'complete statement of the laws of nature' which (ED) refers to. What will the laws look like with the modality of natural necessitation built in? None of the laws we actually have in science contains a modality operator of any kind; it is perfectly consistent with the expression, for example, of Boyle's law[18] or Coulomb's law[19] that they should be merely generalised descriptions of relationships which have made it into the deductive closure of the Lewisian 'best system'. The statement of these sorts of laws, then, if we leave them as they are normally stated, will not do. Perhaps it might be suggested that we might introduce something like a natural necessity operator—call it 'N'—so that we could express law statements them-selves, or at any rate, their deductive consequences, as natural necessities (e.g. $N \forall x[Fx \rightarrow Gx]$); or, alternatively, that we might use strict condi-tionals (e.g. $\forall x N[Fx \rightarrow Gx]$)). But the trouble with these suggestions is that the strengthening of the premises which 'N' has been used to intro-duce is simply not *required* in order for the wanted entailments of future facts by past ones (together with laws) to go through. The entailments will go through anyway, with or without the modal operators. The modal operators are mere idle cogs in the mechanism of the deductions which yield the future facts as conclusions. How then can it be *expressive* of the distinctive thesis of determinism to say that these entailment relations hold (as the entailment definition proposes)? They hold *in any case* (given only that [ED] as I originally conceived it applies) whether the modal operators are there or not, which seems to reveal that mere commitment to the entailments is not properly expressive of the determinist's claim. What (worrisome) determinism is fundamentally about is the claim that the natural laws do indeed *need* to be stated using modal operators of some sort (along with the important additional claim that these laws are all-embracing)—that mere universal generalisations or specifications of functional relationships will not do. But this distinctive claim is not stated, and nor is it implied, by the entailment definition.

One might respond to this difficulty by suggesting that rather than attempting to incorporate modal operators into the laws, it should just be stated to be a *presupposition* of the wanted reading of (ED) that the complete statement of the laws of nature must be a complete statement of *genuine* laws which truly reflect natural necessities in nature, rather than just Ramsey-Lewis laws. That would, I think, ensure an effective equivalence between (MD) and (ED). However, this result comes only at the cost of making it absolutely plain that a substantial part of the burden of ensuring that the doctrine of determinism is at least conceivably a threat to free will is borne by the presupposition, rather than by the explicit content of the so-called definition. And surely if we are trying to *state* a thesis, the most perspicuous way to state it is to bring everything crucial, so far as is possible, into the *explicit content* of our statement. We need the definition of determinism to state *what it is that one believes* in believing in determinism. And so it will not do to attempt to meet my concern that (ED) guarantees no genuine problem of free will by suggesting that we retain (ED), while noting alongside it that it will only do to specify the doctrine, given a certain additional presupposition. For this will not enable (ED) to meet the purpose for which it was wanted in the first place—that of stating as plainly as possible the exact content of what must be believed by someone who thinks determinism is true (rather than [at best] a mere *consequence* of that doctrine). We would need to *add* the content of the presupposition that the laws encode natural necessities to the content of (ED) in order to state the doctrine of determinism. But that seems to be as much as to say that what we *really* need is (MD)—a definition which makes it more perspicuous that what is really crucial to determinism is that there be *natural* necessitation relations between the facts at one time and the facts at another (perhaps, but not necessarily in virtue of the holding of laws, depending on one's view of the ontology of natural necessity). It is (MD), that is, which properly encodes what the worrisome deterministic thesis really is.

The second objection I want to consider is that I am simply arguing for a definition of determinism that will make incompatibilism true by fiat. But it should really go without saying that this is not the case. There are many interesting ways to argue for compatibilism, even if one believes in real, metaphysical necessitation and constraining laws—for example, by arguing that determinism doesn't entail inevitability (see, e.g., Dennett 2003); by endorsing 'ability plus opportunity' conceptions of free will (see, e.g., Kenny 1975); or by arguing that free will *requires* natural necessitation (see, e.g., Hobart 1934). The embrace of (MD) by no means brings incompatibilism inevitably in its wake; there will still be plenty of ground for a wide range of different kinds of compatibilists to occupy. We will simply have removed from the mix as misleading a view of the nature of law which can only muddy the waters—which confuses those I would be inclined to regard as *true* compatibilists, who really *do* believe that free will is compatible with real honest-to-goodness necessitation, with an ersatz sub-group, who secure their compatibilism only by effectively denying with their conception of law the truth of the metaphysical thesis of determinism. So far as the defender of (MD) is concerned, those who believe only in Ramsey-Lewis laws simply *deny* determinism; about (MD), though (supposing they allow its coherence), they might be either compatibilists *or* incompatibilists, for all we know.

Perhaps I should end by saying, in case anyone should be confused about this, that I am no believer in (MD)—nor even a confident believer in its coherence. As stated at the outset of the paper, I think it shares with (ED) a number of problematic concepts; and even if worries about these concepts were to turn out to be unfounded, I think it is vanishingly unlikely that anything like (MD) might conceivably be true—not because I think there is no such thing as natural necessitation, but rather because I do not believe that the reach of natural law is total, it being likely, in my view, that such laws as there are may *constrain* everything without *dictating* everything. I have defended (MD) here, then, not because I think it is true, but because I regard it as an honest attempt, at least, to convey a vision of reality which looks potentially troubling for free will. And if we are going to argue about whether free will is possible, given determinism, we owe determinism the courtesy of expressing it in a form which at least makes it *look* as though it might present some sort of problem for free will. (ED) does not meet this criterion, and nor can we readily adjust it in order to build in the additional assumptions we require. For the purposes of the free will debate, we should ditch the entailment definition of determinism and return to its venerable older relative, the doctrine of necessity.

Notes

1. Of course, it is possible to believe that some of these other, special varieties of determinism might also be threatening for free will; but I restrict
   myself, for the purposes of this paper, to the centrally important *general*
   thesis. It is also important to note here, at the outset, that my questions
   concern determinism *considered as a thesis important to the free will
   debate*. There may be other purposes for which philosophy (or science, or
   theology or economics, say) requires a concept of determinism; none of
   my arguments here need bear on the question what concept might best
   suit those other purposes.
2. I borrow this particular formulation from Fischer (1998, 14), but many
   other philosophers offer very similar definitions. See, for example, van
   Inwagen (1983, 65), Kane (2002, 4), Wiggins (2003, 99) and Vihvelin
   (2013, 1).
3. In fact, one might think we could give an even more general description
   than any of these of what worries us when we worry that determinism
   might be true. One might say that what we worry about is simply that
   something beyond our control somehow completely dictates the whole
   future course of reality (and leave it entirely open whether the 'something beyond our control' is past facts together with the physical laws; or
   God and his wishes or dictates; or God's knowledge of what we will do;
   or the position of the stars .... or something else). But the most prevalent
   source of the worry for most modern philosophers stems from a thought
   that is essentially (1) secular and (2) intended to be at the very least compatible with a scientific world view, if not actually supported by it. I
   therefore focus for present purposes on this specific version of the worry.
4. Plausibly, the idea that something is 'fixed' or 'settled' is the idea that it
   is not possible for it to be otherwise (given that certain things—such as
   the laws of nature, for example—are held fixed).
5. Ontological issues may raise their ugly heads here—there will be those
   who think of facts as essentially linguistic items and hence as things
   which could not be involved in worldly necessitating. So be it. Those
   who have these worries may substitute the term 'state of affairs' or 'event'
   (understanding by 'event' something like an exemplification of a property at a time) if it makes them feel easier. Nothing should turn on this.
6. One possible confusion which might be introduced by the use of the
   word 'metaphysical', which I need to avert: metaphysical determinism is

not committed to the metaphysical necessity of the laws of nature. It is perfectly consistent with metaphysical determinism as I have stated the doctrine that the laws are contingent.

7. Though it may not follow that *no* such future facts are thus entailed, without mention of laws. To take an example of Fischer's, "Smith existed at T1" entails "It is not the case that Smith existed for the first time at T2", without the addition of any laws of nature as extra premises (Fischer 1983, 75). Thanks to Marco Hausmann for reminding me about examples of this sort.

8. In recent years, this view has been most closely associated with Dretske (1977), Tooley (1977) and Armstrong (1983).

9. See, for example, Harré and Madden (1975), Ellis (2001), Mumford (2002), Bird (2007), Vetter (2015).

10. See especially Mumford (2002), for a very explicit repudiation of the idea that belief in natural necessity commits one to the existence of laws.

11. The view that this idea makes no sense also seems to be in accordance with a suggestion made by Fine (2005):

> [T]here are no distinctive *de re* natural necessities. Let us suppose that *x* and *y* are two particles and that it is a natural necessity that they attract one another ... Then it is plausible to suppose that this should follow from (1) its being a metaphysical necessity that each of the particles is of the kind that it is and (2) its being a natural necessity that particles of this kind attract one another. Thus the *de re* natural necessity will reduce to a *de re* metaphysical necessity and a *de dicto* natural necessity; and it might be thought that something similar should be true of any *de re* natural necessity. (243)

12. Ramsey (1978).

13. Lewis (1973, 1986b).

14. Beebee's conception of laws enables her to respond to van Inwagen's well-known Consequence Argument (which, of course, uses the entailment definition of determinism) in a similar way to David Lewis (1986b) by arguing against the premise that claims that no agent can render the laws of nature false (Beebee and Mele 2002). Whilst Beebee and Mele concede that it is true that no agent can render false what *in fact* turns out to be the final set of laws (any more than I can render false what, *in fact*, turns out to be the truths about the future), it is not true that no agent can contribute with their actions to the description of the Universe

which needs codifying as neatly as possible by such laws—and hence it is not true that no agent can indirectly change with their actions what those finalised laws might eventually turn out to be. This seems to me the right response to the Consequence Argument for someone who does not believe in natural necessity.

van Inwagen himself claims that even if something like Lewis's Humean view of laws as mere exceptionless regularities was correct, the Consequence Argument holds up. His reasoning is that it would not follow from the fact that laws were no more than exceptionless regularities that any human being would be able to render any such regularity false:

> Suppose, for example, that the most massive star is 260 times as massive as our sun. 'All stars have masses less than or equal to 260 solar masses' may well be a mere exceptionless regularity: it may well be that there could have been a star with a mass of 261 solar masses. But, no doubt, no human being is (or ever has been or ever will be) able to cause a counterinstance to this regularity to exist. I would suppose that, even if Lewis's Humean conception of laws is right, it would be an even more difficult task to produce a counterinstance to a law—in the sense in which it would be 'even more difficult' for me to lift an object weighing 10,000 kilograms than it would be for me to lift an object weighing 1,000 kilograms. (van Inwagen 2017: 228, fn. 36)

It seems true that there may be some mere exceptionless regularities that cannot be rendered false by a mere human being and hence that it does not follow from a law's merely *being* such an exceptionless regularity that a human being could render it false. But this is not an adequate defence against Beebee. For the Consequence Argument requires that no human being could render false the statement which states *the sum total* of the laws of nature, so it will not do as a response to Beebee to point out merely that *some* exceptionless regularities cannot be rendered false. It must be the case that *none* of those which are at any point in time potential candidates to become laws, should the Universe go in this or that direction, can be rendered false. The Consequence Argument will have a false premise if *any* of those which would otherwise have made it into the Big Book of Laws might have failed to make it onto the statute book after all, should a given agent have acted differently; and the onus is on van Inwagen to show that this is definitely *not* going to be the case. He admittedly appears confident that it is *not* going to be the case ("I would suppose that … it would be an even more difficult task to produce a counterinstance to a law"). But the question is what justifies this confidence. If we are assuming Humeanism about laws, it cannot be faith in natural necessity. And Beebee would doubtless reply to van Inwagen's assertion that it is going to be a difficult task to produce a counterinstance to a law, that if determinism is true, it is going to be plausible that breaking the laws cannot be any more difficult than raising one's hand (for this action, which most of us assume we generally have the ability to undertake whenever we wish, would be bound to amount to lawbreaking on many occasions in a deterministic world). Thanks to Marco Hausmann for alerting me to the relevance of van Inwagen's response to Beebee.

15. This definition is based on that offered by van Inwagen (1983, 65).
16. Laplace (1951/1814).
17. A huge range of work from the last fifty years or so might be mentioned here. Amongst some of the most prominent work in the tradition I have in mind are Harré and Madden (1975), Dretske (1977), Tooley (1977), Armstrong (1983), Ellis (2001), Mumford (2002), Bird (2007), Vetter (2015).
18. Usually stated as P1V1 = P2V2, Boyle's law states that at constant temperature, the pressure of a given quantity of gas is inversely proportional to its volume.
19. Coulomb's law states that the electrical force between two charged objects is directly proportional to the product of the quantity of charge on the objects and inversely proportional to the square of the separation distance between the two objects.

References

Armstrong, David. 1983. *What Is a Law of Nature?* Cambridge: Cambridge University Press.

Austin, John L. 1970. Ifs and Cans. In *Philosophical Papers*, 2nd ed., 205–232. Oxford: Oxford University Press.

Beebee, Helen. 2000. The Non-Governing Conception of Laws of Nature. *Philosophy and Phenomenological Research* 61: 571–594.

Beebee, Helen, and Alfred Mele. 2002. Humean Compatibilism. *Mind* 111: 201–223.

Bird, Alexander. 2007. *Nature's Metaphysics: Laws and Properties*. Oxford: Oxford University Press.

Dennett, Daniel. 2003. *Freedom Evolves*. London: Penguin.

Dretske, Fred I. 1977. Laws of Nature. *Philosophy of Science* 44: 248–268.

Ellis, Brian. 2001. *Scientific Essentialism*. Cambridge: Cambridge University Press.

Fine, Kit. 2005. The Varieties of Necessity, 235–60. In his *Modality and Tense: Philosophical Papers* (Oxford: Oxford University Press).

Fischer, John M. 1983. Freedom and Foreknowledge. *The Philosophical Review* 92: 67–79.

———. 1998. *Responsibility and Control: A Theory of Moral Responsibility*. Cambridge: Cambridge University Press.

Harré, Rom, and E.H. Madden. 1975. *Causal Powers: A Theory of Natural Necessity*. Oxford: Blackwell.

Hobart, R.E. 1934. Free Will as Involving Determination and Inconceivable without it. *Mind* 43: 1–27.

Hume, David. 1975/1777. An Enquiry Concerning Human Understanding. In *Enquiries*, ed. L.A. Selby-Bigge, with Text Revised and Notes by P.H Nidditch, 3rd ed. Oxford: Oxford University Press.

———. 1978/1740. In *A Treatise of Human Nature*, ed. L.A. Selby-Bigge, 2nd ed. Oxford: Oxford University Press.

van Inwagen, Peter. 1983. *An Essay on Free Will*. Oxford: Oxford University Press.

———. 2017. *Thinking about Free Will*. Cambridge: Cambridge University Press.

James, William. 1968. The Dilemma of Determinism. In *Essays in Pragmatism*, 37–64. New York: Hafner.

Kane, Robert. 2002. *The Oxford Handbook of Free Will*. Oxford: Oxford University Press.

Kenny, Anthony. 1975. *Will, Freedom and Power*. Oxford: Blackwell.

Laplace, Pierre-Simon. 1951/1814. *A Philosophical Essay on Probabilities*. Translated into English from the French. 6th ed. by F.W. Truscott and F.L. Emory. New York: Dover Publications.

Lewis, David. 1973. *Counterfactuals*. Cambridge, MA: Harvard University Press.

———. 1986a. *Philosophical Papers*. Vol. II. Oxford: Oxford University Press.

———. 1986b. Are we Free to Break the Laws? In *Philosophical Papers*, vol. II, 291–298. Oxford: Oxford University Press.

Mumford, Stephen. 2002. *Laws in Nature*. London: Routledge.

Ramsey, Frank. 1978. Universals of Law and Fact. In *Foundations: Essays in Philosophy, Logic Mathematics and Economics*, ed. D.H. Mellor, 128–132. London: Routledge and Kegan Paul.

Russell, Bertrand. 1986/1912. On the Notion of Cause. In *Mysticism and Logic*, 173–199. London: Unwin.

Tooley, Michael. 1977. The Nature of Laws. *Canadian Journal of Philosophy* 7: 667–698.

Vetter, Barbara. 2015. *Potentiality*. Oxford: Oxford University Press.

Vihvelin, Kadri. 2013. *Causes, Laws and Free Will: Why Determinism Doesn't Matter*. Oxford: Oxford University Press.

Wiggins, David. 2003. Towards a Reasonable Libertarianism. In *Free Will*, ed. Gary Watson, 2nd ed., 94–121. Oxford: Oxford University Press.

3

Aristotle and the Discovery of Determinism

Dorothea Frede

1   Preface: Three Types of Determinism in Aristotle

That Aristotle can be considered as the 'father of determinism' should come as no great surprise to those who know anything about his philosophy. And it will also not come as a surprise that he discovered all three versions of determinism: logical, physical, and ethical determinism. 'Logical determinism' is concerned with the problem that has been discussed under the title of 'future truth', that is, the truth of propositions about particular contingent events that may or may not occur in the future. 'Physical determinism' addresses the question of whether natural events are the inevitable result of prior events and unchangeable natural laws. 'Ethical determinism' deals with the question of whether psychological conditions determine human actions.

D. Frede (✉)
University of Hamburg, Hamburg, Germany
e-mail: dorothea.frede@uni-hamburg.de

© The Author(s), under exclusive license to Springer Nature Switzerland AG 2021
M. Hausmann, J. Noller (eds.), *Free Will*,
https://doi.org/10.1007/978-3-030-61136-1_3

Although the discovery of all three kinds of determinism can be attributed to Aristotle, this is not to deny that philosophers before him had discussed such questions as whether all things happen out of necessity or whether certain things come to be by chance and in a haphazard way. Certain Presocratics entertained deterministic views;[1] but there is no clear evidence, for instance, that Democritus worked out his theory of atomic interactions in any great detail. As far as we know, the views of the early Greek philosophers were quite general, and it does not seem that any of them so much as raised the question of whether causal constellations necessitate every natural event and human activity.

To be sure, Plato separates the realm of what is eternally selfsame and immobile from the realm of what is changeable and unstable, but this very separation prevents him from raising the question of whether ordinary events, including human actions, are in any way necessitated. And although Plato sometimes speaks about the 'law of destiny' in connection with human lives, he thereby refers to the fate that is in store for human beings after death, depending on how they have lived their lives.[2]

Aristotle thoroughly transformed the discussion of determinism not only by distinguishing between the three versions of determinism, but also by examining each version in considerable detail. Rather than examine the subject in a single work, he addressed the various aspects of determinism in different parts of his philosophy. And, as shown by the way Aristotle deals with the different aspects of determinism, he was apparently not at all vexed by the seemingly insoluble problems that have occupied subsequent generations of philosophers and scientists up to this day.[3]

While Aristotle's treatment of the questions of 'logical' and 'physical' determinism will be sketched here briefly because it sheds light on his position on determinism in general, the focus of this chapter will be on *ethical* determinism, the topic of this volume.

A brief word on terminology is perhaps in order before we proceed. In his discussions, Aristotle does not coin any special terminology; for although he has at his disposition terms like *hôrismenon*, or *aphrorismenon* and its opposite *aortiston*, he uses these terms in the sense of 'definite' and 'indefinite', not of 'determinate' and 'indeterminate'. 'Determinism', like most *-isms*, is an invention of the early modern age, anyway. Aristotle does introduce, however, *endechomenon* as the special term to designate the contingent—that is, as what is neither necessary nor impossible. This term that has come down to us *via* its Latin translation, *contingens*.

2 Logical Determinism: Future Truth

The question of logical determinism arises in the discussion of 'future truth' in the famous ninth chapter of Aristotle's *De interpretatione*.[4] The problem of future contingent events is also called, for short, 'The Sea Battle', because Aristotle uses a sea-battle that is supposedly going to happen tomorrow as his example to illustrate the problem of whether statements concerning particular future contingent events are true or false beforehand.[5] If statements about future events are true or false before the events occur, he claims, then these events must be regarded as settled, that is, as necessary. Aristotle goes to quite some length to point out in a *reductio ad impossibile* the dire consequences of this assumption:

> [T]hat nothing of what happens is as chance has it, but everything happens of necessity. So there would be no need to deliberate and take trouble (thinking if we do this, this will happen, but if we do not, it will not). (9, 18b29–32)[6]

Aristotle clearly expects his readers to find those consequences unpalatable because they contradict basic assumptions about the indispensability of reason, responsibility, and effort:

> For we see that what will be has an origin both in deliberation and in action, and that, in general, in things that are not always actual there is the possibility of being and of not being, and consequently, both coming to be and not coming to be. (19a8–12)

Aristotle's treatment of 'future truth' used to be a hot topic in the years when the 'principle of bivalence' (PB) was still regarded as a kind of sacred cow by logicians.[7] That the general interest in this question has dwindled in recent decades may be due to the fact that logicians have turned to temporal logic, to relevance logic, to many-valued logic, and even to fuzzy logic, so that the PB is no longer regarded as a 'must'. No one seems to be ready any longer to take up the cudgel and attribute a different reading to the text of *De interpretation* 9 in order to protect Aristotle against the reproach of an elementary logical mistake. If Aristotle excepts statements about future particular contingent events from the principle that every proposition must be either true or false, that exception is no longer regarded as outlandish. At any rate, Aristotle is no longer blamed for committing the mistake of distribution, that is, of inferring from: 'it is necessary that p or not p is true' that 'it is necessary that p or it is necessary that not-p': (N: T [p] v T [~p] → N p v N ~ p).

It should be noted that Aristotle makes it quite clear that the way we think or talk about events does not affect their ontological status. Things do not become necessary because we treat them that way. Aristotle's point is, rather, that the way we think and talk about states of affairs should fit the ontological status we attribute to them (*De int.* 9, 19a32–19b4). The dire consequences of treating future events as settled concern *us* and the implications of our commitments; they do not affect the actual status of the events themselves. If we regard an event as 'open either way', in the sense that it may or may not happen, then we should not treat it as fixed by attributing truth-values to the propositions in question while the matter is still undecided. In short: *will be* is not compatible with *may-be* and *may-be-not*. Or to express it more poetically, the assumption that all statements about future events have been true or false since the dawn of creation has the consequence that the book of history must already have been written at that time. Aristotle does not use such poetic metaphors, and he does not believe in creation anyway, but he holds that we should keep separate the states of affairs that we regard as only 'about to happen'—*mellonta*—but that may not actually come to be—and those that are definitely going to happen—*esomena*—of which it must eventually be true to say that they are the case.[8] For Aristotle, 'future truth' is a matter of our semantic treatment of future contingents.

In explanation of why Aristotle does not regard the restriction of truth-values for statements concerning future contingents as problematic it should be said that he does not regard propositions as truth functions. Though he distinguishes between simple sentences that either affirm or deny a predicate of a subject[9] and compound sentences, he nowhere attributes truth or falsity to disjunctions [T (p v q)] or to conditionals [T (p → q)], and he treats the conjunction 'Socrates and Plato are men' as the summary of 'Socrates is a man' and 'Plato is a man'. Truth-carriers are either affirmations or denials of predicates of subjects, not compound sentences.

Though the question of future truth did not present either an ontological or a physical problem for Aristotle, it became a much-debated issue later on in the history of philosophy when the Stoics defended a rigorously deterministic position, a position that was countered by the Epicureans and by the Academic Sceptics.[10] The Stoic position did, indeed, rely heavily on the tenet that propositions about future events are true or false beforehand. This led to a debate that lasted for centuries, because it was continued later on by the Pyrrhonian Sceptics.[11] And in late antiquity and through the Middle Ages, the question of 'future truth' became a problem of great urgency, because philosophers and theologians were concerned with the question of God's omniscience. If God foresees all things, must his foreknowledge and his pronouncements not be true beforehand—and must the respective states of affairs, then, not come to be of necessity?[12] The question of God's foreknowledge and the truth of predictions in his name was not only a hotly debated issue; it also was a dangerous one to engage in, because putting limits on God's foreknowledge was treated as a heresy. Luckily for Aristotle, the Greek gods were not omniscient, so that that aspect of the problem was not among his concerns.

3 Physical Determinism

Aristotle is equally brief about the problem of physical necessity. He holds that in nature only certain events happen of necessity, while others are contingent: even if they are of the kind that happen 'for the most part' (*hôs epi to poly*), particular events may or may not happen, depending on the circumstances. Of course, every event that happens is necessary when it happens—there are no causal gaps in Aristotle's physical word. He adheres not only to the principle that there is no change without cause, but also to the principle that the same causes always have the same effects. But he assumes, at the same time, that in the sublunary world there are no trains of events that cannot, in principle, be interrupted by some interfering event that is not foreseeable because it is not part of the natural nexus. Aristotle calls those interfering factors 'accidental' (*apo t'automatou*) when they concern events in nature, and 'fortuitous' (*apo tychês*) when they concern human affairs. He distinguishes accidental events from those that happen either by nature or by choice (*Physics* II, 4–8). Such accidental results are not the subject of scientific knowledge, because they are neither part of the regular order of nature, nor the intended end of human actions. In Aristotle's universe only the superlunary sphere—the heaven above the moon—is free from accidents; for he holds that only the paths of the heavenly bodies are strictly regular, and not subject to change. He therefore locates comets and other such irregular phenomena in the sublunary sphere.[13]

This does not mean that Aristotle accepts the existence of uncaused events, for accidental causes are causes as well.[14] As he explains in *Metaphysics* E 2–3, accidentals are events that come to be and cease to be; but they are not themselves the products of proper processes of generation (*genesis*) or destruction (*phthora*):

> That there are starting points (*archai*) and causes (*aitia*) which are generable and destructible without ever being in the course of being generated or destroyed (*aneu tou gignesthai kai phtheiresthai*), is obvious. For otherwise all things will be of necessity, since that which is being generated or destroyed must have a cause which is not accidentally its cause. (3, 1021a29–30)[15]

In nature there are natural trains of events that happen regularly, unless something 'from outside' interferes, which is not part of that natural train of events. In human life fortuitous events are due to factors that are neither intended nor foreseeable. Thus, I become an accidental witness of a car-crash if I happen to be on the spot for an unrelated purpose, and if car-crashes do not happen there all the time.[16]

The existence of accidental causes is justified by a *reductio ad absurdum* argument in *Metaphysics* E 3. It construes a causal chain that determines that a certain individual will die by violence: the man will fall into the hands of a murderous gang that happens to be around at the time when the victim leaves his house at night for a drink of water: "This man will die by violence, *if* he goes out; and he will do this *if* he is thirsty; and he will be thirsty *if* something else happens; and thus we shall come to that which is now present, or to some past event" (1027b1–6). If all these conditions are fulfilled, the result is necessary, *if* every event is considered as the proper cause of its consequence. For then the train of events necessarily unfolds, leading up to the man's death. But given the assumption that there is no connection between the two trains of events—the first leading to the presence of the gang, the second leading to the man's leaving his house—the result, the man's dying through violence—is fortuitous. Aristotle therefore claims that there are 'first beginnings' or 'fresh starts', that do not in turn have their own proper beginnings in a causal series (1027b11–14): "Clearly then the process goes back to a certain starting point (*archê*), but this no longer points to something further back. This then will be the starting point for the fortuitous, and will have nothing else as the cause of its coming to be." In explanation of this *prima facie* obscure explanation, it should be said that an *archê*—beginning— must be the *proper* or *specific* cause of its results. An accidental cause has no such principle; accidents are coincidences that do not allow for further explanations beyond the fact that they happened. They are neither uncaused events nor are they totally arbitrary; in the case of my witnessing the car-crash, there is no more to be said in its explanation, except that I happened to be at that particular place at that particular moment.

If the existence of the fortuitous (*to apo tychês*)—of what is neither intended not foreseeable in human life—seems unproblematic, at least to all those who do not believe in divine providence, the existence of the 'accidental' in nature (*apo t'automatou*) does present a problem for scientists who reject the conception of teleological causation. They will point out that there is no difference between intended and unintended results in nature; unforeseeable events are so only because not everything is known to human beings. Aristotle, apart from insisting on the importance of teleology in nature, would reply that only certain types of events are knowable, as a matter of principle, and that chance happenings are not among the 'knowables', because they are not part of the regular train of events. He thereby justifies the distinction between natural processes and chance events.

The Stoics not only rejected Aristotle's restriction of the principle of bivalence, they also rejected his justification of accidental and fortuitous causes, and argued for a rigorous causal determinism. Their account of natural events includes the state of the entire universe from one moment to the next; 'outside interference' is therefore not an option and rare events are determined in the same way as events that happen regularly. Nor do the Stoics acknowledge that the limitations of human knowledge justify the assumption of accidental causes. According to their doctrine everything happens of necessity and in accordance with the laws of nature. The Stoics were not only determinists—they were fatalists as well, because they regarded the laws of nature as the decrees of a divine mind that pervades and determines everything in the universe.

Between the Aristotelians and the Stoics there is, then, a fundamental disagreement on matters of principle, a fact that provoked later Aristotelians to defend Aristotle's conception of contingency and chance against the attacks of the Stoics.[17] The controversy therefore not only continued through late antiquity, but it also influenced Christian philosophers. The early modern scientists rejected both divine providence and teleology. If chance and contingency are still with us, they are so for statistical reasons: different types of events occur with different frequency, so that rare events are treated as chance events, and rare unintended results are treated as fortuitous. However, this does not mean that rare events are not causally determined.[18]

4   Ethical Determinism

Philosophers familiar with Aristotle's ethics may wonder, at first, why ethics should be included in this discussion at all, in view of Aristotle's warning not to expect mathematical precision in that field. As he asserts at the beginning of the *Nicomachean Ethics*, there is a lot of fluctuation in ethical matters, so that one must be satisfied with premises that indicate the truth only "roughly and in outline, and to expect consequences of the same type."[19] In ethics there are, therefore, no strict rules or precepts; they rather apply only 'for the most part'. Given this 'principle of uncertainty', why should ethics be included in a discussion of determinism?

Aristotle's warning against the expectation of undue precision in ethics is often misunderstood. He does not intend to say that the basic concepts and principles of ethics lack precision, or that there are no rules and laws. His *caveat* concerns only the existence of precise general rules about what is right and wrong in particular actions, for adjustments have to be made in order to apply the general ethical rules to the particular circumstances. These adjustments concern such questions as who the agent is, in what relation he stands to the person affected by his action, the moment in time when the action is to take place, the means to be employed, and so on. Aristotle compares the situation of an agent in ethics to that of a captain at sea and to that of a medical doctor.[20] Although there are general rules of the art, adjustments to particular situations may be required (e.g., in order to navigate a ship in a heavy storm, or to treat a particular patient in a critical condition).

The uncertainty concerning what is right or wrong in such situations suggests that Aristotle regards the agent as free to make those adjustments. It might seem strange, therefore, that a question concerning freedom and determinism in Aristotle's ethics should even arise. For Aristotle does not employ the kind of terminology that is typical of the contemporary discussion of freedom and determinism. 'Freedom'—*eleutheria*—is used only in the political sense of free birth and autonomy; and, notoriously, in classical Greek there is no term denoting the 'will' as an independent psychological faculty.[21] But though Aristotle does not address free will as 'the' problem of determinism he does discuss the question under what conditions our actions are 'up to us'—*eph hêmin*. And this is the term that was used after him in the centuries-long debates about freedom and determinism between the Stoics, who were card-carrying determinists, and their opponents—the Platonists, Peripatetics, Epicureans, and the Sceptics.

If Aristotle can be regarded as the father of that debate that is so because in the *Nicomachean Ethics* he is very much concerned with the conditions under which our actions are 'up to us': they must be voluntary, that is, without compulsion by external force and with knowledge of the actions' particular circumstances. Furthermore, actions must be in accordance with the agents' deliberations and choices, and their aims or ends must be in accordance with the agents' wishes. All this is pointed out with care and quite extensively, at least by Aristotle's standards, in *EN* III 1–5. So why should there be a problem concerning determinism with respect to human actions? For it seems quite clear that he regards our actions as 'up to us' in the sense that we can either do them or leave them, according to our wishes.[22]

The question of the determination of human actions according to Aristotle deserves closer inspection, because it concerns the fact that he treats actions as dependent on the agent's character. This is not a side-issue; it is, rather, one of the salient points of Aristotle's conception of ethics. Virtues of character are the dispositions (*hexeis*), which are acquired by habituation from early on—not only to do, but to like doing the proper things under the right circumstances and to dislike doing the wrong ones. The provision of the right moral education by habituation is, therefore, the hallmark of Aristotelian ethics. The right moral training does not just concern the virtues of character; it is also concerns the acquisition of practical reason, of *phronesis*. 'Habituation' is therefore not as simple as it may sound. For Aristotle does not have in mind mere habits that are acquired by routine and drill, like that of using knives and forks, of swimming, or of riding a bicycle. Instead, he is concerned with the acquisition of the right emotional set-up, which determines an agent's motivations, as well as with her acquisition of practical reason. For both jointly determine the agent's deliberations and decisions.

The fact that we are determined by our character and practical reason is not regarded as a problem by Aristotle; it is in fact the very idea and aim of his ethics. For the acquisition of the right dispositions is what moral education is all about: it is to ensure that the morally well-brought-up person will both aim for the appropriate end and choose the right means in every situation. There is a division of labor between character and practical reason: while character determines an agent's wish for a certain end, practical reason determines her choice of the ways and means.[23] Such determinism is at work not just in practical affairs; it also works in purely theoretical disciplines. For example, a person who has understood the premises of a syllogism will immediately draw the right conclusion. Similarly, someone who has mastered arithmetic will do his calculations in the right way. In that sense Aristotle is not just a moral, but also an intellectual determinist. If I happen not to draw the right conclusions or to miscalculate, then either my logical abilities and mathematical knowledge are not as firm as they are supposed to be, or some accidental factor must have interfered with my reasoning and calculation. For instance, something or someone may have distracted me, so that I did not pay sufficient attention to particular flaws in my reasoning. Similarly, I may have been too tired or suffered some other kind of impediment to the proper exercise of my disposition to make use of my knowledge of metaphysics, physics, or mathematics in the right way. The same conditions may have impeded, *mutatis mutandis*, my exercise of practical reason.

Although Aristotle regards the results of moral deliberations and decisions as predetermined in that way, he would find the question puzzling whether a person who has been properly brought up 'cannot help doing the right thing'. For Aristotle, it is not a question of automatically conceiving of the right aims and the appropriate ways and means of action. Agents, rather, have to employ their moral and intellectual faculties to engage in the right kind of deliberations and decisions of how to act in every particular situation. And that can be an intricate business, for the result is not pre-programmed but rather needs to be worked out in every particular case. Routine decisions will do only in routine cases. As Aristotle frequently points out, actions have to concur with the conditions of the case in question, according to what commentators are wont to call the 'parameters of moral actions', that is, what, to whom, by what means, and when something ought to be done.[24] And the same applies to the affections or emotions, the *pathê*. Agents with the right moral frame of mind will feel and act in the appropriate way, unless something interferes. And that is all that is required to meet the condition that our actions be 'up to us', according to Aristotle.

5   Limitations on What Is 'Up to Us'

But if all is well, why should there be a problem concerning determinism in ethics? There is one point in the *Nicomachean Ethics* where Aristotle explicitly raises the question whether we are responsible for our own character and therefore also for our own actions. Aristotle does so in the wake of his explanation that our character is up to us, at *EN* III 5, 1113b3–1114a3. In fact, he raises two objections. The first one he quickly brushes aside, while he seems to be somewhat hesitant concerning the second one.

(1) The first objection takes up the claim that our character is 'up to us', because we not only actively contribute to its acquisition, but we also continue to take care of it. Aristotle's hypothetical objection reads as follows: "But perhaps someone is the kind of person not to take care (*epimelêthênai*)" (1114a3). Aristotle quickly brushes off this objection on the ground that carelessness is an acquired trait too.[25] No one acquires bad moral habits by slack living without being aware of that fact, and only a fool would not know the consequences of a particular kind of conduct. But if a person knows that she is on a slippery slope, so to speak, this means that she accepts her moral deterioration voluntarily. And Aristotle compares such carelessness with the acquisition of an illness of the body by bad living. Such an acquired bad condition will turn out to be irreversible later on, even if the person should then wish to change their character or habits:

> In that case it was *then* open to him not to be ill, but not now, when he has thrown away his chance, just as when you have let a stone go it is too late to recover it; but yet it was up to you to throw it, since the moving principle was in you. So, too, to the unjust and the self-indulgent person it was open at the beginning not to become a person of this kind, and so they are unjust and self-indulgent persons voluntarily; but now that they have become so it is not possible for them not to be so. (1114a13–19)[26]

Just where the beginning of that slippery slope lies is, of course, a good question. One may wonder whether a person is not always either too young or too old to have the first stages of moral deterioration under her own control. At first she is in the hands of her parents and teachers, and later on she has already acquired bad habits, so that she can no longer get rid of them. But Aristotle seems to think otherwise; as he explains elsewhere, reason sets in at age fourteen; it is possible to understand the values of the world and to adopt or reject them at that age, and no one is an inveterate liar or a criminal, as yet.[27]

(2) The second objection against the tenet that our character is 'up to us' is treated with more circumspection. Aristotle acknowledges that humans are not all born alike and are not exposed to the same opportunities through their upbringing. In raising the issue of inequalities of birth, upbringing, and opportunity as factors of moral development, we do not know whether Aristotle is concerned with an actual objection by an opponent, or whether this is a self-fabricated difficulty. At any rate, Aristotle treats with care the contention that, although everyone acts with regard to what they find best, the impression they have of what the best is depends on natural predispositions:

[A]nd the aiming at the end is not self-chosen but one must be born with an eye (*opsis*), as it were, by which to judge rightly and choose what is truly good, and he is well endowed by nature who is well endowed with this. For it is what is greatest and most noble, and what we cannot get or learn from another, but must have just such as it was when given us at birth, and to be well endowed with this will be perfect and true excellence of natural endowment. If this is true, then, how will virtue be more voluntary than vice? To both men alike, the good and the bad, the end appears as it is fixed by nature or however it may be, and it is by referring everything else to this that men do whatever they do. (III 5, 1114b5–16)

That Aristotle should take up such an objection is in itself strange, for earlier in the *EN*, he has rejected the possibility that human beings are by nature good or bad, either as a kind of 'gift of the gods' or 'by chance'.[28] The way in which Aristotle deals with the possibility that character and moral virtue are innate rather than acquired is also strange, because in his further comments he does not reject that possibility offhand, but leaves open the question of whether or not the way in which an aim or end (*telos*) *appears* to be good or bad to a person is determined by nature. Instead, Aristotle concentrates on the fact that the choice of the means is up to the agent, as an argument that his actions are 'up to him'. Nevertheless, Aristotle seems to accept a certain limitation of the agent's responsibility concerning the acquisition of virtue and vice:

If then, as is asserted, the virtues are voluntary, for we are ourselves some-how *co-causes* (*synaitioi*) of our states of character, and it is by being persons of a certain kind that we set the end to be so and so, the vices also will be voluntary, for the same is true of them. (5, 1114b21–25)

The use of *synaitios* ('co-cause') seems to represent an unusual limita-tion of human responsibility on Aristotle's side. The expression *synaitios* is not used elsewhere in Aristotle's ethics.[29] Not only that; but Aristotle nowhere else attributes to the agent a 'natural eye' for what is a good end.[30] Because this concession concerning a 'natural eye' and a 'co-responsibility' of the agent comes only at the very end of the general discussion of virtues of character in Book III, Aristotle may, of course, merely be toying with the idea that there are limiting conditions of an agent's responsibility ('even if …'). But there may be more to it than that. For this concession does accord with Aristotle's notion, expressed earlier, that humans differ in their natural predispositions toward one vice rather than another so that they ought to 'lean over backward' to correct those vices (*EN* II 9). In addition, Aristotle much later on in the *EN* mentions the existence of 'natural virtues' from birth on—predispositions which, however, need training and direction by practical reason, because without the aid of reason people are bound to slip and fall (VI 13, 1144b1–14). Aristotle thereby admits, in a way, that certain people by nature have 'bet-ter cards', morally speaking, than others. For he acknowledges that there can be a difference in 'moral luck': someone who is born altogether ugly, into a bad family, and who is lonely, childless, and friendless, is not suited to live a happy life (*EN* I 1, 1099b2). By that Aristotle does not only mean that such a person will feel miserable, but also that her chances of leading a good life are curtailed.

But there is more to the question of moral determination than concern with the limiting conditions on an agent's responsibility for his or her actions. Aristotle treats it as the hallmark of ethics that we are determined by our character for better or worse. As he sees it, knowledge of the right aim alone is not sufficient. The agent has to have the right emotional dispositions, which affect what aims and goals an agent chooses, as well as the agent's choice of the ways and means to attain that end. The ques-tion is, then, how far these dispositions are in the agent's control. Aristotle often speaks as if actions and emotions are on a par—that is, that they are equally important factors in the determination of our actions. But reflection shows that there is a disparity between them: deliberation and choice concern the 'parameters of action' (e.g., how, on whom, and by what means one acts), and they are a matter of choice. But the respective feelings, the *pathê*, are not chosen by the agent: "We feel anger and fear without choice (*aproairetôs*), but the virtues are modes of choice or involve choice" (II 5, 1106a). Because Aristotle nowhere repeats that restriction concerning the feelings, it is often overlooked by the commentators; it is all the easier to miss the contrast between actions and emotions, because Aristotle most of the time speaks as if they are on a par.

That the emotions (*pathê*) are not a matter of choice but reactive states is confirmed by their treatment in the *Rhetoric*; for an orator must be able to either provoke or assuage the audience's emotions. The definition of anger shows how this works: "Anger may be defined as a desire accompanied by pain, for revenge for an apparent slight at the hands of men who have no call to slight oneself or one's friends and family" (*Rhet.* II 2, 1378a31–33).[31] The orator must be able to create the impression that such an emotional response is called for. But there is more to the emotion of anger than that:

> It must be felt because the other has done or intended to do something to him or one of his friends. It must always be attended by a certain pleasure—that which arises from the expectation of revenge. For it is pleasant to think that you will attain what you aim at, and nobody aims at what he thinks he cannot attain. (1378a39–b5)

The *pathê* of mature persons are highly trained feelings with propositional content; for they do presuppose an assessment not only of the kind of injury that has been inflicted, but also of the satisfaction that is to be expected. These affections clearly are not the 'raw feelings' shared by young children and animals, but they are conditioned responses that determine an agent's aims and decisions.[32]

That the emotions have propositional content is confirmed by Aristotle's explanation of the *pathê* in *De anima*, a work on natural science:

A physicist would define an affection of soul differently from a dialectician; the latter would define e.g. anger as the appetite for returning pain for pain, or something like that, while the former would define it as the boiling of the blood or warm substance around the heart. The one assigns the material conditions, the other the form or account, for what he states is the account of the fact, though for its actual existence it must be the embodiment of it in a material such as described by the other. (1, 403a29–b4)

Feelings are, then, much more complex than the discussion in the *EN* leads one to expect. This is worth noting, for it explains what Aristotle has in mind when he says that the end or aim (the *telos*) of an action is determined by one's character—for better or worse. For it is the 'wish' (*boulêsis*), a kind of desire, that settles the end. Unfortunately Aristotle is not very explicit about how goals are determined by wishes in the short chapter that he dedicates to *boulêsis* (*EN* III 4). But he explains that wishes are caused by what appears to be good to a particular person, regardless of whether it is really so, or only apparently so. The good person has the right impressions, the bad person the wrong ones:

> The good person judges (*krinei*) each class of things rightly, and in each case the truth appears to him. For each state of character has its own noble and pleasant object, and perhaps the good person differs from others most by seeing the truth in each thing, being as it were the norm and measure for them. (1113a29–33)

But it is worth noting that Aristotle does not say that the object of a wish is a matter of choice; choice is concerned, rather, with the actions that lead up to that end. The end is determined by the impression that the person has of what is desirable, and these impressions also depend on one's acquired dispositions, on one's character.

All this is important because it suggests that the determination of one's actions, in so far as the aim or end is concerned, is not a matter of rational choice, but depends essentially on one's character.[33] In the case of grownups, the respective emotions that determine their choices are not 'raw feelings'; although these emotions arise in the non-rational part of the soul, they contain 'trained impressions' of what is good or bad about the prospective ends. A wish is not a purely 'rational desire', as many interpreters assume, but a 'rationally informed desire'.[34]

6   Determinate But 'Up to Us'?

Although the emotions are habitually acquired dispositions to respond to the situation a person finds herself in and not a matter of choice, Aristotle does not regard that conditioning as a negative, but rather as a positive and even as a necessary aspect of human responsibility. For moral conditioning is, at the same time, the guarantee of reliability. A person who lacks moral dispositions will act in haphazard ways and represent a menace to herself and others. Such a lack is, of course, not among the conditions addressed in the discussion of 'free will'. Unpredictable people acting in erratic or bizarre ways are not regarded as the epitome of free agents, but rather as freaks.

Aristotle is quite aware of the fact that there are people with natural deficiencies. He discusses not only morbid states and madness, but also compulsive states (*EN* VII 5). His examples for the latter are not kleptomania or pyromania, but relatively harmless conditions, such as compulsive nail-chewing or the plucking of hair. Apart from such morbid states, he regards human beings as morally malleable both by the right kind and by the wrong kind of education and training. But it is not just such deficiencies of nature that are impediments to the right kind of moral development. Aristotle also admits that some people have better cards than others—and it is not always up to the individuals to compensate for having been dealt with a bad set of cards by playing them well. Apart from an individual's natural endowment, a certain amount of external resources is necessary, not just in order for the individual to be able to act in the right way, but also for the acquisition of the virtues because they presuppose the right training from early on. As mentioned before, Aristotle is quite aware of the fact that a person's development depends on external conditions that are beyond her control. But that is not something that Aristotle would deny, anyway. Not everything is 'up to us', and certain external factors clearly are not. As Aristotle states, one has to make the best use of the available resources, just as a shoemaker will try to make the best kinds of shoes possible, given the kind of leather he has to work with, and a competent general will try to make the best possible use of the troops and equipment at his disposition.[35]

According to Aristotle, the scope of the development of one's moral and intellectual potential clearly has its limitations, as does one's ability to fulfill one's ends and aims; but Aristotle seems not to be worried by such limitations. Nor is he worried about the issue of ethical determinism as such. Once we have acquired a certain personality, we will always act in kind, unless some external or internal factor prevents us from doing so. But Aristotle treats this preconditioning as a positive factor, and not as a limitation of human freedom and responsibility. For actions crucially depend on the agent's deliberation and choice.

Finally, it deserves mention that Aristotle is not worried about the possibility that humans are driven by machines that are operating in their heads, as is suggested by the illustration on the poster of this conference.[36] Aristotle's insouciance is due to the fact that he does not regard thinking as a physical process that is caused by a corporeal organ. This view is not as eccentric as it must seem at first sight. Not only are the objects of thought immaterial, their presence is not *de rigeur* for processes of thought as it is in the case of sense-perception. For all activities of the senses depend on the physical impact of their objects.[37] The mind, by contrast, can conceive of any object, either present or absent; it is also free to conceive of non-existent objects and states of affairs. And while the senses can be disturbed or even destroyed by a strong sensory impact, such as by flashing lights or thunder, the mind is not affected by hard thinking; in fact, it functions all the better in the wake of the most intensive kinds of thought (*De anima* III 4 429a29–b5).

According to Aristotle, the brain has nothing to do with either sense-perception or thought. He regards the brain as a cooling-device, because of its seemingly inert, cold, and bloodless condition; its function is supposedly to cool down the blood that is sent up from the region around the heart and the lungs.[38] But although Aristotle treats the heart as the center of perception, memory, and thought, his explanation of the kind of interaction that is at work between sense-perception and the mind in concept-formation remains hazy. As far as the reception of the sensory qualities is concerned, his comparison with the imprints made by a signet-ring is quite suggestive:

[I]n the way in which a piece of wax takes on the impress of a signet-ring without the iron or gold; what produces the impression is a signet of bronze or gold, but not *qua* bronze or gold: in a similar way the sense is affected by what is coloured or flavoured. (*De anima* II 12, 424a18–23)

It is much harder to see how the soul is supposed to proceed from the sensible forms to the intelligible forms (*De an.* III 4). The explanation that the intelligent part of the soul has no nature of its own, but only receives the intelligible forms, does nothing to fill that gap. This explanation confines itself to the postulate that the soul itself is without matter (*aneu hylês*), on the ground that before the soul thinks anything it is nothing yet also 'potentially all the intelligible forms of the objects' it can think about. Once the soul thinks, on the other hand, it becomes all the intelligible forms in actuality.[39]

There is no further explanation of the reception of the intelligible forms by the soul provided by Aristotle. The depiction of the soul's progress from sense-perception *via* memory to the intelligible content in the much discussed final chapter in *Posterior Analytics* II 19 does not shed further light on the critical step: of how, exactly, the mind (*nous*) is able to progress from sensory experience and to extract the intelligible content from such experience.[40] Aristotle's language is highly metaphorical:

And from experience, or from the universal which has come to rest in the soul (the one apart from the many, i.e. whatever is one and the same in all these items), there comes a principle of skill and understanding—of skill if it deals with how things come about, of understanding if it deals with what is the case) … they come about from perception—as in a battle, when a rout has occurred, first one man makes a stand, then another does, and then another, until a position of strength is reached. And the soul is such as to be capable of undergoing this … Thus it is plain that we must get to know the primitives (*ta prôta*) by induction, for this is the way in which perception instils universals. (100a6–b5)

There is no further explanation of the progress from the particular sensibles to the universal intelligible forms; such progress just happens in the soul that is capable of it.

That Aristotle held an immaterialist position concerning the mind is worth noting, for it explains why he does not envisage problems concerning the way the mind works in decision-making, of the kind that plague modern discussions of free will and responsibility. For Aristotle there is no mind-body problem; for according to him there is no causal mechanism that supposedly 'drives' the mind in the way the brain does, according to the advocates of the primacy of the brain as the center of thought and consciousness in contemporary debates. If Aristotle has a problem, then it is a mind-sense problem. If Aristotle recognized such a problem, however, he does not seem to have regarded it as fatal to his account of the mind and its content. His lack of concern with mechanical explanations explains, at the same time, why he is not worried about determinism in ethics. Aristotle regards as relevant only the way that our choices are determined by our self-acquired moral personality. And that determination, in Aristotle's eyes, is not a negative, but a positive fact. It promises reliability in the case of the good person and at least predictability in the case of the bad one. He would not regard moral indetermination, vacillation, or eccentricity as signs of moral autonomy, but rather of moral weakness.

Could people decide and act differently from the way they do, in fact, decide and act? If Aristotle's assertion holds true that "in those cases where acting is up to us, so is not acting,"[41] then in principle people could think and act differently from the way they do, so far as far as deliberation and choice are concerned; however, they would have to have reasons for deciding otherwise. The 'parameters of action' that Aristotle keeps referring to—that is, how, when, on whom, and by what means one ought to act—are not compelling factors in themselves; they are, rather, factors that are determined by the standards that the morally mature person has accepted.[42] There is no compulsion implied, here, but only an acknowledgment that well-considered decisions are due to a person's character and her judgment of what is the right thing to do, all things considered. These considerations explain why Aristotle regards humans as determined by their character, and also why he regards that kind of determination as a good thing—and politically speaking, also as a necessary thing, if a community is to function properly. That is why citizens must grow up under good laws that regulate their education (*EN* X 9, 1179b31–1180a5).

The citizens have to be able to trust and to rely on each other, and that presupposes that they do, as a whole, act in character.

It was only in later antiquity that moral determinism came to be seen as a problem, once the Stoics had entered into the fray and raised the stakes. They were not only physicalists in the sense that they held that everything that happens has physical causes and that the same causes have the same effects; the Stoics held, in addition, that there are universal cosmic laws that predetermine the outcome of everything by necessity.[43] Thus, according to the Stoics, it had been necessary from the dawn of creation that Oedipus would eventually kill his father and marry his mother.

From the Hellenistic age on an incessant battle waged between determinists, compatibilists, and indeterminists; it is a battle that still goes on in the modern age.[44] In late antiquity that battle was greatly intensified, once God's will became an extra factor in the combatants' arguments in late antiquity and through the Middle Ages.[45] But of those later developments Aristotle could know nothing. According to him, it is up to us how to behave, and it is also, to a more limited degree, up to us what kinds of persons we turn out to be. And that is why Aristotle treats people as responsible for their own actions, certain constraining factors notwithstanding.

Notes

1. In his *On Fate* 39 Cicero mentions various philosophers who held the view that everything is determined and necessitated by fate, including Democritus, Heraclitus, Empedocles, as well as Aristotle. But this is an *obiter dictum* that Cicero neither justifies nor elaborates.

2. In the *Phaedrus*, for instance, Plato speaks of the 'law of destiny' that determines the fate of the different kinds of souls (248b-249c: *thesmos Adrasteias*), and in *Republic* X 616b-617 he vividly describes the revolutions of the 'Spindle of Necessity' (*atraktos Anankês*) and the way her daughters, the three Fates—Lachesis, Clotho, and Atropos—"sing of the past, the present, and the future." The power of fate has been invoked in the poetic tradition from Homer on. But it concerns the inexplicable

turn in the heroes' lives that sometimes even the gods cannot prevent, not the regular course of events (on this issue see Dodds 1951).

3. For an overall account see Sorabji (1980).

4. The question whether Aristotle's suspension of truth values was a reaction to the challenge by certain members of the Megarian School that only what is real is possible must be left aside here (see his discussion in *Met.* Θ 3).

5. Aristotle may have had the famous Sea Battle of Salamis in 480 BC in mind, because it remained uncertain until the last moment whether that battle would actually take place: Xerxes, the Persian king, was lured by a ruse into the narrow straits at Salamis, where his enormous fleet was at a disadvantage against the small but agile Greek fleet.

6. The translation is that of J. L. Ackrill (1963) (repr. (ed.) Barnes 1985).

7. From the 1950s to the 1980s there was a host of literature with ever new suggestions concerning the interpretation of the text; for a summary of that controversy see Frede (1985). The problem of 'future truth' was the subject of several monographs; Weidemann 1994 (^{2}2002); Gaskin (1995); Whitaker (1996). For a judicious reassessment of the problematic see Crivelli (2006, 34–37 (short summary) and 198–233 (detailed discussion)).

8. This distinction is introduced in *De Generatione et Corruptione* II 11, 337a39–b10.

9. *De interpretatione* 6, 17a25–26: "An affirmation (*apophantikos logos*) is a statement affirming something of something, a negation is a statement denying something of something."

10. See Bobzien (1998a).

11. For an orientation see Annas and Barnes (1985); Bett (ed.) (2010).

12. A survey is given by Craig (1988). In recent years the focus has shifted from Aristotle to the later tradition, as witnessed by the fact that the *Stanford Encyclopedia of Philosophy* contains several articles on Medieval theories of future truth and future contingents, but none on Aristotle's discussion of that problem. See, for instance, the articles by S. Knuuttila 'Medieval Theories of Future Contingents' (2006, rev. 2015) and by L. Zagzebski, 'Foreknowledge and Free Will' (2004, rev. 2017).

13. *Meteorologica* I 1; 6–8.

14. On the notion of cause, see Sorabji (1980); Frede (1992); Judson (ed.) (1991).

15. Translation Ross (1924) (ed. Barnes 1985).

16. See Aristotle's *Physics* II 4–8.
17. Alexander of Aphrodisias' *On Fate* (transl. Sharples 2003) is a witness of continued battles between the Stoics and the Aristotelians that lasted into the third century AD.
18. The netherworld of quantum physics is ignored here.
19. *EN* I 3, 1094b11–27; the translation follows W.D. Ross (2009).
20. See *EN* II 2, 1104a3–11.
21. The Greek terms *akôn* and *hekôn* (also *akousion—hekousion*) which are usually translated as 'voluntary' and 'involuntary' do not contain any reference to a will, as do their Latin counterparts. The Greek terms not only apply to what is done wittingly and willingly, they also apply to what is done wittingly but quite unwillingly and *contre coeur*. The lack of a concept of will in antiquity has been discussed ever since Dihle's 1982 monograph. Although his contention that the will was a late innovation by Christian philosophers, based on precedents in Hebrew, met with criticism, it is by now generally acknowledged that the will was a late-comer in Greek philosophy; see Kahn (1988); Bobzien (1998b); M. Frede (2011). The dispensability of the conception of a will is famously argued for by Williams (1993).
22. For a closer analysis of Aristotle's text see Bobzien (2014; Sauvé Meyer (2014).
23. For a detailed discussion see Frede, D. (2014) and Frede, M. (2014).
24. See *EN* II 3, 11104b18–1105a1; 6, 1106b21–23 *et pass.*
25. Care (*epimeleia*) and carelessness (*ameleia*) are not part of Aristotle's canonic catalogue of virtues and vices of character, but he clearly does not ignore such secondary dispositions.
26. Aristotle expatiates somewhat longer on the difference between innate and acquired ills of the body, such as ugliness or blindness from birth on, in contradistinction to the kind of ugliness that is brought on by lack of exercise, or the blindness that is brought on by drinking (1114a22–30).
27. Aristotle approves of the division of life into periods of seven years in *Politics* VII 17, a division that reportedly goes back to Solon.
28. See *EN* I 9, where Aristotle discusses the possibility, raised by Plato in the *Meno*, of whether virtue is acquired by education or training on the one hand, or given by the gods or is acquired by chance (luck), on the other. Aristotle strenuously argues for the point that virtue is the result of both study and care.

29. In other works, the term *synaitios* refers to necessary, but not sufficient conditions. Fire is called a *synaitios* of nourishment in *De anima* II 4, 416a9–18; *Metaphysics* Δ 5 1015a20–26. The original meaning of *synaitios* seems to be a legal one: it designates an accomplice to a crime.

30. Aristotle introduces 'natural virtues' that humans have from birth on in *EN* VI 13, 1144b1–17; he emphasizes, however, that without practical reason people are bound to go wrong and he ends with the assertion that virtues in the proper sense require *phronêsis*.

31. Fear and confidence are also complex responses (*Rhet.* II 5, 1382a22–3): "Fear may be defined as a pain or disturbance due to the imagination of some destructive or painful evil in the future." Confidence depends on the estimate of the absence or remoteness of such an evil.

32. 'Habituation' clearly does not mean that people simply acquire habits of emotional reactions. For these emotional responses are 'in-formed' in quite a sophisticated way. An orator has to be able to provoke or to appease them by carefully chosen reasoning and an appropriate language.

33. In the discussion of the particular virtues and vices in Books III –V of the *EN* Aristotle focuses on actions rather than on emotions, so that in many cases one has to guess what, if any, emotion he has in mind. In the later books of the *EN*, the trained affections or emotions do not play much of a role; Aristotle merely mentions that they belong to the soul's non-rational part.

34. That Aristotle sometimes mentions purely rational wishes seems to contradict this assumption, but such desires as the desire to learn are clearly not determined by the virtues or vices of character.

35. See *EN* I 10, 1100b35–1101a6.

36. "Determinism and Freedom: Historical and Systematic Perspectives."

37. *De an.* II 5, 418a18–27.

38. The mechanism is explained at *PA* II 7. It must remain a moot point whether Aristotle would have given up his immaterialist position had he known anything about the nervous system that was discovered by Herophilus and Erasistratus, two doctors in Alexandria in the third century BC. Their discovery did not end the debate among philosophers between the Platonic encephalocentrists and the Aristotelian cardiocentrists. The controversy was put to an end only as the result of the work of Galen on the anatomy and the function of the brain. For more information on that development see the monograph by Rocca (2003); Chap. 1

provides a judicious account of the tradition from the Presocratics to Galen.

39. *De anima* III 8, 431b2020–432a3: "Let us repeat that the soul in a way is all existing things (ta onta pôs estin panta); for they are either sensible or thinkable, and knowledge of what is knowable *is* in a way what is knowable, and sense-perception *is* in a way what is sensible … It follows that the soul is analogous to a hand; for as the hand is a tool of tools, so is thought the form or forms and sense-perception the form of sensible things."

40. *An post.* II 100a3–100b5. The translation follows, with slight modifications, Barnes (1993). See also his commentary on this difficult text, 259–271.

41. *EN* III 5, 1113b5–14.

42. These parameters are the conditions of both the actions and the affections, as witnessed throughout *EN* Book II.

43. On the intricacies of the Stoic position, see Bobzien (1998a).

44. The most important witnesses are Cicero's *On Fate*, and the defense of the Aristotelian position in Alexander of Aphrodisias' *On Fate*. For an interpretation of the debate as witnessed by Cicero, see Bobzien (1998a); for Alexander, see Sharples (2003).

45. For an overview of the various positions, see Craig (1988).

References

Ackrill, John Lloyd. 1963. *Aristotle's Categories and De interpretatione.* Transl. with Notes. Oxford: Oxford University Press.

Annas, Julia, and Jonathan Barnes. 1985. *The Modes of Scepticism: Ancient Texts and Modern Interpretations.* Cambridge: Cambridge University Press.

Barnes, Jonathan, ed. 1985. *The Complete Works of Aristotle.* 2 vols. Princeton: Princeton University Press.

———. 1993. *Aristotle Posterior Analytics.* Trans. with a Commentary. Oxford: Oxford University Press.

Bett, Richard. 2010. *The Cambridge Companion to Ancient Scepticism.* Cambridge: Cambridge University Press.

Bobzien, Susanne. 1998a. *Determinism and Freedom in Stoic Philosophy.* Oxford: Oxford University Press.

———. 1998b. The Inadvertent Conception and Late Birth of the Free-Will Problem. *Phronesis* 43: 133–175.

———. 2014. Aristotle's Nicomachean Ethics 1113b7–7 and Free Choices. In *What is Up to Us? Studies on Causality and Responsibility in Ancient Philosophy*, ed. Pierre Destrée, Ricardo Salles, and Marco Zingano, 59–74. Sankt Augustin: Academia.

Craig, William L. 1988. *The Problem of Divine Foreknowledge and Future Contingents from Aristotle to Suarez*. Leiden: Brill.

Crivelli, Paolo. 2006. *Aristotle On Truth*. Cambridge: Cambridge University Press.

Destrée, Pierre, Ricardo Salles, and Marco Zingano, eds. 2014. *What is Up to Us? Studies on Causality and Responsibility in Ancient Philosophy*. Sankt Augustin: Academia.

Dihle, Albrecht. 1982. *The Theory of Will in Classical Antiquity*. Berkeley: University of California Press.

Eric R. Dodds. 1951. The Greeks and the Irrational. Berkeley: University of California Press.

Frede, Dorothea. 1985. The Sea-Battle Reconsidered: A Defense of the Traditional Interpretation. *Oxford Studies in Ancient Philosophy* 3: 31–87.

———. 1992. Accidental Causes in Aristotle. *Synthese* 92: 39–62.

———. 2014. Free Will in Aristotle? In *What is Up to Us? Studies on Causality and Responsibility in Ancient Philosophy*, ed. Pierre Destrée, Ricardo Salles, and Marco Zingano, 39–58. Sankt Augustin: Academia.

Frede, Michael. 2011. A Free Will. Origins of the Notion in Ancient Thought. Berkeley: University of California Press.

———. 2014. The 'Eph Hêmin' in Ancient Philosophy. In *What is Up to Us? Studies on Causality and Responsibility in Ancient Philosophy*, ed. Pierre Destrée, Ricardo Salles, and Marco Zingano, 351–364. Sankt Augustin: Academia.

Gaskin, Richard. 1995. *The Sea Battle and the Master Argument: Aristotle and Diodorus Cronus on the Metaphysics of the Future*. Berlin: De Gruyter.

Judson, Lindsay, ed. 1991. *Aristotle's Physics. A Collection of Essays*. Oxford: Oxford University Press.

Kahn, Charles H. 1988. Discovering the Will. From Aristotle to Augustine. In *The Question of 'Eclecticism'. Studies in Later Greek Philosophy*, ed. John M. Dillon and A.A. Long, 234–259. Berkeley: University of California Press.

Knuutila, Simo. 2006, 2015 (rev.). Medieval Theories of Future Contingents. In *The Stanford Encyclopedia of Philosophy*, ed. Edward Zalta. https://plato.stanford.edu/archies/win2015/entries/medieval-futcont/.

Rocca, Julius. 2003. *Galen on the Brain*. Leiden: Brill.
Ross, William David. 1924. *Aristotle's Metaphysics*. Oxford: Oxford University Press.
———. 2009. *Aristotle. The Nicomachean Ethics*. Revised with an Introduction and Notes by L. Brown. Oxford: Oxford University Press.
Sauvé-Meyer, Susan. 2014. Aristotle on What is Up to Us and What is Contingent. In *What is Up to Us? Studies on Causality and Responsibility in Ancient Philosophy*, ed. Pierre Destrée, Ricardo Salles, and Marco Zingano, 75–90. Sankt Augustin: Academia.
Sharples, Robert W. 2003. *Alexander of Aphrodisias On Fate*. Text, Translation and Commentary. London: Duckworth.
Sorabji, Richard. 1980. *Necessity, Cause, and Blame: Perspectives on Aristotle's Theory*. London: Duckworth.
Weidemann, Hermann. 1994. *Aristoteles Peri Hermeias*. Übersetzt und erläutert. Werke in deutscher Übersetzung, Bd. 1.2. Berlin: Akademie Verlag.
———. 2002. De Interpretatione. In *The Oxford Handbook of Aristotle*, ed. Christopher Shields, 81–112. Oxford: Oxford University Press.
Whitaker, C.W.A. 1996. *Aristotle's De Interpretatione: Contradiction and Dialectic*. Oxford: Oxford University Press.
Williams, Bernard. 1993. *Shame and Necessity*. Berkeley: University of California Press.
Zagzebski, Linda. 2004, 2017 (rev.). Foreknowledge and Free Will. In *The Stanford Encyclopedia of Philosophy*, ed. Edward Zalta. https://plato.stanford.edu/cgi-bin/encyclopedia/archinfo.cgi?entry=free-will-foreknowledge.

4

Defending Free Will

Nicholas Rescher

1 Basic Issues

Self-understanding is not a prominent human virtue. The Socratic injunction "Know thyself!" presents a challenge rather than a *fait accompli*. The human agent is not the best—let alone the infallible—judge of his own motivations; his understanding of his wishes is generally imperfect and often confused and mistaken. Accordingly people are far from being a good judge of whether these acts are free.

However the advocates of free will are not engaged in insisting that all human actions are free, and not even that most or many are free, but only that some are so. The correct question is not that of the *processes* of free actions but of their *existence*. The fact that we can be mistaken in this regard, and even the fact (if it is a fact) that we are often or generally mistaken, is beside the point when the product at issue is that of the question if we are sometimes correct in this regard.

But if self-awareness does not establish freedom, what does? And just what is at issue with such freedom?

N. Rescher (✉)
University of Pittsburgh, Pittsburgh, PA, USA
e-mail: rescher@pitt.edu

© The Author(s), under exclusive license to Springer Nature Switzerland AG 2021
M. Hausmann, J. Noller (eds.), *Free Will*,
https://doi.org/10.1007/978-3-030-61136-1_4

We are often told that free will is the capacity to choose and control one's action. But this account is gravely incomplete. The bank manager who opens the safe because the robbers hold his family hostage chooses to do so (for good reason) and is in full control of his actions. But yet his act is not free, because for freedom those choices and actions must be motivated autonomously by the agent's own self-engendered agenda and made at the agent's own discretion. The issue of free agency is obviously complicated.

This chapter will address seven questions regarding freedom of the will:

1. Just what is freedom of the will?
2. Does freedom require control?
3. Does freedom require that the agent could have done otherwise?
4. Does predictability preclude freedom?
5. Is an act's freedom compatible with its causal explanation?
6. How can freedom of the will be evidentiated?
7. Is free will unscientific?

* Question 1: *What Is Free Will?*

Suppose I announce raising my right hand a few seconds hence for the sakes of an example and then proceed to do so. What is it that qualifies my action as free? The answer is simply that nothing discernable whatsoever evert its being free. It does not arise from post-hypnotic suggestion, from threat or bribery, from force majeure or duress, from conditions or brainwashing, or from any other of the various possible impediments of freedom. In a way freedom constitutes a default explanation: when no other impediment appears on the explanatory scene it is freedom that does the job. It is tautologous but nonetheless true that freedom is an absence—the lack of freedom. An act is free if it violates none of the standard impediments, even as it is legal when it breaks no laws, or moral when it breaks no (moral) rules.

Only when there is sound reason for regarding an agent's own naturally formed (i.e., non-manipulated) motivations (preferences, desires, goals) we are entitled to see the agent as proceeding freely.

And one must distinguish between free will and free agency. The former—free will—is presumably a matter of an agent being able to decide actions on his own terms. Free agents should be in a position to decide and choose what they will try to do. But what they actually do generally depends on circumstances and conditions over which the agents have no control. For consider. The agent freely administers the pill he thinks to be a remedy. In fact a poison has been substituted and the agent's act kills the victim. The decision to try to provide aid is free. His actual act of administering the poison is not. Only when things go "according to plan" do free decisions engender free actions.

In the final analysis freedom of the will calls for an agent's capacity for deciding issues of light and action on his own terms.

What has to be the case for it to be said correctly that an agent performed an action "of his own free will"? An agent's action is free when its occurrence can be explained fully and adequately in terms of that agent's consciously formed impulses to act (his own wishes, wants, preferences, desires, etc.) If this requires agent-externally originating impulsion—threat, force majeure, hypnosis, brainwashing, and so on—then that act is no longer freedom. Free agency is a substantially psychological rather than a purely metaphysical concept.

But what if the action, while indeed proceeding from the agent's own preference and motivations, does so when those preferences and motivations themselves are originally imposed upon the agent ab extra by manipulated conditions, brain washing, or the like? Then of course those acts are no longer free. When an agent's motivations are shaped by external manipulation rather than by ordinary and natural means, then freedom is abrogated. For authentic freedom those motivating preferences and aims must originate in the normal course of formative events.

After all, a person's motivations—his preference, tastes, desires, goals, and so on—are not (or at least not generally) external impositions forced upon him against his will. They are formed naturally, autonomously, in the ordinary course of personal development. To be impelled by these motivations is not an ab extra intrusion upon a person's will; they are, on the contrary, fundamentally constituent elements of that will itself; they do not impede its freedom but bring it to expression. They do not block a person's will but enable it to function. When I proceed in the way of doing "what I please" I am not subjecting myself to an external impetus but exercising my free will.

Accordingly, acting from free will is not at odds with more specific modes of motivation (acts done from greed are not unfree)—on the contrary it can be encompassed and encapsulated within them. When I say that X did something "to please his wife" or "to avert going bankrupt," I am not implying that what he did was not an act of free will. Quite to the contrary, I am simply being explicit as to the specific sort of neutral motivation for his free decisions. To reemphasize, acting from the agent's own, appropriately formed motives is the very essence of free will.

Agent control itself is neither necessary nor sufficient for free agency. The victim the robbers have ordered "to put 'em up" controls his action yet is not free; the worshipper whose "Amen" is altogether automatic acts freely yet is no longer actively engaged. What counts for freedom as such is not just control but *ultimate* control, which is something a great deal more complicated because it reaches back into what is authentically one's own.

In the interests of clarity one must distinguish between the metaphysical/ontological freedom at issue with the question "Is the act in question one for which the agent bears *productive* responsibility; is it something he did in line with his decisions and choices?" from the very different *additional* question of moral freedom: "Given that the act is one for which the agent bears such productive responsibility, to what extent does he bear *moral* responsibility for it as reflected by praise or blame?" Metaphysical freedom is only a matter of exercising productivity via notice, while moral freedom, by contrast, also addresses the nature of the motivation at work. Moral freedom is thus a matter of proceeding on one's own account and one's own autonomously self-rooted motivation—acting spontaneously (*sua sponte*) in the Scholastic sense of the expression—"on one's own."[1]

A metaphysically free act is typically one that an agent can do or not do as he chooses via deliberation (however cursory), although even acts performed unthinkingly in line with a naturally formed *policy* of action that has issued in an automatic habit—brushing one's teeth in the morning, for example—will still count as a (metaphysically) free. Just this is what Descartes had in view when he wrote that "The faculty of will consists simply in our having the power of choosing to do something or choosing not to do it."[2] But this is far from the whole of it.

- Question 2: *Does Freedom Require Control?*

Control as such is not *sufficient* for freedom. The pilot whose plane is being hijacked may remain in control of the flight but is not free to direct it as he wishes. Nor is control *necessary* for freedom. For consider John Locke's example of the person who freely chooses to remain in a locked room, so that his remaining is free notwithstanding the fact that he does not control whether or not to remain. One can only say so that normally and in the usual run-of-the-mill situation, people who act freely are in control of what they do—and conversely.

However, one can and should acknowledge that people usually have free and unfettered control over what

- they *intend* to do,
- they *try* to do, and
- they wish or desire to do.

Again, however, there are exceptions to the rule. For even in such matters such control exists only in normal circumstances where motivation is not subject to the interference and control of others.

The freedom of agency hinges on matters of normality and standardness. Freedom is a default—a presumption—a condition of normality and the absence of countervailing factors.

Moral culpability requires free will and the will cannot reach beyond the range of awareness. One escapes culpability for the morally negative consequences of an act when there is no reason to expect them to ensue. Here ignorance—provided it itself is not culpably produced—is a valid excuse. Freedom and its ramifications may not demand control, but they do demand awareness. Only when those consequences form part of the agent's willing intentions is there grounds for reprehension.

- Question 3: *Does Freedom Require That the Agent "Could Have Done Otherwise"?*

Freedom requires that the agent acts in line with self-motivated (autonomous) choices! Does this automatically render unfree an act performed in circumstances where in fact the agent could not have acted otherwise had he chosen to do so? By no means. The idea at issue was demonstrated long ago by John Locke's telling example of the man who freely chooses to remain in a room all exits from which had (unbeknownst to him) been securely locked. There is no reason why a free choice cannot align with what is in fact inevitable. (Were it so, the philosophy of Spinoza and his Stoic antecedents would be a non-starter.) When an agent's action-choices harmonize with an unavoidable course of events then his action still qualifies as free, notwithstanding that "he could not have done otherwise." What is important is that he could have *chosen* otherwise. For what he chooses and what he *tries to do* are matters fully within his power and consequently provide an operative basis for freedom.

* Question 4: *Does Predictability Preclude Freedom?*

  It is sometimes maintained that to be free an agent's act must be spontaneous and unpredictable—that if others can confidently forecast what an agent is going to do, then he is not really free about it. But this idea is simply false. Only where the agent's own characteristic motivations are bypassed can predictability countervail freedom. If I know you prefer chocolate to vanilla ice cream or that you prefer novels to biographies I can confidently predict your choice without any compromise to your freedom. The crucial question is that of the information base for that prediction. If it is based on your own inherent motivations—your tastes, preferences, desires, predilections, and goals—then that choice is not a violation of your freedom but an expression of it. Only those acts that can be predicted without any reference to the agents' own motivations can be deemed unfree.

  Of course if the physical universe were Laplacean—if everything that happens in nature were lawfully predictable from physical conditions existing prior to the agents themselves—then predictability could indeed exclude free agents from nature. But this permission predilection is somewhere between implausible and fanciful.

  At this point we arrive at a clear question:

* Question 5: *Is an Act's Being Free Compatible with Its Causal Explanation?*

  Let it be that every occurrence in nature has a casual explanation in terms of prior antecedent occurrences. Is free will incompatible with this? By no means.

Keith Lehrer envisioned an "ancestral determinism" of human agency where any causally determined action is in turn determined by an earlier one until at least the action is determined by circumstances that pre-exist the agent and thereby fail to be under his control.[3] But there is a big problem here. For deliberations regarding free will are all too often vitiated by what one might call the Zenonic Fallacy. It emerges in the following line of reasoning:

> If every action is determinately fixed in place by the laws of nature and temporally antecedent events, then the chain of causality can be carried back into the distant past.

This Zenonic Fallacy is exemplified in the reasoning which Daniel Dennett formulates on the following terms:

> If [causal] determinism is true, then our every deed and decision is the inexorable outcome, it seems, of the sum of physical forces acting at the moment; which in turn is the inexorable outcome of the forces acting an instant before, and so on to the beginning of time.

And again:

> If determinism is true, then our acts are the consequences of the laws of nature and events in the remote past. But it is not up to us what went on before we were born, and neither is it up to us what the laws of nature are. Therefore the consequences of these things (including our present acts) are not up to us,[4] and we ultimately do not bear responsibility for them.

However, it is exactly in this transit from "and so on" to "the beginning of time" that the Zenonic Fallacy consists. For the reasoning at issue overlooks the prospect of backward *convergence* as illustrated in the following diagram:

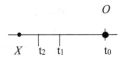

Assume an occurrence O at t_0—the result, so we suppose, of a free decision at X. and suppose a line sequence of t_i with t_{i+1} standing halfway between t_i. And now consider the following situation. Everything at O can be explained causally via events during the interval t_1-t_0 and everything at t_1 can be explained causally via events during the internal t_2-t_1, and so on ad infinitum along an unendingly compressed claim of causation. So *every* event from X to O can in fact be explained causally. But there is now no obstacle to the prospect that *nothing* in this chain can be explained causally via events occurring *antecedently* to X, the juncture at which a free decision occurs. And this sort of causal compression is fatal to any "and-so-on" retrogression into the distant past.

Zeno's notorious paradox of Achilles and the Tortoise led to the conclusion that even an infinite number of steps forward cannot cover a small distance. The Zenonic Fallacy has it that an infinite number of backward steps must cover a great distance. And this latter argument overlooks the fact that, thanks to convergence, an infinity of summands can yield a finite sum, provided merely that the steps get ever shorter. In Zeno's argument, Achilles never catches the tortoise because his progress must go on and on before the endpoint is reached. In the present reasoning explanation will never reach an initiating choice-point because the regress goes on and on ever further. But in both cases alike the idea of a convergence which terminated the infinite process at issue after a finite timespan is simply ignored. The analysis of Zeno's paradox carries exactly this lesson: an infinite succession of steps need not cover an infinite distance. So, once it is granted that, even if a cause must precede its effect, nevertheless there is no specific timespan, however small, by which it need do so, the causal regression argument against free will lose all of its traction. A causal determinism of actions is then perfectly compatible with a causal freedom with respect to decisions and choices.

Surprisingly, it seems somehow to have eluded numerous theorists that it is perfectly possible to have a causal chain tracing back *ad infinitum*, but nevertheless converging on a point of closure only a finite time in the past. For it is simply false that because our present acts are causal consequences of what goes before they must arise from the state of things in the distant past—matters over which we obviously have no control, thus leaving no room for free will.[5] The key point here is that a compressive backward convergence can finalize retrogression. Overlooking this key point is the heart and core of the Zenonic Fallacy.

And fallacy it is. For while every event after the "point of decision" X can be given its causal explanation, nevertheless nothing about the situation prior to X is decisive one way or another with regard to X-subsequent events. With free decisions, it will, accordingly, not be law-determinately predictable antecedently to X what will happen subsequently. With X as the point of decision, we have it that: *The results that issue from a genuinely free decision just are not and cannot be the causally inevitable product of choice-antecedent events.*

Accordingly, the Principle of Causality can easily remain intact in the face of free agency. Events are always predictable from *some* prior world-state, but certainly not in a way that can be traced far back into the past. Within finite timespans there is room for an unending regress of event explanations. The Principle of Causality continues in operation with the effect that every occurrence in the sequence of nature's processual developments would be causally explicable with reference to *some* prior events. But under the here-envisioned conditions, the causal explanation of our actions does nothing to impede the prospect of their origination in acts of free will because every act consequent upon a free decision can in principle be explained by events intermediate between that decision and the commencement of the act.

Ever since the ancient Academic Carneades (214–129 BC) first tried to reconcile free will with universal causality, there has loomed the question of how to fit psychically free agency into a framework of physical causality. The present approach affords a clear-cut resolution to this issue. For it emplaces free agency in a setting that does not suspend causality but envisions a process of "causal compression" that emplaces the regress of causes into a succession of ever shorter timespans converging backward in time to a point of decision.

Thus suppose that I resolve to raise my right hand a few seconds form now to illustrate free agency. The temporal situation is then as follows.

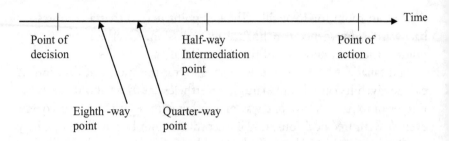

Here the act preferred at the "point of action" can be explained caus-ally at the half-way mark. And the situation at that point can be explained causally at the quarter-way mark. And that situation can in turn be explained causally at the eighth-way mark. And so on as long as you please—and presumably ad infinitum. But the point of decision will never be reached. That claim itself is beyond the grasp of causal regres-sion. And as long as decisions and resolutions terminations are not points of the story of efficient causality, there is no conflict between an act's freedom and its causal explainability.

The crux here lies in the crucially important distinction between *pre-determination* and what might be called *precedence determination*. This crucial difference is illustrated by the following diagram.

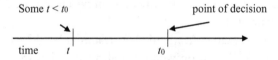

With *predetermination* what happens at t_0 is determined (i.e., law-deducible from) that which happens at some earlier time t. Already at this earlier time the decision becomes settled: a foregone conclusion that is reached in advance of the fact. Some earlier state of affairs renders what occurs at the time causally inevitable. However, with *precedence determi-nation* what happens at t_0 is also determined by what goes before—but only by *everything* that happens from some earlier time t up to but not including t_0.[6]

An occurrence at time t_0 is *precedence-determined* iff its occurrence at that time follows from the relevant laws of nature plus the state of things occurring at *every time* during the interval from $t_0 - \Delta$ to t_0 for some $\Delta > 0$. For predetermination one single prior state-description suffices: for precedence determines the entire manifold of state-descriptions during a final run-up of states is required. (It is the "end-game" that is crucial.) Both alike are modes of determination by earlier history. But the former calls for predictability as of some antecedent time whereas the latter involves no such thing. The claim to precedence determination *requires an infinite amount of input-information* which is of course never available. What we thus have in this latter case is a mode of antecedence determination that does not give rise to predictability but is in fact incompatible with it. Precedence determination can thus coexist with impredictability.

Just exactly such precedence determination can and should be contemplated in relation to free decisions and choices: a determination by the concluding phase of the course of the agent's deliberation that issues in the decision or choice at issue. For the events that constitute a course of deliberation antecedent to a decision or choice here so function as to determine the outcome, *it is only the end-game, the final, concluding phase, that is decisive.* Only the entire course of the agent's thinking as of *some* earlier point up to *but not including* the point of decision suffices to settle the issue. The outcome is never settled in advance—it isn't over "until the fat lady sings." And it should be clear that this sort of precedence determination geared to the unfolding course of deliberation in its final phase is nowise at odds with freedom of the will.

Pre-determination has it that there is some time prior to the (so-called) point of decision when the result of that decision becomes a foregone conclusion. And in denying this a doctrine of free will would have it that

[a]t no time prior to the point of decision will the outcome of the decision be a foregone conclusion: none of the different possible outcomes can be definitively excluded at any time prior to that point. Any and every preceding point of time allows for the prospect of subsequent developments that deflect the outcome from what it otherwise would be.

A critical point of any doctrine of free will is the idea that "it's never over until it's over"—the outcome of a decision is generally not decisively settled as fact until "all returns are in" that is, until the moment of decision itself. And while this principle is also compatible with probabilism and indeterminism, what matters for present purposes is that it allows freedom to be reconciled with a determinism of sorts—not, to be sure, pre-determinism, but what we here characterize as precedence determinism.

This circumstance is crucial for a version of freedom which has it that an issue of choice is only definitely settled when the choice or decision is made as an actually accomplished fact; until then room is always open for a change of mind. The outcome of an authentically free decision is never a forgone conclusion in advance of the fact. And precedence determination creates room for taking exactly this line.

2   Digression: The Crucial Contrast Between Events and Eventuations

In striving for clarity regarding determinism and free will a preliminary bit of process metaphysics will prove useful. For two distinct sorts of occurrences or happenings transpire in the world, namely *events* which are processes that take time, and *eventuations* which are temporally punctiform, instantaneous occurrences. However the processes at issue with events always occupy *a finite interval of time that is* OPEN *at both ends through lacking a first and last moment.* (Event-processes, that is to say, have starting and ending *times*, but not starting and ending *points*, since what occurs at those terminating times does not belong to the event as such: the finishing-point of a race, instead of being the last instant of the race, is the first instant at which the race is no longer in progress.) By contrast, there are also *eventuations* which are temporally punctiform. These are not actually processual doings, but rather are mere junctures of passage—transitions that mark the beginnings and endings of events. Looking for something is an activity but, actually finding it is not. (One can be engaged in looking but not in finding.) One can ask, "How long did it take him to *run* the race?" but not, "How long did he take to *start* the race?" Listening to someone is an activity, but understanding what they say is not. Activities are events, eventuating terminations are not.

Running the race—or any part of it (e.g., the first half) is a process that takes time; finishing it (i.e., reaching the finish line) is effectively instantaneous. Beginnings and endings are eventuations rather than events. The writing of sentence is a process; its completion is not.

The finish of a race is not really a part of it: it is, in effect, the first instant when the race is no longer going on at all. (And its start is the last instant when it can be said that the race has not as yet got underway.)

Such eventuations are beginnings and endings, not processes, and they are thus not events but boundaries to events. By contrast, events are natural processes that have a duration, however short. They are never instantaneous—never temporally punctiform. Such events transpire over intervals, however short (∈-like) in duration. Events as processes are a part of the machinations of nature, whereas mere eventuations—instantaneous beginnings and endings—are artifacts of mind, rational constructions to mark processual beginnings and endings. Eventuations, so understood, do not constitute parts of nature's processual flow but merely just beginnings and endings within it. And even as the terminating period it is not part of the sentence or statement whose completion it betokens, so an eventuation just is not part of the event-process whose beginning or ending it indicates.[7]

The actions in which decisions result belong to the causal processuality in the flow of nature. But the decisions themselves do not. They are precise turning points of processuality.

The processes that constitute the causal flow of nature's time come along in dribbles of finite duration. But eventuations are too short-lived to play a role in the processual commerce of nature. Natural causality relates to events, not eventuations. Instantaneous occurrences are never, as such, items that belong to natural history. Instantaneous occurrences, in sum, are not objective constituents of natural history but thought-imposed contrivances devised for reasons of cognitive convenience.

The crucial point is simply this: A turning in the course of events is an *occurrence* alright but not itself an *event*. A redirection from one potential course to another which could otherwise not have been realized is a structural feature of that course of events but is itself not one of its members. And the *ex ante explainability* of events—even of *all* events—does not entail that of eventuations.[8] Events are purely matters of what does happen. Eventuations involve relating this to what might have happened instead or to what is happening in elsewhere. (Finishing a race is an event; winning it—that is, finishing it before anyone else—is an eventuation.)

And as effectively instantaneous eventuations decisions are not part of Nature's flow of in-principle observable experience. Instead they are purely "theoretical entities" that form a part of the thought-machinery we use in demonstrating and explaining that experience. Even as the North Pole has a place on the globe as we conceptualize it, without occupying space as a physically experientable object, so free decisions have an occurrence in the framework of time without occupying an experientable timespan. And even as the North Pole belongs to theoretical rather than physical geography, so our decisions belong to theoretical rather than phenomenological psychology.

- Question 6: *How Can Freedom of the Will Be Evidentiated?*

We standardly operate in life on the basis of an expectation of one normalcy which provides for certain (defeasible) procedural presumptions—for example that people mean what they say and believe what they affirm as fact. And parallel to these presumptions of communicative credibility there are comparable presumptions of rational agency, namely: (1) that people intend the predictable consequences of their actions, and (2) that they themselves are the responsible authors of their doings in that their actions are done autonomously, on their own account, beheld, and responsibly. To be sure, all of these conventions of normality are default conditions that can be in abeyance: their presumption is defeasible. But they stand firm in the absence of indication to the contrary and together they form the core of the conviction that people can and often do act "on their own free will."

Clearly there are numerous freedom-blockers: force, hypnosis, and so on. Consider an inventory of whole lot B_1, B_2, B_3, … If we had a *complete* inventory we could establish freedom by stepwise elimination. But no complete inventory is actually available. Further complex and often eccentric impediments can always be added. But that exactly is the point.

After the "prime suspects"—the most prominent prospects—have been eliminated and the most plausible successors dealt with, the usual individual considerations come into play. But there is no point in going on beyond a certain stage of the process of elimination. It is of course hard to specify exactly when that point is. In these matters boundaries are hard to fix—think of the Paradox of the Heap here. But a point is eventually reached when for all plausible and practicable purposes the job is done. When a point is reached when the merits of normality are left behind and only the most far-fetched circumstances can be involved to negate freedom, the job is fundamental for all reasonable purposes. Once all of the semantics (plausible) freedom represents are set aside there is no sensible point denying freedom. The burden of proof has shifted and the justificatory onus discharged.

However, the complexity of the issue indicates that while the freedom of particular actions is something that can be evidentiated it is seldom-if-ever something that can be categorically demonstrated. For demonstration would call for the decisive elimination of all principle freedom-blockers and this is something rather difficult to realize. "Give me an example of a fact you will never forget?" is a severe challenge. And so is "Give me an example of a choice by spontaneous freedom whose status as such you will never retract."

- Question 7: *Is Free Will Unscientific?*

Sometimes—when one is drugged, say, or very tired, or when one's brain is electronically stimulated—brain activity can induce and determines thought activity. But sometimes the reverse is the case—when I am excited, say, or fearful or amused. In such circumstances, psychic activity induces and determine brain activity. The relation of mind and brain is a two-way street. Either party can, on given occasion, seize the intuitive in relation to responses by the other.

The possession of free will—of cogency on the basis of suitable reasons—is a human capacity which, like belief on the basis of reasons and evaluation on that basis of reason, is a naturally evolved human capacity. And in the end no reason why a process that has provided for the evolutionary emergence of cognition, reason, and evaluation should not have thrown reason-directed will with its capacity for free decision into the bargain.

Its emergence in that course of human evolution can be observed operationally and explained evolutionally as part of the survival mechanism of the human animal. Our ability to act freely is no more unscientific than our ability to specify relevant facts, to solve problems, to invent possibilities, or to prefer any of the tasks of higher-order intelligence that evolution has put at our human disposal as rational animals.

Modern science is a good deal better at explaining natural phenomena than at explaining psychological phenomena. It is thus not surprising that scientistically inclined determinists prefer addressing free agency rather than free decision. But of course freedom of the will pivots fundamentally on the latter issue, a free action being one that results—however deterministically—from a free choice or decision. In matters of free volition it is decisions and choices that stand in the forefront, not actions.

Free will is not a metaphysical anomaly but a part of ordinary life, the processes of human evolution have brought into being a creature that commands repertoire of characteristic abilities—cognition, and feeling, anticipation and planning, valuing and seeking, willing and doing. The capacity to will freely is every bit as much of our natural human endowment as is the capacity for calculating correctly or imagining vividly.

Notes

1. To be sure, this moral status is also something objective and reflective of the "fact of the matter." Who, after all, said that moral matters could not be so?
2. René Descartes (1641), *Meditations*, IV.
3. See Lehrer (1980).
4. This contention is Peter van Inwagen's "Consequence Argument." See van Inwagen (1983) and also Dennett (1984, 16) and Kane (2005, chap. 3).
5. See Ginet (1990), Kane (1996), van Inwagen and Zimmerman (1998), and compare Dennett (2003, 99 and 134).
6. Note that while predetermination entails precedence-determination, the converse is not the case: precedence determination does not entail predetermination.

7. The presently deployed distinction between eventuations and events has a significant history. It has an ancestry in A. N. Whitehead's distinction between an "actual entity" as a "drop of experience" and a "pretension" which is "a completion or satisfaction." (See Whitehead 1929.) Again it figures in Gilbert Ryle's distinction between ongoing processes and what he called "achievements." (See Ryle 1949.) J. L. Austin's account of verbs of contention which—like "to know," have no present continuous—is also relevant here.

8. Compare Lotze (1885, Vol. III, 292).

References

Dennett, Daniel Clement. 1984. *Elbow Room: The Varieties of Free Will Worth Wanting*. Cambridge: MIT Press.

———. 2003. *Freedom Evolves*. New York: Viking.

Descartes, René. 1641. *Meditationes de prima philosophia*. Paris: Michael Soly.

Ginet, Carl. 1990. *On Action*. Cambridge: Cambridge University Press.

Kane, Robert. 1996. *The Significance of Free Will*. New York and Oxford: Oxford University Press.

———. 2005. *A Contemporary Introduction to Free Will*. Oxford: Oxford University Press.

Lehrer, Keith. 1980. Preferences, Conditionals and Freedom. In *Time and Cause*, ed. Peter van Inwagen, 187–201. Dordrecht: Reidel.

List, Christian. 2019. *Why Free Will Is Real*. Cambridge, MA: Harvard University Press.

Lotze, Hermann. 1885. *Outlines of Practical Philosophy* (=*Grundzuege der praktischen Philosophie*. Leipzig: S. Hirzel, 1882, 2nd ed. 1884). Translated by George Trumbull Ladd. Boston: Ginn.

Ryle, Gilbert. 1949 (2nd ed. 1959). *The Concept of Mind*. London and New York: Hutchinson's University Library.

van Inwagen, Peter, and Dean Zimmerman. 1998. *Metaphysics: The Big Questions*. Oxford: Blackwell.

van Inwagen, Peter. 1983. *An Essay on Free Will*. Oxford: Oxford University Press.

Whitehead, Alfred North. 1929. *Process and Reality*. New York: Macmillan. (Corrected Edition ed. by D. R. Griffin and D. W. Sherburne. New York: The Free Press, 1979.)

5

Some Free Thinking About 'Thinking About Free Will'

Marco Hausmann

1 Introduction: The Problem of Free Will

In his book *An Essay on Free Will* as well as in his new collection of essays *Thinking About Free Will*, Peter van Inwagen has developed a variety of frameworks in which to address the problem of free will. His work has not only led to a revival of incompatibilism, his work has deeply influenced the way in which all participants of the debate nowadays think about the problem. At the heart of van Inwagen's *Thinking About Free Will* lies his repeated insistence on the fact that free will is a mystery. He describes his position as follows:

> Free will is a mystery because [...] there are good arguments for the incompatibility of free will and determinism and good arguments for [the] incompatibility of free will and indeterminism, and [...] no one has ever identified a very plausible candidate for the flaw in any of the arguments in either class. van Inwagen, of course, believes that the arguments he has

M. Hausmann (✉)
Philosophy, Ludwig Maximilian University of Munich, Munich, Germany

© The Author(s), under exclusive license to Springer Nature Switzerland AG 2021   **91**
M. Hausmann, J. Noller (eds.), *Free Will*,
https://doi.org/10.1007/978-3-030-61136-1_5

given for the incompatibility of free will and determinism contain *no* flaws
[...] and that there is some flaw, or are some flaws, in the familiar arguments for the incompatibility of free will and indeterminism. But as to the
latter class of arguments—well, he's damned if he knows what the flaws in
them might be. He simply hasn't a clue. (van Inwagen 2017a, 13–14)

In van Inwagen's view, free will is a mystery because "the following is
certainly the case: *Some* proposition (or maybe there is more than one)
about matters relating to free will, determinism, and moral responsibility
that seems to us to be obviously true is false" (van Inwagen 2017a, 15).

In what follows, I will hint at what, in my view, might be a flaw in van
Inwagen's arguments for the incompatibility of free will and determinism. According to van Inwagen, nobody is able to do anything about the
truth of a complete description of a past state of the world. In my view,
this is a proposition "about matters relating to free will, determinism, and
moral responsibility" that might well be false even though it "seems to us
to be obviously true." However, I will not argue directly against this proposition. Instead, I will only argue that van Inwagen has given us no reason
to believe that this proposition is true. To this end, I will develop (though
not endorse) three arguments that, if successful, will show that van
Inwagen's attempt to argue for this proposition fails. I will argue that van
Inwagen's attempt to argue for this proposition is, first, incompatible
with a theory of propositions according to which necessarily equivalent
propositions are identical; second, incompatible with a description theory of proper names according to which proper names are merely abbreviations for definite descriptions; and, third, incompatible with a
metaphysical theory according to which there is no such thing as the past.
At the end of my chapter, I sketch an independent argument to the conclusion that van Inwagen's attempt to justify his crucial assumption fails.
I will conclude that there is reason to think that van Inwagen has given
us no reason to believe that nobody is able to do anything about the truth
of a complete description of a past state of the world.

As a corollary, I will show that my arguments do not only apply to van
Inwagen's argument for the incompatibility of free will and *determinism*,
but also to a famous argument for the incompatibility of free will and
divine foreknowledge.

2 Peter van Inwagen's Consequence Argument

To start with, it might be helpful to recapitulate the main idea of van Inwagen's Consequence Argument (i.e., van Inwagen's argument for the incompatibility of free will and determinism). To make a long story short, let us say that a truth is untouchable just in case that nobody is (or ever has been) able to do anything about its truth.[1] If we let 'P$_0$' be a proposition that expresses the state of the world in the remote past (at a time long before the existence of the first human being) and if we let 'L' be the conjunction of all laws of nature, then the main idea of his argument seems to be the following:[2] Suppose, for example, that it is true that Epimenides will tell a lie at the meeting of the assembly. If determinism is true, the proposition that Epimenides will tell a lie at the meeting of the assembly follows from the conjunction of P$_0$ and L. But nobody is able to do anything about P$_0$, for nobody is able to do anything about a true description of the past. And nobody is able to do anything about L, for nobody is able to do anything about the laws of nature. It follows that, if determinism is true, nobody (not even Epimenides) is able to do anything about the fact that Epimenides will tell a lie at the meeting of the assembly.

As is well known, one might construct a parallel argument for the incompatibility of free will and divine foreknowledge (and it is not surprising, in this respect, that van Inwagen not only defends the view that free will and *determinism* are incompatible, but also the view that free will and *divine foreknowledge* are incompatible):[3] For consider, again, the proposition that Epimenides will tell a lie at the meeting of the assembly. If we let 'P$_0$' be the proposition that God believed, long before the existence of the first human being, that Epimenides will tell a lie at the meeting of the assembly, then the main idea of the argument seems to be the following: Suppose, again, that it is true that Epimenides will tell a lie at the meeting of the assembly. If so, the proposition that Epimenides will tell a lie at the meeting of the assembly follows from P$_0$ (the proposition that God believed, long before the existence of the first human being, that Epimenides will tell a lie at the meeting of the assembly). But nobody is able to do anything about P_0, for nobody is able to do anything about a true description of the past. It follows that nobody (not even Epimenides) is able to do anything about the fact that Epimenides will tell a lie at the meeting of the assembly.

3   The Fixity of Descriptions of the Past

In what follows, I will identify what, in my view, might be a flaw in both arguments.[4] I will try to show that van Inwagen's attempt to justify the assumption that P_0 is an untouchable truth fails and that he has, therefore, given us no reason to believe that P_0 is an untouchable truth. Besides that, I will show that my reasoning applies not only to van Inwagen's argument for the incompatibility of free will and determinism but also to the argument for the incompatibility of free will and divine foreknowledge. There is, with respect to both arguments, reason to doubt that P_0 is an untouchable truth.

3.1   How van Inwagen Justifies His Assumption

Here, at any rate, is van Inwagen's attempt to justify the assumption that P_0 is an untouchable truth:

> P_0 is obviously an untouchable truth. P_0 is an untouchable truth for the same reason that 'Dinosaurs once walked the earth' is an untouchable truth: both are truths about the past, and, indeed, truths about the pre-human past. (van Inwagen 2008a, 454)[5]

Elsewhere, van Inwagen holds that "no agent is able [...] to render false a true proposition about the past" (van Inwagen 2017e, 227).[6] Before I explain why I have doubts about this argument, I will first try to reconstruct van Inwagen's reasoning. At first glance, he might appear to argue as follows:

(1) P_0 is a true proposition about the past.
(2) Every true proposition about the past is an untouchable truth.
(3) Hence, P_0 is an untouchable truth.

However, it is simply not true that every true proposition about the past is an untouchable truth. For, as is well known from debates about free will and divine foreknowledge, there are propositions about the past that are not *entirely* about the past.[7] Take, for example, the proposition that, yesterday, I smoked for the last time. Without doubt, this is a proposition about the past. It says something about the past, namely, that, yesterday, I smoked. Nonetheless, this proposition is certainly not *entirely* about the past. For it says something about the future as well, namely, that I will never smoke again. And now suppose that, yesterday, I *in fact* smoked for the last time. The proposition that, yesterday, I smoked for the last time then appears to be a true proposition about the past that is not an untouchable truth. For even if I will never smoke again, I am without doubt *able* to smoke again and I am, therefore, *able* to do something about the fact that, yesterday, I smoked for the last time. I conclude that *not* every true proposition about the past is an untouchable truth. We should, therefore, modify van Inwagen's argument as follows:

(1)* P_0 is a true proposition *entirely* about the past.
(2)* Every true proposition *entirely* about the past is an untouchable truth.
(3) Hence, P_0 is an untouchable truth.

However, this argument is equally bound to fail. For it is simply not true that every true proposition entirely about the past is an untouchable truth. To see why, recall that a truth is untouchable just in case that nobody is *or ever has been* able to do anything about its truth. Now, just to mention one example, consider the proposition that Caesar crossed the Rubicon. This is a true proposition entirely about the past that is *not* an untouchable truth. For even though nobody is *now* able to do anything about it, somebody certainly *has been* able to do something about it (presumably, Caesar).[8] Thus, not just *any* true proposition entirely about the past turns out to be an untouchable truth. For this reason, we should come up with a different reconstruction of van Inwagen's argument. We should, as van Inwagen himself suggests, argue that P_0 is an untouchable truth because P_0 is a true proposition entirely about the *prehuman* past. This leads to a (provisionally) final reconstruction of van Inwagen's argument:

(1)** P_0 is a true proposition *entirely* about the *prehuman* past.
(2)** Every true proposition *entirely* about the *prehuman* past is an untouchable truth.
(3) Hence, P_0 is an untouchable truth.

Note, however, that van Inwagen's argument has a premise that, after careful reflection, might seem far from obvious: the premise that P_0 is a true proposition *entirely* about the past (i.e., a proposition that is *not even in part* about the present or the future). As will soon emerge, there are a couple of reasons to reject this assumption.

3.2   Why van Inwagen's Attempt to Justify His Assumption Fails

As I said, I will sketch three arguments to the conclusion that P_0 is not a true proposition *entirely* about the past. For if P_0 is not a true proposition entirely about the past, then it seems that van Inwagen has given us no reason to suppose that P_0 is an untouchable truth.

However, given that a full defense of these arguments is impossible within the bounds of this paper and given that I am not sure whether I want to commit myself to all premises of these arguments (even though *a lot* speaks in favor of them), I have decided to present my arguments in an unusual way. I will present my arguments in the form of a list of advices for compatibilists.

Identity of Necessarily Equivalent Propositions

Here is my *first* advice for compatibilists: defend a theory of propositions according to which necessarily equivalent propositions are identical (e.g., David Lewis's or Robert Stalnaker's theory of propositions).[9] For, as I will argue, *every* true proposition is at least in part about the future if necessarily equivalent propositions are identical. And it is obvious that *no* true proposition is entirely about the past, if every true proposition is at least in part about the future. Therefore, *no* true proposition is entirely about the past if necessarily equivalent propositions are identical. To see why this is so, suppose that necessarily equivalent propositions are identical:[10]

> (*Identity of Necessarily Equivalent Propositions*) P and Q are identical if P and Q are necessarily equivalent.

It straightforwardly follows that necessarily equivalent propositions are about the same time. Thus, if P is (at least in part) about time T and if P is necessarily equivalent to Q, then Q is also (at least in part) about time T:

> (*Equivalence Principle*) If P is (at least in part) about time T and if P is necessarily equivalent to Q, then Q is also (at least in part) about time T.

Take, for example, the proposition that Napoleon lost the battle of Waterloo. And take, further, the necessarily equivalent proposition that Napoleon lost the battle of Waterloo and 2 + 2 = 4. According to the equivalence principle, the latter proposition is about 1815 if the former is about 1815 (and vice versa).

Further, it is plausible to assume that a conjunction is (at least in part) about time T, if it has a conjunct that is (at least in part) about time T:

> (*Conjunction Principle*) If P has a conjunct that is at least in part about time T, then P is *itself* (at least in part) about time T.

Take, for example, the proposition that Newton invented the calculus in 1676 and Leibniz invented the calculus in 1675. According to the conjunction principle, this proposition is about 1675, if it has a conjunct that is about 1675.

Finally, take the proposition that either there will be a sea-battle tomorrow, or there will not be a sea-battle tomorrow. This proposition appears to be a necessary truth that is (at least) in part about the future.[11]

Now let 'P' be an arbitrary truth and let 'Q' be the proposition that either there will be a sea-battle tomorrow, or there will not be a sea-battle tomorrow. P entails Q (given that Q is a necessary truth). Thus, given that P entails Q, P is equivalent to the conjunction of P and Q, that is, P is equivalent to a proposition that has Q as a conjunct. However, Q is (at least in part) about the future. Thus, P is equivalent to a proposition that has a conjunct that is (at least in part) about the future. It follows (from the conjunction principle) that P is equivalent to a proposition that is *itself* (at least in part) about the future. And it follows, further, (from the equivalence principle) that P is *itself* (at least in part) about the future. But, without doubt, no proposition that is *itself* (at least in part) about the future is *entirely* about the past. Therefore, P is not entirely about the past. It follows that *no* true proposition is entirely about the past (given that P is an arbitrary truth). I conclude that *no* true proposition is entirely about the past, if necessarily equivalent propositions are identical.

Let us take a step back: according to van Inwagen's argument for the incompatibility of free will and determinism, P_0 (a proposition that expresses a past state of the world) is an untouchable truth. And according to a parallel argument for the incompatibility of free will and divine foreknowledge, P_0 (a proposition that expresses God's past beliefs) is an untouchable truth. As we have seen, it is highly plausible to assume that P_0 is an untouchable truth, *if* P_0 is a true proposition entirely about the prehuman past. However, as we have also seen, there are *no* true propositions entirely about the prehuman past, if necessarily equivalent propositions are identical. Thus, if necessarily equivalent propositions are identical, there appears to be no reason to believe that P_0 is an untouchable truth.

Descriptivism About Proper Names

Here is my *second* advice for compatibilists: defend a description theory of proper names according to which sentences like 'Saul Kripke gave a famous lecture at the University of Princeton' and sentences like 'The author of *Naming and Necessity* gave a famous lecture at the University of Princeton' express the same proposition (e.g. Bertrand Russell's or Alvin

Plantinga's theory of proper names).[12] The main idea of a description theory of proper names is that proper names such as 'Saul Kripke' are merely abbreviations for definite descriptions such as 'the author of *Naming and Necessity*'. As I will argue, it follows from this idea that P_0 is about everything. And P_0 is certainly *not* entirely about the past, if P_0 is about everything.

To see why a description theory of proper names entails that P_0 is *not* entirely about the past, recall that P_0 is a proposition that expresses the state of the world at a time long before the existence of the first human being. Let 'T_0' denote that time and let us suppose that, at T_0, there is a dinosaur that walks the earth. Let us call that dinosaur 'Rex'.

Now consider the following example: Suppose that I am walking through a forest and I see a stone. I am, of course, able to touch this stone but I don't. Suppose that, if I were to touch this stone, I would come in contact with a very old subatomic particle, a subatomic particle that has existed ever since dinosaurs walked the earth. Let us call this subatomic particle 'Tony' and let us suppose that Rex is the only living being that has ever come in contact with Tony. Now consider the following sentence:

(1) The only living being that has ever come in contact with Tony walked the earth at T_0.

At first glance, this sentence might appear to express a true proposition that is *entirely* about the prehuman past. For given that Rex is the only living being that has ever come in contact with Tony, it says something about what happened in the prehuman past. On the other hand, this statement is certainly *not* an untouchable truth. For, as has been supposed, I am able to touch that stone and, if I were to touch that stone, I would come in contact with Tony. Thus, if I were to touch that stone, it would be false that *the only* living being that has ever come in contact with Tony walked the earth at T_0 (for it would then be false that there is *only one* living being that has ever come in contact with Tony). Therefore, I *am* able to do something about the fact that the only living being that has ever come in contact with Tony walked the earth at T_0. I conclude that this sentence appears to express a proposition that is entirely about the prehuman past even though it is *not* an untouchable truth.

In my view, this example does *not* constitute a counterexample to van Inwagen's view that every true proposition entirely about the prehuman past is an untouchable truth. This example does not constitute a counterexample to van Inwagen's view because, a first impression notwithstanding, this sentence does *not* express a proposition that is entirely about the past. To see this, note that this sentence contains a definite description ('the only living being that has ever come in contact with Tony') and that it, therefore, appears to express the same proposition as the following sentence:

(2) There is something that walked the earth at T_0 and that is such that *everything* is identical with it if and only if it is a living being that has ever come in contact with Tony.

The proposition expressed by this sentence appears to be about *everything*.[13] Thus, in my view, sentences that contain definite descriptions do not constitute a counterexample to van Inwagen's view that every true proposition entirely about the prehuman past is an untouchable truth. The reason is that sentences that contain definite descriptions usually do not express propositions *entirely* about the prehuman past.

Note, however, that van Inwagen is now faced with a dilemma. For according to a description theory of proper names, the proper name 'Rex' is merely an abbreviation for a definite description. Suppose, for example, that 'Rex' is merely an abbreviation for 'the only living being that has ever come in contact with Tony'. Accordingly, the sentence '*Rex* walked the earth at T_0' and the sentence '*the only living being that has ever come in contact with Tony* walked the earth at T_0' express the same proposition. However, the latter sentence contains a definite description and appears to express a proposition that is about everything. Therefore, given that the latter sentence expresses the same proposition as the former sentence, the former sentence appears to express a proposition that is about everything. Now recall that, according to van Inwagen, P_0 is a true proposition that expresses the state of the world at T_0, or, as van Inwagen puts it elsewhere, a true proposition that "gives a complete description of the state of the world at" T_0.[14] Recall, further, that Rex walked the earth at T_0. Now either the proposition that Rex walked the earth at T_0 is a conjunct of P_0, or not. If the proposition that Rex walked the earth at T_0 is *not* a conjunct of P_0, then P_0 does not appear to be "a complete description of the state of the world at" T_0 (contrary to the assumptions). If, on the other hand, the proposition that Rex walked the earth at T_0 *is* a conjunct of P_0, then P_0 has a conjunct that is about everything. It follows that P_0 is *itself* about everything. And P_0 is certainly *not* entirely about the past, if P_0 is about everything.

In the case of the argument for the incompatibility of free will and divine foreknowledge, things get even worse. To see this, let 'P' be the proposition that there will be a fool who says in his heart that the ontological argument is a failure and let 'P_0' be the proposition that God believed, long before the existence of the first human being, that there will be such a fool. According to a description theory of proper names, the proper name 'God' is merely an abbreviation for a definite description. Suppose, for example, that 'God' is merely an abbreviation for 'that than which nothing greater can be conceived'. Accordingly, the sentence '*God* believed that there will be such a fool' and the sentence '*that than which nothing greater can be conceived* believed that there will be such a fool' express the same proposition. However, the latter sentence contains a definite description and appears to express a proposition that is about everything. Therefore, given that the latter sentence expresses the same proposition as the former sentence and given that the former sentence expresses P_0, it follows that P_0 is about everything. It is obvious, however, that no true proposition that is about everything is *entirely* about the past. Thus, it follows from the main idea of a description theory of proper names, that P_0 is not entirely about the past.

Let us take stock: according to van Inwagen's argument for the incompatibility of free will and determinism, P_0 (a proposition that expresses a past state of the world) is an untouchable truth. And according to a parallel argument for the incompatibility of free will and divine foreknowledge, P_0 (a proposition that expresses God's past beliefs) is an untouchable truth. As we have seen, it is highly plausible to assume that P_0 is an untouchable truth, *if* P_0 is a true proposition entirely about the prehuman past. However, as we have also seen, P_0 is *not* a true proposition entirely about the prehuman past, at least according to a description theory of proper names. Thus, at least from the vantage point of a description theory of proper names, it seems that van Inwagen has given us no reason to believe that P_0 is an untouchable truth.

Deflationism About the Past

So far, I have argued *as if I had* an intuitive grasp of phrases like 'being about the past', or 'being entirely about the past'. In my view, these phrases are perfectly legitimate, as long as it is clear that we are expressing ourselves only carelessly or loosely. However, if we want to express ourselves strictly or metaphysically, we are not, as it were, entitled to take these phrases for granted. From now on, I will do my best to express myself strictly and I will, therefore, question the legitimacy of phrases like 'being about the past', or 'being entirely about the past'. The reason why I question the legitimacy of these phrases is that, when embedded in certain sentences, they seem to express propositions that imply that there is such a thing as 'the past'.

Here, then, is my *third* advice for compatibilists: defend a metaphysical theory according to which, strictly speaking, there is no such thing as 'the past'. For if there is no such thing as the past, there is nothing of which it can be truly said that it is about the past. It follows that no proposition is about the past or entirely about the past.

To be sure, my advice is *not* to defend a metaphysical theory according to which there are no past *things*. A deflationist about the past (as I will call an adherent of the view that there is no such thing as the past) might still want to make sense of the view that there are *things* that once existed but do not exist anymore—John F. Kennedy, the Berlin Wall, Gaius Julius Caesar, the Roman Empire, and so on (though I hasten to add that it is by no means mandatory for a deflationist about the past to want to make sense of such a view).[15] My advice is only to defend a metaphysical theory according to which there is no *one single thing* that might reasonably be called 'the past'—that is, no mereological sum or collection of all and only past things (no big container that contains all and only past things). For, as I said, if there is no such thing as the past, then *no* proposition is entirely about the past. And if no proposition is entirely about the past, then P_0 is not entirely about the prehuman past (I take it that if there is no such thing as the past, then there is no such thing as the prehuman past either).

A deflationist about the past, therefore, will simply reject van Inwagen's assumption that P_0 is a true proposition entirely about the prehuman past. He will, instead, try to make sense of van Inwagen's assumption by replacing it with a different, in his view more promising, assumption. It turns out, however, that this is more difficult than one might have expected.

The following proposal suggests itself: A proposition is *entirely* about the prehuman past just in case that it is about past things and *only* about past things, where a thing is a past thing just in case that it existed before there were any human beings but does not exist anymore. Thus, according to this proposal, a deflationist about the past might reconstruct van Inwagen's argument, roughly, as follows:

(1)*** P_0 is a true proposition that is only about things that existed before there were any human beings but do not exist anymore.
(2)*** Every true proposition that is only about things that existed before there were any human beings but do not exist anymore is an untouchable truth.
(3) Hence, P_0 is an untouchable truth.

The problem with this proposal is that P_0 does not seem to be a plausible candidate for a proposition that is only about things that existed before there were any human beings but do not exist anymore.

Take, as a first step, the argument for the incompatibility of free will and divine foreknowledge. It is obvious that P_0 is about God (for, in this argument, P_0 is a proposition about God's past beliefs). However, it is not true, pace Nietzsche, that God existed before there were any human beings but does not exist anymore (either God has never existed, or he still exists). Hence, P_0 is not a proposition that is only about things that existed before there were any human beings but do not exist anymore.

Take, as a second step, van Inwagen's argument for the incompatibility of free will and determinism and recall that, in his argument, P_0 is a proposition that expresses the state of the world at a time long before the existence of the first human being. Let 'T_0' be that time, suppose that, at

T_0, dinosaur Rex came in contact with subatomic particle Tony and suppose, further, that Tony still exists (it seems that subatomic particles have a much longer average life than dinosaurs). It seems that van Inwagen is again faced with a dilemma: either P_0 is about Tony, or not. If P_0 is *not* about Tony then P_0 does not appear to be "a complete description of the state of the world at" T_0 (contrary to the assumptions). If, on the other hand, P_0 *is* about Tony, then P_0 is not a proposition that is only about things that existed before there were any human beings but do not exist anymore. For Tony, as has been supposed, still exists.

For this reason, a deflationist about the past might prefer a different proposal: A proposition is *entirely* about 'the prehuman past' just in case that it is about past things and *only* about past things, where a thing is a past thing just in case that it existed before there were any human beings (regardless of whether it still exists, or not). This proposal leads, roughly, to the following reconstruction of van Inwagen's argument:

(1)**** P_0 is a true proposition that is only about things that existed before there were any human beings.
(2)**** Every true proposition that is only about things that existed before there were any human beings is an untouchable truth.
(3) Hence, P_0 is an untouchable truth.

Admittedly, it is not always clear whether a proposition is *only* about things that existed before there were any human beings. There are, however, strong reasons to doubt that *every* true proposition that is only about things that existed before there were any human beings is an untouchable truth. Take, for example, the proposition that subatomic particle Tony will exist for another thousands of years. If there are any propositions that are only about things that existed before there were any human beings, this proposition appears to be a plausible candidate (for this proposition appears to be only about a subatomic particle that existed before there were any human beings).[16] Suppose, however, that poor old Tony has been captured by crazy scientists from the Large Hadron Collider and suppose, further, that one of these scientists is able to do something that might destroy poor old Tony (e.g., something that might result in a collision of Tony with other subatomic particles). If so, even if Tony will *in fact* exist for another thousands of years, it is *not* an untouchable truth that Tony will exist for another thousands of years. For there *is* someone who is able to do something about the fact that Tony will exist for another thousands of years. I conclude that *not* every true proposition that is only about things that existed before there were any human beings is an untouchable truth.[17]

In general, I conclude that it is more difficult than expected to make sense of van Inwagen's argument, at least if there is no such thing as the past. Again, at least if there is no such thing as the past, we are left with no reason to believe that P_0 is an untouchable truth.

I hope that our reflections about the past will lay the ground for a further argument that is acceptable even for those who believe that there *is* such a thing as the past. For, as we have seen, a past thing may be either a thing that once existed but does not exist anymore, or, on the other hand, a thing that once existed (regardless of whether it still exists, or not). In general, van Inwagen appears to face the following dilemma: either things that once existed and still exist are, if I may so express myself, part of the past, or not.

If things that once existed and still exist are *not* part of the past, then there is reason to think that P_0 is either not a *complete* description of a past state of the world, or not *entirely* about the past. For either P_0 is about things that once existed and still exist, or not. If P_0 is *not* about things that once existed and still exist, then P_0 is not a *complete* description of a past state of the world (at least not a complete description of a past state of the world that includes the existence of such things and, arguably, *any* past state of the world includes the existence of such things). If, on the other hand, P_0 *is* about things that once existed and still exist, then P_0 is not *entirely* about the past. For then P_0 is about things that are not part of the past.

If, on the other hand, things that once existed and still exist *are* part of the past, then there is reason to doubt that every true proposition entirely about the past is an untouchable truth. For then there are true propositions that are entirely about the past even though they are about things that still exist. And if there are true propositions entirely about the past that are about things that *still exist*, then there is no reason to think that *every* true proposition entirely about the past is only about things that are beyond our control. Either way, van Inwagen's argument for his assumption that P_0 is an untouchable truth fails.[18] He has given us no reason to believe that P_0 is an untouchable truth.

4   Conclusion

By way of conclusion: according to van Inwagen, free will "is a mystery because [...] there are good arguments for the incompatibility of free will and determinism and good arguments for [the] incompatibility of free will and indeterminism, and [...] no one has ever identified a very plausible candidate for the flaw in any of the arguments in either class" (van Inwagen 2017a, 13–14). He concludes that some proposition "about matters relating to free will, determinism, and moral responsibility that seems to us to be obviously true is false" (van Inwagen 2017a, 15).

In my chapter, I have tried to identify a flaw in van Inwagen's argument. For, as we have seen, the only reason to believe that P_0 is an untouchable truth is the assumption that P_0 is a true proposition entirely about the prehuman past. However, as we have also seen, there are a couple of reasons to doubt the assumption that P_0 is a true proposition entirely about the prehuman past. I have argued that P_0 is not a true proposition entirely about the prehuman past, if necessarily equivalent propositions are identical, if proper names are abbreviations for definite descriptions, and if there is no such thing as the past. Finally, I have argued that there are independent reasons to think that a description of a past state of the world like P_0 is either *not* untouchable, or only complete if *not* entirely about the past. That is, I have argued that there are independent reasons to think that P_0 is either not untouchable, or not entirely about the past. In sum, there appears to be no reason to assent to the proposition that nobody is able to do anything about P_0. This proposition, even though it *seemed* to us to be obviously true, might well be false.

As a corollary, I have shown that pretty much the same reasoning applies to a famous argument for the incompatibility of free will and divine foreknowledge.

Notes

1. There has been considerable debate over how to best interpret this notion such that van Inwagen's argument comes out as valid. See, for example, McKay and Johnson (1996), Carlson (2000), Schnieder (2004), van Inwagen (2008a, 2017a, 2017b, 2017d, 2017e), and Hausmann (2018, forthcoming). The details of this debate are irrelevant for the argument of my chapter.
2. For a more detailed version of van Inwagen's argument see van Inwagen (1983, 2017b).
3. See van Inwagen (2008b).
4. As is well known, there has been considerable debate about the truth of the premises of van Inwagen's argument, for instance, about whether the conjunction of all laws of nature is an untouchable truth. For this and related debates see, for example, Lewis (1981); Fischer (1994, 67–86); Kane (1998, 44–58); Beebee and Mele (2002); Kapitan (2002, 132–141); Vihvelin (2013, 155–166); and van Inwagen (2017c).
5. See also van Inwagen (1983, 96, 2017e, 228).
6. See also van Inwagen (2017e, 228).
7. At this stage of my argument, I argue *as if I had* an intuitive grasp of what it is to be entirely about the past. Later, I will question the legitimacy of phrases like 'being about the past' or 'being entirely about the past'. For more on the debate about this notion see, for example, Plantinga (1986) and Fischer (1994).
8. Campbell (2007) emphasizes pretty much the same point.
9. See, for example, Lewis (1973, 46–47), and Stalnaker (1976).
10. The following argument is in part inspired by an argument that Alvin Plantinga has developed for a different purpose (1986, 245–248). This is not to say that Plantinga would approve all premises, let alone the conclusion of my argument.
11. There is, of course, only one necessary truth if necessarily equivalent propositions are identical.
12. See, for example, Russell (1918) and Plantinga (1978). Needless to say that Plantinga's view about proper names differs in important respects from Russell's view about proper names. The details of Plantinga's view about proper names need not detain us here.
13. Of course, one might not share this intuition, that is, one might insist that this proposition is not about everything but only about Rex. Note,

however, that van Inwagen's argument fails if this proposition is only about Rex. For if this proposition is only about Rex, then it is a proposition entirely about the prehuman past that is not an untouchable truth. Thus, if this proposition is only about Rex, my example constitutes a counterexample to van Inwagen's assumption that every true proposition entirely about the prehuman past is an untouchable truth.

14. See van Inwagen (2013, 214).

15. As I said, a deflationist about the past need not make sense of the view that there are things that once existed but do not exist anymore. However, if one feels uncomfortable with saying that *there are* things that do *not exist* anymore, one might as well say that *there are* things that are *not concrete* anymore. Following a suggestion of van Inwagen, one might then define a concrete thing as "a thing that can act on or be acted on by other things" (2015, 35).

16. Perhaps, one might object that the proposition that subatomic particle Tony will exist for another thousands of years is not only about a subatomic particle but also about numbers and instants of time. However, numbers and instants of time, if there are such things at all, exist *always*. The proposition that subatomic particle Tony will exist for another thousands of years, therefore, would still be only about things that existed before there were any human beings.

17. Note that a parallel argument can be constructed once we say that a proposition is entirely about the prehuman past if and only if it is about past *events* and only about past *events*. Note, further, that such a proposal would not be acceptable for van Inwagen anyway. For, according to van Inwagen, "there are no events" (2011, 158).

18. Interestingly enough, a similar argument can be constructed if P_0 is a description of God's past beliefs. For either things that once existed and still exist are part of the past, or not. If not, there is reason to think that P_0 is not *entirely* about the past (for P_0 is about God as well as about God's beliefs and, therefore, about things that are, then, not part of the past). If, on the other hand, things that once existed and still exist *are* part of the past, then there is reason to doubt that every true proposition entirely about the past is an untouchable truth. Either way, the argument to the conclusion that P_0 is an untouchable truth fails.

References

Beebee, Helen, and Alfred Mele. 2002. Humean Compatibilism. *Mind* *111*: 201–223.

Campbell, Joseph Keim. 2007. Free Will and the Necessity of the Past. *Analysis* *67*: 105–111.

Carlson, Erik. 2000. Incompatibilism and the Transfer of Power Necessity. *Noûs* *34*: 277–290.

Fischer, John Martin. 1994. *The Metaphysics of Free Will. An Essay on Control.* Oxford: Blackwell.

Hausmann, Marco. 2018. The Consequence Argument Ungrounded. *Synthese* *195*: 4931–4950.

———. forthcoming. The Consequence of the Consequence Argument. *Kriterion.*

Kane, Robert. 1998. *The Significance of Free Will.* Oxford: Oxford University Press.

Kapitan, Tomis. 2002. A Master Argument for Incompatibilism. In *The Oxford Handbook of Free Will*, ed. Robert Kane, 127–157. Oxford: Oxford University Press.

Lewis, David. 1973. *Counterfactuals.* Oxford: Blackwell.

———. 1981. Are We Free to Break the Laws? *Theoria 47*: 113–121.

McKay, Thomas, and David Johnson. 1996. A Reconsideration of an Argument against Compatibilism. *Philosophical Topics 24*: 113–122.

Plantinga, Alvin. 1978. The Boethian Compromise. *The American Philosophical Quarterly 15*: 129–138.

———. 1986. On Ockham's Way Out. *Faith and Philosophy 3*: 235–269.

Russell, Bertrand. 1918. *The Philosophy of Logical Atomism.* Reprinted as: Bertrand Russell. 1988. *The Collected Papers of Bertrand Russell. Volume 8: The Philosophy of Logical Atomism and Other Essays, 1914–19.* Edited by John Slater. London: Routledge.

Schnieder, Benjamin. 2004. Compatibilism and the Notion of Rendering Something False. *Philosophical Studies 117*: 409–428.

Stalnaker, Robert. 1976. Propositions. In *Issues in the Philosophy of Language*, ed. Alfred MacKay and Daniel Merrill, 79–91. New Haven: Yale University Press.

van Inwagen, Peter. 1983. *An Essay on Free Will.* Oxford: Clarendon Press.

———. 2008a. The Consequence Argument. In *Metaphysics. The Big Questions*, ed. Peter van Inwagen and Dean Zimmerman, 2nd ed., 450–456. Oxford: Blackwell.

————. 2008b. What Does an Omniscient Being Know About the Future? In *Oxford Studies in Philosophy of Religion 1*, ed. Jonathan Kvanvig, 216–230. Oxford: Oxford University Press.

————. 2011. Causation and the Mental. In *Reason, Metaphysics, and Mind. New Essays on the Philosophy of Alvin Plantinga*, ed. Michael C. Rea and Kelly James Clark, 152–170. Oxford: Oxford University Press.

————. 2013. A Dialogue on Free Will. *Methode 3*: 212–221.

————. 2015. Nothing is Impossible. In *God, Truth, and Other Enigmas*, ed. Miroslaw Szatkowski, 33–58. Berlin; Munich; Boston: De Gruyter.

————. 2017a. Introduction: van Inwagen on Free Will. In *Thinking About Free Will*, 1–19. Cambridge: Cambridge University Press.

————. 2017b. Free Will Remains a Mystery. In *Thinking About Free Will*, 90–110. Cambridge: Cambridge University Press.

————. 2017c. Freedom to Break the Laws. In *Thinking About Free Will*, 129–148. Cambridge: Cambridge University Press.

————. 2017d. Author's preface to the French Translation of An Essay on Free Will. In *Thinking About Free Will*, 177–191. Cambridge: Cambridge University Press.

————. 2017e. Ability. In *Thinking About Free Will*, 210–229. Cambridge: Cambridge University Press.

Vihvelin, Kadri. 2013. *Causes, Laws, and Free Will. Why Determinism Doesn't Matter*. Oxford: Oxford University Press.

6

Local-Miracle Compatibilism: A Critique

John Martin Fischer

The "Consequence Argument," so-called by Peter van Inwagen (1983), concludes that causal determinism is incompatible with freedom (in the sense putatively implicated in moral responsibility).[1] It is structurally and substantively parallel to arguments for fatalism (the incompatibility of human freedom with future contingents with already determinate truth-values), and theological incompatibilism (the incompatibility of human freedom with God's foreknowledge of future contingents).[2] All of these arguments employ crucially a "fixity of the past" premise. The Consequence Argument employs an additional indispensable ingredient: a "fixity of the laws" premise. A thorough evaluation of the Consequence Argument must be embedded in a framework that includes the histori-cally influential arguments for fatalism and theological incompatibilism.[3]

These argument triplets (or argument-template triplets) have received a huge amount of attention. The arguments for fatalism and theological

J. M. Fischer (✉)
University of California, Riverside, CA, USA
e-mail: fischer@ucr.edu; John.Fischer@ucr.edu

© The Author(s), under exclusive license to Springer Nature Switzerland AG 2021   **111**
M. Hausmann, J. Noller (eds.), *Free Will*,
https://doi.org/10.1007/978-3-030-61136-1_6

fatalism have been discussed for millennia, and the Consequence Argument for centuries. All three arguments come in various different forms: the templates are filled in differently. They are, however, similar in deep ways, sharing at least some regimentation of the intuitive idea of the fixity of the past. The past is over-and-done-with.

Here I wish to focus on what many think is the most powerful compatibilist response to the Consequence Argument: "local-miracle compatibilism."[4] Peter van Inwagen, who has done more than anyone else to persuade contemporary philosophers of the force of the argument, deems this the best response, and he takes it very seriously (van Inwagen 2004). Indeed, van Inwagen writes that Lewis's paper is "the finest essay that has ever been written in defense of compatibilism—possibly the finest essay ever written about any aspect of the free will problem" (2008, 330). This is high praise, especially as it comes from the author of a powerful and influential presentation of incompatibilism: *An Essay on Free Will*.

Lewis-style compatibilism—the local-miracle approach—continues to be the "go-to" reply to the Consequence Argument. Many compatibilists accept it, in some form or other (Vihvelin 2013, 162-6). Here I shall present a critique of this position, one that builds on a previous critical analysis of "multiple-pasts" compatibilism, the view that the fixity of the past premise (as employed in the Consequence Argument) is to be rejected (Fischer 1983, 1988, 1994, 78-83). The problem with local-miracle compatibilism is parallel to the problem with multiple-pasts compatibilism, although different in detail. Further, the problem runs deep: it afflicts even versions of the strategy that don't rely on Lewis's specific views about counterfactuals and related issues (such as the similarity relations among possible worlds).

1   The Consequence Argument: The Conditional Version

As above, the Consequence Argument comes in many different forms. Some, including van Inwagen (1983, 57), have contended that they are all necessarily equivalent.[5] I disagree (Fischer and Ravizza 1996). For our purposes, we can begin by considering a particular version of the argument, which I have dubbed "the conditional version" (Fischer 1994, 63-65; Fischer and Ravizza 1996, Fischer 2016, 5-6).[6] At this point we need not take a stand on whether the various versions are equivalent.

Here's the conditional version of the Consequence Argument. The argument assumes the following regimentations of the intuitive ideas of the fixity of the past (FP) and the fixity of the laws (FL):

> (FP) For any action Y, agent S, and time t, if it is true that if S were to do Y at t, some fact F about the past relative to t would not have been a fact, then S cannot at t do Y at t.
>
> (FL) For any action Y, and agent S, if it is true that if S were to do Y, some natural law that actually obtains would not obtain, then S cannot do Y.

Consider some act X that agent S actually does at $t2$. Take determinism to imply that a complete description of the (intrinsic) state of the world at any time t, in conjunction with a complete formulation of the natural laws (that actually obtain), entails every subsequent truth.[7] Now if determinism is true, and $s1$ was the state of the world at $t1$, then it must be the case that one of the following conditionals is true:

(1) If S were to refrain from doing X at $t2$, $s1$ would not have been the total state of the world at $t1$; or

(2) If S were to refrain from doing X at $t2$, then some natural law that actually obtains would not obtain; or

(3) If S were to refrain from doing X at $t2$, then either $s1$ would not have been the total state of the world at $t1$ or some natural law that actually obtains would not obtain.[8]

But if (1) is true, then (via FP) S cannot refrain from doing X at $t2$. Similarly, if (2) is true, then (via FL) S cannot refrain from doing X at $t2$. And if (1)'s truth implies that S cannot refrain from doing X at $t2$ and (2)'s truth has the same implication, then so does the truth of (3). So the conclusion is that, if causal determinism is true, then S cannot do anything other than what she actually does at $t2$. This conclusion generalizes to the result of incompatibilism. Note (as above) that a parallel argument can be given for theological fatalism, except that we do not need (2), but rather a premise stating that God is essentially sempiternal and omniscient (Fischer 1994, 63; Fischer 2016, 1-52).

2   Local-Miracle Compatibilism

In "Are We Free to Break the Laws?" David Lewis (1981) articulates a reply to the Consequence Argument that is essentially the same as what came to be known as the "standard reply". The standard reply (in its various particular forms) insists on a distinction between a causal and a noncausal way of interpreting (FP) and (FL). Or perhaps better: the proponent of the standard reply contends that the apparent plausibility of (FP) and (FL) relies on implicitly thinking of them as involving causal claims. Recall:

> (FP) For any action Y, agent S, and time t, if it is true that if S were to do Y at t, some fact F about the past relative to t would not have been a fact, then S cannot at t do Y at t.
> (FL) For any action Y, and agent S, if it is true that if S were to do Y, some natural law that actually obtains would not obtain, then S cannot do Y.

Now consider their causal analogues:

> (FPc) For any action Y, agent S, and time t, if it is true that if S were to do Y at t, S would thereby have caused fact F about the past relative to t to not have been a fact, then S cannot at t do Y at t.
> (FLc) For any action Y, and agent S, if it is true that if S were to do Y, S would thereby have caused some natural law that actually obtains to not obtain, then S cannot do Y.

The standard reply to the Consequence Argument has it that (FPc) is plausible, whereas, upon reflection, (FP) is not, and that whatever initial appeal (FP) has comes from a failure to distinguish it from (FPc). Similarly, the view is that (FLc) is plausible, whereas, upon reflection, (FL) is not, and that whatever initial appeal (FL) has comes from a failure to distinguish it from (FLc).[9] Further, the standard reply contends that the plausible versions of the premises (the causal versions) do not entail (when combined) the incompatibilist conclusion (that if causal determinism is true, then no agent S can ever do otherwise), and the versions that do entail incompatibilism are implausible.

This is the core of the standard response. In his book, *Counterfactuals* Lewis (1973) presented a theory of counterfactuals (building on the work of Robert Stalnaker (1968)). On this approach (I simplify and use Stalnaker's version), a counterfactual, "If P had been the case, then Q would have been the case" is true in the actual world iff Q is true in the most similar possible world to the actual world in which P is true. In a paper published after *Counterfactuals*, Lewis (1979) adds various ingredients to get his own specific version of the response: in particular, a "similarity metric" on possible worlds (i.e., a general way of ranking overall similarity of possible worlds) that, together with his theory of counterfactuals, putatively yields the result that if causal determinism obtains, then the "local-miracle counterfactual" (2) is true. In these three works Lewis provides a package of views that issue in his brand of local-miracle compatibilism. On this approach, even if causal determinism holds, sometimes an individual has it in her power to do otherwise, that is, so to act that a natural law that actually obtains would not have obtained just prior to the act in question.

In other words, suppose that $L1$ is a proposition that expresses a natural law, and that causal determinism obtains. On Lewis's view, an agent may have it in her power at a time t to do otherwise than she actually does, because she has it in her power at t so to act that $L1$ would not express a natural law. $L1$ would not have held just prior to t in the closest world to the actual world in which the agent does otherwise. Invoking his philosophical machinery, together with features of our actual world, Lewis contends that (2)—the local-miracle counterfactual—would be true in a deterministic world, and that (FL) is false. Lewis also contends that (1) might also be true, in that the past might have been different just prior to t, but we can put this aside for our purposes. In any case, the acceptance of (2) would not imply that the *remote* past would have been different, if the agent had done otherwise at t.

Lewis's overall approach is systematic and powerful.[10] As Kadri Vihvelin (2013) points out, a proponent of the standard response doesn't have to agree with any of the additional ingredients (ancillary to the core of the standard response) Lewis offers—his theory of counterfactuals and similarity metric—in order to maintain the standard response. All that's necessary for the standard response is the contention that when (FP) and (FL) are interpreted causally, the argument is invalid; and when they are interpreted non-causally, the argument is unsound. Employing Lewis's language in regard to (FL), we cannot *break* the laws of nature, but it does not follow that we cannot so act that some law of nature would not have been a law. (For Lewis, "breaking" a law is a causal notion that implies that one causes a law-breaking event.)

On this view, it is possible for an agent in a deterministic world to perform an act that is such that, if she were to perform it, some actual natural law *L1* would not have been a law. *L1* is a law in the actual world (which we assume to be deterministic), in which the agent raises her hand at *t*, but not in the possible world (or worlds) most similar to (closest to) the actual world in which she does not raise her hand. Although the standard response (in particular as regards [FL]) does not require Lewis's overall philosophical package, I will continue to refer to the denial of (FL) as "local-miracle compatibilism". The denial of (FL) involves the view that a certain sort of counterfactual would be true under causal determinism, but it does not in itself provide an explanation of this view. (It is, of course, an advantage of Lewis's approach—involving his theory of the truth conditions for counterfactuals—that it does.)

Lewis emphasizes that the local miracle compatibilist is *not* committed to outlandish views about what agents can do. A mere denial of (FL) does not imply that an agent could have it in her power to *break* a law of nature, or to cause a law of nature to be false. Lewis writes:

> Thus I insist that I was able to raise my hand (although I actually did not), and I acknowledge that a law would have been broken had I done so, but I deny that I am therefore able to break a law. To uphold my instance of soft determinism, I need not claim any incredible powers. To uphold the compatibilism that I actually believe, I need not claim that such powers are even possible. (1981, 117)

In defending (FL), Peter van Inwagen (1983, 62) pointed out that it would be ridiculous to ask an engineer to construct a spacecraft that would travel faster than the speed of light, given that it is well known to be law of nature that nothing travels faster than the speed of light.[11] In general, it is ludicrous to suppose that any human being can break a law of nature. Lewis would agree with van Inwagen, but he would invoke the distinction between a causal and a non-causal interpretation of the fixity of the laws (FL). Right: we cannot *break* a law of nature; we cannot cause a violation of the law of nature. No breaking the laws—no metaphysical civil disobedience! But Lewis would insist that it does not follow that no human being can so act that an actual law of nature would not be a law. The implausible result that imputes extraordinary powers to human beings is not entailed by local-miracle compatibilism, and the result that is indeed entailed does not impute such extraordinary powers to human beings.

At the end of her discussion of these issues, Vihvelin (2013) points out, and endorses, the compatibilist's contention that a commitment to (FPc) and (FLc), but a rejection of (FP) and (FL), does not result in attributing to agents fantastic powers. She writes:

> The compatibilist is committed only to saying that if determinism is true, we have abilities which we would exercise *only if* the past (and/or the laws) had been different in the appropriate ways. And while this may sound odd, it is no more incredible than the claim that the successful exercise of our abilities depends, not only on us, but also on the cooperation of factors outside our control. Since we are neither superheroes nor gods, we are always in this position regardless of the truth or falsity of determinism.
>
> … The Counterfactual version of the [Consequence A]rgument claims that if we attribute ordinary abilities to deterministic agents, we are forced to credit them with incredible past- or law-changing abilities as well. But no such incredible conclusion follows. All that follows is something that we must accept anyway, as the price of our non-godlike nature… (2013, 165-6)

The upshot: the proponents of the "standard" compatibilist reply to the Consequence Argument contend that the compatibilist is not committed to an attribution of fantastic power to human agents. "Multiple-pasts compatiblism" accepts only that agents can so act that the past would have been different, not that they can bring about a different past. And local miracle compatibilism contends only that agents can so act that a law of nature that actually holds would not have held, not that agents can break the laws of nature. So there's no point in telling the engineer to build that spacecraft that can travel faster than the speed of light, and so forth. The focus of this sort of compatibilism is on the counterfactuals and figuring out which ones would be true, on the assumption of causal determinism. The claim is that once we see precisely which counterfactuals are true, we can make the world safe for compatibilism; the counterfactuals are completely consistent with plausible "can-claims," but not implausible ones.

3   Reply to Multiple-Pasts Compatibilism

So the compatibilist breaks down the relevant claims about our abilities into two parts: a "can-claim" and a counterfactual: for example, "S can do X," and "If S were to do X, some natural law would not have been one." Alternatively: "S can do X," and "If S were to do X, the past would have been different."[12] But what exactly does the truth of the relevant counterfactual (under the assumption of causal determinism) have to do with the can-claim? This question reveals local-miracle compatibilism's Achilles heel. We'll start the philosophical podiatry by reiterating an argument I've made previously against multiple-pasts compatibilism. In the following section I'll extend the same sort of strategy to local-miracle compatibilism. If the sort of compatibilism championed by Lewis and Vihvelin is not a failure, it can at least be seen to be *incomplete* in important ways.

Begin by considering an alternative version of the Consequence Argument.

It will be helpful to accept, as a working hypothesis, the broad outlines of Keith Lehrer's "possible-worlds analysis" of can-claims. Lehrer says:

... when we say that a person could have done something he did not do, we should not, and I believe do not, thereby affirm that *every antecedent* necessary condition of his performing the action is fulfilled. It is enough that there be some possible world minimally different from the actual world restricted in an appropriate way so that the person performs the actions and those conditions are fulfilled. We may speak of worlds restricted in the appropriate way as possible worlds that are accessible to the agents from the actual world. (1976, 253-4)

So on this sort of possible-worlds account of "can," an agent *can* in possible world w perform some action only if she *does* perform the action in a possible world w^* that is *accessible* to the agent from w. Not all possible worlds are accessible to the agent from w; the accessible worlds are "suitably restricted."

There are different and competing views about what these restrictions are. The incompatibilist proponent of the Consequence Argument will insist on strict fixity of the past and laws. Motivating a strong constraint on accessible possible worlds, Carl Ginet puts the point nicely:

If I have it open to me now to make the world contain a certain event after now, then I have it open to me now to make the world contain everything that has happened before now plus that event after now. We might call this the principle that freedom is freedom to add to the given past [holding fixed the laws of nature] or the principle of *the fixity of the given past*. (1990, 102-3)

The basic idea is that an agent has it within his power in possible world w to do X only if his doing X can be an extension of the (temporally intrinsic) past in w, holding the natural laws fixed. The 'can' in the formulation of the principle is not meant to be the 'free will' can, but, rather, a wider notion of possibility, such as logical possibility. On this interpretation, the principle states that an agent has it in his power (in the 'free will' sense) in w to do X only if it is logically possible that his doing X be an extension of the past in w, holding the natural laws fixed.

Put in terms of the possible-worlds framework, we have the Principle of the Fixity of the Past and Laws:

(PFPL) An agent S has it within his power in possible world w to do X at time t only if there is a possible world with the same (temporally intrinsic) past relative to t and the same laws as in w in which S does X at t.[13]

Now we are in a position to present an alternative version of the Consequence Argument, one that employs (PFPL) rather than (FP) and (FL), as in the first version above. Note that (PFPL) doesn't just put the fixity of the past and laws together; it avoids expressing the fixity claims in terms of conditionals.[14]

As in the first version, consider some act X that agent S actually does at $t2$. Assume causal determinism and take determinism to imply that a complete description of the (intrinsic) state of the world at $t1$ (call this state $s1$) in conjunction with a complete formulation of the natural laws (call the total set L) entails every subsequent truth. That is, in every possible world with L that has $s1$ at $t1$, S does X at $t2$. Does S have the power (in the free will sense) at $t2$ or before to refrain from X-ing at $t2$? No, because (PFPL) specifies that if S has this power, there exists a possible world with L and with $s1$ at $t1$ in which S refrains from X-ing at $t2$. Generalizing: causal determinism rules out freedom to do otherwise.

Given that the argument is valid (and I think it is), a compatibilist will need to reject (PFPL). I contend, however, that if one rejects PFPL, one would be committed to implausible results about practical reasoning. That is, rejecting (PFPL) could lead to one's having to say that it is rational to choose certain actions in contexts in which it is manifestly irrational to choose those actions. Remember that the basic point of compatibilists such as Lewis and Vihvelin is that a local-miracle compatibilist need not be committed to implausible results (in particular, about our abilities [in the free-will sense]). Here I will summarize an argument that I have presented before that the multiple-pasts compatibilist (who rejects [PFPL]) is committed to implausible results about practical reasoning (Fischer 1994, 94-98; Fischer and Pendergraft 2013). In the next section I will present a parallel argument that calls into question the Lewis/Vihvelin contention that the local-miracle compatibilist need not be committed to implausible claims about our abilities.

To explain. There are certain examples in which both the relevant can-claim and the paired backtracking subjunctive (counterfactual) conditionals are (arguably, at least) true. Various philosophers have offered examples of this sort, and here is one:

> Consider the example of the Icy Patch. Sam saw a boy slip and fall on an icy patch on Sam's sidewalk on Monday. The boy was seriously injured, and this disturbed Sam deeply. On Tuesday, Sam must decide whether to go ice-skating. Suppose that Sam's character is such that if he were to decide to go ice-skating at noon on Tuesday, then the boy would not have slipped and hurt himself on Monday.
>
> The situation is puzzling. It seems that Sam is able to decide to go and to go ice-skating on Tuesday. [In other words, we can suppose that nothing is preventing Sam from acting out of character by making a decision to go ice-skating. We can be confident that he won't act out of character, but it doesn't follow that he can't.] And it also appears plausible that if he were to decide to go skating on Tuesday, the terrible accident would not have occurred on Monday. So it appears that Sam ought to decide to go ice-skating on Tuesday. And yet, given that Sam knows that the accident did in fact take place on Monday, it also seems irrational for Sam to decide to go ice-skating on Tuesday on the basis of a reason flowing from the truth of the backtracker. Nothing prevents Sam from deciding to go and from going ice-skating on Tuesday [Sam can decide to go and go ice-skating on Tuesday]; and if he were to decide to go ice-skating [on Tuesday], the accident would not have occurred [on Monday]. And yet it seems inappropriate for Sam to decide to go ice-skating. To do so would seem to exemplify something akin to wishful thinking (Fischer 1994, 90).[15]

First, how can both the can-claim (Sam is able—in the free-will sense—to decide to go ice-skating on Tuesday) and the backtracker (If Sam were to go ice-skating on Tuesday, the accident would not have occurred on Monday) be true? The short answer: the can-claim and the counterfactual involve *different modalities*. Put in terms of the possible-worlds framework, the can-claim requires a possible world *suitably related* to the actual world (or world in which the can-claim is putatively true). This sort of relationship underwrites the *accessibility* of the world in question to the actual world. The key point is that such a world, in virtue of which S can at (or just before) $t2$ do X at $t2$, need *not* be the *closest* possible world to the actual world in which the laws of the actual world hold, *s1* obtains at *t1*, and S *X*'s at *t2*. The *can-claim* need not be made true by a "closest" world. In contrast, the *counterfactual* points us to the closest possible worlds in which the laws of the actual world hold and *s1* obtains at *t1*. So it is possible that in all the closest (to the actual world) possible worlds in which the laws of the actual world hold and *s1* obtains at *t1*, S does not *X* at *t2*, but there is a possible world suitably related to the actual world (where this does not require maximal closeness) in which the laws of the actual world hold, *s1* obtains at *t1*, and S does *X* at *t2*.

The intuitive idea is that when we think, as we do, that Sam can decide to go ice-skating at *t2*, we are thinking that he can act out of character and exhibit gross irrationality. That is, we are assuming that Sam can add to the actual past a decision to go ice-skating. In accepting the can-claim, we are holding the past fixed. But we don't hold the past fixed when we evaluate the backtracking counterfactual. Put in terms of possible worlds, here we "look at" the *closest* possible worlds, which may have very different pasts from the actual world.

It is important to note that this analysis of *Icy Patch* shows (FP) to be false. (FP) contends that the truth of the backtracker implies the falsity of the can-claim. This is the way it seeks to capture the intuitive idea of the fixity of the past. But in *Icy Patch* both the backtracker and the paired can-claim are true. If this is correct, it shows that (FP) is not an adequate way to capture the fixity of the past. This helps to motivate the switch by the proponent of the Consequence Argument from (FP) and (FL) to (PFPL). Making this switch, we can see that even if (FP) is rejected, it does not follow that the Consequence Argument is defeated: there is another way of capturing the fixity of the past that can be employed in another version of the Consequence Argument. It is crucial to see that even if examples such as *Icy Patch* lead to the rejection of (FP), these examples do *not* thereby show that (PFPL) is problematic.

These are significant morals of the *Icy Patch* story, but there is another. In *Icy Patch* the rejection of (PFPL) leads to an implausible result: that it is rational for Sam to decide to go ice-skating on Tuesday, or, alternatively, that Sam ought to decide to go ice-skating Tuesday. To see this, start with the intuitively appealing idea that it is appropriate to take the reasons that obtain in all and only worlds accessible from the actual world to the agent at a given time as relevant to the agent's practical reasoning at the time. Intuitively, the agent has access to those worlds—she can get to those worlds from the actual world. Less metaphorically (but still not employing ordinary terms), she can actualize those worlds. Why not then take the reasons that obtain in those worlds as relevant to the agent's practical reasoning? If an agent can't get to a scenario from where he is, then the features of that scenario would seem to be irrelevant to his practical reasoning. But if the agent can indeed get to the scenario from where he is, then why not deem certain features of that scenario relevant to the agent's practical reasoning? It would seem entirely arbitrary not to allow the agent to take into account reasons that obtain in scenarios genuinely accessible to him

Given a rejection of (PFPL), nothing rules it out that in *Icy Patch*, Sam has access on Tuesday to a possible world in which the accident did not occur on Monday. After all, Sam can decide on Tuesday to go ice-skating that afternoon. If this can-claim is rendered true by a possible world w^* accessible to Sam, and on the assumption that we reject (PFPL), nothing rules it out that w^* will contain the accident's not happening on Monday. So Sam would have access on Tuesday to a possible world in which the accident did not occur on Monday. But if this is so, why shouldn't Sam take this as a reason (or as generating a set of reasons) to decide to go ice-skating on Tuesday? If it is appropriate for Sam to take as relevant reasons that obtain in any world genuinely accessible to him at a time, then surely it may well be rational for him to decide to go ice-skating on Tuesday. But, again, this is a manifestly unacceptable result: it is clearly irrational for him so to decide on Tuesday. The problem, then, is that the rejection of (PFPL) leads to unacceptable results for practical reasoning.

A bit more carefully, the problem comes from denying the fixity of the past element of (PFPL). The local-miracle compatibilist, however, will approach things from the fixity-of-the laws angle. She will deny (FL) and thereby resist the Consequence Argument. But in the next section I will show how a similar argument to the one I have just made against the multiple-pasts compatibilist can be deployed against the local-miracle compatibilist.

Spoiler alert: here is a preview. If one denies (FL) on the basis of the "standard response" (distinguishing the causal and non-causal versions of the fixity of the laws), the incompatibilist will switch to (PFPL). Further, denying (PFPL) by denying its fixity-of-the laws component might well lead to implausible results, this time about our abilities (rather than practical reasoning). Even though Lewis and Vihvelin seek to assuage our concern that denying (FL) would lead to the imputation of fantastic abilities, the argument will show that the anxiety cannot so easily be removed. Denying (FL) is not a strong enough philosophical tranquilizer. It is not enough to defeat the Consequence argument, since there is another way of capturing the fixity of the laws that can be employed by the incompatibilist. And rejecting this alternative formulation leads to the possible imputation of fantastic abilities. Out of the frying pan and into the fire!

4   Reply to Local-Miracle Compatibilism

As we noted above, the local-miracle compatibilist distinguishes between (FL) and (FLc), and she contends that the appeal of (FL) comes largely from its conflation with (FLc). According to the local-miracle compatibilist, whereas (FLc) is plausible, (FL) is not. On this view, the truth of a "local-miracle counterfactual," such as "If S were to refrain from X-ing at $t2$, some law $L1$ that is a member of the set of laws $\{L\}$ that actually obtains would not have held," is compatible with "S has it in her power (in the free-will sense) to refrain from X-ing at $t2$".

Lewis argues that if causal determinism were true, the relevant local-miracle counterfactuals would be true, rather than the backtrackers (counterfactuals that backtrack all the way into the remote past). Further, this fact does not threaten the relevant can-claims. Thus, he (and Vihvelin) conclude that (FL) is false.

But our analysis in the previous section points us to the gap in this argument. It is just not clear what the relationship is between the truth of the local-miracle counterfactual and the paired can-claim. It is crucial to Lewis's strategy that we separate the two claims: the can-claim and the counterfactual. We saw, however, in our discussion of multiple-pasts compatibilism, that even if the counterfactual is true, nothing follows about the appropriate constraints on can-claims. Lewis may be right about which counterfactuals are true under causal determinism. But this does not in itself imply that we do not hold the laws of nature fixed, when evaluating can-claims (just as we hold the past fixed when evaluating can-claims, even if the backtracker is true).

Recall (PFPL):

(PFPL) An agent S has it within his power in possible world w to do X at time t only if there is a possible world with the same (temporally intrinsic) past relative to t and the same laws as in w in which does X at t.

Again, the truth of the local-miracle counterfactual in no way bears on the truth of (PFPL); the two are separate claims, dealing with different modalities. The semantics for the counterfactual point us to the closest possible worlds, whereas those for the can-claim need not. And, again (PFPL) can be used in a valid version of the Consequence Argument.

Now what if the proponent of local-miracle compatibilism proposes that we adjust (PFPL) to eliminate the fixity of the laws element? Perhaps she will claim that the truth of the local-miracle counterfactual in the context under consideration at least *suggests* such a modification. Call the new constraint, "the possible-worlds principle of the fixity of the past":

(FPpw) An agent S has it within his power in possible world w to do X at time t only if there is a possible world with the same (temporally intrinsic) past relative to t in which S does X at t.

Determinism implies that in all possible worlds with the same past and laws, the agent does exactly the same thing as in the actual world. It doesn't follow that there is no possible world with the same past but different laws in which the agent does otherwise. So the local-miracle compatibilist is making headway along this route. (FPpw) cannot be employed (without further resources) in a successful version of the Consequence Argument; it is too weak to get the incompatibilist conclusion.

But the problem is that (FPpw) is also too weak to provide a plausible freedom-relevant constraint. That's because once we've relaxed the "same laws" requirement, pretty much anything goes, and we would indeed be in jeopardy of attributing fantastic powers to agents. Keith Lehrer writes:

First of all, the possible world must have the same laws as the actual world. That there are possible worlds with laws different from the actual world in which I perform an action that I do not perform in the actual world hardly shows that I could have performed that action. That there are possible worlds in which whispers move mountains hardly shows that I could have moved the Rincon mountains to Phoenix with a whisper in the actual world (1976, 246 in reprinted version Fischer, ed., 2005).

(FPpw) is presented as only a necessary condition on freedom to do otherwise, and it would clearly need to be beefed up to get a sufficient condition. Otherwise the local-miracle compatibilist would be just as much committed to the imputation of fantastic powers as other compatibilists (and, in particular, those who deny (FLc)). As far as I can see, the beefing-up has to involve something to the effect that natural laws be fixed (at least in some sense).

Perhaps the local-miracle compatibilist will contend that we should learn from Lewis's insightful distinction between (FLc) and (FL) and incorporate this in our possible-worlds analysis:

(PFPL*) An agent S has it within his power in possible world w to do X at time t only if there is a possible world with the same (temporally intrinsic) past relative to t, in which no law $L1$ in the set of laws {L} that obtains in w is *violated*, and S does X at t.

Lewis defines law-violations in terms of the causal notion of "breaking laws," rather than the mere non-holding of laws. So we might re-write (PFPL*) as:

(PFPL**) An agent S has it within his power in possible world w to do X at time t only if there is a possible world with the same (temporally intrinsic) past relative to t as in w, in which no agent breaks any law in the set of laws {L} that obtain in w, and S does X at t.

But (PFPL*) and (PFPL**) are problematic. They do seem to address the problem of the imputation of fantastic powers. But a problem, or at least mystery, remains. These principles imply a weird asymmetry. In the possible world putatively underwriting an agent's power to do X, at least one law may not in general hold, but will apply to the agent's actions and their consequences. More carefully, at least one actually obtaining natural law may not hold in the relevant world prior to an agent's act, but will hold during and after. What explains this asymmetry? Lewis's overall theory of counterfactuals and relative similarity of possible worlds does indeed explain (or in principle could explain) the asymmetry between the counterfactuals in question. The relevant set of possible worlds is related to the actual world via similarity relations that (according to Lewis) imply that under causal determinism, the local-miracle counterfactuals would be true, but not the law-breakers. But these resources are simply unavailable when one *switches* from the version of the Consequence Argument that employs counterfactual conditionals to a version that employs something like (PFPL) or its modifications.

Further, Lewis emphasizes that we can't pick out in advance one specific law or set of laws in advance as the one that would not hold in the counterfactual situation. This would seem to be a problem when we switch from a counterfactual version of the Consequence Argument to a possible-worlds version employing (PFPL). On the (PFPL) version, which laws that actually hold do not obtain in the possible world that putatively underwrites the can-claim? Nothing in (PFPL*) or (PFPL**) rules it out that this possible world have widespread differences from the actual world in the natural laws that hold. Thus, there may be widespread asymmetries of the sort just described, and the worlds may be almost unrecognizable to us. Would such a world really show that an agent has the power to perform an action?[16]

Return to the passage quote above from Kadri Vihvelin:

> The compatibilist is committed only to saying that if determinism is true, we have abilities which we would exercise *only if* the past (and/or the laws) had been different in the appropriate ways. And while this may sound odd, it is no more incredible than the claim that the successful exercise of our abilities depends, not only on us, but also on the cooperation of factors outside our control. Since we are neither superheroes nor gods, we are always in this position regardless of the truth or falsity of determinism.

... The Counterfactual version of the [Consequence A]rgument claims that if we attribute ordinary abilities to deterministic agents, we are forced to credit them with incredible past- or law-changing abilities as well. But no such incredible conclusion follows. All that follows is something that we must accept anyway, as the price of our non-godlike nature... (2013, 165-6).

The second paragraph is explicitly about the counterfactual version of the Consequence Argument, i.e., the version that employs (FP) and (FL). But the first paragraph is about compatibilism more generally. We have seen that it is not at all clear that the version that rejects (PFPL) does not result in the potential imputation of fantastic powers to agents. We all agree that "the successful exercise of our abilities depends, not only on us, but also on the cooperation of factors outside our control." In my view, this is beyond dispute. But the classical compatibilist is committed to more: if she rejects (PFPL), nothing rules it out that her position will countenance fantastic powers—precisely what local-miracle compatibilism is designed to avoid.

5   Freedom and Counterfactuals

Crucial to the Lewis-style strategy, and local-miracle compatibilism more generally, is the notion that we should break claims like "Agent S can bring about a different past" or "Agent S can bring it about that a law of nature would not hold" into two components: the can-claim—"Agent S can do X" and a conditional, "If S were to do X, the past would have been different (or "If S were to do X, the laws would have been different"). The basic point is that it is mistaken to assume that there are conceptual connections between our powers (in the free will sense) and the past and laws that would render the following necessarily true: "No agent can so act that there would have been a different past" and "No agent can so act that there would be different laws of nature." van Inwagen supposes that there are such analytic or conceptual connections; Lewis denies this. Rather, Lewis insists that we break the relevant claims into their parts, and that we focus on the conditionals. He claims that under causal determinism, the "local-miracle counterfactuals" would be true, and seeing this, we can see that the compatibilist need not be committed to implausible attributions of abilities.

I have argued that Lewis's move is successful, at best, against one version of the Consequence Argument. This is because another version employs (PFPL), a principle that specifies constraints on can-claims. These constraints are independent of an evaluation of the counterfactuals, so even if mere local-miracle, and not law-breaking, counterfactuals are true (in a deterministic world), this would be irrelevant to the incompatibilist's argument.

As a classical compatibilist, Lewis must deny that in evaluating the can-claims relevant to free will, we hold fixed the natural laws. This is to deny (PFPL) by denying the possible-worlds regimentation of the fixity-of-the-laws idea. Clearly, any classical compatibilist needs to reject this principle, and the principle itself is contentious. Despite my argument above that rejection of (PFPL) leads to implausible results, we cannot simply take it that (PFPL) is uncontroversially true. My point, rather, is that nothing in a Lewis-style evaluation of *counterfactuals* bears on (PFPL). Whether (FP) or (FL) is true, or whether (FL) or (FLc) is true, is quite beside the point: these issues about counterfactuals are irrelevant to an evaluation of (PFPL). Again: the counterfactuals point us to the closest world or worlds (to the actual world—the world in which the "can-claim" is being considered), whereas the freedom-claim does not.

van Inwagen holds that the two versions of the Consequence Argument we have discussed "stand or fall together". Perhaps this is what lies behind his view that local-miracle compatibilism is such a potent (although ultimately unconvincing) response. On this view, if there is a persuasive objection to one, then there is an objection (presumably, a parallel objection) to the others. On this view, the falsity of (FL) would imply (or at least point to) the falsity of (PFPL). But, as stated above, I don't agree that all the versions of the Consequence Argument stand or fall together. One can just as easily turn the tables and contend that since there are counterexamples to (FL) that are not counterexamples to (PFPL), the arguments are not equivalent and do not stand or fall together.

It is noteworthy that the local-miracle compatibilists focus so much on the counterfactuals. They argue that figuring out precisely which counterfactuals would be true on the assumption of causal determinism is crucial to a proper evaluation of the Consequence Argument. If I am correct, then their attention if misplaced. Or, more charitably, it is instructive with respect to one (prominent) version of the argument, but not another important version. If (PFPL) most effectively captures the basic intuitive idea of the fixity of the past, then the Consequence Argument, in its most basic and menacing form, has not been touched by local-miracle compatibilism.

Consider this passage from Vihvelin:

> … the success or failure of the Consequence Argument turns on a claim about *counterfactuals*. This is significant because it shows that the argument cannot be defended, as van Inwagen originally claimed, only by appealing to uncontroversial premises about our relation to the laws (that *we* aren't able to render them false), and our relation to propositions about the remote past (that *we* aren't able to render them false) (2013, 161, italics in original).

I have shown, however, that the argument can indeed by defended by appealing to a very fundamental and deeply appealing principle: (PFPL). This principle amalgamates uncontroversial and intuitively plausible views about the fixity of the past and natural laws.

The subtitle of Vihvelin's book is, *Why Determinism Doesn't Matter*". In a way it does matter, and in a way it doesn't. The Consequence Argument shows how causal determinism matters for freedom to do otherwise; perhaps it not indisputably sound, but there is no uncontroversial response. Vihvelin thinks determinism does not matter for moral responsibility, because, although responsibility requires freedom to do otherwise, determinism is compatible with such freedom. I do not believe that freedom to do otherwise is necessary for moral responsibility, so I hold that if causal determinism eliminates moral responsibility, it is not in virtue of ruling out alternative possibilities. But this still leaves it open that "Source Incompatibilism" holds; this is the view that causal determinism impugns moral responsibility "directly," and not (solely) in virtue of ruling out alternative possibilities (if it does).[17] I do not accept Source Incompatibilism, but it takes an argument to defeat it. Determinism still matters.

6   The Fixed Future and the Open Past

Recall Carl Ginet's elegant crystallization of the fixity of the past:

> If I have it open to me now to make the world contain a certain event after now, then I have it open to me now to make the world contain everything that has happened before now plus that event after now. We might call this the principle that freedom is freedom to add to the given past [holding fixed the laws of nature] or the principle of *the fixity of the given past* (1990, 102-3).

The basic idea is that an agent has it within his power in possible world w to do X only if his doing X can be an extension of the (temporally intrinsic) past in w, holding the natural laws fixed. The principle states that an agent has it in his power (in the 'free will' sense) in w to do X only if it is logically possible that his doing X be an extension of the past in w, holding the natural laws fixed.

Put in terms of the possible-worlds framework, we have (our good friend) the Principle of the Fixity of the Past and Laws:

> (PFPL) An agent S has it within his power in possible world w to do X at time t only if there is a possible world with the same (temporally intrinsic) past relative to t and the same laws as in w in which S does X at t.

In this paper I have argued for (PFPL), and I have also argued that accepting it shows that the local miracle package of views does not suffice to defeat incompatibilism. In this brief section I wish to sketch how accepting (PFPL) has the further upshot of providing a promising strategy for solving the "Grandfather Paradox," which was originally discussed by David Lewis (1976), in another of his groundbreaking papers, "The Paradoxes of Time Travel."

This is the paradox, in simplified form. If time travel is possible, then Tim could get into his time-machine and travel backward in time to visit his grandfather, whom he hates. Suppose Tim does this and is standing right near grandpa. He has the abilities and skills to shoot (and thereby kill) grandpa, and he has a gun ready. (From now on, I will use "shoot" as short for "shoot and kill.") Intuitively, he can (in whatever sense is relevant to free will) shoot gramps. But he can't shoot his own grandfather, since if were to have done so, Tim would never have existed. Something must give.

Various philosophers have sought to remove the appearance of paradox in different ways. Some contend that, although Tim can indeed shoot grandpa, we know he won't. Further, there is no reason to think that Tim cannot shoot his grandfather; it is only the case that he can't exercise this ability. Others do insist that Tim can't shoot his grandfather, on the basis of views about counterfactuals and their relationship to the relevant freedom or ability-claims. So, for example, Kadri Vihvelin (1996) argues that, although Tim may have a general ability to shoot his grandfather, he can't, in the circumstances, do so, since "If S were to try to shoot his grandfather, he would succeed in at least some cases" is false. Vihvelin's view is based on her contention that the counterfactual is false in Tim's situation and that the freedom claim requires the truth of the counterfactual. David Lewis (1976) has a more complicated analysis of the paradox, purporting to dissolve it.

The Grandfather Paradox has elicited a wide variety of replies, each of which relies on ingredients that some find contentious. We can, however, use (PFPL) to resolve the paradox in a relatively clean and elegant way. Or so I suggest. No doubt some will find features of my approach less than indisputable, but it may be helpful to have a new way through the philosophical thicket. As Lewis pointed out, when we cannot get rid of the intellectual fog entirely, sometimes it is helpful to shift it from one place to another.

Let's think of it this way. Assume time-travel is possible. (Big assumption, I know; but let's make it and see where it leads us [apart from our murky pasts].) So far all we know is that it is possible for (say) Tim to travel back in time. We don't yet know whether he can do anything to affect his surroundings or the world in general (in the past). Grandpa is sitting right there in his reclining chair, next to Tim, and Tim has his gun. Is Tim free to shoot his grandfather? I say no! When causation flows backward, the future must be held fixed, and given this, Tim cannot shoot (and thereby kill) his grandfather.

(PFPL) is built for our world, where causal chains flow forward in time. (Let us put aside certain micro-phenomena, such as tachyons, and ideas from quantum mechanics. We are interested in free will here, and thus we can safely put such things aside.) I contend that our intuitive judgments about fixity are relative to the direction of causation. So, when causation flows forward in time, we accept (PFPL): our freedom is the freedom to add to the given past, holding the laws fixed. But when causation flows backward in time, we accept the idea that our freedom is the freedom to add to the given future, holding the laws fixed. Fixity follows the direction of causation—they are related inversely. One could say that, intuitively, we hold fixed the causally upstream events; so, when causation flows forward in time, we hold fixed the past, and when it flows backward in time, we hold fixed the future.

So, to capture the fixity of the future in the context of backward causation, consider:

(PFPL*) An agent S has it within his power in possible world w to do X at time t only if there is a possible world with the same (temporally intrinsic) future relative to t and the same laws as in w in which S does X at t.

(PFPL) is a very simple, basic, and intuitive principle. I claim that if one accepts it for forward-flowing causal sequences, one ought to accept (PFPL*) for backward flowing causal sequences. And if we accept (PFPL*) in the context of time travel, it straightforwardly follows that Tim cannot kill his Grandfather: there is no possible world with a future that includes Tim in which his grandfather is killed in the past.

Of course, a possible world may have forward-flowing causation on certain paths and backward-flowing causation on others. As I wrote above, fixity is relative to the direction of causation, so our fixity principles are context-relative: (PFPL) applies to forward-flowing causal sequences, and (PFPL*) to backward-flowing sequences.

This strategy of response dissolves the Grandfather Paradox in a simple, elegant way. Note, also, that it avoids any need to evaluate counterfactuals, just as the invocation of (PFPL) within the context of the Consequence Argument obviates the need to evaluate the counterfactuals.[18]

Multiple-Pasts Compatibilism and Local-Miracle Compatibilism often strike people as "tricks"—as clever but desperate attempts to save a theory. People are uncomfortable with these kinds of replies to the Consequence Argument. As one of the best graduate students I've ever had told me, "'Local-Miracle Compatibilism' is hard to wrap my mind around." It is too clever by half. In my opinion, so are many of the strategies of reply to the Grandfather Paradox. But we can cut through all of this complexity by employing a very fundamental and deeply intuitive idea: fixity follows the direction of causation, and our freedom is always the freedom to add to what is fixed (either the future or past). Causally upstream events, past and future, are fixed. What could be simpler?[19]

Notes

1. For an important earlier presentation of the argument, see: Carl Ginet (1966). Ginet (1983).
2. For a recent discussion and analysis, see: John Martin Fischer (2016), "Introduction: God, Freedom, and Moral Responsibility."
3. Discussions of the argument(s) for fatalism go back at least as far as Aristotle's famous analysis of the Sea Battle Argument (*De Interpretatione Bk. II*) and can be traced through David Foster Wallace's (2011) essay, "Richard Taylor's 'Fatalism' and the Semantics of Physical Modality." The argument for theological incompatibilism was first presented by Cicero and remains controversial even now:

   > The Stoics wrestled with such problems, and Cicero framed what may have been the first argument for the incompatibility of foreknowledge and free will, in the form of an argument against divination. The Jewish and Moslem traditions have contributed their share of reflection on these matters. But the fullest and richest development of these questions has occurred in the Christian theological tradition, beginning at least as early as Origen and reaching a climax in the debates of the sixteenth and seventeenth centuries. (Hasker 1989, 1)

   For an overview and discussion of the historical treatments of these arguments, see: William Lane Craig (1991). The essays in my *Our Fate* give an analytical overview.

4. The classic and most influential presentation is David Lewis's (1981). Independently, I discussed this view as worthy of consideration (although I did not endorse it), and I coined the term, "Local-Miracle Compatibilism": Fischer (1983, 1988, 1994).

5. Similarly Michael Slote (1982, 9) writes, "I want to argue, in particular, that [all versions of the Consequence Argument] will rest on [a] questionable [modal] inference…" Slote is here asserting that all versions of the argument depend on the crucial principle employed in the "modal" version of the argument. The modal version employs a "transfer of powerlessness" principle.

6. Kadri Vihvelin (2013, 162-166) calls it, or a relevantly similar version, the "counterfactual version."

7. Note that this claim does not in itself capture the notion of causal determinism, since it does not explicitly state anything about causation. The idea here is that, whatever else causal determinism implies, it implies the claim in the text.

8. I employ "S" as a variable for agents, and "s" to indicate a "state" of the world. So, $s1$ is the (intrinsic) state of the world at $t1$.

9. That laws have a property in virtue of which they are "fixed" (out of our control) is denied by the proponents of a Humean view of natural laws, according to which they are mere generalizations. A view of this sort is developed in Beebee and Mele (2002).

10. I discuss Lewis's overall view in detail in Fischer (1994, 67-78). Also see Vihvelin (2013, 162-166).

11. There is a detailed discussion in Fischer (1994, 67-78).

12. There is another possibility: "If S were to do X, then some natural law would not have been one or the past would have been different." But for our purposes we can put this aside; nothing in our discussion will be affected by doing so.

13. The Humean Compatibilist (Beebee and Mele 2002) will reject (PFPL) insofar as she does not accept the requirement of holding the natural laws fixed. The view then is vulnerable to the challenges presented below in the text to the rejection of (PFPL).

14. In footnote 5, Lewis (1981, 119) seems to anticipate this switch to a "counterfactual-free" version of the argument (my term), along the lines of (PFPL). He contends that it is "uninstructive" to learn (in my terms) that the compatibilist must deny (PFPL). The dialectic here is very delicate, and I cannot pretend to give the issues a fair treatment here. My

co-author and I seek to address them in Fischer and Pendergraft (2013). I contend that the denial of (PFPL), the regimentation of Ginet's deeply intuitive way of expressing the view that the past and laws are fixed, highlights a jarring commitment of the compatibilist about causal determinism and freedom to do otherwise. Is this "uninstructive"? I do not think so, because (PFPL) captures a natural way of thinking about our practical reasoning. We learn that the compatibilist cannot accommodate this intuitive framework.

15. Of course, someone might deny that the backtracker ("If Sam were to decide to go ice-skating on Tuesday, the accident would not have occurred on Monday") is true in the example. After all, if Sam were to decide to go ice-skating on Tuesday, perhaps he would have forgotten about the accident or he would have been acting out of character, and so forth. I do not have any knockdown argument that the backtracker is true in the example, but I believe that the story can be filled in so that it is at least plausible that the backtracker is indeed true. (Nothing in the argument here depends on defending the claim that the backtracker is obviously true; all we need is the claim that it is at least plausible that, if one fills in the details suitably, the backtracking conditional would be true.)

16. Of course, (PFPL*) and (PFPL**) only specify necessary, not sufficient conditions for the relevant power attributions. Fair enough, but it is unclear to me what could be *added* to such principles to rule out the attribution of fantastic powers. What other principle can be invoked? Further, given that (PFPL) does indeed rule out such attributions, this would seem to be *pro tanto* reason to prefer (PFPL).

17. Source Incompatibilism is not available to the incompatibilist about God's foreknowledge and moral responsibility, insofar as one holds that Gods prior beliefs to not cause agents' choices and actions. This is one way in which theological determinism (God's prior beliefs) is less menacing to moral responsibility than causal determinism. Note, however, that Local-Miracle Compatibilism is not available to the theological fatalist, and in this way causal determinism is perhaps less menacing to human freedom. (But, of course, I've argued against Local-Miracle Compatibilism in the text.)

18. I employ (PFPL) to provide a solution to Newcomb's Problem that also avoids the need to evaluate counterfactuals in Fischer (1994, 87-110). The reader might discern a pattern: much ink has been spilled unneces-

sarily in seeking to figure out which counterfactuals are true in all of these puzzling situations.

19. As I state in footnote 4, I began publishing on the Consequence Argument and Local-Miracle Compatibilism in 1983, and through the years I have received invaluable help from colleagues and students at Yale and UC Riverside, and from commentators and audience members at countless colloquia and conferences. I wish I could thank you all individually, but, in any case, thank you! It will be obvious that I have borrowed from my previous published work, as well as extending it. I have benefitted from thoughtful comments on the current paper from Helen Beebee, Marco Hausmann and Andrew Law.

References

Beebee, Helen, and Alfred Mele. 2002. Humean Compatibilism. *Mind* 111 (442): 201–223.

Craig, William Lane. 1991. *Divine Foreknowledge and Human Freedom.* Leiden: E.J. Brill.

Fischer, John Martin. 1983. Incompatibilism. *Philosophical Studies* 43 (1): 127–137.

———. 1988. Freedom and Miracles. *Noûs* 22 (2): 235–252.

———. 1994. *The Metaphysics of Free Will: An Essay on Control.* Oxford: Blackwell Publishing.

Fischer, John Martin, and Mark Ravizza. 1996. Free Will and the Modal Principle. *Philosophical Studies* 83 (3): 213–230.

Fischer, John Martin, and Garrett Pendergraft. 2013. Does the Consequence Argument Beg the Question? *Philosophical Studies* 166 (3): 575–595.

Fischer, John Martin. 2016. *Our Fate: Essays on God and Free Will.* New York: Oxford University Press.

Ginet, Carl. 1966. Might We Have No Choice. In *Freedom and Determinism,* ed. Keith Lehrer, 87–104. New York: Random House.

———. 1983. In Defense of Incompatibilism. *Philosophical Studies* 44 (3): 391–400.

———. 1990. *On Action.* Cambridge: Cambridge University Press.

Hasker, William. 1989. *God, Time, and Knowledge.* Ithaca: New York University Press.

Lehrer, Keith. 1976. 'Can' in Theory and Practice: A Possible-Worlds Analysis. In *Action Theory: Proceedings of the Winnipeg Conference on Humean Action*, edited by Myles Brand and Douglas Walton, 241-70. Dordrecht, Reidel. Reprinted in *Free Will: Determinism* [Volume II *Critical Concepts: Free Will*], edited by John Martin Fischer, 2005, 234-61. London: Routledge.

Lewis, David. 1973. *Counterfactuals*. Cambridge: Harvard University Press.

———. 1976. The Paradoxes of Time Travel. *American Philosophical Quarterly* 12 (2): 145–152.

———. 1979. Counterfactual Dependence and Time's Arrow. *Noûs* 13 (4): 455–476.

———. 1981. Are We Free to Break the Laws? *Theoria* 47 (3): 113–121.

Slote, Michael. 1982. Selective Necessity and the Free-Will Problem. *Journal of Philosophy* 77 (1): 5–24.

Stalnaker, Robert. 1968. A Theory of Conditionals. In *Studies in Logical Theory*, ed. Nicholas Rescher, 98–112. Oxford: Blackwell.

van Inwagen, Peter. 1983. *An Essay on Free Will*. Oxford: Clarendon Press.

———. 2004. Freedom to Break the Laws. *Midwest Studies in Philosophy* 28 (1): 334–350.

———. 2008. How to Think About the Problem of Free Will. *The Journal of Ethics* 12 (3/4): 327–341.

Vihvelin, Kadri. 1996. What Time Travelers Cannot Do. *Philosophical Studies* 81 (2-3): 315–330.

———. 2013. *Causes, Laws, and Free Will: Why Determinism Doesn't Matter*. New York: Oxford University Press.

Wallace, David Foster. 2011. Richard Taylor's 'Fatalism' and the Semantics of Physical Modality. In *David Foster Wallace. Fate, Time, and Language*, ed. Steven M. Cahn and Maureen Eckert, 141–216. New York: Columbia University Press.

7

Backtracking Counterfactuals and Agents' Abilities

Helen Beebee

1   Introduction

John Martin Fischer and Garrett Pendergraft have argued that a non-counterfactual version of the Consequence Argument is not only sound but does not beg the question against the compatibilist (2013; see also Fischer 1994, 94-8). The version they consider is one that has as what we might call its 'ability-constraint' premise the Principle of the Fixity of the Past and Laws (PFPL):

> (PFPL) An agent S has it within his power in possible world w to do X at time t only if there is a possible world with the same (temporally intrinsic) past relative to t and the same laws as in w in which S does X at t. (Fischer, this volume, 120)

In his contribution to this volume, Fischer builds on his and Pendergraft's earlier defence of (PFPL). He argues that the version of the Consequence Argument that deploys (PFPL)[1] is a better argument than

---

H. Beebee (✉)
Department of Philosophy, University of Manchester, Manchester, UK
e-mail: helen.beebee@manchester.ac.uk

© The Author(s), under exclusive license to Springer Nature Switzerland AG 2021
M. Hausmann, J. Noller (eds.), *Free Will*,
https://doi.org/10.1007/978-3-030-61136-1_7

the one he calls the 'conditional version', whose ability-constraint premises are stated in counterfactual terms:

> (FP) For any action Y, agent S, and time t, if it is true that if S were to do Y at t, some fact F about the past relative to t would not have been a fact, then S cannot at t do Y at t.
>
> (FL) For any action Y, and agent S, if it is true that if S were to do Y, some natural law that actually obtains would not obtain, then S cannot do Y.

It is a better argument, Fischer maintains, because it is not susceptible to the broadly Lewisian reply that at least one of (FP) and (FL) is simply false—only *appearing* to be true if one assumes, falsely, that they are jointly implied by the true claim that nobody can do anything that would itself *be or cause* a change in the past or a violation of any law (Lewis 1981a; Fischer 1988; Vihvelin 2013, 162-6). In avoiding stating the ability constraint in counterfactual terms, Fischer argues that no such reply— which relies on appealing to the semantics of counterfactuals—is available to the version of the Consequence Argument that instead deploys (PFPL). According to Fischer, it is (PFPL), rather than the conjunction of (FP) and (FL), that places the correct constraint on what an agent can do because it, and not (FP) and (FL), properly captures the sense in which the past and the laws are fixed.

Fischer's argument that (PFPL) places the correct constraint on agents' abilities has two prongs—one aimed at the 'fixed-laws' compatibilist (who denies (FP)) and one aimed at the 'fixed-past' compatibilist (who denies (FL)). My aim is to show that the first prong of the argument fails: rejecting (PFPL) is entirely reasonable by the lights of the fixed-laws compatibilist.

In §2, I set the scene by giving a quick tour of both Lewis's fixed-past compatibilism and one version of fixed-laws compatibilism, namely the version that combines compatibilism with Jonathan Bennett's 'Simple Theory' of counterfactuals. In §3, after explaining the general set-up of Fischer's argument, I criticise a crucial assumption: that there is a particular pairing of two true propositions—one a backtracking counterfactual (which I'll call '(BACK)') and the other a clam about what an agent can do ('(CAN)'). I'll argue that the assumption is false—both by Fischer's own lights and by the lights of the fixed-laws compatibilist—since accepting the truth of the 'can' claim undercuts the grounds for thinking that the backtracker is true. In §4, I examine Fischer's argument itself, and argue that even if (BACK) and (CAN) *are* both true (or, if not (BACK) and (CAN) themselves, then some other pair of suitably related propositions), the argument still fails. In §5, I briefly discuss what I think is the basic idea that lies behind his argument—roughly, the idea that counterfactuals are relevant to rational decision-making—and explain why anyone who signs up to the truth of backtrackers like (BACK) should steer well clear of that idea.

2   Fixed-Laws Compatibilism: A Primer

Those compatibilists who hold that deterministic agents sometimes have the ability to do otherwise fall into two broad camps, depending on whether they hold that the right account of the semantics for counterfactuals is a 'fixed-past' account or a 'fixed-laws' account. Since the semantics for counterfactuals is going to be crucial to the argument of this chapter, in this section I'll first—by way of scene-setting—give a very brief account of Lewis's fixed-past view before giving a slightly more detailed summary of one particular version of the fixed-laws view, namely the 'Simple Theory', first expounded by Jonathan Bennett (1984) but defended and articulated in more detail by Tomkow (2013) and Tomkow and Vihvelin (2017).[2] Both of these accounts are 'closest-world' accounts—that is to say, the counterfactual 'if it had been the case that A, then it would have been the case that C' is true iff C is true at the closest A-world(s).

As is well known, Lewis's fixed-law account of counterfactuals takes the similarity (and hence closeness) of deterministic worlds under the 'standard resolution of vagueness' (1979, 757)—that is, the resolution we deploy unless we're in an odd conversational context that forces the deployment of some different similarity relation—to be, roughly, a matter of trading off size of spatio-temporal region of perfect match matters of particular fact on the one hand, and size of miracles on the other. So the closest worlds where some event e occurs—Jane's arrival at the pub at *t*, say (when in fact she was a ten-minute walk away at *t*)—will be worlds that are exactly similar with respect to matters of particular fact until shortly before *t*—at *t-minus*, say, whereupon a minor miracle occurs at those worlds (that is to say, a minor violation of the actual world's laws), leading to Jane's arrival at *t*. Thereafter, matters of particular fact at those worlds evolve according to the actual world's laws, thus diverging increasingly, but not in peculiar contra-nomic ways, as time goes on. (The extent of post-*t-minus* divergence makes no difference to similarity, since perfect match is lost at *t-minus* and approximate match counts for nothing.[3])

Size of miracle also matters. The reason why the closest world where Jane arrives at the pub at *t* will not be one in which she somehow instantaneously disappears from her ten-minutes-away location and materialises in the pub at *t* is that that would require a very large miracle indeed. Instead, the closest worlds will be ones with an earlier but smaller miracle, and hence with a 'transition period' between the miracle (at *t-minus*) and *e* (at *t*). (Maybe Jane didn't stop at the shop earlier in the trip. Maybe she left the house a bit earlier. Maybe she took the bus.) The smaller size of the miracle required to get Jane to the pub at *t* in those worlds trumps the fact that at those worlds there is a shorter period of perfect match of particular facts with the actual world than there is at any instantaneous-appearance world.

Crucially, Lewis holds that the competition for the closest world will typically be a tie. There are many and various equally similar worlds in which *e* occurs. For example, suppose that in all the candidate closest worlds Jane leaves the house at the same time as she actually did, but in one she runs rather than walks, in one she jumps on a bus, in another she doesn't stop at the shop, and so on. There will be nothing to choose between these worlds in terms of similarity to the actual world, since they all involve a minor miracle and all lose perfect match with the actual world at the same time.

This claim about tied closest worlds is crucial for Lewis because, for the purposes of giving a counterfactual analysis of causation that doesn't stipulate *a priori* that causes always precede their effects, he needs it to be the case that a certain kind of backtracking counterfactual—that is, a counterfactual where, loosely speaking, the time of the antecedent is after the time of the consequent—is generally, in normal contexts, false. The kind in question is a backtracker whose antecedent and consequent state the occurrence of particular events. In our example, if his account entailed the truth of 'had Jane arrived on time at the pub, she wouldn't have stopped at the shops on the way', it would, according to his account of causation, follow that Jane's late arrival caused her earlier stop at the shops. But (or so he claims) Lewis's account doesn't deliver a true backtracker in this or relevantly similar cases. There is no *one* way things would have gone differently during the transition period from *t-minus* to *t* had Jane arrived on time, but merely many ways things *might* have gone.

As the name suggests, fixed-past *compatibilism* combines the fixed-past account of counterfactuals with compatibilism. Lewis himself falls into this camp (1981a), as does Vihvelin in her (2013, Ch. 7). Consider (FL) again:

(FL) For any action *Y*, and agent *S*, if it is true that if *S* were to do *Y*, some natural law that actually obtains would not obtain, then *S* cannot do *Y*.

According to Lewis's account of counterfactuals and assuming determinism, were *S* to raise her hand at *t*, some law that actually obtains would not obtain. And, Lewis claims, assuming that *S* is a normal agent in normal circumstances, *S can* raise her hand—but her ability to do so does not imply that she is able to act in such a way that her act itself, or any of its effects, violates a law. (Remember, the closest world where *S* raises her hand at *t* is one in which the miracle happens slightly *before t*.)

Bennett's Simple Theory is a fixed-laws rather than a fixed-past account. Its USP is, as its name suggests, disarmingly simple. First—*pace* Lewis—the candidate closest *e*-worlds (where Jane arrives on time at the pub) are worlds with the same laws of nature as the actual world. (Given that *e* itself is nomologically possible—consistent with the actual laws—any world that doesn't have the same laws as the actual world isn't, on this view, even a candidate for closest world.) It follows from this, assuming determinism, that those candidate closest worlds all differ from the actual world at all past times as well.

Sameness of laws, according to *any* closest-world fixed-laws account, is an element in the 'similarity metric' that determines how similar two possible worlds are to each other. But that doesn't narrow the field nearly enough to determine which are the *closest* worlds where *e* occurs. That's because there are many and various possible worlds where Jane arrives at the pub at *t*, which differ from each other at *t* and hence at all other times both past and future. (There are ones where she got the bus, where she ran, where the pub was emptier than it actually was, where she wore a different coat, where Donald Trump lost the 2016 election, and so on, and so on.) Which of these are the closest worlds to actuality? One *might* take similarity or sameness of certain features of the past—though not of course perfect match—to play a role in determining similarity, but it isn't the route Bennett takes. Instead, his view is that—aside from sameness of law—only similarity of the *present* counts. In essence: change the present as minimally as you can, consistent with 'inserting' *e* into it, and hold the laws fixed. That's it. Simple!

It might sound odd to say that similarity with respect to the past counts for nothing, but, as it happens, similarity of the present buys you quite a lot of similarity to the past. After all, past events leave their traces in the present here in the actual world, and so they will be there in other possible worlds that are similar to the actual world with respect to the present unless we need to remove them in order to insert *e*. And, by and large, if you run the laws backwards from those same present traces in those other possible worlds, you'll get back to the same past causes of those traces as you get back to at the actual world. But this is merely a by-product of the present-similarity requirement: similarity of the past *itself* plays no role in the degree of similarity between worlds.

As we saw above, Lewis's own view is that there are many and various ways—all equally similar to the actual world—in which *e* might have come about. Similarly, on the Simple Theory there are generally many and various ways—all equally similar to the actual world—in which we might 'insert' *e* into our close possible worlds at *t*. In fact we might even assume that, roughly speaking, the questions 'how are things *at t* at the closest possible worlds according to Lewis?' and 'how are they at *t* according to the Simple Theory?' get more or less the same answers—but for different reasons. Removing a few customers from the pub at *t* is a gratuitous departure from actuality on both views—for Lewis because it requires further miracles, and for the Simple Theory simply because it's a gratuitous difference to the actual present. We can insert *e* without changing *that* aspect of the present as well. Trump losing the election in 2016 is also a gratuitous departure on both views—for Lewis not only because any world where that happens is a world requires a further miracle but because that world loses perfect match of matters of particular fact much earlier than perfect match is lost in other worlds where *e* occurs, and for the Simple Theory because the very many actual traces of his 2016 win are present, at *t*, in the actual world, and so—plausibly—any world that lacks the 2016 win will lack those traces (having instead traces of Hillary's win), and hence will differ from the actual world at *t* in all manner of gratuitous ways.

The fixed-laws *compatibilist* will, of course, deny (FP):

> (FP) For any action *Y*, agent *S*, and time *t*, if it is true that if *S* were to do *Y* at *t*, some fact *F* about the past relative to *t* would not have been a fact, then *S* cannot at *t* do *Y* at *t*.

Assuming determinism it is *always* true, for any agent *S*, act *Y* and time *t*, that, were *S* to *Y* at *t*, some past fact would not have been a fact; and yet it is often true that *S* can (at *t*) *Y* at *t*.[4]

3   Different Modalities?

Recall (PFPL):

> (PFPL) An agent *S* has it within his power in possible world *w* to do *X* at time *t* only if there is a possible world with the same (temporally intrinsic) past relative to *t* and the same laws as in *w* in which *S* does *X* at *t*.

Fischer holds that a version of the Consequence Argument that deploys (PFPL) is better than the version that deploys (FP) and (FL) because it is not susceptible to the compatibilist manoeuvres described in §1. An obvious response to Fischer's claim is that his preferred version of the Consequence Argument begs the question against the compatibilist; it is, after all, a short step from (PFPL) to incompatibilism. Fischer and Pendergraft (2013) argue that that response fails, and they do so in part by arguing that the denial of (PFPL) leads to trouble. In his contribution to this volume—which is my focus here—Fischer builds on that argument.

On the face of it, it's unclear why invoking (PFPL) rather than (FP) and (FL) strengthens the case for incompatibilism. After all, one might think that (PFPL) entails both (FL) and (FP). If that's so, then it looks as though if we accept that the compatibilist is entitled to block the counterfactual version by denying (FP) and/or (FL), they are thereby entitled to deny (PFPL) too. But, as it turns out, (PFPL) does *not* imply either (FP) or (FL); indeed, Fischer's argument for (PFPL) trades on the falsity of (FP). What's wrong with (FP), Fischer thinks, is that the truth of (FP)'s antecedent is simply irrelevant to the truth of its consequent.

They key to seeing why the inference fails is to appreciate that the claim that an agent is *able* to do something (a 'can-claim') and what *would* be the case if they *were* to do that thing:

> involve *different modalities*. Put in terms of the possible-worlds framework, the can-claim requires a possible world *suitably related* to the actual world (a world in which the can-claim is putatively true). This sort of relationship underwrites the *accessibility* of the world in question to the actual world. (121, n.d.)

In other words, it's true that S *can A* iff there is some possible world w that is (what I'll call) 'agentially accessible' to S, such that S does A in w.[5] But—crucially—the range of worlds that are agentially accessible to S *need not include* the closest possible world where S does A. So let (DM) (for 'Different Modalities') be this combination of claims:

> (DM) (i) S *can A* iff there is some possible world w that is agentially accessible to S, such that S does A in w. But (ii) the range of worlds that are agentially accessible to S need not include the closest possible world where S does A.

(PFPL) and (DM)(i) together explain why (DM)(ii) is true: (PFPL) tells us, via (DM)(i), which worlds are agentially accessible to S with respect to A-ing, and the question which worlds those are is simply a different question to the question of what the *closest* world is in which S does A. That world might or (as in the *Icy Patch* case I'll consider shortly) might not be one of the worlds that is agentially accessible according to (PFPL). And that's why (PFPL) doesn't entail (FP) or (FL). The closest A-world might well be a world where the past or the laws are different, but that's a matter for the semantics of counterfactuals—it has no bearing on which worlds are agentially accessible, that is, on what the agent can and can't do.

Hence a version of the Consequence Argument that deploys (PFPL) might succeed where the conditional version, deploying (FP) and (FL), fails. And—this is where Fischer's argument against the fixed-laws compatibilist comes in—denying (PFPL) is a bad idea, since it leads to what he politely describes as an 'implausible result' when it comes to practical rationality. (Fischer has a different argument against the fixed-past compatibilist's denial of (PFPL). I won't be addressing that argument here. So when I talk about Fischer's 'argument for (PFPL)', I'm really only talking about the first part of his argument—the part aimed at the fixed-laws compatibilist.)

Clearly (DM) is a principle that any sensible incompatibilist should subscribe to. After all, if determinism is true, then the closest possible world where I do *anything* that I don't actually do is a world with a different past and/or different laws. But, according to the incompatibilist, that world will *never* be a world that is agentially accessible to me, since incompatibilism entails that if determinism is true, the only world that is agentially accessible to me is the actual world. So for the incompatibilist (DM) nicely encapsulates the thought that what is the case at the closest A-world is just irrelevant to the question whether S can A.

What should a compatibilist think? Fischer's argument trades on the assumption that, since the compatibilist denies (PFPL), 'nothing rules it out' that, where S can (but doesn't) A, the closest A-world is accessible to S (123, n.d.). That is, Fischer assumes that the compatibilist has no grounds, by her own lights, for endorsing (DM). This assumption undoubtedly has some *prima facie* intuitive appeal; after all, in the absence of a reason to think otherwise (and (PFPL) would have provided such a reason), why *wouldn't* the A-world that's the *most* similar to the actual world be agentially accessible to S? Nonetheless, the assumption is unwarranted. After all, many compatibilists offer accounts of the ability to do otherwise. Any such account will have implications for which worlds are and are not agentially accessible, and, so far as I can tell, there is no reason to think that *no* viable compatibilist account of abilities will entail (DM).

Be that as it may, since I don't want an adequate response to Fischer to turn on any particular compatibilist account of ability I'm going to grant his assumption for the sake of the argument.[6] The basic gist of his argument for (PFPL) is that failure to endorse (DM) leads to trouble. I'll argue on behalf of the fixed-laws compatibilist that it doesn't. That leaves it as an open question whether the fixed-laws compatibilist should accept or deny (DM)—but it leaves them free to deny it without getting into hot water.

Fischer's argument for (PFPL) turns on an example, *Icy Patch*. On Tuesday morning, Sam is deliberating about whether to go ice-skating. (Let *D* be Sam's deciding on Tuesday at noon—*t*—to go ice-staking—a decision he doesn't in fact make.) But on Monday, Sam saw a boy slip on an icy patch and seriously injure himself (*A*). Fischer asks us to suppose that 'Sam's character is such that if he were to decide to go ice-skating at noon on Tuesday, then the boy would not have slipped and hurt himself on Monday' (121, n.d.). (This is a backtracker.) Nonetheless Sam is—on Tuesday morning—able to *D*: 'we can suppose that nothing is preventing Sam from acting out of character by making a decision to go ice-skating. We can be confident that he won't act out of character, but it doesn't follow that he can't' (121, n.d.). So the following two claims are both true:

(BACK) If Sam were to *D* on Tuesday, *A* would not have occurred on Monday.
(CAN) Sam is able to *D* on Tuesday.

The first of my two objections to his argument is that (BACK) and (CAN) are not, in fact, both true—and that undermines one of the argument's assumptions. But since it will take me a while to get through that objection, here's a sneak preview of his argument. Grant that (BACK) and (CAN) are indeed true. Then, given her (assumed) lack of grounds for endorsing (DM), the fixed-laws compatibilist must grant that the closest *D*-world *w*—in which *A* doesn't occur, as per (BACK)—is agentially accessible to Sam. This being so, she also has no grounds for denying that the reasons for *D*-ing that obtain in *w*, *qua* agentially accessible world, are available to Sam in his deliberation about whether or not to *D*. But that is (to put it mildly) 'implausible'. After all, in *w* there is no accident, so Sam has no reason not to go ice-skating. So were Sam to pay attention in his deliberation to the reasons that obtain in *w*, he'd conclude that he should *D* after all. And that's definitely not what he should conclude.

The rest of this section is devoted to considering whether (BACK) and (CAN) really are both true. (Answer: No. Not by Fischer's own lights, and not by the fixed-laws compatibilist's light either.) Note that in endorsing both (BACK) and (CAN), Fischer is claiming that Sam *is* able to do something such that, were he to do it, the past would have been different. That is, along with the fixed-laws compatibilist, he's denying (FP). But his *explanation* for the (alleged) fact that (BACK) and (CAN) are both true trades on (DM): the *D*-worlds that are agentially accessible to Sam need not, and in this case do not, include the *closest* possible world in which he *D*s.

Why, then, according to Fischer, is the closest *D*-world agentially inaccessible to Sam? It's because

> when we think, as we do, that Sam can decide to go ice-skating at *t2*, we are thinking that he can act out of character and exhibit gross irrationality. That is, we are assuming that Sam can add to the actual past a decision to go ice-skating. In accepting the can-claim, we are holding the past fixed. (122, n.d.)

In other words, Sam 'has it within his power' to *D* at time *t* 'only if there is a possible world with the same (temporally intrinsic) past relative to *t*' in which Sam *D*s at *t*. And that's just the fixed-past element of (PFPL).

Fischer thus agrees with the fixed-laws compatibilist that (FP) is false. And he takes *Icy Patch* to 'show (FP) is not an adequate way to capture the fixity of the past' (122, n.d.). In this, he is also in agreement with the fixed-laws compatibilist. But the fixed-laws compatibilist thinks the reason why (FP) doesn't capture the fixity of the past is that it fails to distinguish between the ability to act in such a way that the past would have been different and the ability to *cause* the past to be different—and it is the fact that agents aren't able to do the latter that captures the fixity of the past. By contrast, Fischer thinks (FP) fails to capture the fixity of the past because *only* possible worlds with the same past as ours up until *t* are agentially accessible to Sam at *t*.

Unfortunately, whether we assume a fixed-past or a fixed-laws account of counterfactuals, Fischer's claim that both (BACK) and (CAN) are true is false by his own lights—that is to say, given his story about what it takes for (CAN) to be true. According to (BACK), the closest world *w* where Sam *Ds*—decides on Tuesday at noon (*t*) to go ice-skating—is a world where, on Monday, *A*—the accident—didn't happen. And yet, according to Fischer's story about what it takes for (CAN) to be true, namely (PFPL), there is an accessible *D*-world with the same past and laws as the actual world: it is consistent with the prior-to-*t* facts and the actual laws that Sam does indeed *D*.

Why is that a problem? Well, if (CAN) is true then, according to (PFPL), there is an agentially accessible possible world *w** that is exactly the same as the actual world up to *t*, with the same laws as ours, where Sam—exhibiting 'gross irrationality'—*Ds* at *t*. (Intuitively: Sam is exercising libertarian free will with respect to *D*.) The truth of (BACK) requires that *w** is further away from actuality than is *w*—since if *w** (and not *w*) is the closest *D*-world then, if Sam were to *D*, *A* would still have happened (since it happened at *w**). But *w* is surely *not* closer to actuality than is *w**. After all, *w** accords with *both* the actual world's laws *and* its past. It's hard to see why, on any sensible fixed-laws *or* fixed-past account of counterfactuals, a world with a *different* past to the actual world—one where the boy didn't slip yesterday—is closer than that.

On Lewis's fixed-past view, *w** is manifestly closer than any possible world where Monday's accident didn't happen; after all, *w** retains perfect match of matters of particular fact right up until *t* and contains no miracles. The Simple Theory gets the same result, though for different reasons. As explained in §2, according to the Simple Theory past differences don't matter when it comes to similarity. But *present* differences *do* matter—and *w*, unlike *w**, contains all manner of gratuitous differences to the actual world *at t*. In the actual world, the Monday accident has left all manner of traces at t. The boy in question has his leg in plaster and is mightily regretting leaving the house yesterday. His fingerprints are still present in the hospital ward and the crutches he was given are in his bedroom and not in the hospital store cupboard. His parents are worried about him. And so on, and so on. w^* matches the actual world at t in all of those respects, but w doesn't. Both w and w^*, equally, have the same laws as the actual world, and D, equally, happens in both of them. Hence by Fischer's own lights—that is, given his story about *why* (CAN) is true—according to both fixed-past and fixed-laws accounts of counterfactuals, (CAN) is true iff (BACK) is false. So, *pace* Fischer, they can't both be true together.

We're not done yet, however. Fischer's reasons to endorsing (CAN) leave *him* unable to endorse (BACK). But—since the fixed-laws compatibilist is not going to agree with Fischer about those reasons—it doesn't follow that the fixed-laws compatibilist isn't saddled with the truth of (BACK) and (CAN), and so it doesn't follow that, by *their* lights, Fischer's (soon-to-be-presented) argument isn't sound. So let's consider what the fixed-laws compatibilist should think about (BACK) and (CAN).

Let's assume that Sam's world—the actual world—is deterministic. (As we just saw, if it isn't—specifically, if the laws and the past leave it open on Tuesday that Sam Ds—then, the fixed-laws compatibilist has excellent grounds for denying (BACK).) In fact, assuming determinism and the truth of (CAN) does nothing to undermine the above argument that *any* no-accident world is pretty remote from the actual world. Granted, when we were assuming that whether or not Sam Ds is undetermined by the past and the laws, we could safely assume that the *whole* of the past in the closest D-world exactly matches the actual world's past, since we could hold the laws of nature fixed and still track back to exactly the same just-pre-decision (and hence long-pre-decision) past. If Sam's decision not to D is determined, then we can't do that. In the closest D-world, *something* about the just-pre-decision, and hence long-pre-decision, past must be different to the actual world's past. But we *still* have excellent reason to think that the closest D-world is *not* one where, on Tuesday, all of the traces of A are absent—which is what would be required for (BACK), that is, $D > \neg A$, to be true. There are, unquestionably, possible worlds with the same laws as ours where Sam Ds at t and all of those traces are in place at *t*. Some of those worlds are more similar to actuality at *t* than are the any no-trace worlds. Track the actual laws back from the traces and, come Monday, you'll get to *A*.

Fischer might legitimately complain at this point that I am ignoring his rationale for claiming that (BACK) is true, which is that in assessing (BACK) we, in effect, hold certain facts about Sam's character fixed. After all, his justification for endorsing (BACK) is that 'Sam's character is such that if he were to decide to go ice-skating at noon on Tuesday, then the boy would not have slipped and hurt himself on Monday' (121, n.d.). I take it the idea here is that we hold fixed, in particular, Sam's rational nature: he just isn't the kind of person who is disposed to exhibit gross irrationality. But it is just not clear what justification there might be for claiming that we do indeed hold this aspect of Sam's character fixed in assessing (BACK). As we've just seen, the Simple Theory of counterfactuals does not justify that claim.

Still, one might insist that we *can* hold fixed Sam's disposition to behave rationally fixed in assessing (BACK). That is to say, perhaps in *some* contexts we do indeed do that. An example of Lewis's (taken from Downing 1958–9, 125) is pertinent here:

> Jim and Jack quarreled yesterday, and Jack is still hopping mad. We conclude that if Jim asked Jack for help today, Jack would not help him. But wait: Jim is a prideful fellow. He never would ask for help after such a quarrel; if Jim were to ask Jack for help today, there would have to have been no quarrel yesterday. In that case Jack would be his usual generous self. So if Jim asked Jack for help today, Jack would help him after all. (Lewis 1979, 456)

For Lewis, the problem with the Downing case is that there are two competing counterfactuals—one a backtracker, one not—and it's unclear which is true. He solves the problem by appealing to the context-sensitivity of counterfactuals: 'Counterfactuals are infected with vagueness, as everyone agrees. Different ways of (partly) resolving the vagueness are appropriate in different contexts ... We ordinarily resolve the vagueness ... in such a way that counterfactual dependence is asymmetric ... Under this standard resolution, back-tracking arguments are mistaken' (ibid.).[7] But if we are in a conversational context where, as it were, Jim's prideful nature has taken centre stage, we might resolve the vagueness differently, holding fixed his prideful nature and therefore endorsing the backtracker.

The Downing case parallels *Icy Patch*: on the one hand (we may assume) Jim *could have* asked Jack for help; on the other, in an appropriate and non-standard context it's true to say that had he done so, being the prideful fellow he is, the quarrel would never have happened. So perhaps Fischer could appeal to the context-sensitivity of counterfactuals in order to deliver the truth of both (BACK) and (CAN): if Sam's rational nature (or Jim's pride) is sufficiently salient, it becomes appropriate to suspend the 'standard resolution' of vagueness and resolve it in such a way as to hold that salient feature of Sam (Jim) fixed.

But *in that context*, I submit—that is, a context within which we (non-standardly) judge (BACK) to be true—it would be inappropriate to judge that (CAN) is true. Recall Fischer's grounds for thinking that (CAN) is indeed true: 'nothing prevents' Sam from exhibiting gross irrationality. So in endorsing (CAN) we are precisely *not* holding fixed Sam's rational nature: we are regarding the possibility of his acting irrationally as an open one. So, in effect, we can grant that each of (CAN) and (BACK) *may* be true, but only in different contexts: they are not true in the *same* context.

Of course Fischer will presumably—given his endorsement of (PFPL) –disagree with Lewis that 'can' claims are themselves context-sensitive (Lewis 1976, 150; see also Kratzer 1977), and hence maintain that (CAN) is true in all contexts and therefore in contexts in which (BACK) is true. In that case, what's the right thing to say? Well, consider a parallel case: suppose you think it's just true—and not context-dependent—that the sun is 92,955,807 miles away from Earth. Nonetheless, there are contexts where 'the sun is 93 million miles away from Earth' is … well, true or merely false-but-assertable-in-the-context? Either way, what one can't coherently do is hold, at the same time and in the same context, that the sun is both 92,955,807 *and* 93 million miles away from Earth. That's just a flat-out contradiction. Similarly, I claim, for (BACK) and (CAN).

I conclude that Fischer is not, in fact, entitled to his starting-point. Not only do his *own* grounds for endorsing (CAN) undermine the claim that (BACK) is true; the fixed-laws compatibilist has good grounds not to endorse both claims.

4   Fischer's Argument for (FPFL)

So much for that particular example. Fischer and Pendergraft say (2013, 587): 'We do not have any knockdown argument that the backtracker is true in the example, but we believe that the story can be filled in so that it is at least plausible that the backtracker is indeed true'. Well, can it? The prospects for doing so are, I think, bleak. Recall the Simple Theory's story about backtrackers. The idea is that, in general, there will be a tie for the closest D-world because there are many and various equally small ways in which the various close possible D-worlds differ from one another at the time of D. (Perhaps Sam's decision might be realised by very many precise brain-states. He might make the decision while breathing in or breathing out. He might make it emphatically ('Right! That's what I'll do then!') or somewhat reluctantly ('Well OK, I guess I'll go skating after all then') or impulsively ('To hell with it: I'm going skating!'). And so on. Run the (actual) laws backwards at each of those worlds, and you'll get to different pasts—increasingly different as we progress further away from t. We'll only get a true backtracker if there is some common feature of *all* of the pasts of the tied-closest worlds that does not obtain at the actual world.

That's quite a rare thing to happen. Why? Because, as Tomkow and Vihvelin 2017, 23-6) explain, it will happen only if the consequent C of our backtracker is some *nomologically necessary condition* for its antecedent A. In other words it will happen only if, *however*, we tinker with the actual world's present to get us a tied-closest possible world where A is true, running the laws back from those tinkered-with presents will entail truth of C. There are *some* true backtrackers—it's true that if JFK had been re-elected in 1964, he wouldn't have been assassinated in 1963 (Tomkow and Vihvelin 2017, 25)—but *that's* not a problematic one in the current context: nobody thinks that anyone could, in 1964, do anything such that, were they to do it, JFK wouldn't have been assassinated in 1963.

Still, for all I've said maybe Fischer is right that there is *some* way of fleshing out the Sam story—or perhaps some other story—that (if his argument, which I'm just about to get to, works) will give us a true (BACK)/(CAN) pair that makes trouble for the fixed-laws compatibilist. Indeed, here's a (BACK)/(CAN) pair that the fixed-laws compatibilist really *must* endorse, where *P* is the following rather ugly proposition:

P   The true proposition (call it *Q*) stating the whole truth about the actual world's past at some point prior to *t* is false.
(BACK*)   Were Joti to *D* at *t*, *P* would be true.
(CAN*)   Joti is able (shortly before *t*) to *D*.

After presenting Fischer's argument I'll explain why, as applied to (BACK*) and (CAN*), it doesn't make trouble for the fixed-laws compatibilist, and then generalise to *Icy Patch*-style cases (if there are any). Conclusion: even if there *are* such cases, Fischer's argument fails.

Fischer argues that rejecting (PFPL)—the claim that what an agent can do is constrained by facts about the whole of the past plus the laws—leads to an 'implausible result' when it comes to *Icy Patch*, namely that 'it is rational for Sam to decide to go ice-skating on Tuesday, or, alternatively, that Sam ought to decide to go ice-skating Tuesday' (122, n.d.). So—admittedly putting it in stronger terms than Fischer does—we can think of the argument as a *reductio* of fixed-laws compatibilism.

The argument depends on the 'intuitively appealing idea that it is appropriate to take the reasons that obtain in all and only worlds accessible from the actual world to the agent at a given time as relevant to the agent's practical reasoning at the time' (122-3, n.d.). After all: If 'an agent can't get to a scenario from where he is [i.e. a possible world is not agentially accessible to them], then the features of that scenario would seem to be irrelevant to his practical reasoning. But if the agent can indeed get to the scenario from where he is [the possible world *is* agentially accessible to them], then why not deem certain features of that scenario relevant to the agent's practical reasoning? It would seem entirely arbitrary not to allow the agent to take into account reasons that obtain in scenarios genuinely accessible to him' (123, n.d.). So the first premise of the argument is:

(REASON) The reasons that obtain in all and only worlds that are agentially accessible to S at t are relevant to S's practical reasoning at t.

Moreover, 'Sam can decide on Tuesday to go ice-skating that afternoon [since (CAN) is true]. If this can-claim is rendered true by some possible world [w] accessible to Sam, and on the assumption that we reject (PFPL), nothing rules it out that [w] will contain the accident's not happening on Monday [given the truth of (BACK)]. So Sam would have access on Tuesday to a possible world in which the accident did not occur on Monday' (123, n.d.). (Recall the discussion of (DM) in §3 above: if we deny (PFPL), as the compatibilist must, we have no grounds for denying (DM)(ii): the claim that the closest D-worlds need not be agentially accessible to Sam.) So we have:

(ACC) There is at least one possible world that is agentially accessible to Sam at t where Sam (at or shortly after t) Ds. For short: There is at least one agentially accessible D-world (since (CAN) is true).

(No-A) In at least one agentially accessible D-world, call it w, A—Monday's accident—does not occur (since (BACK) is true and (PFPL) is false).

It follows that

(REL) The non-occurrence of A at w is relevant to Sam's practical reasoning with respect to D.

But (REL) is 'implausible': the fact that there is some possible world in which the accident does not happen on Monday surely cannot be relevant to Sam's practical reasoning, on Tuesday, with respect to whether or not to go ice-skating. (Roughly: if Sam *can*, as it were, 'get to' that world from where he is, then he surely *should*. After all, it's a world where the accident didn't happen.) So there must be something wrong with the argument. And, in effect, Fischer's contention is that it is (No-A) that should be rejected: there are no agentially accessible no-accident worlds, and so any plausible constraint on agential accessibility must rule that possibility out. (PFPL) achieves that—but the fixed-laws compatibilist rejects (PFPL), and hence has no grounds for denying (No-A).

As I argued in §3, the fixed-laws compatibilist has no reason to endorse (BACK) given the truth of (CAN), and hence can safely agree with Fischer that (No-*A*) is false. But how does the argument fare with respect to (BACK*) and (CAN*), which the fixed-laws compatibilist *must* endorse? Well, the fixed-laws compatibilist must agree with Fischer that there is at least one agentially accessible *D*-world, and that at least one such world, *P* is true. (Recall, *P* is the mouthful: 'The true proposition, call it *Q*, stating the whole truth about the actual world's past at some point prior to *t* is false'. In fact, *P* is true at *every* nomologically possible non-actual world.) So analogues of (ACC) and (No-*A*) are true. That leaves (REASON). So the question is: are those agentially accessible *P*-worlds 'relevant to' Joti's practical reasoning?

Well, let's suppose Joti is a committed determinist. So one thing she can reasonably take herself to know while she's deliberating—assuming she thinks that she can, shortly before *t*, both *D* and not-*D*—is that whatever she *actually* decides, all the nomologically possible worlds in which she decides otherwise are worlds in which *P* is true. What she is *not* in a position to know, however, is (BACK*), that is, *D* > *P*. She doesn't know—and isn't in a position to know until she's decided what to do—whether the actual world is a world where *D* is true, or instead a world where *D* is false. If she *did* take herself to know that, then she'd already know what she's going to decide—and that, plausibly, would make her incapable of deliberating about what to do. As Ginet says: 'It is conceptually impossible for a person to know what a decision of his is going to be before he makes it' (1962, 50). It follows that Joti does not and cannot take herself to know, while deliberating, that *D* > *P*.[8] After all, if she in fact ends up deciding to *D*—which is most certainly a live epistemic possibility for her—it will turn out that the actual world is a *D*-world, in which case *P* will turn out to be false (since *Q*—whatever proposition it is that states the whole truth about the actual world's past—will turn out to be true), and hence *D* > *P* will turn out to be false. And Joti, to repeat, is in no epistemic position to rule that possibility out.

More generally, Joti can take herself to know very little about what the prior-to-*t* facts are like at the non-actual agentially accessible worlds. That's partly for the reason explained earlier: normally there will be a tie for the closest *D*-world, so even if Joti did (*per impossibile*) know that she was going to refrain from D-ing, then plausibly—absent knowing that some specific nomologically necessary condition N for D-ing is absent from the actual world, in which case she would know $D > N$—all she could infer from that would be that P would be false. But it's also partly because, since she does *not* know that she's not going to D, she has no idea whether the closest non-actual agentially accessible worlds are D-worlds or *not-D* worlds.

Where does that get us? Recall (REASON): 'The reasons that obtain in all and only worlds that are agentially accessible to S at t are relevant to S's practical reasoning at t.' The above considerations give us no good grounds for accepting (REASON). Was Joti *can* legitimately take herself to know about the agentially accessible worlds is that at the non-actual ones, P is true. She knows what her reasons are at *one* agentially accessible world, of course, namely the reasons she actually has, since however things turn out, the actual world is definitely agentially accessible to Joti, and she knows what her *actual* reasons are. But that doesn't tell her anything at all about what her reasons are at the non-actual agentially accessible worlds.

Joti knows, then, that there are agentially accessible worlds where she does otherwise than what she actually ends up doing, and hence where the past is different to the way it is at the actual world. Indeed she knows that the *closest* such worlds are worlds where the past is different to the actual world. But what she doesn't have any clue about is whether, or in what ways, her reasons for acting in those worlds are any different to what they are in the actual world. Maybe her reasons *are* different in some such worlds: maybe the differences from actuality that are required to, as it were, implement her non-actual decision (whatever that is) nomologically imply differences in her reasons. But so what? She cannot possibly know what those differences might be, and so she is not in a position to deploy them in her deliberation.

Let's pause to take stock of the dialectic for a moment. Since Fischer's argument depends on the truth of some (BACK)/(CAN)-type pairing, my strategy so far has been to see how the argument fares against a particular (BACK)/(CAN)-type pairing—namely (BACK*)/(CAN*)—that the fixed-laws compatibilist must endorse. The upshot is that, since Joti is not in a position to know anything about the specific reasons she has at all the non-actual agentially accessible worlds, (REASON) is false in her case—and hence, since it is a general principle, false *simpliciter*.

That leaves open the possibility that (REASON) applies in some special set of cases, and in particular in the special case of Sam, if we assume for the sake of the argument that (BACK) and (CAN) are both true. I'll argue that it doesn't.

As with Joti, while deliberating Sam doesn't know whether or not he'll *D*: again, he *can't* coherently take himself to know that before having made up his mind. This being so, as we saw with Joti and (BACK*), Sam cannot possibly take himself to know that (BACK) is true, since the truth of (BACK) depends on the assumption that *D* doesn't actually happen. Perhaps Sam can legitimately take himself to know that *if he in fact* decides not to *D*, then (BACK) will turn out to be true, and hence it will turn out that in some agentially accessible world, his reasons for acting are different from his actual reasons: it will turn out that there is an agentially accessible world in which he has no reason not to go ice-skating because the accident never happened. But that is not relevant to his decision-making, because he *also* knows that if *in fact* he decides to *D*, (BACK) will turn out to be false.

Thus (REASON) is not only false as a general principle (since it fails in the Joti case); it doesn't even hold in Sam's case, even assuming that (BACK) and (CAN) are both true. It's not the case that the reasons that obtain in all and only worlds that are agentially accessible to Sam at *t* are relevant to his practical reasoning at *t*. Sam cannot know enough about which world will be actual to deploy facts about what his reasons are at *non*-actual worlds in his deliberation. Moreover, *no amount* of further information will plug that epistemic gap, because it is crucial to Sam's ability to deliberate about whether or not to *D* that he doesn't yet know whether the actual world will be a *D*-world or a ∼*D*-world; hence he cannot take himself know prior to making up his mind whether, in any agentially accessible *D*-world, the Monday accident didn't occur.

Fischer's argument therefore fails not only because (BACK) and (CAN) themselves aren't both true, but because even if we assume that there's some way to flesh out the story in such a way that they *are* both true, one of the argument's premises, (REASON), is false. The fixed-laws compatibilist is not, *pace* Fischer, compelled to reject premise (No-*A*), and hence can happily reject (PFPL) without getting into trouble.

5   Counterfactuals and Rationality

The attentive reader may have noticed that in fact Fischer's argument—as he presents it and not as I somewhat more formally rendered it in the previous section—attempts to capture the key idea that Sam's reasons at the closest *D*-world are somehow relevant to his decision in several different and not obviously equivalent ways. The 'implausible result' that he thinks the fixed-law compatibilist is saddled with is variously described as the result that those reasons are 'relevant to [Sam's] practical reasoning at the time' (123, n.d.) and the result that 'it is rational for Sam to decide to go ice-skating on Tuesday, or, alternatively, that Sam ought to decide to go ice-skating Tuesday' (122, n.d.).

The response I gave in §4 was in effect targeted at the first of these: at the idea that Sam himself, while deliberating, is in a position to take account of those reasons. One might contend that the argument would fare better if focused squarely on the rationality of Sam's decision itself—viewed from an objective perspective—rather than on (what I argued is) Sam's necessarily epistemically limited point of view *qua* deliberator. It is, after all, very natural and plausible to think that the truth of counterfactuals is crucially relevant to what an agent ought to do: it is by virtue of the facts about Sam's preferences together with the truth of counterfactuals such as (say) 'If Sam were to *D*, then he'd almost certainly fall over (because he's nervous after Monday's accident)' and 'If Sam were to stay home, he definitely wouldn't hurt himself but he'd be missing out on seeing his friends at the ice rink' that we get to the result that what Sam ought to do is to stay home. So—assuming that (BACK) or some relevantly similar pesky backtracker is true—what grounds does the compatibilist have for *not* taking into account the truth of 'If Sam were to *D*, the accident wouldn't have happened' when considering the rationality or otherwise of his decision?

Well, one answer to that question has nothing at all to do with compatibilism and everything to do with the connection between counterfactual dependence and causation. The claim that what it's rational for Sam to do is determined by the truth of counterfactuals is *hostage* to the assumption that there are no true pesky backtrackers in the offing—since precisely what is pesky about the relevant class of backtrackers is that they deliver counterfactual dependence without causation. After all, the idea that counterfactuals tell us what it's rational for agents to do stems, roughly, from a combination of casual decision theory and the view that counterfactual dependence lines up neatly with causal dependence (as per, e.g., Lewis 1981b). That combination will be toxic to anyone who endorses a theory of counterfactuals that delivers true pesky backtrackers since, if such backtrackers are true, causation and counterfactual dependence will fail to line up and bad things will follow.

Fischer's argument against fixed-laws compatibilism is, in effect, an attempt to show that what happens at the closest D-world is, by fixed-laws compatibilist lights, somehow relevant to the rationality of Sam's decision (or, alternatively, to his 'practical deliberation') even though—we can all agree—what happens at that world doesn't line up with what Sam's D-ing would *cause*.[9] But we only have reason to care—when it comes to Sam's decision-making—what happens at the closest D-world if we *already* have reason to care about what *would* happen were Sam to D. And we only have reason to care about *that* if we already think that counterfactual and causal dependence line up—which of course we shouldn't, if we think there are true pesky backtrackers in the offing. But none of that has anything to do with compatibilism. In the end, then, the original fixed-laws compatibilist response to the Consequence Argument had things right: what's important is what Sam can *do* or *cause by* D-ing, and not what *would* be the case were he to D.[10]

Notes

1. It's unclear that an argument for incompatibilism that deploys (PFPL) really deserves to be called a 'version' of the Consequence Argument. Such an argument has no need for a so-called transfer principle, since

(PFPL) entails all by itself that nobody has the power to do anything that is incompatible with facts about the past or with the laws. But I'll ignore this quibble.

2. Other fixed-laws accounts, and defences thereof, are available. See for example Albert 2015; Dorr 2016; Kutach 2002; Loewer 2007; Wilson 2014. I take it the argument I give in §4 is available to all such accounts; the argument of §3 is a different matter since it depends on making a specific claim about backtrackers, and, at least in principle, different fixed-past accounts might take different lines on how prevalent true backtrackers are.

3. Actually Lewis says that approximate match is of 'little or no importance' (1979, 472), but the reason for his hedging on that issue is irrelevant here.

4. While the fixed-past compatibilist denies (FL) and the fixed-laws compatibilist denies (FP), we should not assume that they *accept* (FP) and (FL) respectively. In particular, Lewis's own outline theory of ability (Lewis 2020; Beebee et al. 2020) entails that (FP) is false.

5. I have borrowed this term from List (2014). List's definition of agential accessibility is specific to his own theory of the ability to do otherwise, but it fits with the more general conception I have in mind here.

6. In Beebee (2003) I argue—*contra* Lewis's response to the Consequence Argument—that, for all Lewis says in his (1981a), it might be that a deterministic agent S is able to B, and the closest possible worlds in which he Bs are worlds where he performs some prior mental action A that directly violates a law of nature. And so, since such worlds will also be the closest worlds where S As, Lewis is forced to concede that S is *able* to A. The argument implicitly trades on the denial of (DM). (So it's certainly true that *some* compatibilists have—implicitly at least—denied (DM).) Peter Graham, in his response (2008), denies on Lewis's behalf that that world is agentially accessible to S—that is, he endorses (DM). But Graham offers no account of what agential accessibility requires; and, as I've said, that's a matter to be decided on the basis of a compatibilist theory of ability. (For what it's worth, I now think what was wrong with my 2003 argument was that it assumed the truth of a backtracker: if S had B-ed, she would have A-ed. Since I'd like a counterfactual analysis of causation to be true and I'm on the fence with respect to fixed-past and fixed-laws accounts of counterfactuals, in retrospect I'd like that assumption to be false.)

7. Bennett's own view about this kind of case—which is of no help at all to Fischer—is that we should simply reject the backtracker. ('The answer to "Why are [Downing stories] plausible?" is "They are not." Our falling for them was merely careless' (1984, 72).)

8. Here I take issue with Vihvelin (2013, 223).

9. Stefan Rummens summarises Fischer's view as follows: 'the rejection of (PFPL) fails to explain why Sam should not commit to the manifestly irrational conclusion that he can bring about the non-occurrence of the accident' (2019, §9). I think Fischer is very careful *not* to attribute that particular irrational conclusion to Sam.

10. Many thanks to Christian Loew, Christian List, Michael Townsend, John Fischer, and especially Kadri Vihvelin for comments and suggestions.

References

Albert, David. 2015. *After Physics*. Cambridge, MA: Harvard University Press.

Beebee, Helen. 2003. Local Miracle Compatibilism. *Noûs* 37: 258–277.

Beebee, Helen, Maria Svedberg, and Ann Whittle. 2020. *Nihil Obstat*: Lewis's Compatibilist Account of Abilities. *The Monist* 103 (3): 245–261.

Bennett, Jonathan. 1984. Counterfactuals and Temporal Direction. *The Philosophical Review* 93 (1): 57–91.

Dorr, Cian. 2016. Against Counterfactual Miracles. *The Philosophical Review* 125 (2): 241–286.

Downing, P.B. 1958–9. Subjunctive Conditionals, Time Order, and Causation. *Proceedings of the Aristotelian Society* 59: 125–140.

Fischer, John Martin. 1988. Freedom and Miracles. *Noûs* 22 (2): 235–252.

———. 1994. *The Metaphysics of Free Will: An Essay on Control*. Oxford: Blackwell Publishing.

———. n.d. Local Miracle Compatibilism: A Critique. This volume, 112–38.

Fischer, John Martin, and Garrett Pendergraft. 2013. Does the Consequence Argument Beg the Question? *Philosophical Studies* 166 (3): 575–595.

Ginet, Carl. 1962. Can the Will be Caused? *The Philosophical Review* 71 (1): 49–55.

Graham, Peter. 2008. A Defense of Local Miracle Compatibilism. *Philosophical Studies* 140: 65–82.

Kratzer, Angelika. 1977. What 'Must' and 'Can' Must and Can Mean. *Linguistics and Philosophy* 1 (3): 337–355.

Kutach, Douglas N. 2002. The Entropy Theory of Counterfactuals. *Philosophy of Science* 69: 82–104.

Lewis, David K. 1976. The Paradoxes of Time Travel. *American Philosophical Quarterly* 12 (2): 145–152.

———. 1979. Counterfactual Dependence and Time's Arrow. *Noûs* 13 (4): 455–476.

———. 1981a. Are We Free to Break the Laws? *Theoria* 47 (3): 113–121.

———. 1981b. Causal Decision Theory. *Australasian Journal of Philosophy* 59: 5–30.

———. 2020. Outline of '*Nihil Obstat*: A Theory of Ability. *The Monist* 103 (3): 241–244.

List, Christian. 2014. Free Will, Determinism, and the Possibility of Doing Otherwise. *Noûs* 48 (1): 156–178.

Loewer, Barry. 2007. Counterfactuals and the Second Law. In *Causation, Physics, and the Constitution of Reality: Russell's Republic Revisited*, ed. Huw Price and Richard Corry, 293–326. Oxford: Oxford University Press.

Rummens, Stefan. 2019. The Counterfactual Structure of the Consequence Argument. *Erkennnis*. https://doi.org/10.1007/s10670-019-00117-2.

Tomkow, Terrance. 2013. The Simple Theory of Counterfactuals. https://tomkow.typepad.com/tomkowcom/2013/07/the-simple-theory-of-counterfactuals.html

Tomkow, Terrance and Kadri Vihvelin. 2017. The Temporal Asymmetry of Counterfactuals. https://vihvelin.typepad.com/vihvelincom/2017/12/the-temporal-asymmetry-of-counterfactuals.html.

Vihvelin, Kadri. 2013. *Causes, Laws, and Free Will: Why Determinism Doesn't Matter*. New York: Oxford University Press.

Wilson, Jessica M. 2014. Hume's Dictum and the Asymmetry of Counterfactual Dependence. In *Chance and Temporal Asymmetry*, ed. Alastair Wilson, 258–279. Oxford: Oxford University Press.

8

Moral Necessity, Agent Causation, and the Determination of Free Actions in Clarke and Leibniz

Julia Jorati

1   Introduction

When reading the 1715–16 correspondence between Samuel Clarke and Gottfried Wilhelm Leibniz, it is easy to get the impression that these two authors have diametrically opposed views on a wide range of issues. One of these issues is freedom of the will. While Leibniz holds that free actions are determined by the balance of the agent's reasons or motives, Clarke appears to object vehemently to such a determination. Free actions, he seems to insist, cannot be determined by anything. Hence, there are reasons to think that Leibniz and Clarke occupy opposite sides in the free will debate: while Leibniz is what we would today call a compatibilist and a soft determinist, Clarke is what we would call an incompatibilist and a libertarian—he holds that freedom is incompatible with determination. This is indeed the standard interpretation.[1]

J. Jorati (✉)
University of Massachusetts Amherst, Amherst, MA, USA
e-mail: jjorati@umass.edu

© The Author(s), under exclusive license to Springer Nature Switzerland AG 2021   **165**
M. Hausmann, J. Noller (eds.), *Free Will*,
https://doi.org/10.1007/978-3-030-61136-1_8

Yet, this chapter will show that when we look more carefully at Leibniz's and Clarke's theories of freedom, it becomes clear that the initial impression is misleading. Even though there are some real differences between these theories, the similarities are much more significant than the dissimilarities. On several important and controversial issues, they are on the same side. For instance, they both reject Baruch Spinoza's necessitarianism as well as the Hobbesian claim that free actions can be the products of causal chains that originate outside of the agent. Likewise, they both reject the indifferentism and voluntarism of Molinists, according to whom free agents can act independently of reasons even in cases in which there are strong reasons for one specific action. At the same time, both Clarke and Leibniz believe—*pace* Thomas Hobbes and John Locke—that what matters for freedom is not only whether we can act in accordance with our choices, but also whether our choices are themselves free. Even more interestingly, both understand free actions in terms of agent causation. Moreover, they both believe that there are necessary truths about goodness that in some sense determine the actions of wise agents; they both call this determination 'moral necessity'. As a result, both acknowledge that there is a sense in which God must do what is best. Indeed, Clarke and Leibniz pursue a very similar goal in their theories of freedom: both aim to find a middle way between necessitarianism and simple (or Hobbesian) compatibilism on the one hand and indifferentism or voluntarism on the other hand (see Harris 2005: 51).

The most important difference between Clarke's and Leibniz's theories of freedom, as we will see later, concerns what I will call equipoise cases. Equipoise cases are situations in which two or more courses of action are tied for best. Clarke thinks it is crucial that free agents can choose one of these equally good options, without needing a reason to choose any one in particular. Leibniz, on the other hand, finds it extremely important that free agents are unable to choose any option in situations like that. For him, not even the freest agent can choose an option without a sufficient reason for choosing it over all other available options. This is a genuine difference between Leibniz and Clarke, but I will argue that it is not all that significant for the two theories of freedom. Their disagreement about equipoise cases springs from their disagreement on other issues, rather than from anything that is directly related to the necessary and sufficient conditions for freedom.

Most other apparent differences between the two theories are merely differences in terminology. The most important such difference concerns their usage of the terms 'determine' and 'necessitate'. As I will argue, Clarke uses these terms in an idiosyncratic way, which makes his theory sound libertarian.[2] He appears to define 'determination' and 'necessitation' in such a way that only efficient and external causes determine or necessitate. Final and occasional causes, or reasons that motivate an agent to act, are by definition non-determining or non-necessitating, according to this usage. Leibniz, on the other hand, is often happy to apply these terms to instances of non-efficient and internal causation.[3] Underneath this terminological difference, Clarke and Leibniz agree: wise agents cannot act contrary to what they perceive as best. Hence, I will argue that on a more standard understanding of the relevant terms, both authors hold that free actions can be determined.

Let me explain the sense in which I use the terms 'necessitate' and 'determine' when I claim that both authors believe that free actions can be determined or necessitated. I use these two terms interchangeably in the following way, which I take to capture a common usage:

x necessitates/determines y in circumstances C if and only if (a) y occurs because of x, and (b) x's occurring in C without y would violate at least one physical, psychological, metaphysical, or logical law or axiom.

It is important to note that this definition does not require that x efficiently causes y. The definition is hence compatible with a non-efficient causal relation, or in fact a non-causal explanatory relation, between x and y. This is significant for this chapter because both Clarke and Leibniz embrace agent-causal theories according to which free agents cannot be efficiently caused to act.

If, as I argue, both Leibniz and Clarke believe that free actions can be determined in the sense just specified, there are good reasons to interpret both of them as compatibilists.[4] This term is admittedly anachronistic. Yet, its usage is warranted because the question of whether freedom is compatible with necessitation was central to the early modern free will debate. Hence, I will occasionally use the terms 'compatibilist' and 'incompatibilist' in this chapter. It will also become clear, however, that one must be extremely careful when applying these terms to early modern theories. Philosophers in that period commonly distinguish not just several different types of necessity, but also several types of causation, such as efficient, final, and occasional causation. In combination with inconsistencies in how they use the term 'determine', this makes it hard to classify some early modern theories as compatibilist or incompatibilist. Clarke is a good example of this, as we will see—even though I contend that he should ultimately be classified as a compatibilist.

Because Leibniz's theory of freedom is far better known than Clarke's, and because I have explored it in depth elsewhere, I will keep my discussion of Leibniz very brief and concentrate mostly on Clarke. Clarke's theory of freedom has several important facets that I will discuss separately, after providing a very brief overview of Leibniz's theory in Sect. 2. The first and most important facet of Clarke's theory is his claim that freedom requires, or consists in, self-motion; I will discuss this in Sect. 3. Another important aspect of Clarke's theory is his notion of moral necessity and its relation to freedom and determination; this will be the topic of Sect. 4. A final facet of the theory is the insistence that it is possible for free agents to act even in situations of equipoise. That will be the topic of Sect. 5. In my discussion of Clarke's theory of freedom, I will draw on his two Boyle Lectures, which are titled *A Demonstration of the Being and Attributes of God* (1704) and *A Discourse Concerning the Unalterable Obligations of Natural Religion* (1705), his 1707–08 public correspondence with Anthony Collins, the five letters to Leibniz that he composed in 1715 and 1716, his 1716–17 correspondence with John Bulkeley, his 1717 review of Anthony Collins's book *A Philosophical Inquiry Concerning Human Liberty*, and a few of his sermons.

The comparison between Leibniz's and Clarke's theories has a few upshots that might interest contemporary philosophers of action. The most important such upshot is the following: A metaphysical framework that includes final causation and agent causation has distinct advantages for theories of freedom. It allows authors like Clarke and Leibniz to advance sophisticated compatibilist theories that avoid many of the problems associated with simple compatibilism[5] while also avoiding the notorious problems that face libertarian theories. For instance, it allows these authors to deny that free actions are the products of causal chains originating outside of the agent. At the same time, they can deny that free actions or choices are ultimately random and unintelligible, or that they lack a firm connection to the agent's character, values, or judgments.

2   Brief Overview of Leibniz's Theory of Freedom

Leibniz's theory of freedom has the following five components:[6]

A. *Freedom requires spontaneity and agent causation.* For Leibniz, one necessary condition for freedom is what he calls 'spontaneity', which means that free actions cannot be caused by external efficient causes—they must originate entirely within the agent.[7] Thus, freedom requires self-determination. While Leibniz views all substances as spontaneous in a general sense, he holds that free, intelligent agents possess a particularly elevated type of spontaneity: they can determine themselves rationally, on the basis of their judgments about the good.[8] Although this is somewhat controversial, I interpret Leibniz as holding that the spontaneity of free actions is a form of agent causation. In other words, the agent causes the action for a reason that they understand and endorse. Agents themselves—rather than their motives, perceptions, desires, or other mental states—are the efficient causes of their actions. This becomes clear, for instance, in Leibniz's fifth letter to Clarke: "properly speaking, motives do not act on the mind as weights do on a balance, but it is rather the mind that acts by virtue of the motives, which are its dispositions to act" (§15, 2000: 38).[9]

B. *Freedom requires rationality and control over the passions.* On Leibniz's theory, free actions must be preceded by rational deliberation about the relative merits of different possible courses of action. Agents must understand these options clearly and determine themselves to act in accordance with their assessment of what is best overall.[10] Moreover,

Leibniz insists that in agents that possess non-rational inclinations or passions, freedom requires that they are able to master these passions, or over-rule them, so that they can act in accordance with reason.[11] In many cases, Leibniz admits, we can control the passions only indirectly, by acquiring better habits of mind and body and thus making our future actions more rational (e.g. *Theodicy* §§326f., 1985: 322f.).

C. *Freedom is compatible with a determination by reasons.* Leibniz is a determinist and holds that all actions are determined by the agent's inclinations: agents must always do what they are overall most strongly inclined or disposed to do, or what they have most reason to do.[12] Thus, he views freedom as compatible with determination.[13] The most perfectly free actions are determined by the wisdom and goodness of the agent plus the agent's perception of an action as best. Leibniz calls this kind of determination 'moral necessity'.[14]

D. *Freedom requires contingency and an ability to do otherwise.* While Leibniz is a determinist and views freedom as compatible with moral necessity, he holds that freedom is incompatible with metaphysical and absolute necessity, or a brute determination that is "blind" or indifferent to goodness (*Theodicy* §288, 1985: 303; §349, 1985: 334). Hence, free actions must be (metaphysically) contingent. The relevant contingency, as I argue elsewhere, has to do with final causation, the Principle of Sufficient Reason, and inclinations toward a perceived good. Free actions are no less determined than other actions; they are simply determined by something different, namely by the agent's judgments about the good and hence via final causes (Jorati 2017a: 121–147). Sometimes Leibniz refers to this contingency by saying that free actions are completely certain or infallible without being (metaphysically) necessary,[15] or that free agents are merely inclined, rather than necessitated, by their reasons or motives.[16] This means that there is a sense in which free agents can do otherwise: even though it may be morally necessary for the agent to act as they do, it is not metaphysically necessary; hence, it is metaphysically possible for the agent to do otherwise (*Theodicy* §234, 1985: 271). Leibniz sometimes makes this point by distinguishing an agent's power, or what is metaphysically possible for this agent to do, from her will, or from what the agent is most strongly motivated to do.[17]

In God's case, everything that does not imply a contradiction is within God's power, since God is omnipotent. Yet, God's perfect goodness guarantees that God will in fact only do what is best (e.g. *Theodicy* §171, 1985: 233; fifth letter to Clarke §76, 2000: 54).

E. *Free agents cannot choose without contrastive sufficient reasons.* Leibniz insists that if two options are tied for best, even the freest agent cannot choose one of them over the other (*Theodicy* §49, 1985: 150; fourth letter to Clarke §3, 2000: 22). Indeed, if there were no best possible world, God would not have created any world (*Theodicy* §8, 1985: 128). There must always be a sufficient reason why an agent chooses one specific option rather than any of the other options.

My aim in this chapter is to show that in all of these respects, except (E), Clarke agrees with Leibniz, aside from some terminological differences. Hence, their theories of freedom are much more similar than commonly thought. In Sect. 3, I will discuss Clarke's versions of (A) and (B); Sect. 4 will address (C) and (D), and Sect. 5 will be about (E).

3 Activity, Self-Motion, and Agent-Causation in Clarke

One key feature of Clarke's theory of freedom is the close connection that it posits between freedom, activity, self-motion, and agent-causation. Those connections are the topic of the present section.

In a letter to Bulkeley, Clarke states unequivocally that "action and freedom are ... perfectly identical ideas" because insofar as something is passive, it is necessitated, whereas something is free insofar as it is active (1998: 125). He makes the same point in his review of Collins (1998: 136) and in *Demonstration*, where he adds that "a necessary agent is an express contradiction" (§10, 1998: 74f.). Thus, he holds that something is necessitated or unfree just in case it is passive,[18] and that something is free just in case it is active.

Clarke furthermore understands activity as self-motion or agent causation; that is, he holds that the only way for a thing to be active is for it to introduce a new motion or start a new causal chain. More specifically, agents cause changes without being efficiently caused by anything else to cause those changes.[19] That this is Clarke's view becomes clear in his fifth letter to Leibniz, where he defines 'action' as "the beginning of a motion where there was none before from a principle of life or activity" (§§93–95, 2000: 76; see also review of Collins, 1998: 133). All activity, in other words, is agent-causation or self-motion. As a result of this identification of activity with self-motion, Clarke holds that there is no activity whatsoever in mechanical causation, which for him is the only type of causation that exists among inanimate things (fourth letter §33, 2000: 33; fifth letter §§93–95, 2000: 76).[20] A queue stick that moves a billiard ball is completely passive, according to Clarke, because this stick is not the originator of its own motion; it merely moves because the player's hands caused it to move. Even machines like clocks, Clarke stresses, "are in no sense agents; neither is their motion, in any sense, an action" (review of Collins, 1998: 133).

The idea here seems to be that a mechanistic system in which any change in the motion of one body is caused by the impact of other bodies is a system of entirely passive things. John Carriero describes this intuition nicely in a paper about Leibniz: no body in a purely mechanistic system is an "originator of activity"; each body is merely "a conduit through which the impulses of earlier members in some indefinitely extended causal series are relayed to subsequent members in the series" (2008: 123). Hence, no body in such a system is truly active, or an agent.[21] Because activity requires self-motion, and because there is no self-motion in inanimate, purely material things, Clarke holds that only living things with immaterial souls—which include both human beings and animals—can act (*Demonstration* §10, 1998: 58; letter to Bulkeley, 1998: 129f.).

Given Clarke's identification of freedom with activity, and his identification of activity with self-motion, it makes sense that he often identifies freedom with self-motion, or with the power to begin motion (e.g. *Demonstration* §9, 1998: 53; 1998: 47; review of Collins, 1738 vol. 4:727). Hence, whatever possesses self-motion is free, and whatever is free possesses self-motion. Clarke hence aligns himself with the tradition that understands freedom in terms of self-determination.[22]

Because even brute animals and young children have the power of self-motion, this means that they are free. Indeed, Clarke claims that this is true for "the *Actions of every living Creature*" (review of Collins, 1738 vol. 4:729), even "the meanest Insect" (Sermon XXXV, 1738 vol. 1:218). Interestingly, Clarke sometimes uses a slightly different terminology, reserving the term 'liberty' for rational agents and calling the power of self-motion in non-rational agents 'spontaneity' (letter to Bulkeley, 1998: 126). Yet, in his review of Collins, Clarke describes the spontaneity of non-rational actions as a type of freedom. He notes that animals possess the same "physical Liberty or self-moving Power" that adult human beings possess; animals are merely unable to sense, be conscious of, or make judgments concerning moral goodness or badness (1738 vol. 4:729). Hence, the physical liberty of adult humans who can cognize moral qualities is "*eminently* called *Liberty*," whereas the physical liberty of non-rational animals is "vulgarly called *Spontaneity*" (ibid.). This means that both animals and human beings are free in the broader sense because they are equally capable of self-motion. The difference is merely that human beings additionally possess reason or intelligence and can thus self-move in accordance with rational judgments.

The most helpful discussion of the distinction between the freedom of rational and that of non-rational agents occurs in Clarke's sermon "Of the Liberty of Moral Agents." There, he distinguishes between the "mere *physical* or *natural* Liberty" that both rational and non-rational agents possess and the "Liberty of a *Moral* Agent and of a *rational* Being." The former consists merely in the ability to act in accordance with one's appetites, instincts, desires, or wills (sermon XXXV, 1738 vol. 1:218). The latter, in contrast, is the ability to do what is morally right and what reason demands (ibid.). Or, more specifically, it consists in "a clear unbiassed Judgment, and in a Power of acting conformably thereunto" (1738 vol. 1:219). Hence, the freedom of moral agents allows them to control or "over-rul[e]" their natural appetites in order to act on their rational judgments (1738 vol. 1217; see also sermon XXXIX, 1738 vol. 1:244).[23] This ability is necessary for moral agency. Thus, moral agency requires not just freedom in the physical sense, but also the ability to determine oneself rationally and to control "the violent impetus of ... blind and headstrong

Passion[s]" (sermon XXXV, 1738 vol. 1:220; see also sermon XXXIX, 1738 vol. 1:244).

There is a potential problem with the discussion of freedom in this sermon, however: its definitions of physical liberty and the liberty of moral agents do not explicitly invoke the power of self-motion. Indeed, the definition of physical liberty sounds quite similar to Hobbes's, Locke's, or Collins's definitions of freedom, against which Clarke argues elsewhere. Does that mean that this definition is incompatible with the other definitions that we examined earlier?[24] I do not think so. After all, Clarke holds that the only way to act on the basis of appetites or judgments is through self-motion. As we will see in the next section, Clarke holds that it is metaphysically impossible for pleasure, pain, reasons, or motives to cause an action efficiently (review of Collins, 1998: 134/1738 vol. 4:723). Thus, for Clarke, both physical liberty and the liberty of moral agents, as they are defined in the sermon, presuppose self-motion.

4   Determination, Moral Necessity, and Final Causation in Clarke

So far, we have explored the connections that Clarke draws between freedom, activity, and self-motion, or agent causation. Now we are in a position to address one of the most critical issues: the question of whether free actions can be determined. It might be tempting to think that because Clarkean freedom requires agent causation, it must also require indeterminism. Yet, that would be too fast. Historically speaking, it is not at all uncommon for philosophers to combine agent causation with determinism. Leibniz, as we have already seen, is a case in point. A deterministic agent-causal theory can hold, for instance, that agents have natures or natural inclinations that determine them to agent-cause specific actions.[25] These natures or inclinations can determine specific actions without causing them efficiently and hence without undermining agent causation. After all, it is historically very common to view natures and natural inclinations as dispositions, tendencies, or powers, which in turn were not always viewed as the kinds of entities that can be efficient causes.

Substances (or agents) cause changes because of their natures or inclinations, that is, because they are naturally disposed to cause those changes in specific circumstances. Describing dispositions or natures as efficient causes, for at least some historical philosophers, would be a category mistake.

What, then, are Clarke's views about the compatibility of freedom and determination? Can an action be both free and determined? This is a complex question, in part because Clarke uses the relevant terminology in non-standard and confusing ways. A good place to start finding answers to this question are Clarke's remarks about divine freedom, because the issue is more straightforward in God's case. Hence, let us first investigate determination in the context of divine freedom and then turn to human freedom. For Clarke, as we will see, humans are free in exactly the same sense as God, except that humans are free to a lower degree because of their passions and defects in their knowledge. I aim to show that for both God and humans, freedom is compatible with determination—though not in the idiosyncratic sense of 'determination' in which Clarke often uses that term.

4.1 God's Inability to Choose Sub-optimal Options

When examining Clarke's theory of freedom, it is important to distinguish between cases in which there is an option that the agent recognizes as best overall, and cases in which there is not. Let us call the former 'rankable cases' and the latter 'equipoise cases'. We will examine equipoise cases in Sect. 5 and focus on rankable cases in the current section.

Clarke states repeatedly that God cannot perform sub-optimal actions in rankable cases. Consider, for instance, the following claim from section 12 of *Demonstration*: "though God is a most perfectly free agent, yet he cannot but do always what is best and wisest in the whole" (1998: 87). This is nicely clear: God can only do what is best or wisest, all things considered; that is, he cannot perform a sub-optimal action. Nevertheless, God is perfectly free. Hence, freedom is compatible with this particular kind of determination.

In the continuation of the passage under discussion, Clarke elaborates further and also explains the source of God's inability to do anything but the best:

> The reason is evident, because perfect wisdom and goodness are steady and certain principles of action as necessity itself. And an infinitely wise and good being endowed with the most perfect liberty can no more choose to act in contradiction to wisdom and goodness, than a necessary agent can act contrary to the necessity by which it is acted, it being as great an absurdity and impossibility in choice for infinite wisdom to choose to act unwisely, or infinite goodness to choose what is not good, as it would be in nature for absolute necessity to fail of producing its necessary effect. (*Demonstration* §12, 1998: 87)

Here, Clarke uses slightly different terminology to describe the fact that God cannot but do what is best: he says that it is completely *certain* that God will do the best, and it is *absurd* and *impossible* for God to choose or perform something other than the best option. Indeed, he says that God's choosing a sub-optimal course of action is as impossible as the non-occurrence of some natural event that is absolutely necessary.[26] Clarke avoids saying that God's choices and actions are determined. Yet, he does say explicitly that it is impossible for God to do what is not best.

In the passage just quoted, Clarke furthermore identifies the source of God's inability to choose sub-optimal options: the divine attributes, particularly wisdom and goodness. Elsewhere it becomes clear how exactly God's attributes make it impossible to choose sub-optimal options. Clarke defines 'goodness' as "a fixed disposition to do always what in the whole is best" (sermon XIV, 1998: 143). This fixed disposition, when combined with omniscience and omnipotence, makes it "truly and absolutely impossible for God not to do, or to do anything contrary to," what goodness and justice require of him (*Demonstration* §12, 1998: 86). In other words, God's nature is such that he must always know what is best, want to do what is best, and have the power to do what is best. As a result, it is necessary that God will in fact always do what is best. Acting sub-optimally would contradict God's attributes, which he necessarily possesses and of which he therefore cannot divest himself; it is "as much a contradiction to suppose [God] choosing to do anything inconsistent with his justice, goodness, and truth, as to suppose him divested of infinity, power, or existence" (*Demonstration* §12, 1998: 87).

Sometimes Clarke provides a slightly different explanation for God's inability to choose sub-optimal options. He first notes that truths about what is good, just, or fitting, are necessary and eternal truths that are grounded in the natures of things (*Discourse*, 1738 vol. 2:612; see also *Demonstration* §12, 1998: 83). Then, he argues that any intelligent being, unless its intellect is very imperfect or very depraved, must know these truths. Similarly, he notes, the wills of all intelligent beings must be "constantly directed [by this knowledge], and must needs be determined to act accordingly," unless those will are either corrupted or subjected to strong passions (*Discourse*, 1738 vol. 2:612; see also *Demonstration* §12, 1998: 84). The idea here seems to be that it is natural for wills to be attracted to a clearly recognized good. Based on these premises, Clarke argues that since God possesses infinite knowledge, wisdom, and power, he must also be perfectly good: "'tis manifest *His* Divine Will cannot but always and necessarily determine itself to choose to Do what in the whole is absolutely Best and Fittest to be done; that is, to act constantly according to the eternal Rules of infinite Goodness, Justice, and Truth" (*Discourse*, 1738 vol. 2:612; similarly in *Demonstration* §12, 1998: 84). This argument appears to rely implicitly on the Principle of Sufficient Reason: a good will that is not subject to any passions or corrupting influences must choose what is best in rankable cases, because it has no reason to do anything but what is best.[27]

4.2 Divine Freedom and Moral Necessity

Clarke often refers to the necessitation of divine choices as a "necessity … of fitness and wisdom" (*Demonstration* §9, 1998: 51), a "necessity … of wisdom and choice" (*Demonstration* §9, 1998: 49) or, interchangeably, as a "moral necessity" (*Demonstration* §10, 1998: 73). The concept 'moral necessity' has a long and complicated history. It is used in many late medieval and early modern discussions of freedom and traditionally denotes a modality that is compatible with freedom. It is often contrasted with absolute, physical, or metaphysical necessity, which are typically described as incompatible with freedom. Interestingly, this term is used both by philosophers who view freedom and determination as incompatible, and by philosophers who view them as compatible.[28] Hence, we need to look carefully at Clarke's own discussions to figure out what he means by it and whether it is a form of determination.

Clarke describes moral necessity, or the necessity of fitness and wisdom, as "*that Inclination*, ... which every rational Being does so much the more constantly and regularly follow, as the Being is more rational and perfect" (review of Collins, 1738 vol. 4:728).[29] This suggests that God, who is perfectly rational, always follows the relevant inclinations. The relevant inclinations, as Clarke makes clear elsewhere, are the inclinations to do what one recognizes as best. That is, moral necessity is the necessity by which the will of a wise and good agent chooses what the agent understands to be best (*Demonstration* §10, 1998: 73).[30] For instance, Clarke claims that this necessity is founded on "such an unalterable rectitude of will and perfection of wisdom as makes it impossible for a wise being to resolve to act foolishly, or for a nature infinitely good to do that which is evil" (*Demonstration* §9, 1998: 51). This fits well with what Clarke says elsewhere about God's inability to choose sub-optimal options: choosing such an option would contradict some of God's attributes, which is impossible because God cannot lose these attributes—they are "unalterable," as the previous quotation puts it.[31] Moral necessity, of course, is entirely compatible with freedom (*Demonstration* §9, 1998: 51).

Clarke contrasts moral necessity with natural or physical necessity, which is incompatible with freedom, and which is a necessitation that has nothing to do with the will or with goodness (letter to Bulkeley, 1998: 128; *Demonstration* §9, 1998: 46; sermon XXXV, 1738 vol. 1:220). Sometimes, he says that what is morally impossible for God is contrary to his moral attributes—which include goodness, justice, and truthfulness—or to the rectitude or goodness of his will. In contrast, what is physically or naturally impossible for God is contrary to his natural attributes—which include God's omnipotence, omnipresence, and omniscience (*Demonstration* §12, 1998: 87f.; sermon XIV, 1998: 143; sermon XI, 1998: 142; letter to Bulkeley, 1998: 128).[32] For instance, being ignorant is naturally impossible for God, while being cruel is morally impossible.

This distinction allows Clarke to say that certain actions are physically possible but morally impossible for God. For instance, breaking a promise is physically possible for God, since he has the physical power to perform that action, or since the action is compatible with God's natural attributes. Yet, breaking the promise is morally impossible for God, since it contradicts his moral attributes (review of Collins, 1738 vol. 4:725). This means that when God keeps a promise or does what is best, he is only physically able to do otherwise; he is morally unable to do otherwise.[33] In contrast, as we will see later, God is both morally and physically able to do otherwise when he chooses among options that are tied for best (review of Collins, 1738 vol. 4:728).

Clarke sometimes calls the absence of physical necessity 'physical Liberty', and the absence of moral necessitation 'moral Liberty' (review of Collins, 1738 vol. 4:728). As should already be clear, however, many of the most perfectly free actions are free only in the sense of physical liberty, because they are morally necessitated. Moral necessity, for Clarke, does not in the least diminish freedom. Thus, this usage of the term 'moral Liberty' is not to be confused with what Clarke elsewhere calls 'the liberty of a moral agent', and which we discussed in the previous section. As we saw, the liberty of a moral agent is the ability to do what reason demands and what is morally right (sermon XXXV, 1738 vol. 1:218). Clearly, many actions that are free in that sense are morally necessary; that is, they are not instances of moral liberty.

There is, however, a potential objection to what I have so far stated about divine freedom. This objection is connected to the traditional distinction between the liberty of exercise (sometimes called 'liberty of contradiction') and the liberty of specification (sometimes called 'liberty of contrariety').[34] Liberty of exercise is, roughly, the power to either act or refrain from acting, whereas liberty of specification is the power to pursue either one course of action or another. For example, if I am considering my options for dinner, liberty of exercise would give me the power to either have dinner or refrain from having dinner altogether, whereas liberty of specification would give me the power to choose either the pasta or the salad. Some authors argue that God lacks liberty of specification, because God can only choose to do what is best. Yet, they maintain that God possesses liberty of exercise, because God has the power to refrain from acting. Thus, while God may be unable to create a non-optimal world, he is able to refrain from creating altogether.[35]

Might Clarke hold that free agents can be morally necessitated only with respect to specification, but not with respect to exercise?[36] If so, we might have to classify Clarke as a libertarian after all. There is at least one passage that can be taken to suggest this interpretation: Clarke writes in his review of Collins that "All power of acting essentially implies at the same time a power of not acting, otherwise it is not acting but barely a being acted upon by that power (whatever it be) which causes the action" (1998: 133.). This passage clearly refers to a liberty of exercise, rather than specification, and it clearly states that all genuine agents must possess a liberty of exercise—if they lacked it, they would not be agents. Conversely, this means that agents cannot be necessitated with respect to exercise. Yet, this passage does not settle the question we are currently considering, because it is unclear whether the power to refrain from acting is supposed to be a moral possibility or merely a physical possibility. If it is merely a physical possibility, and if free agents can be morally necessitated with respect to exercise, then this passage does not contain any evidence against a compatibilist reading of Clarke. As we will see later, Clarke typically associates physical necessity—not moral necessity—with passivity, which suggests that in the passage under discussion, he may merely be ruling out a physical necessitation of exercise.

A passage from *Demonstration* supports this reading:

There was indeed no necessity in nature that God should at first create such beings as he has created, or indeed any beings at all, because he is in himself infinitely happy and all-sufficient ... But it was fit, and wise, and good, that infinite wisdom should manifest, and infinite goodness communicate itself. And therefore, it was necessary (in the sense of necessity I am now speaking of) that things should be made at such time, and continued so long, and endowed with various perfections in such degrees, as infinite wisdom and goodness saw it wisest and best that they should. (*Demonstration* §12, 1998: 87)

Here, it is much clearer that Clarke merely wants to deny that God was physically necessitated (or determined by a "necessity in nature") to create a world in the first place. Indeed, Clarke then seems to assert that eternal truths about goodness and "fitness" required God to create: it is more fit to create than not to create, and hence God was morally necessitated to do so. This strongly suggests that Clarke does not after all exempt liberty of exercise from moral necessitation; perfectly free actions can be morally necessary both with respect to exercise and with respect to specification. This interpretation is also confirmed earlier in the same text, where Clarke states that it is "truly and absolutely impossible for God not to do, or to do anything contrary to," what goodness and justice require of him (*Demonstration* §12, 1998: 86). This quotation states very plainly that even refraining from acting (i.e. "not to do" what goodness requires) is impossible for God. Therefore, Clarke appears to hold that free agents can be morally necessitated with respect to specification as well as exercise.

4.3 Human Freedom

Let us now take a look at what Clarke says about human freedom. We already saw a hint earlier: the only reason why an intelligent agent would fail to choose the best is depravity or a lack of intelligence (*Discourse*, 1738 vol. 2:612; *Demonstration* §12, 1998: 84). As he elaborates in *Discourse*,

> *[N]egligent Misunderstandings* and *wilful Passions or Lusts*, are … the only Causes which can make a reasonable Creature act contrary to Reason … For, was it not for these inexcusable corruptions and deprivations, 'tis impossible … but the same eternal *Reasons of Things* must … have Weight enough to determine constantly the Wills and Actions of all Subordinate, Finite, Dependent, and Accountable Beings. (1738 vol. 2613)

This suggests that even for humans, the ability to choose something other than the best is not a result of some human perfection, and thus not something that is necessary for human freedom. In fact, Clarke says that humans ought to be determined in all of their actions by the kinds of reasons that determine God's actions (*Demonstration* §12, 90; *Discourse*, 1738 vol. 2:612).

Indeed, it becomes clear in several texts that for Clarke, humans are sometimes morally necessitated in the same sense in which God is morally necessitated, and that this is entirely compatible with human freedom (*Demonstration* §10, 1998: 73). For instance, Clarke states that humans were naturally and originally—which presumably means prior to original sin—subject to moral necessity, just as God is (*Discourse*, 1738 vol. 2:613). In our current state, we of course do not always do what is most rational because sin has corrupted us. Yet, we sometimes do—and, as already seen, always ought to. In his review of Collins, Clarke claims that all rational beings are subject to moral necessity, and that the constancy and regularity with which they are subject to it varies according to their degree of rationality and perfection (1738 vol. 4:728). The more perfect someone's moral character is, and the more clearly they recognize what is best, the more frequently they are subject to moral necessity. This also becomes clear in a letter to Bulkeley: "It is indeed a contradiction in terms, *morally* speaking, that a wise man should do a foolish thing, or an honest man a dishonest thing" (1998: 128). Thus, wise people cannot act unwisely while retaining their wisdom, and honest people cannot act dishonestly while retaining their honesty (see fifth letter to Leibniz §§4–13, 2000: 67).

Of course, unlike God, human beings can lose their character traits; a wise and honest person can become foolish and dishonest. Yet, as already seen, those things cannot happen unless there are sufficient reasons, such as temptations and other corrupting influences.[37] When wise people are not faced with strong temptations, it is morally impossible for them to act foolishly (*Demonstration* §10, 1998: 74). Clarke provides a helpfully concrete example of moral necessity in human beings: "a man entirely free from all pain of body and disorder of mind judges it unreasonable for him to hurt or destroy himself; and being under no temptation or external violence, he cannot possibly act contrary to this judgment" (*Demonstration* §10, 1998: 73). Clarke stresses that this man clearly has the physical power to hurt himself. Yet, he does not do so because "it is absurd and mischievous, and morally impossible, for him to choose to do it" (1998: 74).

Hence, in the human case, moral necessity depends on certain background conditions, such as the absence of temptations as well as physical and mental health. That is not the case for God, since God is immune from disorders and temptations, and will therefore do what is best in any circumstance. Yet, when the background conditions are in place, humans can be morally necessitated in just the same way as God. This means that human freedom is just as compatible with moral necessity as God's freedom. Human beings are not always morally necessitated, but they are when they act the way they ought to act. Hence, if moral necessity is a type of determination, then both human and divine free actions can be determined.

4.4   Clarkean Determination and Freedom

Is moral necessity a type of determination? Clarke's own usage of the terms 'determine' and 'necessitate' is somewhat idiosyncratic, as already mentioned. Hence, let us first examine how Clarke uses those terms in the context of free actions. After that, in Sect. 4.5, we can examine whether free actions can be determined on a more standard conception, namely the one I defined in the introduction.

Clarke is sometimes happy to talk about the determination of free actions by reasons or by the agent's character. For instance, he writes in *Demonstration* that "God is unalterably determined to do always what is best in the whole" by the perfection of his will (§9, 1998: 46). Similarly, he says later in the same work that in rankable cases, "reasons ... always and necessarily ... determine the will of God" (§12, 1998: 90; repeated almost verbatim in *Discourse*, 1738 vol. 2:612). Along similar lines, he writes in his third letter to Leibniz that the agent's knowledge of the differences between the options "always determines an intelligent and perfectly wise agent" (§§7–8, 2000: 19). And even the wills of intelligent creatures who are not perfectly wise "must needs be determined to act" in accordance with their knowledge of the good, at least when they are not corrupted or subject to strong temptations (*Discourse*, 1738 vol. 2:612).

Clarke is also happy in some places to describe free actions as necessary, as already seen: they can be necessary in the sense of a moral necessity, or a necessity of wisdom and fitness (e.g. *Demonstration* §9, 1998: 49; 51; §12, 1998: 84). And, as we saw in Sect. 4.1, he sometimes says that it is impossible for God to do what is not best; in fact, he claims in *Demonstration* that this is "as great an absurdity and impossibility" as the non-occurrence of something that is naturally necessary (§12, 1998: 87). Likewise, as we saw in Sect. 4.3, it is impossible for humans not to do what they clearly understand to be best, unless they are in unfavorable circumstances.

Elsewhere, however, Clarke insists that it cannot be literally true that free actions are either necessary or determined by reasons. For example, he sometimes claims that 'necessary agent' is an oxymoron (*Demonstration* §10, 1998: 75). Likewise, he stresses in his review of Collins that it is a "mere figure [of speech] or metaphor" to describe an agent as determined by reasons or motives, because in philosophical strictness it is the agent who determines herself (1998: 134).[38] He says the same about moral necessity: whereas physical necessity is a literal necessity, moral necessity is merely a figurative or metaphorical necessity and is "philosophically speaking, *no necessity* at all" (letter to Bulkeley, 1998: 130; see also 1998: 126; review of Collins, 1998: 136f.; fifth letter to Leibniz, §§4–13, 2000: 67).

Metaphorical expressions, of course, point to some similarity. According to Clarke, the similarities in this case are certainty and dependability: morally necessitated actions are as certain to occur as physically necessitated ones and we can rely on their occurrence "as firmly and reasonably" in our reasoning (letter to Bulkeley, 1998: 130; see also review of Collins, 1998: 136f.; *Demonstration* §12, 1998: 86; fourth defense against Collins, 2011: 277). Thus, Clarke does not hold that morally necessary actions or choices are merely extremely likely, though not guaranteed, to happen:[39] he is very clear that they are as certain as events that are physically necessary. He even says that we can depend on the effects of moral necessity "with infallible certainty" (fourth defense against Collins, 2011: 277). All of this suggests that moral necessity and physical necessity do not differ in modal strength. That makes sense, of course, given how Clarke explains divine moral necessity: God's doing something non-optimal would contradict his moral attributes, of which he cannot divest himself any more than he can divest himself of his natural attributes.

Why, then, does Clarke sometimes insist that free actions are not strictly speaking necessary, or determined by reasons? The answer, I contend, is that he associates the terms 'determine' and 'necessitate' with a particular kind of determination, namely a determination by efficient and external causes. This means, given his understanding of activity and passivity, that whatever is determined in this sense is passive rather than an agent, and hence cannot be free.

There is textual evidence that Clarke sometimes understands determination and necessitation in this way.[40] For instance, he argues in his fourth defense against Collins that necessity is incompatible with self-determination (2011: 277). In his review of Collins, Clarke explains: "To be an agent signifies to have a *power of beginning motion*; and motion cannot begin necessarily, because necessity of motion supposes an efficiency superior to, and irresistible by, the thing moved; and consequently the beginning of the motion cannot be in that which is moved necessarily" (1998: 133). This passage is somewhat difficult to unpack, but it appears to make the following point: an entity is necessitated only if it is being forced to move by an extrinsic efficient cause whose influence this entity cannot resist. Since being forced to move by such an extrinsic efficient cause makes this entity passive, necessitation is incompatible with activity or agency.[41]

Hence, Clarke often appears to use the terms 'determined' and 'necessitated' in the sense of 'externally determined', and hence as opposed to 'self-determined'. That usage makes perfect sense. Yet, this means that Clarke's claims that free actions cannot be determined must not be taken to mean that there cannot be determination in the sense that I defined in the introduction. As already noted, it is entirely possible to hold that agents are exempt from any external efficient-causal influences, while also holding that agents are completely determined by their natures, reasons, or inclinations.

4.5   The Determination by Final and Occasional Causes

So far we have seen that, according to Clarke, free actions can be determined neither externally nor efficiently. Hence, in order to answer the question of whether Clarke holds that free actions can be determined in the sense specified in the introduction, we need to examine whether they can be determined internally and non-efficiently. That is the task of the current subsection. I will argue that Clarke grants that free actions can indeed be determined in a non-efficient way by factors internal to the agent's mind. More precisely, I will argue that motives and reasons, or the last judgment of the intellect, can determine actions, as either occasional or final causes.

It is already obvious that motives and reasons cannot be efficient causes for Clarke, because that would undermine agent-causation or self-motion. By definition, an agent who exercises its self-moving power "is itself the only proper, physical, and immediate *CAUSE* of the Motion or Action" (review of Collins, 1738 vol. 4:728). Clarke provides an additional reason why motives cannot efficiently cause human actions:

> If the *Reasons* or *Motives* upon which a Man acts, be the *immediate* and *efficient Cause of the Action*, then either *abstract Notions*, such as all *Reasons* and *Motives* are, have a *real Subsistence*, that is, are themselves *Substances*; or else *That which has itself no real Subsistence*, can *put* a Body into *Motion*: either of which is manifestly absurd. (Review of Collins, 1738 vol. 4:734; similarly ibid., 723 and 728)

What he says here is that only substances, or things with real subsistence, are capable of putting bodies into motion. Mental states, which he classifies as 'abstract notions', cannot move bodies. Elsewhere, Clarke justifies this claim through the widely accepted causal axiom that "Nothing can possibly be the cause of an effect more considerable than itself" (review of Collins, 1998: 134).[42] He takes this to mean that passive things cannot cause active things, and that judgments or perceptions in the intellect, which he classifies as passive,[43] cannot cause physical motion. After all, the production of a new motion requires an active cause.

Even though judgments, reasons, and motives cannot be efficient causes of actions for Clarke, he insists that they must have some influence on the action. Indeed, he criticizes Collins for assuming that the only alternative to viewing reasons as efficient causes is a theory according to which the agent is completely indifferent to reasons and acts without any regard for them (review of Collins, 1998: 135). The implication is clear: Clarke views this as a false dichotomy and contends that on his theory, motives have a genuine influence on the action, even though they do not efficiently cause the action. Similarly, he notes in *Demonstration* that the self-moving power "exerts itself freely *in consequence of* the last judgment of the understanding" (§10, 1998: 73; emphasis mine).[44] This is of course a very sensible stance for an agent-causation theorist; it would be extremely implausible to claim that reasons cannot influence free actions in any way.[45]

But what kind of influence can motives and reasons have? Sometimes Clarke calls them 'moral causes' or 'moral motives', which he contrasts with efficient or physical causes. In *Demonstration*, for instance, he writes that a rational agent's action "is not determined or caused by the last judgment as by the physical efficient, but only as the moral motive," and that the agent's self-moving power begins acting "upon" this moral motive (§10, 1998: 73). This statement is helpful because, when taken at face value, it states that the last judgment *causes* and even *determines* the action as a moral motive. Thus, Clarke appears to be invoking some kind of non-efficient determination and causation here. Elsewhere, he uses the term 'moral cause', apparently for the same notion (review of Collins, 1738 vol. 4:732).

One helpful way to understand Clarke's talk of moral causes and moral motives is in terms of final causation. After all, final causes are non-efficient, as Clarke himself states explicitly (review of Collins, 1738 vol. 4:732). Moreover, it is common to think of free, rational actions as explained by final causes: rational agents choose to act in a certain way because they think it is overall best, that is, because they are attracted by the goodness of that particular course of action. Clarke clearly believes in final causation, and even appears to hold that there is a connection between final causation and freedom, or contingency (*Demonstration* §9, 1998: 51). He also describes God as acting "not necessarily but voluntarily with particular intention and design, knowing that he does good and intending to do so freely and out of choice" (*Demonstration* §12, 86). This strongly suggests that free actions are instances of final causation: they are performed for the sake of the goodness that they aim to bring about. That would also fit extremely well with Clarke's description of moral necessity as an inclination toward something that the agent judges to be best (review of Collins, 1738 vol. 4:728).

Intriguingly, in at least one passage, Clarke suggests that motives and reasons are not final but occasional causes: "reasons, motives, and arguments … [are] Occasions … upon which that substance in man wherein the self-moving principle resides freely exerts its active power" (review of Collins, 1998: 134).[46] Occasional causation is a type of non-efficient causation that quite a large number of early modern authors acknowledge. It is most commonly associated with occasionalism. According to occasionalism, created things are incapable of being efficient causes. This means, among other things, that human decisions do not directly cause bodily motions because the human mind lacks the power to be the efficient cause of such motions. Instead, human decisions are merely the occasions upon which God exercises his power to move human bodies. In other words, human decisions are occasional causes for God's activity. This means that they are the reasons for God's activity, even though they are not efficient causes of God's activity.[47]

Clarke, of course, is not an occasionalist.[48] Yet, quite a few early modern authors invoke occasional causation without being occasionalists. The idea behind this usage is simply that the relation that occasionalists posit between human decisions and God's exercise of his powers can also exist between two created entities. Steven Nadler describes this causal relation as follows: occasional causation occurs "when one thing or state of affairs brings about an effect by inducing (but *not* through efficient causation …) another thing to exercise its own efficient causal power" (2011: 33). This causal relation is *sui generis*, irreducible, and governed by special causal laws (2011: 37).[49]

Early modern substance dualists sometimes invoke occasional causation in their theories of sensation (Nadler 2011: 38f.). That is because, for dualists, it is problematic to claim that bodies or their modes can efficiently cause mental states. After all, these philosophers view mind and body as radically heterogeneous and they typically view minds as more perfect than bodies. These two doctrines strongly suggest that bodies or their modes cannot be efficient causes of mental states, since efficient causes must traditionally be homogeneous with and at least as perfect as the effect.[50]

Clarke sometimes invokes occasional causation in just this context: in his fourth defense against Collins, he claims that "the power by which matter acts upon the soul is not a *real quality* inhering in matter, ... but it is only a power or occasion of exciting certain *modes* or *sensations* in another substance" (2011: 261; similarly second defense, 2011: 100). What he seems to be saying here is that the soul produces sensations on the occasion of a specific physical stimulus. In *Demonstration*, Clarke uses a parallel account in order to explain secondary quality perceptions like colors, sounds, and tastes, which do not resemble anything in the physical world. These sensations, Clarke says, "are by no means effects arising from mere figure and motion ... and are not properly caused but only *occasioned* by the impressions of figure or motion" (§8, 1998: 41). This usage is helpful because it suggests that occasional causation can be deterministic: it is quite likely that for Clarke, there are deterministic laws that govern the relation between physical stimuli and sensations. After all, we do not appear to have any direct voluntary control over sensations and they seem determined by physical facts.

Given this background, it is plausible that when Clarke states that reasons and motives are occasions upon which the self-moving principle exercises its own active powers, he is invoking precisely the causal relation that Nadler describes.[51] Clarke's motivation, after all, is exactly parallel to the motivation of other authors who appeal to occasional causation: motives and reasons cannot be efficient causes of the action, but they nevertheless must have a genuine influence on the action. Occasional causation fits the bill perfectly, because it is a genuine but non-efficient type of causation. It allows Clarke to maintain that motives have a real influence, without having to say that motives are active or that agents are acted upon by anything.

Now we can finally answer the question of whether Clarke holds that free actions can be determined, and if so, how. Recall my definition from the introduction: x necessitates/determines y in circumstances C if and only if (a) y occurs because of x, and (b) x's occurring in C without y would violate at least one physical, psychological, metaphysical, or logical law or axiom. Can motives determine actions in this sense? It should be easy to see that condition (a) is met: the relevant actions occur because of the motives. As just seen, it is likely that Clarke understands this explanatory relation as either final or occasional causation. We have already seen strong evidence that in rankable cases, condition (b) is met as well. God's failing to act in accordance with his motives would be a violation of his moral attributes, which it is metaphysically impossible to violate. Similarly, when a human being is morally necessitated by a judgment, failing to act accordingly in the same circumstances would be a violation of Clarke's Principle of Sufficient Reason, as I argued earlier. This suggests—although Clarke does not say it explicitly, to the best of my knowledge—that the occasional-causal or final-causal influence of motives and reasons is deterministic.[52] Hence, in the human case, failing to act based on those motives would violate the Principle of Sufficient Reason, or whatever laws govern occasional and final causation. Therefore, Clarke holds that both divine and human free actions can be determined. This makes him a compatibilist: even though he does not believe that all free actions are determined, he believes that some are—and that is all it takes to be a compatibilist.

5   Equipoise in Clarke

Let us finally turn to Clarke's theory that in equipoise cases—that is, in cases in which multiple options are tied for best—free agents can choose to perform any of these options, without needing a reason to choose one over another. As I mentioned in Sect. 4.2, Clarke contends that both in equipoise and in rankable cases, free agents possess physical liberty; that is, they have the physical power to choose or perform any of the options. Yet, in equipoise cases they additionally possess moral liberty; that is, they are not even morally necessitated to choose one specific option (review of Collins, 1738 vol. 4:727f.). This means that choosing any of the equally good options is compatible with perfect wisdom and perfect goodness. In rankable cases, in contrast, only one option is compatible with perfect wisdom and perfect goodness and hence the agent lacks moral liberty.

In Clarke's letters to Leibniz—by far his most extensive discussion of equipoise cases—it becomes clear why he holds these views. One reason appears to be this: being unable to choose an option when there is no sufficient reason to choose any particular one is incompatible with the activity of free agents. His thinking seems to be that such a dependence on reasons indicates that the agent cannot in fact determine herself to act, and hence is no agent at all, but a passive entity that can only move when something else moves it. This is particularly explicit in the third letter:

> [W]hen two ways of acting are equally and alike good, ... to affirm in such case that God cannot act at all, ... because he can have no external reason to move him to act one way rather than the other, seems to be ... denying God to have in himself any original principle or power of beginning to act, but that he must necessarily be (as it were mechanically) always determined by extrinsic things. (§§7–8, 2000: 19f.)

Here, Clarke explicitly associates the need for external reasons with mechanical causation and hence with passivity.[53] In his next two letters, he makes the same point in the context of the analogy between a balance and an agent (fourth letter, §§1–2, 2000: 29; fifth letter, §§1–20, 2000: 66f.).

Another reason for Clarke's stance on equipoise cases appears to be the following. Not being able to act when two or more options are tied for best, and when choosing either of the equally good options is better than doing nothing, would be an imperfection (fourth letter, §§1–2, 2000: 29; fifth letter, §§1–20, 2000: 67). After all, that kind of paralysis would prevent the agent from doing something of great value. This, of course, is quite plausible. Consider, for instance, a case in which an agent has the opportunity to throw a life saver to one of several drowning people who are equidistant from the agent. In such cases, it clearly seems better to pick one person at random than to refrain from throwing the life saver altogether. Or consider a case in which someone receives two equally amazing job offers. Saying that this agent would be forced to turn down both offers because she cannot choose between them appears very unattractive; this kind of paralysis does seem like an imperfection.

Of course, Clarke's views about equipoise cases come at a cost: he cannot accept psychological determinism, nor can he accept a strong or contrastive version of the Principle of Sufficient Reason. After all, he must acknowledge that there is no sufficient reason to choose one of the equally good options rather than another. Even though there is a reason to act—since acting is better than refraining to act—there is no contrastive reason to perform this particular action rather than another, equally good action. In rankable cases, in contrast, there is always a contrastive reason.

How important are Clarke's claims about equipoise cases for his theory of freedom? J.B. Schneewind argues that they are very important because they make it possible for God, and presumably humans, to "have completely free choices that are yet not entirely arbitrary" (1998: 320). Yet, I do not find this compelling. After all, Clarke gives no indication that agents are less free in rankable cases, when they are completely determined by motives. For Clarke, the determination by motives is clearly compatible with the highest degree of freedom. Nor is it obvious how the freedom that agents possess in rankable cases could somehow depend on what happens in equipoise cases. Indeed, it is clear that what makes us free in rankable cases is precisely what makes us free in equipoise cases, namely our activity or capacity for self-motion.[54] Furthermore, one would expect Clarke to mention equipoise cases much more frequently in his extensive discussions of freedom if they were so important to his theory. Yet, he rarely mentions them at all outside of his letters to Leibniz, in which the Principle of Sufficient Reason and the Principle of the Identity of Indiscernibles are important for reasons other than freedom. In fact, in that correspondence, Clarke seems to be motivated more by his desire to defend Newton's theory of space than by anything having to do directly with freedom.

Hence, I contend that Leibniz's and Clarke's disagreement about equipoise cases is at bottom a disagreement about (a) whether the Principle of Sufficient Reason always requires contrastive reasons, and hence rules out choices among equally good options, (b) whether choosing randomly among equally good options is compatible with wisdom and goodness, and (c) whether being unable to choose among equally good options entails passivity. Leibniz affirms (a) and denies (b) and (c); Clarke denies (a) and affirms (b) and (c). Yet, these are not differences in anything that is central to their theories of freedom.

6   Comparison and Conclusion

I hope to have shown that Clarke is not the libertarian that many interpreters think he is. On my interpretation, we should instead classify him as a compatibilist. Yet, his theory is very different from the simple compatibilism of philosophers like Hobbes and Collins. Clarke insists that freedom requires a capacity for self-motion and hence agent causation, which means that free actions cannot be the products of efficient-causal chains. Nevertheless, he is perfectly fine with the determination of free actions by the agent's judgments about the good, as long as this determination does not take the form of an efficient-causal or external determination.

This means that Clarke's theory of freedom is extremely similar to Leibniz's theory, which—as I argued in Sect. 2—has the following five components:

A. Freedom requires spontaneity and agent causation.
B. Freedom requires rationality and control over the passions.
C. Freedom is compatible with a determination by reasons.
D. Freedom requires contingency and an ability to do otherwise.
E. Free agents cannot choose without contrastive sufficient reasons.

Clarke clearly disagrees with Leibniz about (E), as we saw in Sect. 5. Yet, this disagreement does not appear to be a deep disagreement about freedom. Instead it appears to spring from a disagreement about the Principle of Sufficient Reason as well as about the question of whether the ability to choose among equally good options is a perfection and entailed by activity.

Much more significant than Clarke's denial of (E) is the fact that he embraces versions of each of the other four components of Leibniz's theory. As seen in Sect. 3, he agrees with Leibniz about (A): freedom requires agent causation or spontaneity; free agents must start new causal chains and cannot be efficiently caused to act. Moreover, while Clarkean freedom does not generally require rationality and a control over passions, the type of freedom that is necessary for moral agency does, as we also saw in Sect. 3. The fact that Clarke sometimes calls the spontaneity of non-rational animals 'freedom' is merely a terminological difference between him and Leibniz that does not point to any genuine disagreement. This means that, terminology aside, they agree about (B). As seen in Sect. 4, Clarke furthermore agrees with Leibniz about (C): freedom is compatible with a determination by reasons, or a moral necessitation. While Clarke sometimes insists that this is not a genuine determination or necessitation, we saw that this appears to be due to an idiosyncratic understanding of these terms rather than a commitment to a libertarian conception of freedom. According to the definition I provided, Clarke holds that many free actions are determined. After all, he holds that these actions occur because of the agent's reasons or motives. Likewise, he holds that in the specific circumstances of the action, those reasons or motives could not fail to give rise to that specific action without violating the Principle of Sufficient Reason—or, in God's case, without contradicting God's moral attributes. Finally, Clarke and Leibniz agree about (D), as we also saw in Sect. 4: for both authors, freedom requires that agents are physically or metaphysically able to do otherwise; that is, that they are necessitated only by wisdom and goodness, rather than by something brute or independent of their wills and value judgments. This means that Clarke's and Leibniz's theories of freedom are strikingly similar and that both are compatibilist.[55]

Notes

1. Interpreters who interpret Clarke as a libertarian include Vailati (1997: 79); Greenberg (2013: 249); Harris (2005: 50); Yenter (2020). Only after finishing this chapter did I come across the unpublished manuscript "Was Clarke a Voluntarist?" by Lukas Wolf, which argues against the standard interpretation, though not in the way that I do.

2. This idiosyncrasy, in combination with Clarke's claims about equipoise cases, is among the main reasons why many interpreters read Clarke as a libertarian. There are at least two additional reasons, which I will address in this chapter as well: (a) Clarke's insistence on agent causation, which is often assumed to entail libertarianism, and (b) his public arguments against compatibilists like Anthony Collins.

3. Even Leibniz insists that free actions are contingent, or non-necessary, in an important sense. I will say more about that in Sect. 2.

4. It is crucial to remember that compatibilists need not be determinists. Compatibilism is merely the view that it is possible for an action to be free and determined, or that it is possible for there to be freedom in a fully deterministic world. Given what Clarke says about equipoise cases, it seems that he is not a determinist. Nevertheless, he appears to be a compatibilist.

5. See Markosian (2012) for a contemporary case for agent-causal compatibilism.

6. I explain my interpretation in detail in Jorati (2017a: 114–147). For a shorter and less technical summary, see Jorati (2017b).

7. Leibniz states this explicitly in *Theodicy* §288, 1985: 303, among other places.

8. See e.g. *Theodicy* §291, 1985: 304. For a detailed analysis of the different kinds of spontaneity, see Jorati (2015, 2017a: 37–58).

9. Leibniz says something very similar in an essay criticizing William King, which is appended to the *Theodicy*: "When we say that an intelligent substance is moved by the goodness of its object ... [the object's] representation acts in the substance, or rather, the substance acts on itself, insofar as it is disposed and influenced by this representation" (§21, 1985: 428; translation altered). For a more thorough argument in favor of understanding Leibnizian spontaneity as agent causation, see Jorati (2017a: 29–31).

10. This becomes clear, for instance, in *Theodicy* §299, 1985: 303.

11. He discusses this mastery, for example, in *Theodicy* §301, 1985: 310; §337, 1985: 327f. For more on my interpretation of Leibniz's views about mastery over the passions, or rational control, see Jorati (2017a: 149–162).

12. Leibniz says this, for instance, in *Theodicy* §45, 1985: 148; §48, 1985: 150; fifth letter to Clarke §4, 2000: 36. See also my discussion in Jorati

(2017b: 298f). This, of course, is connected to Leibniz's endorsement of the Principle of Sufficient Reason.

13. He says this explicitly in *Theodicy* §288: "infallible determination ... destroy[s] neither freedom nor contingency" (1985: 303). See also §369, 1985: 346.

14. For some passages in which Leibniz discusses moral necessity, see *Theodicy* §174, 1985: 236; §282, 1985: 299; fifth letter to Clarke §7, 2000: 37. See also Jorati (2017a: 126–128).

15. He mentions this in his fifth letter to Clarke §9, 2000: 37. See also Leibniz's essay about William King §14, 1985: 419.

16. He states this, for example, in his fifth letter to Clarke §8, 2000: 37. See my discussion in Jorati (2017a: 124–126).

17. Leibniz explains this at length in his fifth letter to Clarke, §§73–76, 2000: 53f. See my discussion in Jorati (2017a: 129–131).

18. Further evidence for the connection between passivity and necessitation is in *Demonstration* §9, 1998: 46.

19. As Clarke puts it in his review of Collins, "That active Substance, in which the Principle of Self-Motion inheres, is itself the only proper, physical, and immediate *CAUSE* of the Motion or Action; For, that any thing *extrinsick* to the Agent, should be the Mover, or physical Cause of the *Self-Motion*, is a Contradiction in Terms" (1738 vol. 4:728). For a careful explication of the coherence of Clarke's theory of agent causation, see Rowe (1987).

20. For a helpful discussion of Clarke's views about mechanistic causation and Newtonian gravitation, see Wolf (2019).

21. This illustrates that in order to make sense of Clarke's claims that there is no activity among material things, we do not need to interpret him as an occasionalist about the physical world, as some interpreters suggest (e.g. Sangiacomo 2018: 440ff.).

22. See Chappell (2005) for a helpful introduction to the early modern self-determination tradition. Clarke himself sometimes talks of self-determination or the determination of one's own actions; see e.g. 2011: 277 and 1998: 64.

23. This control, of course, need not require indeterminism. It could simply consist in the agent's developing virtuous habits and strengthening their character, such that their inclinations to do what reason demands will reliably be stronger than even the most violent passions.

24. Yenter and Vailati worry that they are incompatible (2018: section 3.2). They interpret the power of self-motion as libertarian, which makes it more difficult to reconcile with the definition from the sermon under discussion. Yet, they also propose, as I am about to, that self-motion might be a necessary condition for the type of freedom described in the sermon.

25. For discussions of why it can be extremely advantageous for determinists or compatibilists to adopt an agent-causal theory of freedom, see Markosian (2012), Jorati (2017a: 117–119), and Jorati (2019: 269f).

26. Saying that something is as impossible as something else may sound odd. Yet, because Clarke acknowledges different types of necessity and possibility—most importantly, physical and moral—this comparison is highly significant. It suggests that the moral necessity that governs divine choices and actions is not modally weaker than an absolute natural necessity.

27. He appears to use the same line of argument in sermon XXXV (1738 vol. 1:220). For a clear expression of Clarke's understanding of the Principle of Sufficient Reason, see his fifth letter to Leibniz (§§124–130, 2000: 86f.).

28. For a relevant example of the latter, see the preface to Anthony Collins's *A Philosophical Inquiry Concerning Human Liberty* (1717: iii). Another example, as already mentioned, is Leibniz. For an example of the former, see Bramhall and Hobbes, "Defence" §28h, 1999: 56.

29. The reference to inclinations is relevant because, as Sven Knebel argues, one of the two major traditions of moral necessitarians ties moral necessity to inclinations (2000: 197ff.).

30. Erin Kelly appears to interpret Clarke's term 'moral necessity' differently, namely as referring to a moral obligation, or to the fact that rational beings ought to act in accordance with their rational judgments (2002: 306).

31. This comes out nicely in Clarke's fifth letter to Leibniz, in which he explicates moral necessity as the thesis that "a good being continuing to be good cannot do evil, or a wise being continuing to be wise cannot act unwisely, or a veracious person continuing to be veracious cannot tell a lie" (§§4–13, 2000: 67). If a good being did something evil, it would thereby cease to be good. Hence, it is impossible for God, who cannot cease being good, to do evil.

32. In a letter to Bulkeley, Clarke explains that natural attributes are attributes that "have no dependence on [God's] will or power of acting" (1998: 128).

33. William Rowe argues that this attempt to safeguard God's power to do otherwise ultimately fails because God's choosing to do what is incompatible with his moral attributes is logically impossible (2004: 29f.; Harris [2005: 52] voices a similar worry). Thus, Rowe concludes, Clarke is unable to reconcile divine freedom with this type of necessitation (2004: 30). My own assessment is that Rowe would be right about this if Clarke were trying to make room for libertarian freedom, as Rowe assumes. Yet, if my compatibilist interpretation is correct, Clarke's solution makes perfect sense: the distinction between what God must do (or is unable to do) because of his moral attributes, and what God must do (or is unable to do) because of his natural attributes can be important for freedom even if there is ultimately no modal difference between them. For instance, as Clarke himself points out, this distinction is important for moral praiseworthiness (sermon XI, 1998: 142; sermon XXXV, 1738 vol. 1:220; letter to Bulkeley, 1998: 128): it does not make sense to praise or thank God for being eternal; but it does make sense to praise or thank God for being merciful. After all, the latter is determined by God's goodness and hence has to do with God's moral character and his will, whereas the former is not.

34. For an early modern usage of this distinction, see Bramhall, "Discourse" §4 in Bramhall and Hobbes (1999: 1).

35. For an expression of this type of view, see Bramhall, "Discourse" §4 and §19, in Bramhall and Hobbes (1999: 1 and 9).

36. That appears to be Andrea Sangiacomo's interpretation, even though he uses a different terminology (2018: 431–433).

37. Interestingly, Clarke states in a sermon that the biblical claim that good men cannot sin means "their having their *Liberty so perfect*, in Imitation of God, as (abating the unavoidable infirmities of human Nature) to be in *no danger* of being biassed or seduced" (sermon XXXV, 1738 vol. 1:220). This confirms that in the absence of temptations or faulty judgments, human beings must do what is best.

38. It might be relevant in this context that there is precedent for describing the influence of motives or final causes as a metaphorical influence; see e.g. Bramhall, "Defence" §20o: "the end draws the will to it by a metaphorical motion" (Bramhall and Hobbes 1999: 58). The claim that final

causes exert their influence through a metaphorical motion is also found in the influential sixteenth-century philosopher Francisco Suárez (e.g. *Disputationes Metaphysicae* 23.4.8, 1861: 861).

39. This is important because it shows that Clarke's moral necessity is not the same as what some early modern authors call 'moral certainty', which is not an absolute certainty.

40. My interpretation also has the advantage of making good sense of Clarke's claim that agency cannot be necessitated. If we fail to see that Clarke is using 'necessitation' in a non-standard way, his claim looks extremely question-begging, as some interpreters think it is (e.g. Vailati 1997: 81).

41. Clarke says something similar elsewhere in the same text: "every *Necessary Agent* is *moved necessarily* by something else; and then *that which moves* it, not the *thing itself which is moved*, is the *true and only Cause* of the Action" (1738 vol. 4:734).

42. In *Demonstration*, in a different context, he phrases this axiom as follows: "it is impossible that any effect should have any perfection which was not in the cause" (§8, 1998: 39).

43. Clarke describes the last judgment of the intellect as passive, among other places, in a letter to Bulkeley (1998: 128) and in his fifth letter to Leibniz (§§1–20, 2000: 66).

44. See also the fifth letter to Leibniz, which states that "The doing of anything, *upon and after or in consequence of* that perception, is the power of self-motion or action" (§§1–20, 2000: 66; emphasis mine).

45. For more on how agent-causal views can handle reasons, see Griffith (2017: 75–76).

46. Bramhall says something similar about the relation between external things and the will: "outward objects … have no natural efficacy to determine the will. Well may they be occasions, but they cannot be causes of evil" (*Defence* §14d, in Bramhall and Hobbes 1999: 52).

47. They cannot be efficient causes of God's activity because, among other reasons, it is theologically problematic to portray God as passive, or acted upon.

48. Or, more precisely, he is clearly not an occasionalist about free human actions. At least one interpreter argues that he is an occasionalist with respect to causation among material things (Sangiacomo 2018: 440ff.). That issue, however, is irrelevant for the purposes of this chapter.

49. See also my discussion of occasional causation in Emilie du Châtelet, who appears to have been strongly influenced by Clarke's theory of freedom (Jorati 2019: 266–268).

50. As already noted, Clarke accepts the axiom that "it is impossible that any effect should have any perfection which was not in the cause" (*Demonstration* §8, 1998: 39; similarly in review of Collins, 1998: 134). In these passages, he is arguably talking about efficient causation.

51. Some interpreters appear to assume that invoking occasional causation entails occasionalism, and are hence puzzled by Clarke's talk of occasions; see e.g. Vailati (1997: 94).

52. Clarke might be hinting at this in his review of Collins with respect to occasional causation: a judgment may be "An *occasion* [of the action], … and action may be consequent (though without any physical connection) upon perception and judgment; nay, it may easily (if you please) be supposed to be *always* consequent upon it" (review of Collins, 1998: 134).

53. His reference to 'external' causes appears connected to his claim that in equipoise cases, the sufficient reason to pursue one of the equally good courses of action can be the agent's own will (e.g. second letter to Leibniz, §1, 2000: 11). As he puts it earlier in the third letter, "in things indifferent in their own nature, mere will, without anything external to influence it, is alone that sufficient reason" (§2, 2000: 18). Hence, 'external' might refer either to factors external to the will, such as reasons perceived by the intellect, or to differences among the objects of choice. The latter would fit with Clarke's claim in the fifth letter that in one sense, motives are extrinsic to the mind because they are real entities in the world that we perceive; in another sense, they are our perceptions of those extrinsic objects, and hence intrinsic (§§1–20, 2000: 66).

54. As just seen, Clarke holds that this activity entails that we can choose any option in equipoise cases and that the only alternative is an extrinsic, quasi-mechanical determination. Yet, he appears to be mistaken in this respect. As Leibniz's theory of freedom shows, it is perfectly consistent to view free agents as active agent-causes of their actions, and to view them as unable to act in equipoise cases.

55. This chapter has benefited immensely from discussions with the participants of the LSNA/SELLF Congress at the University of Montréal in 2018 and the virtual Early Modern work-in-progress workshop in May 2020. I also thank Stephan Schmid, Andrea Sangiacomo, Lukas Wolf, and Ruth Boeker for extremely helpful written feedback on an earlier draft.

References

Bramhall, John, and Thomas Hobbes. 1999. *Hobbes and Bramhall on Liberty and Necessity*, ed. Vere Chappell. Cambridge: Cambridge University Press.

Carriero, John. 2008. Substance and Ends in Leibniz. In *Contemporary Perspectives on Early Modern Philosophy: Essays in Honor of Vere Chappell*, ed. Paul Hoffman, David Owen, and Gideon Yaffe, 115–140. Peterborough: Broadview Press.

Chappell, Vere. 2005. Self-Determination. In *Early Modern Philosophy: Mind, Matter, and Metaphysics*, ed. Christia Mercer and Eileen O'Neill, 127–141. Oxford: Oxford University Press.

Clarke, Samuel. 1738. *The Works of Samuel Clarke*. 4 vols. Ed. B. Hoadly. London: Knapton.

———. 1998. *A Demonstration of the Being and Attributes of God and Other Writings*, ed. Ezio Vailati. Cambridge: Cambridge University Press.

———. 2000. Letters to Leibniz. In *Correspondence*, ed. Roger Ariew. Indianapolis: Hackett.

———. 2011. *The Correspondence of Samuel Clarke and Anthony Collins, 1707–08*, ed. William L. Uzgalis. Toronto: Broadview.

Collins, Anthony. 1717. *A Philosophical Inquiry Concerning Human Liberty*. 2nd ed. London: Robinson.

Greenberg, Sean. 2013. Liberty and Necessity. In *The Oxford Handbook of British Philosophy in the Eighteenth Century*, ed. James A. Harris, 171–193. Oxford: Oxford University Press.

Griffith, Meghan. 2017. Agent Causation. In *The Routledge Companion to Free Will*, ed. Kevin Timpe, Meghan Griffith, and Neil Levy, 72–85. New York: Routledge.

Harris, James A. 2005. *Of Liberty and Necessity: The Free Will Debate in Eighteenth-Century British Philosophy*. Oxford: Clarendon Press.

Jorati, Julia. 2015. Three Types of Spontaneity and Teleology in Leibniz. *Journal of the History of Philosophy* 53 (4): 669–698.

———. 2017a. *Leibniz on Causation and Agency*. Cambridge: Cambridge University Press.

———. 2017b. Gottfried Leibniz [on Free Will]. In *The Routledge Companion to Free Will*, ed. Kevin Timpe, Meghan Griffith, and Neil Levy, 293–302. New York: Routledge.

———. 2019. Du Châtelet on Freedom, Self-Motion, and Moral Necessity. *Journal of the History of Philosophy* 57 (2): 255–280.

Kelly, Erin. 2002. Moral Agency and Free Choice: Clarke's Unlikely Success Against Hume. *Archiv für Geschichte der Philosophie* 84 (3): 297–318.

Knebel, Sven K. 2000. *Wille, Würfel und Wahrscheinlichkeit: Das System der moralischen Notwendigkeit in der Jesuitenscholastik 1550–1700*. Hamburg: Meiner.

Leibniz, Gottfried Wilhelm. 1985. *Theodicy*. Trans. E. M. Huggard. La Salle: Open Court.

———. 2000. Letters to Clarke. In *Correspondence*, ed. Roger Ariew. Indianapolis: Hackett.

Markosian, Ned. 2012. Agent Causation as the Solution to All the Compatibilist's Problems. *Philosophical Studies* 157: 383–398.

Nadler, Steven. 2011. *Occasionalism: Causation Among the Cartesians*. Oxford: Oxford University Press.

Rowe, William L. 1987. Causality and Free Will in the Controversy Between Collins and Clarke. *The Journal of the History of Philosophy* 25: 51–67.

———. 2004. *Can God Be Free?* Oxford: Oxford University Press.

Sangiacomo, Andrea. 2018. Samuel Clarke on Agent Causation, Voluntarism, and Occasionalism. *Science in Context* 31 (4): 421–456.

Schneewind, J[erome] B. 1998. *The Invention of Autonomy: A History of Modern Moral Philosophy*. Cambridge: Cambridge University Press.

Suárez, Francisco. 1861. *Opera Omnia*. Vol. 25. Paris: Vivès.

Vailati, Ezio. 1997. *Leibniz and Clarke: A Study of their Correspondence*. New York: Oxford University Press.

Wolf, Lukas. 2019. Clarke's Rejection of Superadded Gravity in the Clarke-Collins Correspondence. *History of Philosophy Quarterly* 36 (3): 237–255.

Yenter, Timothy. 2020. Clarke, Samuel. In *Encyclopedia of Early Modern Philosophy and the Sciences*, ed. Dana Jalobeanu and Charles T. Wolfe. Cham: Springer.

Yenter, Timothy, and Ezio Vailati. 2018. Samuel Clarke. *The Stanford Encyclopedia of Philosophy*. Ed. Edward N. Zalta. https://plato.stanford.edu/archives/fall2018/entries/clarke/.

Part II

Free Will and Indeterminism

9

Indeterministic Compatibilism

Carolina Sartorio

1   Introduction

Free will compatibilists are typically focused on arguing that the truth of determinism would not undermine our freedom and responsibility. Most compatibilists also think, however, that the truth of determinism is not *required* for free will—in other words, they think that the truth of indeterminism is compatible with free will too. Unsurprisingly, given compatibilism's main aim, little work has been done on this aspect of compatibilism.[1] Still, it is important to think about this, if one is interested in developing a view of free will that doesn't hinge on determinism being actually true or false—and I am one of those compatibilists.

In this chapter, I will look at this issue from the perspective of a compatibilist view that I have developed and defended elsewhere (Sartorio 2016): a view where the type of freedom or control required by responsibility is accounted for in terms of responsiveness to reasons, and where

C. Sartorio (✉)
University of Arizona, Tucson, AZ, USA
e-mail: sartorio@arizona.edu

responsiveness to reasons is in turn a feature that is directly reflected in the causal histories of our behavior. Thus, this is a view according to which acting freely is a matter of our acts having the right kinds of causes, and it is a form of compatibilism because the right kinds of causes can be deterministic. Now, under the assumption that our acts fail to be determined, the causal histories of our acts will be, at least partly, indeterministic. An examination of the compatibility of this view with indeterminism will then lead us into a discussion of how our free will could be grounded in causes that are not fully sufficient for their effects, as well as into the intriguing nature of indeterministic causation.

In the first part of the chapter I will argue that, assuming this compatibilist view of free will, indeterminism does not constitute an obstacle to our freedom and responsibility. What is important, on this view, is the existence of causal histories that are rich or robust enough to ground our reasons-responsiveness, but not in a sense that requires them to be deterministic. Still, as we will see, the assumption of indeterminism gives rise to some novel and interesting questions. The second part of the chapter will be concerned with motivating and discussing those questions.

One issue that I cannot take up in this chapter is the question of whether there is a (potentially new and worrisome) problem of luck that may arise for compatibilists as a result of the application to indeterministic contexts. This is an important issue that I cannot get into here, since it would require its own extended treatment. My main focus will instead be on the more basic or fundamental issue of how compatibilist views could be applied to indeterministic contexts, and the special questions that arise at that earlier stage.

2   The Compatibility of Compatibilism with Indeterminism

I will illustrate with an example of a kind analyzed in detail by Kane (1996, chapter 8), an incompatibilist (and libertarian) about free will, one that involves "self-forming" or will-setting acts. Imagine that at a certain point in your life you are forced to choose between satisfying your own self-interested goals and providing needed assistance to someone else. Imagine, for example, that you are on your way to a very important meeting, one that is likely to advance your career in significant ways, when you see a wounded man who needs your immediate assistance. If you stop to help him, you won't make it to your meeting on time, and you will miss the only chance you have (and will likely have in years) to advance your career in the way you wanted and you think you deserve. On the other hand, if you don't stop to help the wounded man, you have reason to believe that, although he will survive, his wounds might get infected, which could result in complications for his long-term health. So, this is a case where you have strong reasons to do the selfish thing (continue on to your meeting) and also strong reasons to do the selfless thing (help the man).[2] We are to imagine that, given those compelling reasons pulling in opposite directions, you feel very torn about what to do. But, regardless of what you end up deciding to do, this is an important decision that will help shape your future character in significant ways (by turning you into a more selfish or selfless person, say); hence the label "self-forming." Moreover, we are to imagine that your decision is causally undetermined, so it is in fact compatible with the past and the laws of nature that you will make either decision.

Call this case *Choice*. Kane argued that, if there are instances during our life stories where we make important decisions of this kind, then those self-forming choices can constitute the locus of our free will (Kane 1996). But, Kane argued, it is crucial that these be causally undetermined decisions, since this is the only way in which we can be the ultimate originators or ultimate sources of our wills, which he thinks is a fundamental requirement for acting freely. Thus, according to Kane, your decision in *Choice* can be made freely to the extent that you make that decision voluntarily and rationally, or on the basis of compelling reasons, and to the extent that it fails to be causally determined.

The details of Kane's view are not important for our purposes here. The reason I will focus on a case like *Choice* is that, despite being an indeterministic case, by design it has the potential for meeting the conditions for free action set out by the compatibilist view that I am assuming here. And this is regardless of what you end up deciding to do. If you decide to stop to help the man, then you do it for reasons, and those reasons are arguably part of the causal history of your act, even if that causal history is indeterministic. Similarly, if you decide not to stop to help the man, you also do it for reasons, and those reasons, again, are arguably part of the causal history of your act, even if the causal history is indeterministic. In fact, examples like *Choice* are of special interest because they suggest that there can be instances where, although it is genuinely undetermined *what* we will do (say, whether we will do A or B instead), we act freely regardless of what we do (if we do A or if we do B)—roughly, because we are acting for reasons either way. (This is also Kane's own position on this, although he would add that the fact that your choice was undetermined was, in addition, a requirement for you to have free will.[3])

Now, things are in fact more complicated than this because being reasons-responsive in the sense required to act freely and to be responsible is not simply a matter of acting for the *actual* reasons that you had. This is too simplistic, for it would entail that someone who acts for reasons automatically acts freely, which is clearly false. For example, a compulsive behavior can be done for reasons (say, to satisfy an irresistible urge) but it is not free. Compulsive behaviors are not free because they are not reasons-responsive in the relevant sense.

At this point, different reasons-responsiveness views give different accounts of how compulsive and other unfree behaviors come apart from free behaviors. But the common strategy used by reasons-responsiveness views is, roughly, to expand the set or pattern of reasons to which one has to be sensitive in order to be sufficiently reasons-responsive. On the view that I favor, one has to look at the role played by, in addition to the actual reasons, the *absence* of various other (counterfactual) reasons. In a nutshell, and simplifying quite a bit, the view can be stated as follows:

Causal Reasons-Responsive Compatibilism (CRRC): Reasons-responsiveness is causal sensitivity to an appropriate range of reasons and absences of reasons, one that includes *actual* reasons to do what you are doing as well as the *absence of* (counterfactual) sufficient reasons to refrain from doing what you are doing.[4]

Very roughly, the idea is this. Imagine that you decide not to help the wounded man in *Choice* on the basis of the selfish reasons. The thought is that, if you do this freely (not, e.g., as a result of some irresistible compulsion to act selfishly), then in making that choice you are also responding or being causally sensitive to the absence of a range of sufficient reasons to do otherwise (reasons to help the man). Imagine, for example, that you would have stopped to help the man if you had reason to believe that others were watching (you care very much about what others think about you). Or imagine that you would have stopped to help the man if you had been informed of the existence of a substantial financial reward for doing so, one that would help you and your family immensely. And so on. In fact, conditions like these didn't obtain. But the point is that we can account for the fact that you acted freely (and not, for example, compulsively) by thinking about the role played by the absence of reasons of this kind in an explanation of your behavior. Given that you were not acting compulsively and you were disposed to act differently if conditions of that kind had been present, part of the explanation of your actual behavior seems to be that such conditions did not in fact obtain. This suggests that free behaviors are behaviors whose causal histories are quite rich in that they include, in addition to the actual reasons, the absence of several other (counterfactual) reasons. And it is in this way that free behaviors differ from unfree behaviors such as things that we may do compulsively.[5]

Although CRRC is a compatibilist view of free will, and this means that the causal histories in question can be deterministic, they don't in fact need to be deterministic. According to CRRC, the difference between free and non-free behaviors amounts to a difference in the content of the causal histories of those behaviors; it does *not* amount to a difference in the type of causal relation that ties those contents (the causes of the behaviors) to the behaviors. For example, even if the past and the laws didn't guarantee that you would make the selfish choice in *Choice*, if you do end up making that choice and your choice is indeterministically caused by an appropriate range of actual reasons and absences of counterfactual reasons, your choice is free, according to CRRC.

The easiest way to see that free will is compatible with indeterminism according to CRRC is by focusing on a simple version of *Choice*, which I will call *Choice 1*, and to which I already alluded above (I discuss other more complex variants later in the chapter). Imagine, again, that you decide not to help the man on the basis of the selfish reasons, and that this choice was undetermined by the past and the laws. Also, imagine that you are psychologically constituted in such a way that, if others had been watching or if there had been a substantial financial reward for helping the man, then you *would* have chosen to help him. (That is, I am assuming that this is a *deterministic* relation: if either of those conditions had obtained, then the chance that you'd decide to help the man in those circumstances would have been 1.) In that case it seems clear that the absence of reasons of that kind is part of what accounts for your choice to not help the man in the actual scenario—that is, those absences of reasons are part of the causal history of your choice. As a result, CRRC entails that you were responding to reasons in the relevant sense when you made the choice and, thus, that you acted freely.

But notice that all of this is consistent with the initial assumption that the causal history of your choice was indeterministic. For the past and the laws didn't have to guarantee that you would choose to do the selfish thing in the actual conditions, where those other reasons were not present (we may still assume that the past and the laws were compatible with your making the opposite choice). Thus, CRRC entails that you acted freely in *Choice 1*, even if the causal history of your choice was indeterministic.

We can imagine a similar variant of the case where you make the opposite choice (you choose to help the man). Imagine, for example, that you wouldn't have made that choice (i.e. the chance of your making that choice would have been null) if you had reason to believe that your spouse would divorce you, or that your whole family will be ruined as a result of your missing the only chance you had to advance your career. Then the causal history of your choice would include the absence of facts like these. As a result, you would be reasons-responsive, according to CRRC. And, again, this is so even if the causal history of your choice was indeterministic—even if those reasons and absences of reasons, in conjunction with any other causes of the choice, did not guarantee that you would act selflessly.

This strongly supports the compatibility of CRRC with indeterminism. If acting freely is a matter of having the right kind of actual causal history, one including the relevant combination of reasons and absences of reasons, then acting freely is in fact consistent with the causal histories of our acts not being deterministic.

Now, all of this works only under certain assumptions about the nature of causation—and, in particular, indeterministic causation—which I have been implicitly taking to be true. More discussion of these assumptions would be helpful. Also, it's not clear what would happen if one tried to generalize to other cases that have a more complex structure than *Choice 1*. I take these issues up, in turn, in the following two sections.

3   Indeterministic Causation and Probability-Raising

One assumption I have obviously been relying on is that causation *can* be indeterministic: causes needn't be sufficient for their effects (even when we take the "whole cause" of an effect, or the combination of all the factors that causally contributed to it). This assumption is widely accepted nowadays.[6] And this isn't something that we can only conceive happening at the microscopic or quantum level, where the possibility of indeterminism being real usually comes up. If a terrorist manages to build an indeterministic bomb (one that has a chance smaller than 1 of going off) and the bomb actually goes off, the terrorist causes the explosion, even if the explosion wasn't causally necessitated by the terrorist's act in conjunction with anything else.[7] Surely, events like this still have causes, even if they are not sufficient causes. Plus, it is easy to see how indeterministic causal relations of this kind could potentially ground the responsibility of agents. For example, if the terrorist is morally responsible for the explosion, his responsibility would be partly grounded in the fact that he caused the explosion to happen, even if he didn't guarantee that it would happen.

But how are we to make sense of indeterministic causation? A natural and quite popular way to think about it is in terms of objective probabilities (or chances) and, in particular, in terms of the idea of *probability-raising*.[8] The main motivation behind this thought is that, even if indeterministic causes don't guarantee the occurrence of their effects, they can still make them more likely to occur (than if they had been absent). In light of this, they can make a contribution to the occurrence of those effects, by virtue of having raised the probability of their occurrence, *when* and *if* they occur. (Of course, if the effects don't come about, as it's bound to happen in some cases, then there is no such causation simply because causation is factive and the effects did not in fact occur.)

Understanding indeterministic causation in terms of probability-raising can help us see, for example, how causes can bring about their effects even in cases where the effects had only a small chance of occurring. Imagine that it was much more probable, given the past and the laws, that you would help the man in *Choice* than that you would not. Imagine, for example, that this time the chances were 0.9 and 0.1, respectively, but you still decided to do the unlikely thing, the selfish thing, on the basis of the same set of reasons (and thus, we would like to say, freely).[9] An account in terms of probability-raising can explain how those reasons caused your choice even if the event of your making that choice was highly unlikely. For example, the selfish reasons may have raised the chance of your making the selfish choice from 0 to 0.1, if the choice had no chance at all of occurring in the absence of those reasons (because you wouldn't have at all been motivated not to help the man if you didn't have a very important meeting to attend, one with potentially life-changing implications). In that case it is clear that the reasons caused the choice.

Now, accounts of indeterministic causation in terms of probability-raising face important challenges. This is not the place to review them all.[10] For now I will just touch on one of them that is relevant for my purposes here. It is the problem posed by certain kinds of *preemption* cases (Lewis 1986: 179). Imagine that Suzy, an unreliable terrorist, and Billy, a reliable terrorist, are simultaneously trying to make a bomb go off. They each do this by throwing a switch that is part of a mechanism that is hooked up to the bomb; however, whereas Suzy's mechanism is very unreliable (it only has a 0.1 chance of success), Billy's mechanism is very reliable (it has a 0.9 chance of success). Imagine that Suzy's and Billy's mechanisms are also connected with each other in such a way that, when Suzy throws her switch, it shuts off Billy's reliable mechanism at the same time that it starts its own unreliable process. Imagine that, despite this, the unlikely happens and the bomb still goes off. This case threatens to undermine the idea that indeterministic causation can be understood in terms of probability-raising. For notice that Suzy's throwing her switch doesn't raise, but instead considerably lowers, the probability of the bomb going off; however, it still clearly causes that outcome. The unreliable process started by Suzy *preempts* the reliable process started by Billy, and thus it (and not Billy's process) causes the explosion, despite having made the explosion less probable.

Causation theorists have tried to deal with this problem in different ways. One main strategy has been to tinker with the probability-raising requirement in a way that unreliable preempting causes like Suzy end up being probability-raisers, in the relevant sense. One way to do this is to understand the probability-raising requirement as claiming that, when there is more than one potential causal route or path to an outcome, in assessing whether an event raises the probability of the outcome, one must hold fixed facts involving the other potential paths. In other words, the relevant sense of probability-raising is in an important way path-specific, or restricted to a particular causal pathway.[11] This way of understanding the probability-raising requirement yields the desired result in the preemption case. For, holding fixed the fact that Billy's process is no longer active after a certain time, Suzy's act of throwing the switch does raise the probability of the outcome (because Suzy's process is the only active process that could potentially lead to it). But not everybody would agree that this type of strategy fully addresses the problem, and this (as other challenges that arise for the probability-raising view) is still an issue of much debate.

The reason this is relevant for our purposes here is that we can easily imagine a kind of preemptive structure underlying cases like *Choice*, one that mimics other cases widely discussed in the free will literature ("Frankfurt-style" cases, originally from Frankfurt 1969). Imagine, again, that the chance that you would help the man is much higher than the chance that you would do the selfish thing, say, 0.9 versus 0.1. Now add a preempted alternative involving a resourceful and evil neuroscientist. Imagine that the neuroscientist wanted you to do the selfish thing, so earlier in the day he installed a chip in your brain that started a process that deterministically guarantees that you will do the selfish thing, by causing you to make the selfish choice, but only if the (unreliable) indeterministic process started by your own selfish reasons doesn't do it on its own.[12] Imagine that the unlikely happens, and you decide to do the selfish thing on your own, on the basis of the selfish reasons. So, again, the unreliable process preempts the reliable process (which in this case is a completely reliable or fully deterministic process). Your selfish reasons caused your choice even if they didn't raise the probability of that choice. In fact, in this case, the chance that you would make the choice was already 1 by the time you considered those reasons, so the reasons clearly couldn't have raised that chance any further. Call this case *Frankfurt-style Choice*.

The CRRC account of free will would say that all that matters to your freedom is the actual causes of your behavior. So, if your choice is caused by your own deliberation and selfish reasons, and not by the process started by the neuroscientist, then you act freely in *Frankfurt-style Choice* (and this is despite the fact that you couldn't have done otherwise). Moreover, views like CRRC are typically *motivated* by intuitions about Frankfurt-style examples. For those examples are taken to show that all that matters to freedom is actual causal histories, or actual explanations of behavior, and not something like having alternative possibilities of action or being able to do otherwise. Thus, the thought that an agent in a Frankfurt-style case is responsible for his choice because he made the choice for his own reasons, or because his own reasons caused the choice, is central to a view like CRRC. If this causal claim couldn't be sufficiently supported, then this would be a serious blow to the view. But, as we have just seen, it seems that we cannot substantiate such a causal claim by appealing to a probability-raising view of indeterministic causation, which is the most natural way to try to understand that form of causation.

However, this isn't a problem for the CRRC view. For, as we have also seen, this is a problem that probability-raising views have with preemption cases in general. And it is a problem for those views precisely because it seems clear what the causal structure of those cases is, and the probability-raising view has trouble accommodating it. The apparent failure of those views does not make us doubt the causal structure of such cases; if anything, it's the other way around: the causal structure of the cases makes us doubt the truth of those views (or to look for refinements). In this respect, the preemption problem that arises for probability-raising views of indeterministic causation is just like the preemption problem that arises for most reductive views of *deterministic* causation (which is, in and of itself, a big problem).[13] In both cases, they are problems because the views don't seem able to accommodate the causal facts, which we take to be clear (or clear enough).

To conclude this section, the main assumption that underlies the extension of the compatibilistic view to indeterministic settings is just this: there can be indeterministic causation, and, in particular, there can be indeterministic causal processes that have the potential to ground our reasons-responsiveness. In this section I argued that this assumption is not undermined by worries concerning the prospects of a probability-raising account of causation, or, in general, by any uncertainty concerning the underlying metaphysics.

4   Indeterminism, Causal Underdetermination, and Causal Indeterminacy

Still, indeterminism raises some interesting new questions. To establish the compatibility point all we needed was the simplest case of a certain kind, *Choice 1*. Recall that a feature of that case was that, although the causal history of the choice was in fact indeterministic, there were other (counterfactual) relations that I assumed to be deterministic. In particular, I was assuming that, had certain sufficient reasons to do otherwise been present, then you would have done otherwise (it was deterministically guaranteed that you would). You actually chose to do the selfish thing, and this was not determined, but, had other people been watching or had there been a substantial financial reward for helping the man, then you would have helped the man (the chance of your helping the man would have been 1). The reason I focused on that case is that, under those assumptions, it seems perfectly clear that the absence of those reasons partly accounts for your actual choice, and thus it is easy to see that you are reasons-responsive, according to a view like CRRC.

But, of course, this isn't the most natural case to consider under the assumption of indeterminism. What if those chances would not have been 1, but some number in between 0 and 1? That is to say, what if there is some chance, but not a full guarantee, that you would have responded to those reasons if they had been present? Are you reasons-responsive in that case? Call this new version of the case *Choice 2*.

CRRC would say that you are reasons-responsive in *Choice 2* to the extent that those absences of reasons still caused your choice. But, *did* those absences of reasons cause your choice in this case? Here matters are much less clear than before. Imagine, for example, that the chance of your choosing to do the selfish thing on the basis of the selfish reasons was 0.5, and so was the chance of choosing to help the man on the basis of the selfless reasons. Imagine that you actually chose to do the selfish thing. Moreover, imagine that, had other people been watching, then the chance of your helping the man would have been higher (say, 0.7 instead of 0.5) and your chance of doing the selfish thing lower (0.3 instead of 0.5). In these conditions, did the absence of that reason actually cause your choice? Did the fact that nobody was watching causally contribute to your choosing to do the selfish thing?

Note that a probability-raising account of indeterministic causation would entail that such a causal connection exists. For the fact that nobody was watching raised the probability that you would choose to do the selfish thing (it was more likely that you would do the selfish thing given that nobody was watching than if someone had been watching). Plus, you in fact did the selfish thing.

However, there is reason to be wary here. For one, as we have seen, we shouldn't blindly trust everything that a probabilistic account says. But, also, people's judgments are likely to be less clear at this point. Some would agree with the judgment entailed by the probabilistic account. But others would disagree. Instead, they would suggest that there are *two* distinct possibilities that are compatible with the setup of the case: one where there is a causal connection of the kind we were imagining and one where there is not. And the probabilities don't settle which possibility is the actual one.

This is sometimes called the problem of *underdetermination* (for reductive theories of causation), and it has been discussed in the causation literature as part of an argument for primitivism about causation. Basically, the thought is that probability-raising examples can be used to show that the non-causal facts underdetermine the causal facts. The causal facts are primitive in that they are not reducible to other facts—in particular, they are not reducible to probabilities or probability-raising. All we can say in underdetermined cases is that it is possible that a certain causal relation exists and also possible that it doesn't, or how likely it is that there is one and how it likely it is that there isn't one.

Consider, as another example to motivate this, the following scenario discussed by Schaffer: Two sorcerers, Merlin and Morgana, simultaneously cast spells with a 0.5 chance of turning the prince into a frog. Each spell has an independent 0.5 chance of succeeding. If the prince turns into a frog, who caused it to turn into a frog? Call this case *M&M*.[14]

In magic-involving cases like *M&M* it is assumed that, when spells work, they work directly (not through any intermediate events). This is important because it means that we cannot hope to establish which spell was the cause by looking for causal intermediaries or their absence; *all* we have is the probabilities. In light of this, a probability-raising account would simply entail that Merlin and Morgan are both causes because both of them were probability-raisers. But somebody with primitivist leanings would protest that there are in fact *three* distinct possibilities in this case: either Merlin is a cause, or only Morgana is a cause, or both are causes. And there are no non-causal facts about the situation that determine which is the actual scenario. Again, the causal facts are brute: they are what they are, and they cannot be reduced to non-causal facts (in particular, probabilities).

Now, note that *Choice 2* is relevantly like *M&M* in that all we have to go by is the relevant probabilities. If, for example, the absence of other people watching is indeed a cause of your choice, then this is an instance of absence causation. As a result, there won't be an ordinary process linking cause and effect via intermediate events. When there is absence causation, it works "directly" or without any causal intermediaries.[15] This is why the cases are equally prone to eliciting primitivist intuitions about causation.

In turn, other philosophers with reductivist leanings would counterargue that this results in unacceptable metaphysical burdens. It commits us to causal differences that "float free" in that they are not grounded in any other feature of the world. Moreover, they would argue, the primitivist intuitions elicited by these kinds of cases can be explained away. Lewis (1986: 180-3) tries to explain them away by arguing that they are the result of not taking genuine indeterministic chances seriously, and thus of assuming that there are features of the world that remain hidden from us when we give the probabilistic descriptions of the cases. In turn, Schaffer (2008: 89) argues that we can explain away the primitivist intuitions by attributing them to errors of reification (mistaking mere concepts for real things). Given that we have the concepts needed to describe the different causal possibilities, we tend to think that they are real possibilities when in fact they aren't.

So, what would the reductivist say about the causal structure of these cases? Lewis sticks to his guns and says that whenever an event C raises the chance of another event E that actually occurs, it automatically follows that C is a cause of E (Lewis 1986: 180). In other words, probability-raising is sufficient for causing, at least when the effect actually occurs.[16] It follows that, in *M&M*, both spells caused the enchantment, and, in *Choice 2*, the fact that nobody was watching caused your choice to do the selfish thing.

Schaffer (2008) would agree with Lewis about these specific causal judgments. But, as he notes elsewhere, the view that probability-raising is sufficient for causation needs further refinement (Schaffer 2000). Schaffer asks us to consider the following "overlapping" variant on the *M&M* case, which we may call *Overlapping M&M*: Merlin casts a spell with a 0.5 chance of turning the *king and prince* into frogs. Morgana casts a spell with a (probabilistically independent) 0.5 chance of turning the *prince and queen* into frogs. As it happens, the king and prince, but not the queen, turn into frogs. Now consider the actual event of the *prince* turning into a frog. Schaffer asks: What caused that event? Clearly, it was Merlin's spell and not Morgana's. However, Morgana's spell also raised the probability of that event happening. So, raising the probability is not sufficient for causing an actual event. The reductivist story in terms of probability-raising needs further refinement.

Schaffer also notes that the reductivist story may have to include the possibility of causal indetermination in order to account for the structure of some special cases. Imagine yet another variant on the *M&M* case (taken from Schaffer 2000: n. 21), which we may call *Enhanced M&M*. Simply add to the description of the *M&M* case that, when more than one spell works, the effect is enhanced, say, the prince-turned-into-frog becomes extra-green. Imagine that this time the enhanced effect does not obtain. So, we know that this isn't an overdetermination case where both spells were causes. In this case the primitivist would say that either Merlin or Morgana caused the effect and it's a brute fact who did. But the reductivist will have to say that it is indeterminate who did: there is simply no fact of the matter.[17]

As suggested by the brief discussion above, this is a lively and ongoing controversy. I think it is fair to say that there is no consensus on what the causal facts are in these cases. But note that there is also quite a bit of uncertainty about the *responsibility* facts themselves. Are you, in *Choice 2*, responsible for making the selfish choice?

This is much less obvious than in *Choice 1*. In *Choice 1*, it was perfectly clear that you were reasons-responsive because it was perfectly clear that the relevant absences of reasons causally contributed to your choice (and thus that you were not acting compulsively, for example). But, in *Choice 2*, all of this is less clear. If all we can say is that you *might* have responded to the sufficient reasons to help the man, or that the probability that you would help the man would have been *higher* than it would have been otherwise, without being a full guarantee, is this enough to satisfy the reasons-responsiveness requirement? This doesn't seem obvious one way or the other.

Now, those with reductivist leanings about indeterministic causation should probably say that it is. For, again, given that those absences of reasons considerably raised the probability of your making the selfish choice, and given that you actually made the selfish choice, it follows from the probability-raising account that those absences of reasons caused your actual choice. After all, this is basically what indeterministic causation *is*, on these kinds of views. If that is the case, then you are reasons-responsive, and thus responsible, in *Choice 2*.

On the other hand, those with primitivist leanings would say that there are two distinct possibilities consistent with the setup of the case: one where the absences of reasons caused the choice and one where they didn't. The former possibility would make you reasons-responsive but the latter would not. And it is a brute fact which of these possibilities is the actual one. Hence, although there is a fact of the matter about which possibility is in fact actualized, we don't know (and in principle cannot know) what it is. As a result, we don't know (and in principle cannot know) if you are indeed responsible in *Choice 2*.

In sum, in this case it is much less clear that you are responsible, and this is because the underlying causal facts are less clear. Even if you are a committed reductivist about causation, and for that reason you believe that you are indeed responsible in *Choice 2*, you may use the primitivist intuitions (which everybody agrees have some force) to explain away the initial uncertainty about this case. Following CRRC, you may say that it is less obvious that you are responsible (although you are in fact responsible) because it is less obvious that the causal history of your choice includes everything that is needed to make you reasons-responsive.

Could there be cases where there is simply no fact of the matter as to whether an agent is responsible? This depends, again, on your views on causation. Imagine a variant on *Choice* that shares the structure of the scenario that drew Schaffer to commit to causal indeterminacy (*Enhanced M&M*). Let this case be *Enhanced Choice*: As in the *Enhanced M&M* case, there are two indeterministic potential causal routes to your making the selfish choice, each with a 0.5 chance of succeeding. One of them involves a spell by Merlin, but the other involves the relevant absences of reasons to help the man. Imagine that when they are both causally active this results in an enhanced effect (say, you act particularly selfishly in that you leave the scene without even feeling worried about the man's condition). Imagine that this time the enhanced effect doesn't obtain, so we know that this is not an overdetermination case where both potential causes are causally active.

In this case, the uncertainty about your responsibility seems even more pronounced. The primitivist would explain it by noting that there are two distinct possibilities, one where you are responding to reasons and one where you are manipulated by Merlin, and we have no way of telling which is the actual one. A reductivist like Schaffer, on the other hand, would explain it by arguing that this is a case of fundamental causal indeterminacy: there is no fact of the matter as to which was the cause. So, according to one of the views, it would follow that there is a fact of the matter as to whether you are responsible; we just don't know what it is. According to the other view, it would follow that there simply is no fact of the matter. Either way, the uncertainty or indeterminacy about the causal structure grounds the uncertainty or indeterminacy about your responsibility.

5   Conclusions

As we have seen, the assumption of indeterminism raises some interesting questions about the nature of indeterministic causation and its application to our theories of responsibility. But note that, regardless of how those questions are answered, the discussion in the previous section reinforces the idea that responsibility is closely tied to causation (via reasons-responsiveness) in the way posited by CRRC. For it is arguably due to that close connection between responsibility and causation that we see that, when the causal facts are less clear, so are the responsibility facts. Thus, the remarks in the previous section are further confirmation of the idea that our free will is grounded in the actual causal histories of our behavior, as CRRC says.

In particular, I think this provides further reason to prefer a *causal* version of reasons-responsiveness to a more traditional "counterfactualist" version like Fischer and Ravizza's (a view that appeals to counterfactual scenarios).[18] Very roughly, Fischer and Ravizza's view states that the relevant mechanism is reasons-responsive when it issues in the agent's doing otherwise in *some* counterfactual scenarios where sufficient reasons to do otherwise are present. As far as I can tell, this condition is easily met in all of these scenarios that we have been considering. For example, in *Choice 2*, there are certainly counterfactual scenarios where the reasons to do otherwise are present and your practical reasoning results in your helping the man. So the requirement of reasons-responsiveness seems to be met in this case, and thus the account seems to entail that you are responsible for your selfish choice.[19] But, again, it is not clear that this is the right result. Perhaps it is, at the end of the day, but matters are not as clear as with other simpler cases (such as *Choice 1*). Plus, a counterfactualist account like Fischer and Ravizza's account doesn't have the resources to explain the source of that lack of clarity.

Again, I think that the source of this uncertainty is that what we want to know, in order to determine whether you are responsible in *Choice 2*, is whether in the *actual* case you were responding to certain absences of reasons. In other words, it is a matter of actual (causal or explanatory) relevance. Of course, I don't mean to suggest that counterfactual possibilities are simply useless in answering this kind of question. Typically they are not. But in *this* case they do appear to be useless—or so the primitivist would say. Again, the primitivist intuition (which others also agree we have, even if they try to explain it away) is that those kinds of facts don't settle whether an actual causal connection obtains. So, by appealing to the uncertainty about the causal connection, a causal account of reasons-responsiveness can accommodate the uncertainty in responsibility about *Choice 2*, whereas a counterfactualist account cannot.

More generally, I think this supports CRRC over other compatibilist accounts of free will. As we have seen, if it is less clear that agents act freely in some of the cases we have reviewed, it is because it is less clear that the relevant *absences of reasons* played a role in accounting for their behavior. Thus, this helps bring out the importance of the role played by absences of reasons in grounding free will, which is unique to CRRC. And note that this is something that we can only see by thinking about indeterministic cases. For this lack of clarity about the causal structure of the situation doesn't arise in deterministic settings; it arises only in indeterministic settings given the probabilistic nature of those cases and the special metaphysical questions they give rise to. Thus, reflecting on the indeterministic case can be particularly illuminating at the time of formulating a promising compatibilist account of free will, and it can help support CRRC over other forms of compatibilism.[20]

Notes

1. Mackie 2018 and McKenna Ms. are two notable exceptions. Both Mackie and McKenna are mostly concerned with addressing the problems of luck and control that compatibilists would inherit from libertar-

ians, given the assumption of indeterminism (and, in McKenna's case, given the assumption of determinism too). As I note below, this is an important issue that unfortunately I cannot take up in this chapter.

2. This is so even if it might be the case that one set of reasons outweighs the other—for example, if helping the man were the only morally permissible thing to do in the circumstances. We don't need to decide this issue here.

3. Mackie (2018) and McKenna (Ms.) also focus on a case of this kind to motivate a similar point. Mackie writes about that kind of case: "But if, whichever of these things she does, it will be a decision for which she has (or takes herself to have) good reasons, why shouldn't the *two-way compatibilist* [a compatibilist who thinks free will is compatible both with both determinism and indeterminism] say that, whichever way she decides, she does so freely—at least if certain other standard compatibilist conditions are fulfilled...?" (Mackie 2018: 281). As will be apparent later, I think those "other standard compatibilist conditions" are where the main action lies.

4. See Sartorio 2016 (chapter 4) for a full development of the view. A standard—causalist—theory of agency is assumed throughout the book. As I explain in Chap. 2, the assumption that absences can be causally efficacious is only a simplifying assumption, one that can be replaced with an assumption involving other explanatory kinds of relations that absences can participate in, if causation isn't one of them. The main idea is that absences of reasons must be part of what *accounts for* or *explains* our behavior when we act freely. The simplest way of understanding this idea is, of course, in terms of causal explanation.

5. Notice that the relevant counterfactual reasons must be *sufficient* reasons to do otherwise (or else we shouldn't expect the behavior of a reasons-responsive agent to be explained by the absence of such reasons). But also note that sometimes reasons-responsive agents fail to respond to the *actual* sufficient reasons to do otherwise (*Choice* could be an example of this if, for example, stopping to help the wounded man were in fact morally required in the circumstances). All that is required to be sufficiently reasons-responsive is sensitivity to an appropriate *range* of reasons or absences of reasons, and these needn't include the actual sufficient reasons.

6. Anscombe (1971) forcefully argued for this, and many others have claimed to find the main idea extremely plausible.

7. Lewis gives an example of this kind in his 1986: 176.

8. This can be done in terms of conditional probabilities (the classical example is Suppes 1970) or in terms of counterfactual conditionals with objective chances in the consequent (the classical example is Lewis 1986, Postscript B).

9. You may wonder, though, whether low chances make the problem of luck particularly pressing. Again, unfortunately, this is something I cannot take up here. For a discussion of the problem of luck that arises for compatibilists under the assumption of indeterminism and a comparison with the parallel problem for libertarians, see Mackie 2018 and McKenna Ms.

10. For discussion of the different challenges, see the contributions in Dowe and Noordhof 2004.

11. See, e.g., Dowe 2004 and Hitchcock 2004a.

12. This example has the causal structure of a case discussed in Mele and Robb 1998. It involves a special variety of preemption known as "trumping" preemption. Trumping is a particularly tricky kind of preemption because the preempted process is never interrupted or cut off (it just fails to be causally efficacious), and this rules out the use of several strategies that are commonly used to deal with preemption, such as the one discussed above in the text.

13. For example, but not exclusively, for counterfactual theories of causation. See the discussion in Paul and Hall 2013, chapter 3.

14. Schaffer 2008: 88. Similar examples are discussed by Armstrong (1983: 133; 2004: 450), Tooley (1987: 199-202), Woodward (1990, 215-16), and Carroll (1994: 134-41). Armstrong writes: "Suppose that there are two bombardments of an atom, with the same chance of the atom emitting a particle, which the atom duly does. Does there not seem to be an objective question, which of the two bombardments actually did the job?" (Armstrong 2004: 450). In general, the most interesting cases to think about are cases without causal intermediaries, and the atom case could be one of them. As noted below in the text, magic cases like Schaffer's do that simply by stipulation about how magic works, so they are particularly well suited for these purposes. Ordinary absence causation doesn't involve magic, but it works in the same kind of way, as I argue next.

15. This is one of the reasons why some think absence causation is spooky and should be rejected. But recall that the possibility of absence causa-

tion isn't strictly speaking necessary for the view to work (see n. 4 above). And note that similar questions would arise if, for example, we were to rephrase the point in terms of the explanatory power of absences instead of in terms of their causal efficacy.

16. As others have noted, this seems to work only for cases without causal intermediaries (see, e.g., the discussion in Schaffer 2000 and Hitchcock 2004b). But, again, recall that the cases under discussion contain no causal intermediaries.

17. It wouldn't be the first time a causation theorist commits to this. For instance, Bernstein (2016) offers reasons to believe that *deterministic* causation can also be indeterminate.

18. See Fischer and Ravizza 1998, and also McKenna 2013. In Sartorio 2016 I give other reasons to prefer a causal account of reasons-responsiveness and free will.

19. The Fischer and Ravizza view also requires a coherent counterfactual pattern of reasons-responsiveness. So perhaps Fischer and Ravizza could argue that, if you respond to the reason in some worlds but fail to respond to it in other worlds where everything else is equal, then it is not clear that this makes for a coherent pattern of reasons-responsiveness, and thus it is not clear that you are responsible. But I don't think that this would be a satisfying response. For it doesn't seem to get to the heart of the uncertainty about responsibility. Intuitively, the source of the uncertainty is something else: it is that we are uncertain, more fundamentally, about whether you are *in fact* responding to reasons.

20. For helpful feedback, thanks to Al Mele, Michael McKenna, the students in our metaphysics seminar at the University of Arizona (co-taught with Michael in the spring of 2020), and audiences at the University of Maryland, Florida State University, and the College of William and Mary. Thanks, also, to Marco Hausmann and Jörg Noller for inviting me to contribute to this volume.

References

Anscombe, Gertrude Elizabeth Margaret. 1971. *Causality and Determination: An Inaugural Lecture.* London: Cambridge University Press.
Armstrong, David. 1983. *What Is a Law of Nature?* Cambridge: Cambridge University Press.

————. 2004. Going Through the Open Door Again: Counterfactual Versus Singularist Theories of Causation. In *Causation and Counterfactuals*, ed. John Collins, Ned Hall, and L.A. Paul, 445–457. Cambridge, MA: The MIT Press.

Bernstein, Sara. 2016. Causal and Moral Indeterminacy. *Ratio* 29 (4): 434–447.

Carroll, John. 1994. *Laws of Nature*. Cambridge: Cambridge University Press.

Dowe, Phil. 2004. Chance-Lowering Causes. In *Cause and Chance: Causation in an Indeterministic World*, ed. Phil Dowe and Paul Noordhof, 28–38. London: Routledge.

Dowe, Phil, and Paul Noordhof, eds. 2004. *Cause and Chance: Causation in an Indeterministic World*. London: Routledge.

Fischer, John, and Mark Ravizza. 1998. *Responsibility and Control: A Theory of Moral Responsibility*. New York: Cambridge University Press.

Frankfurt, Harry. 1969. Alternate Possibilities and Moral Responsibility. *Journal of Philosophy* 66 (23): 829–839.

Hitchcock, Christopher. 2004a. Routes, Processes, and Chance-Lowering Causes. In *Cause and Chance: Causation in an Indeterministic World*, ed. Phil Dowe and Paul Noordhof, 138–151. London: Routledge.

————. 2004b. Do All and Only Causes Raise the Probabilities of Effects? In *Causation and Counterfactuals*, ed. John Collins, Ned Hall, and L.A. Paul, 403–417. Cambridge, MA: The MIT Press.

Kane, Robert. 1996. *The Significance of Free Will*. New York: Oxford University Press.

Lewis, David. 1986. Causation. In *Philosophical Papers II*, 159–213. New York: Oxford University Press.

Mackie, Penelope. 2018. Compatibilism, Indeterminism, and Chance. *Royal Institute of Philosophy Supplement* 82: 265–287.

McKenna, Michael. 2013. Reasons-Responsiveness, Agents and Mechanisms. In *Oxford Studies in Agency and Responsibility*, ed. David Shoemaker, vol. 1, 151–183. New York: Oxford University Press.

McKenna, Michael. Ms. n.d. Facing the Luck Problem for Compatibilists.

Mele, Alfred, and David Robb. 1998. Rescuing Frankfurt-Style Cases. *The Philosophical Review* 107 (1): 97–112.

Paul, L.A., and Ned Hall. 2013. *Causation: A User's Guide*. Oxford: Oxford University Press.

Sartorio, Carolina. 2016. *Causation and Free Will*. Oxford: Oxford University Press.

Schaffer, Jonathan. 2000. Overlappings: Probability-raising without Causation. *Australasian Journal of Philosophy* 78: 40–46.

————. 2008. Causation and Laws of Nature: Reductionism. In *Contemporary Debates in Metaphysics*, ed. Theodore Sider, John Hawthorne, and Dean Zimmerman, 82–107. Oxford: Blackwell Publishing.

Suppes, Patrick. 1970. *A Probabilistic Theory of Causality*. Amsterdam: North-Holland Publishing Company.

Tooley, Michael. 1987. *Causation: A Realist Approach*. Oxford: Clarendon Press.

Woodward, James. 1990. Supervenience and Singular Causal Statements. In *Explanation and Its Limits*, ed. Dudley Knowles, 211–246. Cambridge: Cambridge University Press.

10

The Culpability Problem and the Indeterminacy of Choice

Thomas Buchheim

1 Peter van Inwagen's Description of the Problem

If it is not true that a human agent, when faced with a choice between mutually incompatible actions, is at least on some occasions *able* to perform each of them, then the bad consequences of his choice are never his own fault; that is, he is then never to blame for them (= "Culpability Problem"). In his book *Thinking About Free Will* (a collection of old and new essays on the topic),[1] Peter van Inwagen connects two plausible theses about what we usually call "free will":

(1) The *first* plausible thesis is that we human agents, when faced with a choice between mutually incompatible actions, are at least on some occasions able to perform each of them (= Thesis One)

T. Buchheim (✉)
Faculty of Philosophy, Ludwig Maximilian University of Munich, München, Germany
e-mail: Thomas.Buchheim@lrz.uni-muenchen.de

© The Author(s), under exclusive license to Springer Nature Switzerland AG 2021
M. Hausmann, J. Noller (eds.), *Free Will*,
https://doi.org/10.1007/978-3-030-61136-1_10

(2) The *second* plausible thesis is that if the consequences of an action are to be attributed to an agent who decided to perform that action, there have to be occasions in which that agent was able to perform each of the actions between which he was trying to decide; that is, the first thesis is then not only plausibly true but true.

It is my firm conviction that it is right to assume such a connection between these two theses. However, by invoking additional theses, van Inwagen goes on to describe a "dialectical" or even dilemmatic situation that has received special attention in the contemporary debate. These additional theses are, first, two theses about the concepts of determinism and indeterminism (where indeterminism is the negation of determinism and both form an exclusive contradiction):

(3) "*Determinism* is the thesis that the past and the laws of nature determine a unique future." (van Inwagen 2017, 199)
(4) "*Indeterminism* is the thesis that the past and the laws of nature do not determine a unique future." (van Inwagen 2017, 199)

Additional are, in the second place, also the theses concerning two famous arguments according to which the Thesis One can neither be true if determinism is the case, nor be true if indeterminism (i.e., the negation of determinism) is the case. However, a sentence that is incompatible with both members of an exclusive contradiction is impossibly true and, therefore, false.

The two famous and much discussed arguments that are part of van Inwagen's aforementioned theses are, on the one hand, the so-called "Consequence Argument" (according to which, if determinism is true, my actions are always logical consequences of inevitable conditions in the remote past together with equally inevitable laws of nature such that what I decide is not "free" but also inevitable) and the so-called "Mind Argument" (according to which, if my decision were indetermined, my action would not be the result of a controlled and free decision but a mere matter of chance).

The dilemmatic situation, therefore, is the following: Our main thesis (Thesis One) about our controlled ability to choose among at least two mutually incompatible actions has to be false, if none of the two arguments is refutable on plausible grounds. As van Inwagen puts it:

(5) "The seemingly unanswerable arguments for the incompatibility of Thesis One and *determinism* are in fact answerable; these arguments are fallacious" (van Inwagen 2017, 200).

(6) "The seemingly unanswerable arguments for the incompatibility of Thesis One and *indeterminism* are in fact answerable; these arguments are fallacious" (van Inwagen 2017, 200).

2   Are Forms of Determinism and Indeterminism Conceivable That Might Not Be Contradictory?

In what follows, I will not attack directly one of van Inwagen's "unanswerable arguments" (the Consequence Argument or the Mind Argument). Instead, I will focus on the distinction between determinism and indeterminism. I will distinguish between a stronger and a weaker form of determinism (between nomological and logical determinism) and I will argue, contrary to van Inwagen's contention, that the weaker form of determinism (and not the stronger form of determinism) is required for free and controlled decisions (decisions that are not a pure matter of chance). I conclude, given that the weaker form of determinism is, unlike the stronger form, compatible with indeterminism (as van Inwagen understands it), that van Inwagen's reasoning does not support the conclusion that Thesis One is impossibly true.

Let me use one of van Inwagen's remarks about his distinction between determinism and indeterminism as a starting point:

There are seemingly unanswerable arguments that [...] demonstrate that Thesis One is incompatible with determinism. I allude, of course, to the various versions of the Consequence Argument, as it is known in the trade. And there are seemingly unanswerable arguments that [...] demonstrate that Thesis One is incompatible with indeterminism (this part needs a little work, since indeterminism does not imply that a *given person's* actions are undetermined; the work can be done). (van Inwagen 2017, 199)

Interestingly enough, in the case of his definition of indeterminism, van Inwagen thinks that "a little work" needs to be done in order to apply this thesis to the actions of a given person at a given time. In contrast, such a work is not required in the case of his definition of determinism: it seems that, if determinism is true, it is not necessary to apply determinism to the actions of a given person at a given time. Instead, according to van Inwagen, if determinism is true, it is automatically also true of the actions of a given person at a given time. Whereas, in the case of indeterminism, additional work needs to be done in order to apply indeterminism also to, for example, the actions of a given person at a given time. van Inwagen has on numerous occasions already done this little additional work for the case of indeterminism; that is, he has described a form of indeterminism that applies to the decision to act of a given person at a given time. I shall now turn to one of these descriptions.

However, let me first suggest to call indeterminism as applied to the actions of a given person "personally localized indeterminism" and to call determinism—as not applied to a person through additional work— "general determinism."

My guiding question is the question whether, even granted that determinism and indeterminism as quoted above are contradictory, there is a form of general determinism that does not contradict a personally localized indeterminism as described by van Inwagen. That is to say, whether there is a form of general determinism that is not wholly incompatible with the conditions of a personally localized indeterminism as van Inwagen has specified them.

In general, my aim is to find a form of determinism, that is weak enough to not exclude a personally localized indeterminism and that is, therefore, weak enough to escape the unanswerable Consequence Argument, but that, on the other hand, is strong enough to escape in a way the Mind Argument according to which it seems that in the case of a personally localized indeterminism a person's decision has to be a mere matter of chance.

3 Personally Localized Indeterminism and Its Aporetic Consequences for the Possibility of Controlled Decision

Let me now turn to the "little work" that van Inwagen has already done and in virtue of which indeterminism gets applicable to the actions of a given person in a given situation of choice:[2]

> *Indeterminism* with respect to "a *given person's* actions":
> "Let us say that it is at a certain moment up to one whether one will do A or do B if one is then faced with a choice between doing A and doing B and one is then able to do A and is then able to do B. And let us say that it is *at a certain moment undetermined whether* one will do A or do B if there is a possible world in which the laws of nature are the same as those of the actual world and whose state at that moment is identical with the state of the actual world at that moment and in which one will do A and a world satisfying those same two conditions in which one will do B." (van Inwagen 2017, 166; my italics)

The first part of this paragraph restates Thesis One, according to which we human agents are at least sometimes, when trying to decide between mutually incompatible actions, able to perform each of them:

> *Thesis One* "On at least some occasions when a human agent is trying to decide between two or more incompatible courses of action, that agent is able to perform each of them." ('The Problem of Fr** W*ll', in: van Inwagen 2017, 197)

Thus, given that the agent is able to perform each of the actions between which he is trying to decide, according to van Inwagen, it is only up to him which of the actions he is going to perform. The phrase "it is at a certain moment up to one whether one will do A or do B" indicates that the future action depends on the human agent who is trying to decide.

Thus, according to the first sentence of "A Promising Argument," van Inwagen assumes two things with respect to an upcoming decision: *First*, he assumes that it is only up to the human agent what action he is going to perform (= being up to one whether one will do A or do B). *Second*, he assumes that the human agent is able to perform each of the incompatible actions (= ability in the Relevant Sense[3] to do each of them).

Note, however, that this is not strictly true according to van Inwagen's own standards: For before someone has made a decision, it is, strictly speaking, not true that he is able to *do* each of the actions he is trying to decide between. Instead, it is at most true that he is able to *choose* (= to decide for) each of them. In fact, van Inwagen defines free will elsewhere as follows:

> x has free will = $_{df}$ x must sometimes choose among two or more alternative courses of action and, on at least some of these occasions, x is able$_{RS}$ [able in the Relevant Sense] to choose each of them. (van Inwagen 2017, 227)

In his article 'A Promising Argument' he gives a slightly weaker formulation of the "Free-will Thesis": "Various human agents […] were faced with a choice between alternative courses of action […] and it was then up to them which of these courses of the action they would pursue" (166). This latter thesis can be true even in cases where the agent is, at time t_1 before making a decision, able to *choose* any of the incompatible courses of action, but becomes able in the relevant sense at time t_2 to perform the action he has chosen only after and *in virtue of* his decision. The upshot is that in cases where somebody is able to perform an action according to van Inwagen's own standards, the *future* decision is already part of his *ability*; that is, van Inwagen does not speak of being able$_{RS}$ tout court, but of being able$_{RS}$ by making a choice or decision. Otherwise decision making would be pointless.

But the main difficulty with upcoming decisions in order to sufficiently ground culpability that van Inwagen goes on to describe in "A Promising Argument" lies in the fact that on the one hand, according to the premises specified above, the first element (= being up to one whether one will do A or do B) entails personally localized indeterminism—a thesis van Inwagen calls incompatibilism:

> *Incompatibilism* "If one is at a certain moment faced with a choice between doing A and doing B, it is then up to one whether one will do A or do B

only if it is then undetermined whether one will do A or do B—and *necessarily so.*" (van Inwagen 2017, 167)

While on the other hand, one and the same personally localized indeterminism appears to exclude the second element of decision competence (= ability in the Relevant Sense to do each of them), according to van Inwagen's Indetermination-Inability-Principle:[4]

New Indetermination-Inability-Principle "Where t_2 is a future moment and t_1 is a future moment earlier than t_2: If one is now faced with a choice between doing A at t_2 and doing B at t_2, and if, at t_1, it will be undetermined whether one will do A at t_2 or do B at t_2 (and if this *would* then be undetermined whatever one might do between now and t_1), then one is not now able to do A at t_2 and one is not now able to do B at t_2." (van Inwagen 2017, 170)

Hence, according to van Inwagen, a decision competence that is allegedly free and justifies culpability imposes incompatible requirements and is therefore—as the article tries to demonstrate—impossible: Before a human agent decides what to do it has to be *undetermined* what she is going to do, if her decision between mutually incompatible actions is supposed to be only up to her (up to one whether one will do A or do B). However, she *cannot be able in the relevant sense* to pursue the courses of action in question before she decides, if it is at that time undetermined what she is going to do.

What, then, is to be done?

4 Decisions in a Situation of Personally Localized Indeterminism

Let us first consider what, according to van Inwagen, is required for the truth of personally localized Indeterminism:

[L]et us say that it is at a certain moment *undetermined whether* one will do A or do B if there is a possible world in which the laws of nature are the same as those of the actual world and whose state at that moment is identical with the state of the actual world at that moment and in which one will do A *and* a world satisfying those same two conditions in which one will do B. (van Inwagen 2017, 166)

a. There has to be an actual world in which a decision is upcoming at a given time. Let us call this world "temporal-choice-world" or "TC-world."
b. Further, there have to be (at least) two possible worlds that are congruent with the TC-world up to that time and that, from this time on, differ from one another without contradicting their own past (congruent with the TC-world). I call them the possible A-world and the possible B-world.[5]
c. Finally, in both of these possible worlds there have to be laws of nature that are the same in the A-world and in the B-world and that are, moreover, in accordance with the laws of nature of the TC-world.

Let us first consider the (at least) two possible worlds with the same past that, according to van Inwagen, have to be assumed given personally localized indeterminism.

It seems plain to me, given the above-mentioned conditions for a personally localized indeterminism that the TC-world has to be identical with *a* possible world but that, at a time prior to the decision, it is undetermined (in the sense of van Inwagen's definition of indeterminism) to which one of these (possible worlds) the TC-world is identical. For, given personally localized indeterminism, this depends on how the human agent is going to decide: if he decides to perform action A, the TC-world is identical to the possible A-world; if he decides to perform action B, the TC-world is identical to the possible B-world. It is, therefore, undetermined whether the TC-world is the possible A-world or the possible B-world. But is it, at least, not undetermined that the TC-world is *either* the possible A-world *or* the possible B-world? That is, is it true that the TC-world is the possible B-world, if it is *not* the possible A-world, and that it is the possible A-world, if it is *not* the possible B-world?

It seems to me that this doesn't follow—at least as long as a personally localized indeterminism as described by van Inwagen is in place. For as things presently stand at the TC-world nothing excludes that the TC-world is the possible A-world. Further, nothing excludes that the TC-world is the possible B-world. Consequently, nothing excludes that it is not the possible A-world and, likewise, nothing excludes that it is not the possible B-world. In fact, the TC-world *might*, as things stand prior to the decision, neither be the possible A-world nor the possible B-world and, instead, a different possible world—depending on how someone would decide in a situation of personally localized indeterminism.

In fact, van Inwagen appears to admit in a footnote that when an agent is trying to decide in a situation of personally localized indeterminism there might be much *more* possibilities than only the possibilities that the agent is taking into account in his decision; therefore, much more possible worlds might be compatible with the past of the TC-world than only the A-world and the B-world:

> None of the three propositions »Sally is now faced with a choice between doing A and doing B«, »It is now up to Sally whether she will do A or do B«, »It is now undetermined whether Sally will do A or do B« entails that Sally will either do A or do B. It might be, for example, that at a certain point in her life Sally was faced with a choice between becoming a physician and becoming a concert pianist, that it was then up to her whether she would become a physician or a pianist, that it was then undetermined whether she would become a physician or a pianist—and that she eventually decided to pursue neither of those vocations and became a journalist. ("A Promising Argument," in: van Inwagen 2017, 166 n. 2)

It follows that even after an agent has, in the course of making her decision, *excluded* one of the alternative courses of actions—A or B—there might still be an indeterminacy with respect to a whole range of alternative courses of actions. We are, therefore, entitled to assume that, when it comes to a decision between A and B, personally localized indeterminism is *more closely focused* on alternative courses of action that have *not* been excluded than on alternative courses of actions that have been excluded. It makes a difference for Sally's decision making, whether she contrasts all possibilities that come in question only with the possibility to become a physician, or whether she contrasts them with all possibilities she wavered between before eventually excluding one of them. If it is legitimate to assume something along these lines without contradicting the conditions of personally localized indeterminism, it implies that excluding alternative courses of action according to certain principles *narrows* the range of remaining options. These remaining options are then according to that principles, despite a personally localized indeterminacy of choice as a whole, *closer* to the choice of the agent *than other* options. That is, the possible worlds that according to personally localized indeterminism have to be compatible with the TC-world might have *different degrees of closeness* with respect to an agent at a certain time in the actual world, without thereby contradicting the conditions of personally localized indeterminism.

David Lewis has described this difference of closeness or nearness between possible worlds as "degree of similarity" between possible worlds and he has tried to defend it against the charge of obscureness (Lewis 1973, 50 sqq.). Building on this concept of degrees of similarity, he has in turn developed a concept of "comparative possibility." In what follows, I feel inspired by this concept of Lewis's, without having the opportunity to discuss it further.

> It is more possible for a dog to talk than for a stone to talk, since some worlds with talking dogs are more like our world than is any world with talking stones. It is more possible for a stone to talk than for eighteen to be a prime number, however, since stones talk at some worlds far from ours, but presumably eighteen is not a prime number at any world at all, no matter how remote. (Lewis 1973, 52)

We can therefore say with respect to a given locality of personally localized indeterminism in the TC-world: that, if a person is wavering between alternatives, then, depending on what kind of principles that person refers to in order to exclude alternatives, *different* possible continuations of the TC-world are *more possible* than the excluded ones.

However, it is evident that it is *not* the case that the two or more possible worlds that have to be possible continuations of a decision between alternative courses of actions in the TC-world (according to van Inwagen's conditions for a personally localized indeterminism) have to be *equally* possible worlds with respect to the locality of personally localized indeterminism and the adopted principles, by which the person proceeds in making her decision. Instead, they *might* have (and I hasten to add that this is plausible to assume) different degrees of possibility and, therefore, different degrees of *closeness* or *nearness* with respect to their connection to the TC-world in a given situation of personal localized indeterminism.

As the foregoing reasoning has shown, somebody who is faced with a choice between explicit alternative courses of actions in a situation of personally localized indeterminism might well retain a whole range of different and mutually incompatible courses of action such that, even if personally localized indeterminism holds, it is up to her which of them she is going to pursue—and this, even after she has excluded *one* or more of the alternative courses of action between which she has to decide. The fact that a human agent in the course of decision making *excludes* just one out of several possibilities according to adopted principles of decision does not imply that she has also decided what she is going to do instead. She rather has to decide, in addition, *for* a certain action within the range of remaining possible actions. I want to maintain, however, that, depending on which exclusions had already been carried out, the range of possible actions may be more closely focused on the remaining possibility A, or more closely focused on the remaining possibility B, without thereby contradicting the conditions of the originally assumed personally localized indeterminism.

If it is admitted that, when a human agent is faced with a choice in a situation of personally localized indeterminism, *some* of all alternative courses of action that come into question might be *closer* to the choice of the agent *than other* of these alternative courses of action (without thereby contradicting the conditions of this form of indeterminism), then it must also be admitted that only one of these alternative courses of action might, according to certain principles, be *closer* to the choice of the agent *than any other* of these alternative courses of action—and this depending on which exclusions the agent carries out. We may say that such a course of action is, according to the adopted principles of decision, *the most possible* course of action for a certain agent.

What we have seen so far is that, depending on what principles a person adopts in a situation of personally localized indeterminism in order to exclude apparently reachable alternatives, *some* of the remaining alternatives are, according to that principles, closer and, therefore, *more possible* than the excluded ones. And if this is compatible with the conditions of personally localized indeterminism, then it is also compatible with those conditions that after a series of steps, according to the same principles, exactly one of the possible continuations is *the most possible* according to these principles. The claim, then, is that there are certain requirements for a decision to be a decision according to *rational* principles:

a. the whole sequence of exclusions has to be guided by the same principles.
b. the same principles according to which an excluded alternative is less favorable than the others support consistently the finally chosen alternative as the reachable alternative that fits better with these principles than any other apparently reachable alternative.
c. the principles enable the deciding person to map the abilities and general goals that person ascribes to him- or herself onto the alternatives between which he or she has to decide.

Of course, these are only three necessary conditions for principles of a decision qualifying as rational. A decision that has been made according to principles that fulfill at least these three characteristics of rationality can be called, because of these characteristics, a "rationally bridged decision" with respect to the life of the deciding person up until before the decision. Taking it all together, the conditions of personally localized indeterminism according to van Inwagen would not exclude that exactly one of the possible continuations of the TC-world is the most possible for the deciding person according to a rationally bridged decision of hers.

5 The Most Possible Course of Action According to Rational Principles: Aquinas's Idea of a Rational Consilium of Free Decisions

In the late thirteenth century, Aquinas has, pretty much in the same spirit, put forward a thesis about a faculty of reason he called "libera electio humana," that is, free decision or free choice of human beings. What I want to highlight is this: the upshot of Aquinas's reasoning lies in the fact that, not unlike van Inwagen's view, a free decision presupposes a form of *indeterminism* with respect to alternative courses of action. That is, Aquinas agrees that there is only a free or culpable decision, if an agent overcomes a situation of indeterminacy by deciding in favor of exactly one of the alternatives.

> Human beings [unlike things of nature] have an intellectual form and an inclination of the will resulting from understood forms, and external acts result from these inclinations. But there is this difference [in contrast to the inclination of natural things], that the form of a thing of nature is a form individuated by matter, and so also the inclinations resulting from the form are determined to one thing, but the *understood* form is universal and includes many individual things. And so since actualities regard singular things, and none of them exhausts the potentiality of the universal, inclinations of the will remain indeterminately disposed to many things. (Aquinas 2003, 257–258)[6]

That is, according to Aquinas, a human being, when making a potentially *free* decision, has to overcome a certain indeterminacy of his will (= voluntative indeterminism). For the will of such a human being is by necessity "indeterminately disposed to many things" which cannot all be realized simultaneously. Therefore, a human being, when he is deciding freely (= culpable and not necessarily determined), has to overcome *always* a situation of voluntative indeterminism in favor of one alternative course of action by taking operative steps. This overcoming of voluntative indeterminism of free decision, which does not advance by necessity, takes place, according to Aquinas, in virtue of a rational *consilium* which involves intellect and will in two different respects. On the one hand, it involves intellect and will with respect to the performance of a concrete act of the will (= *exercitium*) and, on the other hand, with respect to the object or the precise content of action on which the will is directed (= *specificatio*).

> Therefore, in order to show that the will is not moved necessarily, we need to consider the movement of the will both regarding performance (*exercitium*) of the will's act and regarding specification of the act, which is by the object. (Aquinas 2003, 259)[7]

In both respects in which will and intellect are involved in a rational *consilium*, there is, according to Aquinas, a procedure that, though not necessarily, realizes unambiguous determination. With respect to the performance of a concrete act of the will, Aquinas calls this process *libertas exercitii*. With respect to the determination of the content of action, Aquinas calls this process *libertas specificationis*.

Both special modes of execution of intellect and will which Aquinas describes in great detail are meant to *explain* how and why it is *possible* that, in the course of deliberation, a voluntative indeterminism with respect to alternative courses of action is overcome not by necessity but determinately, that is, *determinately according to rational principles*. As we have already seen, it is the human agent that, because of his decision, builds a rational bridge to the reachable alternative that is the most compatible with his or her past according to rational principles.

If indeterminism is therefore overcome by both modes of execution (*et quantum ad exercitium actus, et quantum ad determinationem actus, qui est ex obiecto*) according to rational principles, then the will of a person is rationally *self*-moved (i.e., not moved by an additional will of other things) with respect to his performance and tends, on the other hand, to an object of will which it pursues not necessarily.

Thus, the mark of rational principles for a decision is, also according to Aquinas, that the person consistently proceeds from indeterminate will and relevant consilium to a decision and a determinate will. It is only true to say that it is the *same* will at the beginning of the decision that determines itself further to a determinate will because the principles that guide the procedure are rational. The principles according to which other possibilities are excluded are not only at each step consistently the same; they are at each step of the decision rationally coherent with respect to the pursued goal.

I cannot expand on this, but Aquinas explains the possibility and conceivability of this in much more detail. What matters is Aquinas's thesis that from a situation of voluntative indeterminism of choice, pretty much like van Inwagen's personally localized indeterminism, a self-determined path may lead to exactly one most possible action relative to the person.

6   Sameness of Laws of Nature with a Potential Difference of Principles of Choice

This brings me to the second condition of personally localized indeterminism according to van Inwagen, that is, to the question whether it is consistent, in my view (if exactly one world among many possible continuations of the TC-world may be the most possible according to rational principles for a person that has to make a decision) that at least two of the possible worlds that are possible continuations of a decision that was made in a situation of personally localized indeterminism in the TC-world (the A-world and the B-world) may have the same laws of nature as the TC-world.

I think that this requirement can be fulfilled, if it is denied that a past state of the world together with a conjunction of all laws of nature entails *every other* state of the world. As we have seen at the beginning, this thesis is equivalent to the thesis of *nomological* determinism as defined by van Inwagen: the thesis that *everything* that takes place follows entirely from an arbitrary state of the past solely together with the laws of nature. Even though, in my view, nothing that ever happens is a contradiction of the laws of nature or, as they say, "violates" a law of nature, it does not follow, assuming a past state, that it is *implied* solely by a law of nature.—Instead, there might be *other* rules or *other* true generalizations without exception, according to which something in the world occurs or happens—other principles, that is to say, that are *not* laws of nature.

According to personally localized indeterminism as van Inwagen describes it, a controlled decision has to be *in*determined, at a time before that decision, only with respect to facts of the past and laws of nature of the TC-world. This is obviously consistent with *a general determinism in a weaker sense* according to which that decision is determined with respect to *all* relevant principles for the future decision making progress. These principles, however, need not be laws of nature, nor need they be "unavoidable" for the agent that is about to make that decision. It is not unavoidable for me that I regard something as "good" or "right" according to certain principles what according to other principles is sometimes regarded as "bad" or "wrong." The general (logical) determinism that I want to uphold is the thesis that the future is determined by *all* principles that, starting from a given past state of the world, play a part in the proceeding of the history of the world.

In my view, the principles that play a role in the thesis of such a general determinism need not be laws of nature. True generalizations that are not laws of nature might *differ* among worlds with the same past and laws of nature as the TC-world. And there might be exactly one of those worlds in which these true generalizations are, all things considered, maximally rational and favorable for all human and other rational beings that have to make decisions and conform to *Thesis One* of the "Culpability Problem." According to Leibniz, to just mention one famous example which matters with regard to the philosophy of freedom, such a possible world would not only be the "best" of all possible worlds, but also identical to the actual world, in which a rational determinism is consistently conceivable with the culpability of persons that make rational decisions—at least according to Leibniz.

It seems, therefore, that the conditions of a personally localized indeterminism, as van Inwagen specifies it, can be combined with a weak determinism of the general sort that includes rational principles of decision (or other true generalizations that are up to us). For these rational principles might be consistent with the same laws of nature, regardless of which alternative course of action is pursued.

7   General Determinism and the Ability to Decide Otherwise

Thus, it seems that we can claim in general—without contradicting our-selves—that at a certain time t_1 in the TC-world personally localized indeterminism holds and there are more than one alternative courses of action (= more than one possible continuations of the present) that are all up to the agent that is about to make a decision. And this, even though only one of these alternative courses of action is the *most* possible for the person in question according to rational principles of decision; *and* that, further, a rational person might be able and capable, due to a *consilium* according to rational principles that begins after t_1, to determine the most convenient course of action, that is, the course of action that, according to such a rational *consilium*, appears to be the most advisable. If it is legitimate to uphold the thesis that several worlds in the situation of per-sonally localized indeterminism that are subject to a decision of a person are *possible*, but only one of them is *rationally* the most possible for the person according to rational principles of decision making, then a weak form of *general* and logical (i.e., neither temporally nor personally speci-fied) determinism might hold—if we consider all principles (rational as well as non-rational) that are relevant for what will take place. If so, there is no reason to believe that a person that in general sticks to rational prin-ciples and consequently makes a rational decision this time too should not prefer the most possible world according to rational principles—and this, even if God repeatedly causes the TC-world to revert to the time of decision.

At the end of my chapter, I would like to look back on the two ele-ments that, according to van Inwagen's thesis, are required for a culpable decision. As he puts it in the first sentence of "A Promising Argument":

> Let us say that it is at a certain moment up to one whether one will do A or do B if one is then faced with a choice between doing A and doing B and one is then able to do A and is then able to do B. (van Inwagen 2017, 166)

How, then, can we reconcile a general determinism in the weak sense (as indicated above) with these two elements, "being up to one whether one will do A or do B" on the one hand and "being then able to do A and able to do B" at the time of decision? For, according to van Inwagen, these elements could not both be true given that the first element implies personally localized indeterminism and given that personally localized indeterminism is incompatible with the second element, that is, with the ability to perform each of the incompatible courses of action.[8]

Following Aquinas, we can hold with respect to the first element that exactly one course of action depends only on a self-determined decision of the agent (and is, therefore, *a fortiori* up to him under conditions of personally localized indeterminism), namely the course of action that, due to an exerted *consilium*, is the most possible for the agent according to rational principles of choice. And this holds, while the other alternative courses of action do not only depend on the agent, but are influenced by factors that are outside of his control. Thus, we can say in this sense (following Aquinas) that it is "up to one" whether one will perform that course of action that conforms to the possible world that is most possible according to rational principles. If it is only up to him whether he will choose the action that conforms to the possible world that is most possible according to rational principles, then it is also only up to him whether he will *not* choose the action that conforms to the possible world that is most possible according to rational principles. For this depends only on whether someone sticks to the same rational principles in the given case, as she proves to have done in numerous other cases. But this would not be a matter of the choice she's faced with. Taking it all together: it is up to her whether she will choose the action in question or an alternative course of action.

With respect to the second required element, namely being able in the Relevant Sense to perform each of the alternative actions, there is no longer any reason to believe that in a situation of personally localized indeterminism there can be *no* ability in the Relevant Sense. In fact, the only reason van Inwagen cites in favor of his view is that a person sufficiently informed about the problem of indeterminacy of decision could not be sure, before his decision, how he or she is going to decide. As van Inwagen argues, such a person, if faced with a decision (e g., with a decision between keeping silent about the transgression of a friend in a public consultation, or not), could not promise with certainty to do something:

> Am I in a position to promise you that I will keep silent?—knowing, as I do, that if there were a million perfect duplicates of me, each placed in a perfect duplicate of my present situation, forty-three percent of them would tell all and fifty-seven percent of them would hold their tongues? [...] I do not see how I could be in a position to make it. But if I believe that I am able to keep silent, I should, it would seem, regard myself as being in a position to make this promise. (van Inwagen 2017, 169)

However, it should be obvious by now that, if we assume that the conditions of personally localized indeterminism hold together with the weak form of determinism that I want to uphold, that one of these alternative decisions conforms to the possible world that is most possible according to rational principles. I could, therefore, now be *sure* that, if my upcoming decision stays conform with rational principles I'm used to apply, I will do what in that situation is the most possible according to rational principles. Therefore, I can legitimately be sure that I am *able* in the Relevant Sense to keep silent (if it is that what seems to conform with the principles I usually hold to be rational) and that I am, therefore, in a position to make such a promise in advance: All perfect duplicates of me placed in a perfect duplicate of my present situation would, to 100 percent, always make the same decision according to these principles. If so, however, there is no reason to exclude the *possibility* that, before making definitely a decision, one and the same person may be able to perform each of the alternative actions between which he or she is supposed to be going to decide (in a culpable way).

Note, that this would not be the case, if the principles which I adopt in my upcoming decision would be arbitrary ones. For in being careless or inattentive in adopting principles of my decision or changing them step by step in the course of making up my mind, there would not be a consistently *most* possible of all the possible worlds in the range of my choice. It is plain, therefore, that van Inwagen's *New Indetermination-Inability-Principle does not hold:*

Where t_2 is a future moment and t_1 is a future moment earlier than t_2: If one is now faced with a choice between doing A at t_2 and doing B at t_2, and if, at t_1, it will be undetermined whether one will do A at t_2 or do B at t_2 (and if this *would* then be undetermined whatever one might do between now and t_1), then one is not now able to do A at t_2 and one is not now able to do B at t_2. (van Inwagen 2017, 170)

For before starting at t_1 to exclude reachable alternatives, it is only true (as a general rule) that somebody who sticks to rational principles of decision making can expect that there is exactly one most possible world according to that principles—and this, even though from before t_1 up to the decision van Inwagen's conditions for a personally localized indeterminism hold.[9]

Notes

1. van Inwagen (2017).
2. 'A Promising Argument', in: van Inwagen (2017, 166–176).
3. See van Inwagen's definition in his article "Ability" in the same collection of essays (van Inwagen 2017, 225): "Someone is able in the Relevant Sense (is »able$_{RS}$«) to do something just in the case that that person is able to do that thing in the *strongest* sense of »able« such that, if one made a promise and did not believe that (did not have the belief that) one was able (in that sense) to keep that promise, that promise would be defective."
4. The same holds, a fortiori, with respect to van Inwagen's "original Indetermination-Inability Principle":

   "*The Indetermination-Inability Principle* If one is at a certain moment faced with a choice between doing A and doing B, and if it is then undetermined whether one will do A or do B, it is not then up to one whether one will do A or do B; in fact, one is not then able to do A *and* not then able to do B."

5. Every reachable possible world (from the perspective of somebody's decision), is, strictly speaking, a whole sheaf of possible worlds that have, as a common feature, the alternative that is reachable from that perspective. For in one and the same maximally consistent possible world, there are

many localities of indeterminism that are independent from the locality of indeterminism in question.

6. "in homine invenitur forma intellectiva, et inclinatio voluntatis consequens formam apprehensam, ex quibus sequitur exterior actio: sed in hoc est differentia [sc. in contrast to the inclination of natural things], quia forma rei naturalis est forma individuata per materiam; unde et inclinatio ipsam consequens est *determinata ad unum*, sed forma intellecta est universalis sub qua multa possunt comprehendi; unde cum actus sint in singularibus, in quibus nullum est quod adaequet potentiam universalis, remanet inclinatio voluntatis *indeterminate se habens ad multa*" (*Quaestiones disputatae De malo*, qu. 6, *Respondeo*).

7. "Sic ergo ad ostendendum quod voluntas *non ex necessitate* movetur, oportet considerare motum voluntatis *et* quantum ad exercitium actus, *et* quantum ad determinationem actus, qui est ex obiecto" (*Quaestiones disputatae De malo*, Qu. 6, *Respondeo*).

8. See 'The Problem of Fr** W*ll', in: van Inwagen (2017, 197).

9. In working on this topic, I have benefited from an ongoing exchange of ideas with Marco Hausmann. I thank him for this as well as for the translation of the text from German into English. I want to thank, further, Helen Beebee, Thomas Pink, Peter van Inwagen, and others for thoughtful questions and objections that helped me to find and to (possibly) close gaps in the original argument.

References

Aquinas. 2003. *On Evil*. Trans. Richard Regan, S.J. and Edited with Introduction and Notes by Brian Davies, O.P. Oxford: Oxford University Press.

Lewis, David. 1973. *Counterfactuals*. Cambridge, MA: Harvard University Press.

van Inwagen, Peter. 2017. *Thinking About Free Will*. Cambridge: Cambridge University Press.

11

Ambivalent Freedom: Kant and the Problem of *Willkür*

Jörg Noller

1 The Problem of *Willkür*

From a philosophical point of view, the notion of *Willkür* (*arbitrariness*) is highly problematic.[1] The German word "Willkür" can be etymologically explained as "choice of the will." It is composed of "Wille" ("will") and "kiesen" ("to choose"), the latter being an old German word for "reflection, examination, choice," and originally meaning as much as "choice according to one's own will" (Seebold 2011, 490, 550, 989). The two words—the German "kiesen" and the English "to choose"—are etymologically related. Although "Willkür" denotes the individual free decision of a person, it has experienced a semantic pejoration of meaning in modern philosophy. The Greek and Latin equivalents—ἐξουσία and *arbitrium*—also possess the meaning of free willing, but cannot be reduced to the pejorative meaning of "Willkür" because of their semantic range, which also includes justified and deliberate willing (Ritter 2004, 809). *Willkür* therefore often seemed to be a wrong kind of freedom, a

J. Noller (✉)
Philosophy, Ludwig Maximilian University of Munich, Munich, Germany
e-mail: joerg.noller@lrz.uni-muenchen.de

© The Author(s), under exclusive license to Springer Nature Switzerland AG 2021   **251**
M. Hausmann, J. Noller (eds.), *Free Will*,
https://doi.org/10.1007/978-3-030-61136-1_11

kind freedom that does not involve reasons and is therefore just random and arbitrary. Hegel famously called it "the will in the form of chance" (Hegel 1986, TWA 8, 261), and many other philosophers followed him.

In what follows, I will address the philosophical ambivalence of the concept of *Willkür* in and after Kant. The aim of my chapter is to defend it against the charge of irrationality and mere chance, and to rehabilitate it from a historical and analytic point of view. I will analyze Kant's use of the word "Willkür" (*power of choice*), and chronologically follow the semantic and systematic changes in his philosophical work. Finally, I address recent attempts to revitalize the concept of "Willkür" in the analytic debate by referring to the work of Harry Frankfurt and Robert Kane. I shall argue that we need to distinguish between two kinds of *libera arbitria*. Whereas the *liberum arbitrium indifferentiae* can be interpreted in terms of the pejorative sense of "Willkür"—as mere chance—the *liberum arbitrium voluntatis* equals a reflective kind of *Willkür*—literal *Willkür* ("choice")—which involves freedom of the will.

2   The Conceptual History of *Willkür*

It is worth noting that the word "Willkür" experienced a semantic pejoration especially in the time of the Enlightenment. The *Grimmsches Wörterbuch* (1854) notes: "Since the second half of the 18th century, [...] reigns [...] the reproving meaning" (Grimm 1854, 216) and lists in addition to the "new meaning, mostly with reproving sense" (Grimm 1854, 210) numerous "older meanings, without reproving sense" (Grimm 1854, 205). This shifting and narrowing of meaning is especially found in the adjective "willkürlich" (*arbitrary*). In the "older use of language, without blaming sense" it meant as much as "voluntary" or "acting according to free self-determination" (Grimm 1854, 214), whereas in the "newer use of language, with reproving sense" it contains pejorative meanings such as "unjustified, unlawful, violent, unrestrained" or "out of the air, unfounded, unwise" (Grimm 1854, 216; my translations).

This tendency toward a pejorative meaning of the word "Willkür," which was already evident in the nineteenth century, has continued to the present day. The word "Willkür" (arbitrariness) and "willkürlich" (arbitrary) can now be understood as being synonymous with "random" or even "involuntary," so that its original meaning has turned into the exact opposite (Duden 2010, 1086; my translation). Whoever acts *willkürlich* (arbitrarily) acts in the bad sense of the word, without reasons or deeper sense. It is only by the meaning of the word "unwillkürlich" (involuntary) that we recognize *ex negativo* that the total absence of *Willkür* seems to exclude any control of a certain action. Thus Rudolf Eisler's *Wörterbuch der philosophischen Begriffe (Dictionary of Philosophical Terms)* (1904) states both opposed meanings: "Willkür (*arbitrium*) is: 1) in contrast to drive, the independent will, the ability to choose, 2) the lawless-individual, unmethodical will and action" (Eisler 1904, 785; my translation).

Such a negative understanding, however, does not do justice to the philosophical concept of *Willkür*, for it overlooks its long tradition as *arbitrium liberum*: "Willkür" does not mean, according to its origin, a merely "arbitrary" choice, but a well-founded decision, which is closely connected with the capacity of reason. The close connection between rationality and *Willkür* is already indicated by etymology of the word, for it is anything but a groundless, decisionistic act: Whoever is "chosen" (*auserkoren*) is chosen after careful consideration and judgment (*arbitrium*), often not only for individual reasons, but for many good reasons, including different perspectives, arguments, and opinions.

How does this striking pejoration of the German word "Willkür" fit in with the enthusiasm for freedom during the period of Enlightenment and classical German philosophy? Reasons for the increasingly negative connotation can be seen in the changed political situation of the second half of the eighteenth century, in which freedom was demanded less as a concentration of power in the sense of "prince arbitrariness," for instance, which does not require any justification, but happens merely according to individual preferences, than as a public, general or moral capacity. One decisive historical event here is the French Revolution, but already Rousseau's *Contrat Social* published in 1762 points in this direction, according to which freedom consists precisely in "obedience to the self-given law."[3] Against this background, the conception of an autonomy of reason and its orientation toward morality can also be seen as a counter-project to the problematic individual abuse of freedom, insofar as it was now normatively determined, precisely by a general and universal faculty, as reason is.

It is striking that the pejorative change in meaning of *Willkür* coincides with the development of Kant's philosophy. More precisely, the turning point from the positive to the negative meaning of the term coincides with the emergence of Kant's theory of freedom. For in Kant's *Critique of Pure Reason*, the concept of *Willkür* is used in terms of the *liberum arbitrium* and thus demonstrates its positive meaning. Especially in Hegel's philosophy, however, the concept of *Willkür* was more and more criticized, so that since then it could generally be regarded as a prime example of a false understanding of freedom. Hegel defines *Willkür* as "the will in the form of chance" (Hegel 1986, TWA 8, 286). As a mere "appearance of freedom," *Willkür* is in this respect "to be banished from the concept of the sciences of the absolute" (Hegel 1986, TWA 2, 108). According to Hegel, *Willkür* is "false freedom," since it is only an "empty opinion of freedom." Hegel also speaks of Willkür as being "blind" (Hegel 1986, TWA 17, 178), even "wild" (Hegel 1986, TWA 17, 85), and "raw" (Hegel, 1986, TWA 11, 398; my translations).

It can be shown, however, that the tension within the concept of *Willkür*—between mere chance in the sense of unfounded freedom and a judgment of the will based on reasons of consideration (as an *arbitrium liberum*)—has not only been discussed in history before and after Kant, but also in Kant's philosophy *itself.* One could thus say that Kant's philosophy marks a critical point also with regard to the conception of *Willkür*. Therefore, the general thesis according to which "the notion of *Willkür* undergoes a process of pejoration which seems to be completed in the second half of the 18th century" (Eisler 1904, 811; my translation) is to be subjected to a critical examination.

3   Kant and the Problem of *Willkür*

3.1   *Willkür* and Transcendental Freedom in the *Critique of Pure Reason*

It is striking that Kant does not treat in detail the concept of *Willkür* as the capacity of individual free choice in his three transcendental major works, which he understood as critiques of the rational human faculties—understanding, reason, will, and judgment.[4] Remarks on the capacity of individual choice can often be found outside the three Critiques, not least in Kant's reflections and preliminary works. The word "Willkür" can be found more than 20 times in the *Critique of Practical Reason*, only twice in the *Groundwork of the Metaphysics of Morals*, almost 20 times in the *Critique of Pure Reason*, even more than 80 times in his *Religion*, and finally around 150 times in the late *Metaphysics of Morals*.

The ambivalence of Kant's transcendental-philosophical evaluation of *Willkür* is already evident at the beginning of his *Critique of Pure Reason*. While according to the 1st edition "the concepts of pleasure and displeasure, of desires and inclinations, of choice (*Willkür*), etc., [...] are all of empirical origin" and in contrast to the objects of a transcendental philosophy only "belong among empirical sources of cognition," Kant strikingly leaves the concept of *Willkür* unmentioned at the parallel place of the 2nd edition (Kant 1998, CPR, B 29) with otherwise identical listing (Kant 1998, CPR, A 15). It thus seems that Kant, in the 2nd edition of the *Critique of Pure Reason*, no longer wanted to exclude with certainty *Willkür* from transcendental philosophy as a mere empirical concept and therefore left its conceptual status open.

This ambivalence in the treatment of the concept of *Willkür* can be further substantiated. Probably the best known definition of *Willkür* can be found in the 2nd edition of the *Critique of Pure Reason*:

> The human power of choice is indeed an *arbitrium sensitivum*, yet not *brutum* but *liberum* because sensibility does not render its action necessary, but in the human being there is a faculty of determining oneself from oneself, independently of necessitation by sensible impulses. (Kant 1998, CPR, B 526)

Kant thus determines the capacity of *Willkür* at this point in the sense of a negative and positive freedom. The freedom of *Willkür* is negative insofar as it is not necessitated (as, for example, animal choice) by inclinations and thus has no volitional scope for judgment and reflection ("arbitrium"). *Willkür* is positive inasmuch as it represents a capacity for self-determination; that is, it stands at a reflexive distance from natural causal inclinations or first-order desires. Kant characterized this capacity somewhat later as the source of "motives that can only be represented by reason" (Kant 1998, CPR, B 830) and which determine our free choice. *Willkür* thus consists in the ability to suspend desires that directly affect the will ("first-order desires"):

> For it is not merely that which stimulates the senses, i.e., immediately affects them, that determines human choice, but we have a capacity to overcome impressions on our sensory faculty of desire by representations of that which is useful or injurious even in a more remote way; but these considerations about that which in regard to our whole condition is desirable, i.e., good and useful, depend on reason. (Kant 1998, CPR, B 830)

Kant defines "freedom in the practical sense" as "the independence of the power of choice (*Willkür*) from necessitation by impulses of sensibility" (Kant 1998, CPR, B 562). The concept of *Willkür* as developed in the *Critique of Pure Reason* is primarily related to Kant's concept of transcendental freedom as absolute spontaneity. The relationship between *Willkür* and autonomy becomes thematic in Kant's *Critique of Practical Reason*.

3.2   *Willkür* and Autonomy in the *Critique of Practical Reason*

While Kant's work contains the phrase "autonomy of will" more than ten times, the phrase "autonomy of choice (*Willkür*)" occurs only once: "What is to be done in accordance with the principle of the autonomy of choice is seen quite easily and without hesitation by the most common understanding" (Kant 1997, CPrR, 5:36). Nevertheless, it can be shown that Kant uses both phrases synonymously. In the Second Chapter of the

Analytic of the *Critique of Practical Reason*, Kant speaks of the fact that the categories of freedom "are directed to the determination of a free choice (*Willkür*)" and that "all precepts of pure practical reason have to do only with the determination of the will, not with the natural conditions (of practical ability)" (Kant 1997, CPrR, 5:66). This shows that for Kant "free determination of will" and "free choice (*Willkür*)" can be used synonymously.

Kant further distinguishes between a "pathologically affected" and a "free choice (*Willkür*)" (Kant 1997, CPrR, 5:32). This equivalence can also be found in the following place, where Kant again defines *Willkür* as the free determination of will: "*Autonomy* of the will is the sole principle of all moral laws and of duties in keeping with them; *heteronomy* of choice (*Willkür*), on the other hand, not only does not ground any obligation at all but is instead opposed to the principle of obligation and to the morality of the will" (Kant 1997, CPrR, 5:33). In his second *Critique*, Kant conceives of the decisive moment of choice as moral respect. The moral feeling of respect represents a kind of "moral necessitation" and an "internal but intellectual constraint" (Kant 1997, CPrR, 5:32). However, this kind of "volitional necessity" is restricted to the faculty of pure practical reason and not to the contingent and individual person's decision.[5]

3.3   *Willkür* and Maxim in Kant's *Religion*

While Kant, in the 2nd edition of the *Critique of Pure Reason*, had left open whether *Willkür* be an object of transcendental philosophy, and had even excluded this in the A edition, he now positively determines "free choice (*Willkür*)" in his *Religion*, insofar as it is "not empirical," but "purely intellectual" (Kant 1996, RBMR, 6:35). While Kant in the *Critique of Practical Reason* had discussed the "autonomy of choice (*Willkür*)" in the sense of the autonomous determination by the moral law, he is now concerned with the failed, that is, evil determination of the will as "the actual resistance in time of the human power of choice (*Willkür*) against the law" (Kant 1996, RBMR, 6:35). In this respect, his *Religion* can be read as a "critique of the power of choice (*Willkür*)." Kant defines the individual freedom of man in the face of evil in connection with his concept of transcendental freedom as "absolute spontaneity of the power of choice (*Willkür*)" (Kant 1996, RBMR, 6:24). What is the positive freedom of *Willkür*? Since the ground of evil cannot lie in matter—neither in that of inclinations nor in the moral driving force of pure practical reason itself—only the possibility remains that it exists in a purely *formal* relationship to the determinants of the will, as "the formal ground of every deed contrary to law" (Kant 1996, RBMR, 6:31). Kant no longer locates the spontaneity of the freedom of choice (*Willkür*) in the general causality of reason, but in the individual decision, which stands in a reflexive relation to the moral law, although it has likewise a "rational origin" (Kant 1996, RBMR, 6:43). According to Kant, the "freedom of the power of choice (*Willkür*)" "cannot be determined to action through any incentive *except so far as the human being has incorporated it into his maxim* (has made it into a universal rule for himself, according to which he wills to conduct himself); only in this way can an incentive, whatever it may be, coexist with the absolute spontaneity of the power of choice (of freedom)" (Kant 1996, RBMR, 6:23-4).

Central to Kant's analysis of individual freedom is the concept of maxim, which he now characterizes as "a rule that the power of choice (*Willkür*) itself produces for the exercise of its freedom" (Kant 1996, RBMR, 6:21). This definition of the maxim shows that Kant does not understand the freedom of *Willkür* as an indifferent capacity, as *libertas indifferentiae*, but as grounded by an individual rule and based on reasons. Through the analysis of individual freedom, Kant adds further distinctions to the concept of maxim in contrast to the theoretical profile of the *Critique of Practical Reason*. While Kant there had distinguished the maxim as subjective rule—as "mere maxim""—of a "pathologically-affected will" from the objective practical laws of pure reason (Kant 1997, CPrR, 5:19), now he understands a maxim as the result of a weighing of first-order desires, which finally lead to a decision and action by reflection. The process of the evaluation of first-order desires is nothing groundless, nor is it founded in pure and general practical reason. Rather, it consists in a maxim which can be defined as a second-order maxim or "supreme maxim" (Kant 1996, RBMR, 6:31).[6]

3.4   *Willkür* and Will in the *Metaphysics of Morals*

The importance of Kant's late *Metaphysics of Morals* consists in the fact that it attempts to clarify the relation between will, power of choice (*Willkür*), reason, and moral law. For this reason, the concept of the power of choice (*Willkür*) is of special interest. Kant attempts to situate it within his system of transcendental philosophy and to clarify its determining ground. Kant's final remarks to the problem of *Willkür* can be found in the fourth section of the *Metaphysics of Morals* and encompass roughly one single page (Kant 1991, MM, 226–7). They read more like explications or annotations than a genuine theory. The fact that these final remarks are very short, however, must not hide the fact that they are of special systematic importance.[7]

Like in his *Religion*, Kant defines individual freedom as a maxim, namely as the "rule that the agent himself makes his principle on subjective grounds" (Kant 1991, MM, 6:225). Moreover, Kant defines the concept of a deed as an action "insofar as it comes under obligatory laws and hence insofar as the subject, in doing it, is considered in terms of the freedom of his choice ('Willkür')" (Kant 1991, MM, 6:223). It is striking that Kant defines the "capacity for desiring in accordance with concepts" as the "capacity for choice" ("Willkür") (Kant 1991, MM, 213), and not, as he did in his *Critique of Practical Reason*, as the "higher faculty of desire" ("höheres Begehrungsvermögen"), that is, pure practical reason Kant 1997, CPrR, 5:23–5). At this point, Kant sharply distinguishes between will ("Wille") and faculty of choice ("Willkür"):

> The capacity for desire whose inner determining ground, hence even what pleases it, lies within the subject's reason is called the will. The will is therefore the capacity for desire considered not so much in relation to action (as the capacity for choice is) but rather in relation to the ground determining choice to action. The will itself, strictly speaking, has no determining ground; insofar as it can determine the capacity for choice, it is instead practical reason itself. (Kant 1991, MM, 6:223)

It follows from this that it is not pure practical reason that immediately produces an action as the *principium executionis* through the moral feeling of respect; rather, the faculty of the power to choose takes up this intermediate position between will and action. Hence, Kant situates the faculty of choice *below* the will as a kind of faculty to realize the will in the empirical world (Kant 1991, MM, 6:213).

This definition of the faculty of choice has as a consequence the fact that the will has only a legislative function, whereas the power to execute the will lies in the faculty of choice: "Laws proceed from the will, *maxims* from choice ('Willkür')" (Kant 1991, MM, 6:226). Since the will "is directed to nothing beyond the law itself, [it] cannot be called either free or unfree, since it is not directed to actions but immediately to giving laws for the maxims of actions (and is, therefore, practical reason itself). Hence the will directs with absolute necessity and is itself subject to no necessitation" (Kant 1991, MM, 6:226). It follows that "[o]nly *choice* ("Willkür") can [...] be called *free*" (Kant 1991, MM, 6:226). This is due to the fact that it can choose the concrete *matter* of the maxim, whereas the will *qua* moral law always provides the *form* to which the faculty of choice can freely refer. Kant's attempt to locate autonomy and *Willkür* together in the realm of the intelligible is limited to the extent that the realm of the intelligible is exclusively restricted to the realm of pure practical reason. There is still the question to be answered, how a both *individual* and *free* decision is possible.

4   *Willkür* and Free Will in the Analytic Debate on Freedom

The fact that the concept of *Willkür* is also part of current concepts of freedom can be shown by a closer look at the theories of freedom of the will by Harry Frankfurt and Robert Kane. In the wake of his epoch-making essay "Free Will and the Concept of a Person," Harry Frankfurt distinguished the individual will from the pure will and general faculty of reason: "[T]he pure will is thoroughly *impersonal*. The commands that it issues are issued by no one in particular" (Frankfurt 1994, 436). Frankfurt opposes Kant's view that free will and pure be identical:

Kant argues that someone whose conduct is motivated merely by his own personal interests is inevitably heteronomous. What interests a person is a contingent matter, of course, which is determined by circumstances that are outside his control. Kant understands this to entail that personal interests are not integral to the essential nature of a person's will. In his view, they are volitionally adventitious: they do not depend wholly upon the person's inherent volitional character, but at least partly upon causes that are logically external to it. (Frankfurt 1994, 436)

At the center of Frankfurt's theory of freedom is the concept of the individual person, which is distinguished by a reflexive structure of the will. This structure can be further analyzed as a hierarchical model of first-order desires and second-order volitions. Frankfurt conceives freedom of will in analogy to freedom of action. Just as freedom of action basically means being able to *do* what you want, so freedom of will means being able to will what you will. While first-order desires are always object-oriented, that is, oriented toward concrete purposes, second-order volitions are normatively oriented to the extent that they contain personal standards of value that refer to first-order desires. The object-oriented desires represent the operative starting point from which a uniform and harmonious will is then produced by different deliberative achievements such as prioritization, integration, and separation by second-order volitions. According to Frankfurt, the essence of the person lies precisely in her ability to self-evaluate and form herself.

Just as freedom of action consists in the fact that directly action-oriented desires can be transformed into action, freedom of will consists in the fact that normative second-order volitions have control over first-order desires, and are thus able to produce a harmony which then leads to a unified will as an action-effective desire: "It is in securing the conformity of his will to his second-order volitions, then, that a person exercises freedom of the will" (Frankfurt 1971, 16). The free person identifies herself with a selection of first-order desires and thus takes responsibility for the actions resulting from this formed will. First-order desires thus represent for the person a reservoir of volitional possibilities, so to speak the voluntative "raw material" (Frankfurt 1994, 442), out of which she forms her will deliberatively, and which finally expresses her individuality: "It is these acts of ordering and of rejection—integration and separation—that create a self out of the raw materials of inner life. They define the intra-psychic constraints and boundaries with respect to which a person's autonomy may be threatened even by his own desires" (Frankfurt 1987, 39).

By this two-stage model of will, Frankfurt is referring to the original meaning of *Willkür* as the "choice of will." Freedom of the will is not about individual reasons that are successively taken into consideration, but about a holistic constellation of reasons in their personal context. With a view to such a holistic effect of the network of reasons on the person, Frankfurt coined the term "resonance effect":

> When a person identifies himself decisively with one of his first-order desires, this commitment 'resounds' throughout the potentially endless array of higher orders … The fact that his second-order volition to be moved by this desire is a decisive one means that there is no room for questions concerning the pertinence of desires or volitions of higher orders. (Frankfurt 1971, 16)

Only if the right personal frequency and coherence is achieved through the "arbitrary" adjustment of reasons, which corresponds to the individual nature of the person, that is, if a certain selection and order of first-order desires is appropriately arranged in relation to second-order volitions, a volitional integration and unity can be achieved. Instead of excluding empirical incentives from the formation of will, as Kant's theory of freedom as autonomy demands, Frankfurt holds that "[p]assions such as jealousy and craving merely provide him [scil. the person] with psychic raw material, as it were, out of which he must design and fashion the character and the structure of his will" (Frankfurt 1994, 442). A rational way of weighing reasons can maximize resonance, so that freedom of will is understood as a process of volitional formation that has various degrees. This volitional formation finally leads to a state of the person that Frankfurt calls "volitional necessity" (Frankfurt 1982, 264). Volitional necessity is just an expression of the result of an inner volitional formation that has come to a definite end, which is a decisive action. Volitional necessity, in other words, can be understood in terms of strength of the will or as a kind of volitional coherence by identification, which Frankfurt calls "wholeheartedness" (Frankfurt 1987, 33). Volitional necessity is fully compatible with freedom, since it is the result of a deliberate process, a process of reflecting and balancing reasons for an action, and of integrating different volitional tendencies into a unified will. Therefore, Willkür as individual decision is neither indifferent nor exclusively bound to pure practical reason. It is rather an expression of the individual person's will—a will that is essentially reflexive.[8]

Robert Kane, too, has revitalized the traditional concept of *Willkür*. He regards the concept of will as being divided by two equally strong motives: "[T]he indeterminism thus arising from a tension-creating conflict in the will" (Kane 2003, 230). These conflicting, contingent motives or first-order desires do not represent heteronomous determinants that would in principle be negligible for the free decision. Whatever the decision in view of the complete alternative of both determinants would be, it is based on the person's own will.

However, it must be shown how exactly the free decision can be conceived in the sense of positive freedom. According to Kane, the tension of indeterminism initially appears as a kind of obstacle due to the lack of overweight on one side. According to Kane, such a state of equilibrium turns out to be precisely the reason for enabling positive freedom, insofar as it enables the formation of second-order volitions:

> [B]y being a hindrance to the realization of some of our purposes, indeterminism paradoxically opens up the genuine possibility of pursuing other purposes—of choosing or doing *otherwise* in accordance with, rather than against, our wills (voluntarily) and reasons (rationally). (Kane 2003, 235–6)

According to Kane, this complexity of the will, which is transformed into an equilibristic state by conflicting desires, is virtually necessary for the opening of alternative possibilities and the development of the person through "self-forming actions" (Kane 2003, 225).

Kane here explicitly refers to the tradition of the *liberum arbitrium voluntatis*, which he translates as "free judgment of the will":

Imagine a writer in the middle of a novel. The novel's heroine faces a crisis and the writer has not yet developed her character in sufficient detail to say exactly how she will act. The author makes a "judgment" about this that is not determined by the heroine's already formed past, which does not provide unique direction. In this sense, the judgment (*arbitrium*) of how she will react is "arbitrary," but not entirely so. It had input from the heroine's fictional past and in turn gave input to her projected future. (Kane 2002, 425)

Free will persons are therefore " 'arbiters' of their own lives," which form themselves out of indeterminacy in a deliberate judgment. In this context, however, "arbitrary" does not mean mere arbitrariness in the bad sense, but a rational decision making process through judgment. Referring to the etymology of the word, Kane stresses that "'arbitrary' comes from the Latin *arbitrium,* which *means* 'judgment'. [...] "there is a kernel of in sight in this etymological connection for understanding free will." Kane therefore argues that "free agents are both authors of, and characters in, their own stories all at once. By virtue of their free choices *(arbitria voluntatis),* they are 'arbiters' of their own lives—'making themselves' as they go along out of a past that (if they are truly free) does not limit their future pathways to one" (Kane 1998, 145–6). Therefore, "free choices, decisions, and practical judgments may be viewed as instances of *liberum arbitrium,*" as Kane (1998, 22) argues.

5   Conclusion

A historical and analytic investigation of the philosophical concept of *Willkür* shows that it is by no means to be equated with groundless freedom or mere chance. Rather, it shows that it stands in the context of a long philosophical tradition in which the judgmental character of individual freedom plays a major role as the *liberum arbitrium voluntatis.* Understood in this way, and distinguished from the concept of a *liberum arbitrium indifferentiae,* that is of indifferentism, the concept of *Willkür* can also be revitalized in contemporary philosophical discourse, if one reflects on the process of volitional self-formation as well as on the role of reasons that are involved in individual free decisions.

Notes

1. For a more detailed discussion of the notion of *Willkür* see Noller (2020a). For an extensive historical and systematic analysis of *Willkür* as individual freedom and choice, especially with regard to immoral actions, see Noller (2016). If not indicated otherwise, the German translations are mine.
2. The Cambridge Edition of Kant's works translates "Willkür" as "power of choice" or "choice." However, other translations are likewise possible, such as "faculty of choice" or "capacity of choice."
3. "[L]'obéissance à la loi qu'on s'est prescrite est liberté."
4. Citations of Kant's works refer to the volume and page number in the Academy Edition of Immanuel Kant, *Gesammelte Schriften* (Berlin: Walter de Gruyter and predecessors, 1900 sqq).
5. For a historical and systematic discussion of Kant's notion of moral respect see Noller (2019b).
6. See Timmermann (2003, 150 sqq).
7. For a discussion of the concept of *Willkür* in Kant's *Metaphysics of Morals*, see Noller (2019a, 858-9).
8. For a historical and systematic discussion of individual freedom and volitional necessity in Kant, Schelling, and Frankfurt see Noller (2020b).

References

Duden-Redaktion. 2010. *Duden*. Mannheim: Duden.

Eisler, Rudolf. 1904. *Wörterbuch der philosophischen Begriffe. Second volume.* Berlin: Mittler.

Frankfurt, Harry G. 1971. Freedom of the Will and the Concept of a Person. *The Journal of Philosophy 68 (1)*: 5–20.

Frankfurt, H.G. 1982. The Importance of What We Care About. *Synthese 53 (2)*: 257–272.

Frankfurt, Harry G. 1987. Identification and wholeheartedness. In *Responsibility, Character, and the Emotions. New Essays in Moral Psychology*, ed. Ferdinand David Schoeman, 27–45. Cambridge: Cambridge University Press.

———. 1994. Autonomy, Necessity and Love. In *Vernunftbegriffe in der Moderne: Stuttgarter Hegel-Kongress 1993*, ed. Hans Friedrich Fulda and Rolf-Peter Horstmann, 433–447. Stuttgart: Klett.

Grimm, Jacob, and Wilhelm Grimm, eds. 1854. *Deutsches Wörterbuch*. Vol. 30. Leipzig: Hirzel.

Hegel, Georg Wilhelm Friedrich. 1986 sqq. *Theorie Werkausgabe* [TWA]. Edited by Eva Moldenhauer and Karl Markus Michel. Frankfurt a.m.: Suhrkamp.

Kane, Robert. 1998. *The Significance of Free Will*. New York/Oxford: OUP.

———. 2002. Some Neglected Pathways in the Free Will Labyrinth. In *The Oxford Handbook of Free Will*, ed. Robert Kane, 406–437. Oxford: Oxford University Press.

———. 2003. Free Will: New Directions for an Ancient Problem. In *Free Will*, ed. Robert Kane, 222–246. Malden, MA: Blackwell.

Kant, Immanuel. 1991. *The Metaphysics of Morals (=MM)*. Introduction, translation, and notes by Mary Gregor. Cambridge, UK: Cambridge University Press.

———. 1996. *Religion within the boundaries of mere reason (=RBMR)*, in *Religion and Rational Theology*. Edited by Allen W. Wood and George Di Giovanni and translated by George Di Giovanni, 31–191. Cambridge, UK: Cambridge University Press.

———. 1997. *Critique of Practical Reason (=CPrR)*. Edited and translated by Mary Gregor. Cambridge, UK: Cambridge University Press.

———. 1998. *Critique of Pure Reason (=CPR)*. Transl. by Paul Guyer and Allen Wood. Cambridge: Cambridge University Press.

Noller, Jörg. 2016. *Die Bestimmung des Willens. Zum Problem individueller Freiheit im Ausgang von Kant*. 2nd ed. Freiburg/München: Alber.

———. 2019a. 'Practical Reason Is Not the Will': Kant and Reinhold's Dilemma. *European Journal of Philosophy* 27 (4): 852–864. https://doi.org/10.1111/ejop.12448.

———. 2019b. Reason's Feeling. A Systematic Reconstruction of Kant's Theory of Moral Respect. *SATS. Northern European Journal of Philosophy 20* (1): 1–18. https://doi.org/10.12857/10.1515/sats-2019-0012.

———. 2020a. Kant und die Tradition des *liberum arbitrium*. Plädoyer für einen wohlverstandenen Begriff von Willkür. *Archiv für Begriffsgeschichte* 60/61a: 185–207.

———. 2020b. Higher Necessity: Schelling's Volitional Compatibilism. *Idealistic Studies* 1. https://doi.org/10.5840/idstudies202061112.

Ritter, Joachim, ed. 2004. *Historisches Wörterbuch der Philosophie*. Vol. 12. Schwabe: Basel.

Seebold, Elmar. 2011. *Kluge. Etymologisches Wörterbuch der deutschen Sprache*. Berlin/Boston: De Gruyter.

Timmermann, Jens. 2003. *Sittengesetz und Freiheit. Untersuchungen zu Immanuel Kants Theorie des freien Willens*. Berlin/New York: De Gruyter.

12

Determination, Chance and David Hume: On Freedom as a Power

Thomas Pink

1 Freedom and the Distinctiveness of Blame

In a famous discussion in *A Treatise of Human Nature* Hume argued that actions were produced solely by 'causes'. These causes, he claimed, were prior occurrences, including motivations or passions within the agent, that determined and necessitated the actions they produced. If freedom, or as Hume termed it 'liberty', required the absence of such necessitating causes, then freedom would come to nothing more than chance:

> [L]iberty, by removing necessity, removes also causes, and is the very same thing with chance. (Hume 1978, 407)

But then our moral responsibility for action could not depend on freedom. For how could our moral responsibility for our actions be based on

T. Pink (✉)
Department of Philosophy, King's College London, London, UK
e-mail: tom.pink@kcl.ac.uk

© The Author(s), under exclusive license to Springer Nature Switzerland AG 2021   **267**
M. Hausmann, J. Noller (eds.), *Free Will*,
https://doi.org/10.1007/978-3-030-61136-1_12

mere chance—on a mere absence of determination of our actions by anything else?

Hume is an important proponent of scepticism about the relevance to moral responsibility of freedom conceived, in incompatibilist terms, as inconsistent with the determination of action by prior occurrences for which the agent is not responsible. Incompatibilists view the causal power of past occurrences—happenings involving the agent but not the agent themselves—as a threat to the agent's responsibility for their actions. And perhaps the incompatibilists are right. But even if they are right, removing or reducing this causal power is at best to remove a threat to the agent's responsibility for what they do. It does nothing to provide a positive basis for that responsibility.

There is an opposing view of what freedom might amount to, however. Freedom is not, or not simply, an absence of determination of action by one kind of power, causal power exercised by prior occurrences. Rather freedom is a power in its own right, a power to determine action exercised not by occurrences, but by the agent themselves. If the agent has a moral responsibility for what they do, this is not, or not simply, because of an absence of determination of what they do by prior occurrences. It is because what the agent does is determined by the agent.

It seems that freedom does indeed matter to moral responsibility as a distinctive power of determination belonging to the agent. This becomes clear when we consider the content of moral blame—the criticism that asserts our moral responsibility for what we do.

Someone may have motivations that are entirely self-interested and act only on the basis of these. That is clearly enough to establish that they are selfish and that they act selfishly. The selfishness follows from the content of their motivations. Even if everything in the agent's life, their agency included, was predetermined by past occurrences (the product of upbringing, genetic inheritance or the like) we could still criticise them as thoroughly selfish. But this criticism very importantly does not amount to moral blame. For our criticism of them as selfish still leaves open the question whether that they so acted was their fault.

It makes perfect sense to criticise someone as thoroughly selfish, but to concede that perhaps, because of their upbringing or genetic inheritance, this selfishness, their selfish actions included, is simply not their fault.

The question of whether the selfishness is their fault is the question raised and answered in moral blame. When we blame someone morally for their selfish actions, we do not only criticise the selfish character of their motivations and actions, but we put their performance of the actions down to them as their fault.

So there are two importantly different levels of ethical criticism that can be made of people. One level does not raise the issue of a distinctively moral responsibility at all. An event in someone's life or a state of them is faulty, bad or foolish, and we criticise them simply by reference to that event or state. We may criticise people as selfish just insofar as their motivations or actions are selfish, or as foolish just insofar as their attitudes or actions are foolish. But in moral blame we go further and raise the question whether the fault in them, the defective event or state, was their fault. Moral blame asserts that it was, and this means that we move from criticism of someone as merely involved in defective events or states to someone as a determiner of them. The fault has to do not simply with the character of those events or states, but with the agent's own power to determine those events and states. The fault occurred because the agent exercised this power, or because they had the power but failed to exercise it. The selfish action is not only a fault in the agent, but the agent's own fault, only because its origin lies in the agent's own power to determine.

Hume ignored the possibility that freedom might be a power to determine action belonging to and exercised by the agent themselves. It is not surprising, then, that he failed to recognise that moral blame is a distinctive ethical criticism. For Hume blame is simply a heightened case of the general criticism of people for various kinds of deficiency:

> A blemish, a fault, a vice, a crime; these expressions seem to denote different degrees of censure and disapprobation; which are, however, all of them, at the bottom, pretty nearly of the same kind or species. (Hume 1975, 322)

And others have taken the same view of blame since. Consider Robert Merrihew Adams:

> Perhaps for some people the word 'blame' has connotations that it does not have for me. To me, it seems strange to say that I do not blame someone

though I think poorly of him, believing that his motives are thoroughly selfish. Intuitively speaking, I should have said that thinking poorly of a person in this way is a form of unspoken blame. (Adams 1985, 21)

For both Hume and Adams, to blame someone is simply to criticise someone for their faults. To blame someone morally no more assumes a power on their part to determine what they do than to criticise them for, say, being bad at history. Hume and Adams crucially ignore moral blame's very distinctive content—its criticism of faults within the agent as their fault.

Event-causal libertarianism makes the same mistake as Hume and Adams.[1] Event-causal libertarians are incompatibilists about freedom. They treat freedom as something that determination by prior occurrences would remove. But they do not think that freedom requires the agent to exercise any power of their own over what they do, beyond such power as is exercised (without determination) by their motivations—by occurrences within them. They effectively concede to Hume that, indeed, freedom 'is the very same thing with chance'. But having conceded that, they insist against Hume that freedom does still matter to moral responsibility.

But this view is quite self-undermining. By removing the agent as a determinant of occurrences, these libertarians remove the basis for moral blame as a distinctive form of criticism. We are left simply with the faultiness of the agent's motivations and actions; the question of whether any of these arise through the agent's fault can no longer arise. And if moral blame goes as a distinctive form of criticism, with it goes any rationale for incompatibilism about moral responsibility. If in blame all we are doing is criticising the agent as selfish or the like, how might that criticism be blocked by the predetermination of what the agent does? The selfishness has simply to do with what the agent aims at and the content of their motivations; and the truth or falsehood of determinism is irrelevant to that.

2 Freedom as Agent-Causation

If moral responsibility is distinctive in the way that we suppose it to be, so that faults in an agent can really be their fault, what must freedom as the power basing this responsibility be like?

We have seen that the power of freedom must, at the very least, be a power exercised by the agent. So it is tempting to reason as follows. The power is the same power that we find at work in causation through general nature—as when a brick hits a window and this causes it to break. Only instead of being exercised by occurrences, such as by the event of a brick hitting a window, freedom is simply causal power exercised by a persisting substance—an agent—to determine what they do. Freedom is causation—but agent-causation as opposed to event-causation. Causal power amounts to freedom when the bearer of the power, the cause, is a substance.

This would not be enough for a satisfactory account of freedom, however. First, it assumes that causes are not often substances in any case. But the ancient and medieval theories of causation that entertained causes as substances supposed not only that free agents but other substances too could be causes, so that substance-causation extended further than the exercise of freedom or control. A brick hits a window and causes it to break: the cause of the breakage might be the brick, on hitting the window, and not the event of its hitting the window. After all, the bearer and exerciser of power or force seems to be the brick. It is the brick, not the event of its hitting the window, that possesses the mass that impacts the window.

But even were the brick itself a cause, the brick is not free, and this is because the operation of the brick not up to it. The brick does not determine 'for itself' what outcomes it produces. Given that it is thrown so hard against the window, the brick can produce but one outcome—that the window breaks. The brick exercises a power to determine; but the operation of the brick is necessitated, like that of a cog in a machine. Even though the brick itself, and not some mere occurrence, may determine that the window breaks, it cannot be the brick's own fault that it operates so destructively.

That of course is not how we understand a free agent's power to determine. We think of freedom as power that leaves us able to determine 'for ourselves' what we do. We are not mere cogs within a mechanism, playing a merely instrumental role in the production of our actions. This is connected with something that seems central to freedom—its nature as a power to determine alternatives, a power that leaves us in control over which of a range of options by way of action we perform. The expression we commonly use in English to report this power has reference to alternatives baked in. 'It is up to me whether I raise my hand or lower it'—the very syntax of that expression 'up to me whether … or …' serves to report a plurality of contrary outcomes that I can determine and that are thereby left 'within my control' or 'up to me'. So freedom as a power of control over whether my hand is raised or lowered is a power both to produce the outcome that my hand is raised or, alternatively, the outcome where it is lowered.

As we have seen from the case of the brick, by contrast to freedom ordinary causation can perfectly well obtain as a power to produce but one outcome. When the brick hits the window, there may be but one outcome that can be produced—that the window breaks. Central to understanding freedom, then, is how freedom involves a capacity to produce and determine more than one outcome. And that understanding is clearly not provided just by identifying the bearer of the power as a substance. Whether or not it is true that unfree causes can be substances too (and though I shall often write as if they could be, nothing depends on this), more still needs to be said about how agents determine their actions 'for themselves', and in a way that involves control over alternatives.

3   Determination and Contingency

It is tempting to suppose that the missing element needed to complete the story is simply this. Freedom is substance-causation, but with just one further element—that the operation of the substance-cause is not itself causally determined. Supposing bricks were substance-causes too, that would be the difference between a free agent and an unfree brick. Both the free agent and the brick exercise the same power—causation—to determine outcomes. But the free agent is not determined by prior causes to produce one particular outcome, while the brick is. The brick is already determined by prior causes to break the window—causes that have determined the brick so to hurtle with its mass towards the window. But no prior cause determines that the free agent exercises his power to produce one action rather than another. That lack of predetermination is what provides the free agent's capacity to produce and determine more than one outcome.

But as we shall now see, that does not explain the difference. For the difference between freedom as a power and the causal power of a brick (or of events involving a brick) has to do not with prior causal determination, but with the differing natures of the powers themselves, and specifically with the way that those powers determine outcomes. The two powers must be of importantly different kinds, because they determine outcomes in a fundamentally different way.

Power or force involves a capacity to produce outcomes. But to produce an outcome is not always to determine it. A cause may produce an effect, but without determining that the effect occurs. The cause may merely influence whether the effect occurs. So too with the power of freedom. An agent may exercise their power of freedom or control to determine which outcome follows. Or they may merely exercise a lesser degree of control over the outcome, influencing but not determining whether it occurs.

Consider again that brick thrown against a window. Perhaps there is no chance of its not cracking the window. But whether beyond cracking the window the brick actually breaks it can still depend on chance. In which case the brick may in the relevant circumstances (when hurled against the window) have the power to determine that the window cracks; but it lacks the power to determine that the window breaks. The brick may still have some power to break the window. Indeed this is a power that may have been exercised in any case, just in causing the window to crack. Given the force applied to crack the window, no additional force beyond that which cracked the window would have had to be applied for an actual breakage to occur. But though the brick's power determines that the window cracks, it still leaves the window's actual breakage dependent on chance. Even if the brick does break the window, it will not have determined that the window breaks.

With causation, it is clear what is required for a cause to possess the power to determine an outcome. If an ordinary cause is to count as a determining cause of that outcome, then under the relevant circumstances the presence of the cause with its determining power must remove any chance of the outcome not occurring. To count as determining that the window breaks, the brick, when hurled at the window, must leave no chance of a breakage not occurring. If that condition is not met, then even if the cause does actually produce the outcome, it will not have determined its occurrence.

Contrast the case of a free agent and their power to produce or determine outcomes. It is clearly not a condition of an agent's power to determine, as opposed to merely influence, his performance of a given action that his presence with the power to determine remove any chance of that action's non-performance. That cannot be so, otherwise an agent could not possess, under one and the same circumstances, the power to determine incompatible alternatives by way of action.[2]

A power to determine a given outcome is of course, by its very nature, a power to remove the chance of that outcome not occurring. That is what the brick's power to crack the window constitutes—a power to remove any chance of the window not cracking. And a power to remove any chance of an outcome not occurring is what freedom gives me when it gives me complete control over what happens. If it is completely up to me whether or not I perform a given action A, I have a power the exercise of which, whether to do A or refrain, would leave which I do no longer up to chance. But by contrast to causal power in determining form, my mere possession of freedom as a power to determine a given outcome need not in itself, prior to the power's exercise, remove the chance of that outcome's non-occurrence.

The presence of a truly determining cause must remove any chance of the effect not occurring. But my presence with the power to determine that I do A does not of itself remove the chance of my refraining. Far from it. The very nature of freedom as a multiway power—a power to determine more than one outcome—is to be consistent with the production of more than one outcome. Prior to my exercise of freedom, though

I possess the power to determine that I do A, there might indeed be a chance of my refraining from doing A.

Power generally is the capacity to produce outcomes, and whether as causation or as freedom it can take determining form—a form which, once exercised, removes any remaining dependence of the outcome produced on chance. But ordinary causation and freedom are importantly different cases of power. For they determine outcomes in quite different ways. The power of a cause determines a given outcome only when the presence of the cause with its determining power excludes alternatives. But freedom is a power to determine outcomes that operates in quite a different way. And that is because the nature of freedom is to put outcomes within the power or control of the free agent. The nature of freedom is to make alternatives available to the power's possessor, not to exclude them.

4   Hume's Argument Again

Hume's argument assumed there were only two possibilities. Either there was a cause to determine the outcome. But then the cause operated by necessity. Or there was no such determining cause. But then there was no power to determine, and how the agent acted, far from being determined by the agent, was a matter of mere chance.

We now see that Hume's argument imports a way of looking at power that does apply—but only to ordinary causation. With causation there are indeed only two possibilities. Either the cause determines the outcome that it produces. But then the cause operates in a way necessitated by the very nature of its power and its circumstances of operation. If the cause really does have the power, under those very circumstances, to determine the outcome—the conditions required for exercise of the power to be successful are all met—the cause must produce the outcome.

Or else we have a case of causal power that is not determining—a case of probabilistic causation. Such a cause may influence towards a given outcome, but the outcome can still depend on chance. I throw a probabilistic brick at a window and the operation of its force might determine that the window cracks. But though the force of the brick is clearly operative, whether the window actually breaks might still depend on chance. The possibility of causal influence without determination allows incompatibilists to reconcile the evident influence of our desires and emotions over our actions with those actions remaining free. Even though our desires exercise a causal power over us—we feel ourselves moved by them to act one way rather than another—those desires need not determine how we act. It can be left to another power, our own freedom, to determine whether we finally act as our desires influence and incline us to.

The operation of a probabilistic cause is open. Its production of a given outcome is not necessitated by its power to produce it. The cause might or might not produce that outcome. But then the cause lacks power, because it at best influences what happens without determining it. So either causes lack power, or they operate in the fixed and inevitable way of a cog within a mechanism.

But where freedom is concerned, we think of power in quite a different way. The openness of freedom is essential to it. Freedom is by its very nature power over alternatives, a power that might be exercised to perform an action or to refrain. But this openness does not imply a weakening of the power. The openness of freedom does not prevent it from being a power to determine, and not merely influence, how the agent acts. Given the agent's exercise of this power, the outcome—how the agent acts—need no longer depend on chance. So the openness of freedom does not reduce to chanciness and lack of determination in the outcome—in the free action. But though the power is determining, instead of the power's operation being necessitated by its very nature, its operation is left contingent. Freedom is a power to determine—but to determine contingently.[3]

Hume argued that if you remove causal necessity from human action you are left with randomness rather than freedom. Hume was of course right if ordinary causation is the only power operative in nature. Then an action that is not determined by prior causes is not determined by any power. Its occurrence must depend on mere chance; it must be random. But if there can be a power that, unlike causation, determines contingently, Hume's claim is just false. An agent can determine how he acts, so that given the exercise of his power how he acts is not left to chance. But whether and how he exercised the power can still have been left open both by the nature of the power itself and by prior causes.

This distinguishing feature of freedom—contingency of determination—does not obviously imply incompatibilism about freedom. The contingency of operation involved in freedom is not the contingency of incompatibilist freedom. It is not an absence of prior determining causes. The contingency has to do instead with compatibility of freedom's nature as a power to determine one outcome with its operation to produce another. Freedom's nature as a power to determine outcomes is consistent with its being exercised in any one of alternative ways, to determine alternative outcomes. So freedom may be possessed as a power to determine a given outcome, and yet still not produce that outcome. The contingency has to do with the nature of freedom as a power to determine; it has to do with the way freedom determines outcomes when it does so. It is another question whether the operation of the power itself can ever be causally determined.

The theory of freedom as a determining power exercised by agents themselves is associated in modern philosophy with an incompatibilist conception of freedom. It is commonly treated as a form of libertarianism—a conception of freedom that while incompatibilist is non-sceptical, treating freedom as real and as important to moral responsibility. The theory of freedom as a power of agents is presented, then, as a libertarian alternative to event-causal libertarianism. It is still assumed, moreover, that the only power or capacity to produce outcomes in play is causation; agent-causal and event-causal libertarians dispute merely about whether agents themselves are causes.[4]

But now we see what really distinguishes freedom as a power. It is not enough that the bearer of the power is a substance. Nor does the power's identity as freedom come from its exercise being itself causally undetermined. What distinguishes freedom is its nature as a power to determine. You can still call freedom 'causation' if you like, but that is simply to use 'causation' as a general term for any capacity to produce outcomes. Freedom is clearly importantly different from what we ordinarily recognise as causation, such as the power of bricks, or of events involving bricks, to crack and break windows. Freedom is a power that can combine openness in operation with determining punch—properties that in ordinary causation are inconsistent.

Since we are distinguishing freedom by reference to the contingent way the power determines outcomes, and not by appeal to any supposed absence of determining causes for the power's own exercise, that leaves open a compatibilist view of the power. Belief in freedom as power of agents to determine alternative outcomes is not, or at least not trivially, a form of libertarianism. And we find in philosophical history examples of freedom understood as a power of agents to determine alternatives by way of action, but where some causal determination of the power's exercise was viewed as entirely possible.[5] Recognising freedom as a power of agents to determine outcomes contingently still leaves the debate between incompatibilism and compatibilism open. That debate remains, but now as a debate about the relations between two very different kinds of power, one (causation) whose mode of operation is fixed and restricted by its nature, the other (freedom) whose mode of operation as a power is left open by its nature.

The operation of freedom cannot be tied to the actual production of one outcome just by its nature as a power to determine that outcome. But could the exercise of freedom ever be determined to produce that outcome, not by its own nature, but by some prior cause? Could compatibilism about freedom be true? The answer to that question is far from obvious. Indeed, it is not even obvious by what method of inquiry this question of the relation between distinct forms of power should be pursued.[6]

Hume's argument against the existence of a specifically moral responsibility based on freedom does not, after all, really depend on incompatibilism about freedom. It depends instead on the assumption that all power is (ordinary) causation—the same power that operates when a brick cracks or breaks a window. That assumption makes a distinctively moral responsibility impossible from the outset, because it removes the agent as the distinctive object of moral blame. Either there is determination. But then the bearer of the power, be it event or substance, functions like a mere cog. The very nature of the power to determine a given outcome dictates its exercise to produce it. Or to the extent that the power's operation is open, we have nothing more than diminution of power—mere chance.

On the other hand, Hume's argument does nothing to support the assumption on which it so crucially depends: that all power is indeed causation. Hume has done nothing whatever to show that power—the capacity to produce outcomes—cannot come in more than one form. One form (causation) determines outcomes by excluding alternatives; the other (freedom) determines outcomes while making alternatives available. What is impossible about that?

Notes

1. I take the term 'event-causal libertarianism' from Clarke (2003, chapter 2).
2. For this argument see also Pink (2004, 114–115).
3. Freedom's involvement of contingency of determination, and its consequent distinction from causation, is explored in greater detail in Pink (2017)—see especially chapters 7, 8 and 14.
4. A modern pioneer of libertarian theorising about freedom as a causal power of agents was Roderick Chisholm—see, for example, Chisholm (1971).
5. Consider the Thomist-Augustinian theory of grace and predestination defended by Dominicans such as Domingo Banez in the early modern period and Reginald Garrigou-Lagrange in the twentieth century. Grace operates in those predestined to salvation as a cause determining their meritorious action, but without removing freedom as a power of the agent to determine that they act otherwise.
6. Relations between distinct cases of power in nature cannot always be resolved conceptually. That is certainly true when the only kind of power in question is causation, and we are looking at distinct cases of causal power. Is the exercise of one force by this cause compatible with the exercise of another force by that cause? Unless physics is turned into an entirely armchair science, conceptual inquiry alone may not produce the answer. We may have to experiment and look.

   As for the relations between one causal power and another, so too perhaps for the relations between freedom and causation. In the final chapter 15 of Pink (2017) I argue that conceptual argument has not proved decisive in establishing either compatibilism or incompatibilism about freedom. But much intuition in favour of incompatibilism seems not to be conceptually based in any case. It derives instead from phenomenology—from the way experience represents the impact of prior causation on freedom. (E.g.: to feel oneself being determined to do something by a prior cause outside the will itself, such as by intense fear or anger, is to feel oneself losing control. But this link in experience between representation of the operation of one power or force and representation of the removal of another seems to be a matter of human phenomenology; it need have nothing to do with relations between concepts.)

But then the key issue is not what causal determination implies conceptually, but the phenomenology. How are powers such as causation and freedom represented in experience, and what epistemic authority does such representation carry? David Hume is of course importantly responsible for the neglect of experience and phenomenology here. Not only was causation the only kind of power to produce outcomes he allowed for, to the extent that he allowed for the existence of power at all. He also insisted (dubiously) that power or force was never represented in experience in any case.

References

Adams, Robert Merrihew. 1985. Involuntary Sins. *Philosophical Review* 94 (1): 30.

Chisholm, Roderick. 1971. Reflections on Human Agency. *Idealistic Studies* 1: 33–46.

Clarke, Randolph. 2003. *Libertarian Theories of Free Will*. Oxford: Oxford University Press.

Hume, David. 1975. In *An Enquiry Concerning the Principles of Morals*, ed. P.H. Nidditch. Oxford: Clarendon Press.

———. 1978. In *A Treatise of Human Nature*, ed. P.H. Nidditch. Oxford: Clarendon Press.

Pink, Thomas. 2004. *Free Will: A Very Short Introduction*. Oxford: Oxford University Press.

———. 2017. *Self-Determination (The Ethics of Action, Volume 1)*. Oxford: Oxford University Press.

Part III

Free Will and Moral Responsibility

13

Kant's Justification of Freedom as a Condition for Moral Imputation

Claudia Blöser

Kant holds that transcendental freedom of the will—"a faculty of absolutely beginning a state, and hence also a series of consequences" (Kant 1998, 485; A445/B473)—is a necessary condition for moral imputation.[1] The question of whether we are really free is a vexed issue. In this contribution, I pursue two aims: On the one hand, I provide an account of how, according to Kant, theoretical and practical reason work together in a way that allows us to affirm that we are free. On the other hand, I bring Kant's position into contact with the contemporary debate and defend Kant's decidedly *practical* justification of freedom against objections. I will proceed as follows. In the first part, I introduce Kant's account of moral imputation and argue that it captures central aspects of what today is often discussed under the title of "moral responsibility". Further, I clarify the sense of freedom required for moral imputation. In the second part, I present an overview of Kant's resolution of the third Antinomy in the *Critique of Pure Reason*, where he argues that freedom and determinism are compatible. In the third part, I turn to Kant's practical

C. Blöser (✉)
Goethe University Frankfurt, Frankfurt, Germany

283

M. Hausmann, J. Noller (eds.), *Free Will*,
https://doi.org/10.1007/978-3-030-61136-1_13

philosophy, where he argues that, on the basis of practical considerations, notably our consciousness of the moral law, we can go beyond the mere logical possibility established by theoretical reason. Being conscious that we unconditionally *ought* to do something gives us reason to "postulate" that we are free. In the last part, I discuss Derek Pereboom's objections to Kant's practical justification of freedom (Pereboom 2001, 2006). I argue that contrary to what Pereboom suggests, Kantian ought judgments cannot do without the presupposition of transcendental freedom and that our practice of holding each other responsible relies on transcendental freedom as a necessary condition, even though freedom is not sufficient to justify every aspect of this practice. It turns out that Kant's practical justification of freedom is stronger than Pereboom suggests.

1   Moral Responsibility, Imputation and the Required Sense of Freedom

One central question animating the contemporary debate on freedom is whether we are free in the sense required for moral responsibility.[2] Kant rarely uses the term "moral responsibility".[3] It would be hasty, however, to infer from this that he does not have anything relevant to contribute to contemporary debates on this topic. Kant's approach to what most people today call "moral responsibility" can be found in his account of *moral imputation*. This becomes apparent when considering Derek Pereboom's view of moral responsibility and comparing it with Kant's characterization of imputation. Derek Pereboom holds that "for an agent to be morally responsible for an action is for this action to belong to the agent in such a way that she would deserve blame if the action were morally wrong, and she would deserve credit or perhaps praise if it were morally exemplary" (Pereboom 2001, xx). According to this view, the important features of moral responsibility are, first, the special connection between an agent and an action (the action's *belonging* to the agent in a particular way), and second, the idea that it is in virtue of this connection that the agent *deserves* praise or blame if the action is evaluated according to moral principles.[4] In Kant's characterization of imputation from the introduction to the *Metaphysics of Morals*, we find both of these features. The idea of a special connection between agent and action is expressed by calling the agent the "author" of an action:

> *Imputation* (*imputatio*) in the moral sense is the *judgment* by which some-one is regarded as the author (*causa libera*) of an action, which is then called a *deed* (*factum*) and stands under laws. (Kant 1996a, 19; 6: 227)

For Kant, being the "author" of an action is linked to the idea of freedom: Being an author is tantamount to being the free cause (*causa libera*) of the action. Understanding the person as a free cause suggests that reference to the person's will suffices to explain the action, without being led to ask for further previous causes.

Kant does not immediately connect the idea of being an author to the idea of being praiseworthy or blameworthy. Right after introducing the concept of imputation, however, Kant continues with the evaluative cat-egories of merit and culpability:

> If someone does *more* in the way of duty than he can be constrained by law to do, what he does is *meritorious* (*meritum*); if what he does is just exactly what the law requires, he does what is *owed* (*debitum*); finally, if what he does is less than the law requires, it is morally *culpable* (*demeritum*). (Kant 1996a, 19; 6: 227)

Even though Kant never identifies merit and culpability with praise- or blameworthiness, these pairs of concepts are closely connected.[5] An agent to whom an action is morally imputable is blameworthy (or praisewor-thy) for that action if the action is evaluated according to moral principles and found to be less than (or exactly what) the law requires.[6] Thus, the question formulated at the beginning—Are we free in the sense required for moral responsibility?—can be reformulated in Kant's terms as the question: Are we free in the sense required for moral imputation?

Before addressing Kant's answer to this question, we need to clarify what sense of freedom is required for moral imputation. Kant envisages two possible answers to this question, namely absolute and relative free-dom, which are characterized by either absolute or relative independence from natural causes. He characterizes these possibilities as transcendental, absolute freedom—"independence from everything empirical and so from nature generally" (Kant 1996b, 217; 5:97)—and "psychological and comparative" (Kant 1996b, 218; 5:97) freedom—independence from outer coercion and acting in accordance with an "internal chain of representations of the soul" (Kant 1996b, 217; 5:96). Kant emphatically expresses the view that moral responsibility requires an absolute sense of freedom. Without transcendental freedom, he claims, "no moral law is possible and no imputation in accordance with it" (Kant 1996b, 217; 5:97). This was Kant's view as early as in the first *Critique*, where he claims that the "transcendental idea of freedom [...] constitutes [...] the absolute spontaneity of an action, as the real ground of its imputability" (Kant 1998, 486; A448/B476).[7] Kant's reason for insisting on transcendental freedom is clearly stated in the *Critique of Practical Reason*. If our choices were only free in a comparative sense, they would be determined by antecedent states of affairs that reach back in time. However, "since time past is no longer within my control, every action that I perform must be necessary by determining grounds *that are not within my control*, that is, I am never free at the point of time in which I act" (Kant 1996b, 216; 5:94). The idea is that freedom—at least the kind of freedom "which must be put at the basis of all moral laws and the imputation appropriate to them" (Kant 1996b, 217; 5:96)—requires control and that this control is undermined if the action is necessarily determined by natural causes that precede it in time. That is, the worry is not so much that natural determinism is incompatible with the idea that the agent could have acted otherwise than she in fact did, but that natural determinism undermines the idea that the action is 'up to' the agent.

This leads to the question of how transcendental freedom can guarantee that the action is under the agent's control. In order to see this, we need to turn to the positive aspect of transcendental freedom. If Kant had characterized transcendental freedom only negatively (as independence from natural determination), this would have left open the possibility that free actions are due to mere chance. The idea that our actions are either determined by natural causality or due to chance is also referred to as "Hume's Fork".[8] There are legitimate doubts, however, concerning whether actions from chance are imputable—they do not show any relation to the person's character or intentions and hence are not signs of a person's moral qualities.[9] The clue to seeing how Kant circumvents Hume's Fork and guarantees the agent's control lies in the positive aspect of transcendental freedom. In the most abstract sense, Kant characterizes the positive aspect as "absolute causal spontaneity beginning from itself a series of appearances" (Kant 1998, 484; A446/B474). While this is the most general characterization—Kant introduces the notion of a transcendental idea of freedom in the first *Critique* as "freedom in the cosmological sense" (Kant 1998, 533; A533/B561)—Kant also applies it to human agency. In the *Dialectic*, Kant characterizes "[f]reedom in the practical sense" (Kant 1998, 533; A534/B562) as transcendental freedom applied to the human will.[10] Negatively, it is "the independence of the power of choice from necessitation by impulses of sensibility"; positively, it is "a faculty of determining oneself from oneself, independently of necessitation by sensible impulses" (Kant 1998, 533; A534/B562). Still, this does not answer the question of what it means to determine "oneself from oneself". Kant's answer is that a free action is determined by the person's own reason, more precisely by ought statements or imperatives (see, e.g., A534/B562, A802/B830, 6:213–214).

One difficulty at this point is the fact that Kant describes the relation between freedom and determination through imperatives differently in the *Critique of Pure Reason* and in the practical writings from the *Groundwork* onward. Accordingly, two positions can be found in Kant scholarship regarding the question of what transcendental freedom of the will consists in.[11] The first, which mirrors Kant's approach in the first *Critique*, holds that transcendental freedom of the will consists in the capacity to act on imperatives in general, that is, moral as well as prudential imperatives.[12] This capacity allows for independence from natural causes in the sense that actions are not determined by any particular inclination and can instead be performed on the basis of rational deliberation. The second interpretation holds that transcendental freedom of the will consists in the capacity to act on the categorical imperative, for the sake of the moral law.[13] This is how Kant characterizes freedom of the will in the third section of the *Groundwork*, where he calls it "autonomy, that is, the will's property of being a law to itself" (Kant 1997, 52; 4:447). Kant explains:

But the proposition, the will is in all its actions a law to itself, indicates only the principle, to act on no other maxim than that which can also have as object itself as a universal law. This, however, is precisely the formula of the categorical imperative and is the principle of morality; hence a free will and a will under moral laws are one and the same. (Kant 1997, 52–53; 4:447)

Freedom as autonomy, as Kant conceives of it in this passage, constitutes independence not only from any particular inclination but from inclinations in general and is the capacity to act from a purely rational motive, namely the formal criterion that one's maxim should be apt to be a universal law.[14]

For the purposes of this contribution, we do not need to decide which of the two interpretations offers the correct reading of transcendental freedom in general. The more specific question is how to understand transcendental freedom as required for moral imputation. Freedom as a condition for moral responsibility, in Kant's framework, has two functions: First, freedom secures the idea of authorship by designating the person's will as the first cause of the action. Because an action is independent of natural determination and originates in a choice according to principles of the person's own *reason*, that person has the required control over her action. The second function comes into view when considering the claim that an imputable action "stands under laws" and can be evaluated according to those laws, which leads to merit or culpability. The person must therefore be an appropriate addressee of these laws; that is, she must possess the capacity to comply with them. For *moral* imputation, the relevant laws are *moral*. Thus, we must presuppose transcendental freedom of the will as autonomy.

Let me close this section by relating Kant's conception of freedom to the contemporary debate. In this section, the central question was how to characterize the kind of freedom required for moral imputation. In arguing for the requirement of transcendental freedom, Kant takes a side on the question of whether freedom and natural determinism are compatible. In general, there are two options: Compatibilists affirm, while incompatibilists deny the compatibility of freedom and natural determinism. It is tricky to locate Kant in this debate. On the one hand—as we will see in the next section—he argues that absolute freedom can be reconciled with the determination, by natural causality, of everything empirical. This reconciliation is possible on the basis of transcendental idealism. On the other hand, we have seen in this section that his main reason for requiring transcendental freedom rather than comparative freedom is that natural determinism undermines the agent's having control over her action and therefore her freedom.[15] This argument can be seen as a predecessor of a famous argument for incompatibilism, the "Consequence Argument" (van Inwagen 1983). On this basis, Kant can be seen as an incompatibilist who denies the compatibility of freedom and determinism but affirms that we are free—a position that we today call "libertarianism".[16] Pereboom aptly describes Kant as "a source rather than a leeway incompatibilist, stressing that the key notion of freedom is not the ability to do otherwise, but rather being the undetermined source of one's actions" (Pereboom 2006, 542). The ability to do otherwise in every situation does not characterize free will, according to Kant. However, Kant does assume that a person with a free will could have acted otherwise when she *violates* a moral law. This is just the retrospective perspective on the idea that "ought implies can":[17] If one morally ought to do something, one must be able to do it—in other words, one must have the capacity to act morally. If one fails to exercise that capacity properly and acts wrongly, one must acknowledge—looking back—that one could have acted otherwise.

2 Making Room for Freedom: The Compatibility of Transcendental Freedom and Determinism

Kant is not a "pure" incompatibilist; in the *Critique of Pure Reason*, he argues that natural determinism and freedom are compatible. He frames the problem of compatibility in terms of an antinomy, that is, a contradiction between a thesis—there is more than natural causality, namely causality from freedom (Kant 1998, 484; A444/B472)—and an antithesis—everything happens according to laws of nature (Kant 1998, 485; A445/B473). The resolution of this antinomy, which he presents as the third Antinomy of pure reason, constitutes his argument for the compatibility of freedom and determinism. Having introduced Kant's notion of transcendental freedom in Sect. 1, let me sketch what kind of determinism Kant has in mind as a threat to freedom. Kant makes clear that the "correctness of the principle of the thoroughgoing connection of all occurrences in the world of sense according to invariable natural laws is already confirmed as a principle of the transcendental analytic" (Kant 1998, 534; A536/B564). This transcendental principle of causation, which Kant defends in the second Analogy in the Analytic, holds that "[a]ll alterations occur in accordance with the law of the connection of cause and effect" (Kant 1998, 304; B232). Further, cause and effect follow in an irreversible temporal order, "inevitably and necessarily" (Kant 1998, 310; A198/B244). This principle that every event has a necessary, temporally preceding cause belongs to the conditions of the possibility of empirical experience. In presupposing this transcendental principle of causation in the context of the Antinomy, Kant claims to show the compatibility of freedom with *every* kind of determination through temporally preceding causes, according to all kinds of special causal laws, such as the laws of physics and psychology.[18]

Kant's resolution of the antinomy hinges on the central distinction within transcendental idealism: that between appearances (or *phenomena*) and things in themselves (or *noumena*). As Kant puts it pointedly, "if appearances are things in themselves, then freedom cannot be saved" (Kant 1998, 535; A536/B564). Kant does not withdraw or weaken his claim that all objects of experience are necessarily subject to complete causal determination. Rather, his solution consists in *limiting the scope* of natural causality to the realm of appearances, while freedom finds application in the realm of things in themselves.

Thus, the appeal of Kant's suggestion for how to reconcile freedom and determinism depends on an account of "things in themselves". The distinction between things in themselves and appearances, as Kant draws it in the Transcendental Aesthetic, is a consequence of the fact that human beings can cognize the world only by way of a specific human cognitive apparatus. To gain cognition, we must equally draw on sensibility and understanding by connecting intuitions and concepts to form judgments. Kant argues that space and time are necessary forms of sensible intuition that shape every empirical experience and are therefore necessary features of things as they "appear" to us. Abstracting from the sensible conditions of experience yields the concept of a "noumenon in the negative sense" (Kant 1998, 360; B307). Beyond this merely negative concept, Kant introduces the notion of a "noumenon in a positive sense" (Kant 1998, 361; B307). The idea is that things might have not only empirical features but also features that are not accessible by empirical cognition, as long as those "intelligible" features do not conflict with observable features.[19] Kant assumes the possibility of ascribing such features when he states at the beginning of the resolution of the Antinomy that he calls "*intelligible* that in an object of sense which is not itself appearance" (Kant 1998, 535; A538/B566).

Just as one can view objects as having intelligible features, one can view objects as having a "faculty which is not an object of intuition, through which it can be the cause of appearances" (Kant 1998, 535; A538/B566). The causality of such a faculty can be considered "in two aspects, as intelligible in its action as a thing in itself, and as sensible in the effects of that action as an appearance in the world of sense" (ibid.). Kant finally also applies this distinction between the intelligible and the empirical to the "law of its [the cause's, CB] causality", which Kant calls "character":

> But every effective cause must have a character, i.e., a law of its causality, without which it would not be a cause at all. And then for a subject of the world of sense we would have first an empirical character, through which its actions, as appearances, would stand through and through in connection with other appearances in accordance with constant natural laws [...]; and thus, in combination with these other appearances, they would constitute members of a single natural order. Yet second, one would have to allow this subject an intelligible character, through which it is indeed the cause of those actions as appearances, but which does not stand under any conditions of sensibility and is not itself appearance. The first one could call the character of such a thing in appearance, the second its character as a thing in itself. (Kant 1998, 536; A539/B567)

Thus, the distinction between empirical and intelligible character is analogous to the distinction between appearances and things in themselves.

Correspondingly, empirical character is "part of the world of sense" (Kant 1998, 537; A540/B568) and subject to conditions of time, while intelligible character "would not stand under any conditions of time" (Kant 1998, 536; A539/B567). Kant ascribes to intelligible character freedom in the negative and the positive sense: Regarding its intelligible character, a subject would "have to be declared free of all influences of sensibility and determination by appearances" (Kant 1998, 537; A541/B569), and "[o]f it one would say quite correctly that it begins its effects in the sensible world from itself" (ibid.). In sum, the answer to the question of how freedom and determinism are compatible is that on the basis of the distinction between appearances and things in themselves, "nothing hinders us" (Kant 1998, 536; A538/B566) from ascribing freedom as a special kind of causality to things in themselves.

To be sure, there are many controversial issues surrounding Kant's transcendental idealism that I cannot address here. Let me close this section by addressing one question, which is especially relevant to Kant's practical treatment of freedom: Does Kant's claim that things in themselves can be thought of as free causes contradict the central thesis of the *Critique of Pure Reason*—the idea that we can only have cognition (*Erkenntnis*) of objects of experience and not of things in themselves? The thesis that we cannot have cognition of noumena is grounded in the fact that cognition of an object presupposes concepts and intuition, but things in themselves are not given to us in intuition. Still, Kant holds that the concept of causality "can be used even of noumena" (Kant 1996b, 183; 5:54), as long as we keep in mind that "this concept cannot be determined in the least and thereby produce a cognition" (ibid.). Kant clearly makes this point in the first *Critique*, where he says that

> the categories are not restricted *in thinking* by the conditions of our sensible intuition, but have an unbounded field, and only the *cognition* of objects that we think, the determination of the object, requires intuition. (Kant 1998, 264; B166n.)

What is shown in the first *Critique* is the logical, but not the real, possibility of freedom. Kant uses the distinction between logical and real possibility in the sense of 'concerning the non-contradictoriness of a concept' (see Kant 1998, 344; A244/B302) and 'concerning the object'.[20] Kant has shown in the resolution of the antinomy "that nature at least does not conflict with causality through freedom" (Kant 1998, 546; A558/B586), and hence the non-contradictoriness of the combination of nature and freedom. Still, Kant emphasizes that "we have not even tried to prove the possibility of freedom" (Kant 1998, 546; A558/B586), where he seems to mean *real* possibility. For Kant, the question of the real possibility of a concept is whether it relates to an object (see Kant 1998, 342; B303, fn). As we will see in the next section, it is precisely this relation to an object that the practical philosophy is able to establish.

3   The Practical Justification of Freedom

As early as in the first *Critique*, we find precursors of a practical justification of freedom when Kant claims: "that this reason has causality, or that we can at least represent something of the sort in it, is clear from the imperatives that we propose as rules to our powers of execution in everything practical" (Kant 1998, 540; A547/B575). This idea is spelled out in Kant's practical writings. One difficulty in approaching Kant's justification of freedom on practical grounds is that he presents a different argument in the third section of the *Groundwork* and in the *Critique of Practical Reason*. In the *Groundwork*, Kant formulates the following in an assertive mode:

> I say now: every being that cannot act otherwise than under the idea of freedom is just because of that really free in a practical respect, that is, all laws that are inseparably bound up with freedom hold for him just as if his will had been validly pronounced free also in itself and in theoretical philosophy. (Kant 1997, 53; 4:448)

The full argument in the third section of the *Groundwork* is complicated, but let me address three questions that point to aspects that are improved in Kant's later approach in the second *Critique*. First, what does it mean to act "under the idea of freedom"? Is acting under the idea tantamount to *believing* that one is free? This is questionable, as it seems to be an option to deny the belief that one is free (for instance on the grounds that one is incompatibilist and believes that everything is determined) and set this aside in action.[21] Rather, acting under the idea seems to point to a presupposition in acting that need not be identified with (justified) belief. Kant's doctrine of the postulates in the second *Critique* can be understood as clarifying the nature of this presupposition. Second, why should we think that a being cannot act otherwise than under the idea of freedom? In contrast to the second *Critique*, Kant is not making specific reference to the capacity to act on *moral* laws. Rather, he links the presupposition of freedom to consciousness of being a rational agent in general and draws on the symmetry between theoretical and practical spontaneity. Reason "shows in what we call 'ideas' a spontaneity so pure that it thereby goes far beyond anything that sensibility can ever afford it" (Kant 1997, 57; 4:452), which implies that any being with reason must regard itself "as belonging to the intelligible world" and therefore as free, even in his or her actions. Kant's move from theoretical to practical spontaneity is problematic—it is at least unclear whether they are similar or isomorphic in the relevant sense. In particular, it is not clear whether or how one can infer autonomy ("the will's property of being a law to itself", Kant 1997, 52; 4:447), which is required for the bindingness of the categorical imperative, from the spontaneity expressed in developing 'ideas'.[22] Thus, many interpreters view the new approach in the second *Critique*, which makes no reference to theoretical spontaneity, as an implicit acknowledgment on Kant's part that the strategy of the *Groundwork* is defective. A third question arising from the *Groundwork* is the "bindingness problem" (Allison 2013, 289): If Kant's argument shows that we must *presuppose* freedom, then this seems at most to be able to show that we must *presuppose* that we are bound by the categorical imperative, not that we *really are* bound by it.

This third problem is solved by the new strategy in the *Critique of Practical Reason*. Here, Kant does not argue from a presupposition of freedom to the (presupposition of) the moral law. Instead, he argues the other way around: From consciousness of the moral law (the "fact of reason"), we can infer that we are free. In the rest of the section, I present the argument in the Analytic of the second *Critique* and relate it to the doctrine of the postulates, which answers the question of the sense in which practical reason is able to complement the account of the logical possibility of freedom provided by theoretical reason. Kant argues, in a first step, for the reciprocity thesis: "[F]reedom and unconditional practical law reciprocally imply each other" (Kant 1996b, 162; 5:29). In a nutshell, the argument for this thesis is that a will that is determinable by the "mere lawgiving form of maxims" (Kant 1996b, 162; 5:28) must be "independent of the natural law of appearances" (Kant 1996b, 162; 5:29); that is, it must be transcendentally free. The reciprocity thesis amounts to a conditional: If a will is determinable by the moral law, it is transcendentally free. The second step is meant to show that the antecedent is true: The "fact of reason", that is, consciousness of the moral law, shows the person that the moral law is valid for her. Kant illustrates this with the famous gallows example, in which a person is asked by a powerful ruler "on the pain of […] immediate execution, that he give false testimony against an honorable man" (Kant 1996b, 163; 5:30). In such a situation, Kant holds that one is immediately aware that one unconditionally ought to tell the truth; that is, one is immediately conscious that one's will is determinable by the moral law. Hence, together with the reciprocity thesis, one "cognizes" (Kant 1996b, 164; 5:30) that one is free.

Kant cannot mean here that the fact of reason allows for theoretical cognition, since we still lack an intuition of freedom. Still, the *Critique of Practical Reason*, according to Kant, shows that freedom (along with the other transcendental ideas of god and immortality) indeed has "objective reality" (Kant 1996b, 139; 5:4). Kant uses different formulations for this point: Freedom has "objective reality" (Kant 1996b, 139, 175, 248; 5:4; 5:44; 5:135), "practical reality" (Kant 1996b, 185, 5:56), "objective and, though only practical, undoubted *reality*" (Kant 1996b, 179; 5:49), and the concepts of freedom, god and immortality "are real and really have their (possible) objects" (Kant 1996b, 248; 5:134). These are alternative ways of putting the same thought: On practical grounds, we cognize that the concept of freedom refers to a specific *object*. The "fact of reason" allows for this cognition insofar as it is consciousness of the fact that one's will is determinable by the moral law and therefore—drawing on the reciprocity thesis—that the will is free.

What remains a difficult question, however, is exactly what kind of epistemic attitude we can take toward freedom on practical grounds. Key to understanding the practical extension of Kant's account of freedom is his doctrine of the postulates. In the Dialectic of the *Critique of Practical Reason*, Kant argues that we can postulate the immortality of the soul (Kant 1996b, 238–239; 5:122–123), god's existence (Kant 1996b, 239 ff.; 5:124 ff.) and freedom of the will (Kant 1996b, 246; 5:132). He defines a "postulate of pure practical reason" as "a *theoretical* proposition, though one not demonstrable as a such, insofar as it is attached inseparably to an a priori unconditionally valid *practical* law" (Kant 1996b, 238; 5:122), which is the moral law. The two distinctive features of postulates can thus be called (1) theoretical undecidability and (2) practical necessity.[23] Theoretical undecidability was the result of the first *Critique*: Freedom cannot be an object of knowledge, but it also cannot be shown to be impossible. The second aspect, practical necessity, is at issue in the second *Critique*. With regard to god and immortality, Kant presents extended arguments for why they are "attached inseparably" to the moral law. These arguments, which I will not consider here, rely on the concept of the "highest good", which Kant introduces as the necessary end of moral willing. Kant argues that both god and immortality are necessary presuppositions of the possibility of the highest good and in this sense practically necessary.

The section on the postulates does not offer an argument for the practical necessity of freedom. Instead, Kant briefly states that the postulate of freedom is grounded in "the necessary presupposition of independence from the sensible world and of the capacity to determine one's will by the law of an intelligible world" (Kant 1996b, 246; 5:132). Freedom, Kant claims here, must be postulated as a necessary presupposition of the moral law, without thereby gaining any further theoretical insight: "But how freedom is even possible and how this kind of causality has to be represented theoretically and positively is not thereby seen; that there is such a causality is only postulated by the moral law and for the sake of it" (Kant 1996b, 247; 5:133).

The relation between Kant's idea of freedom as a postulate and his idea in the Analytic of the second *Critique* that one "cognizes" (Kant 1996b, 246; 5:30) freedom through the "fact of reason" (Kant 1996b, 246; 5:31) has troubled many interpreters.[24] I cannot do justice to this question here. I am sympathetic to the idea that Kant does not provide an explicit argument for the postulate of freedom in the Dialectic because he already provided an argument in the Analytic, based on the fact of reason.[25] On this reading, it is not the case that Kant justifies the belief in freedom in two different ways, first through the fact of reason and second through the doctrine of the postulates. The fact of reason does not give us access to our freedom directly but is an awareness of the validity of *moral obligation*. By reflecting on the presuppositions of the validity of the moral law, we can cognize that we are free. This is tantamount to saying that freedom must be postulated as a presupposition of the moral law. The doctrine of the postulates, however, cannot fully replace the idea of a fact of reason; without consciousness of the moral law, we would not be aware that the moral law is valid *for us*, and hence we would not be aware that we must postulate freedom for *our will*.

In sum, whereas the first *Critique* showed that freedom is logically possible, that is, can be thought without contradiction, the second *Critique* introduced the notion of a postulate: We do not have to suspend judgment as to whether we are free but are rationally entitled to postulate that we are free because this is a necessary presupposition of acknowledging the moral law. This argument for why we can affirm our freedom—and indeed the transcendental freedom required for moral imputation— employs a *practical* justification. Whether we are free cannot be answered by theoretical considerations, for example, by pointing to the evidence or to general claims about nature, such as the truth or falsity of determinism. To be sure, Kant's practical justification presupposes a theoretical claim, namely that theoretical reason leaves *open* the question whether we are free. The positive reason for affirming freedom is a *moral* one, however. Unconditional ought judgments are valid only for a transcendentally free will, since only such a will is able to obey unconditional demands. Our consciousness of being bound by unconditional demands (the "fact of reason") allows us to infer that transcendental freedom—as a necessary presupposition of such a demand—must be affirmed, as well.

4   Pereboom on Kant's Practical Justification of Freedom

Having presented Kant's practical justification of freedom, I now want to discuss Derek Pereboom's objections to this approach. Pereboom argues "that it is not clear that the practical reasons Kant adduces provide practical justification for the belief that we are transcendentally free" (Pereboom 2006, 548).[26] Pereboom presents what he views as Kant's two practical reasons for this belief and voices skepticism against both of them. The first reason is that the truth of ought judgments, in particular moral principles, is incompatible with natural determinism; the second is that judgments of moral responsibility are incompatible with natural determinism as well. Let us consider Pereboom's interpretation of these two reasons in turn.

In order to show that Kant is committed to the claim that ought judgments presuppose transcendental freedom, Pereboom adduces Kant's idea, from the first *Critique*, that we can recognize reason's causal power from ought statements, namely practical imperatives. The argument is that we are subject to imperatives, that these imperatives contain an ought, and that the idea that something ought to be other than it is cannot be grounded in nature, since on the basis of nature we can only cognize what is. Pereboom connects this argument to Kant's affirmation of an ought-implies-can principle: "If one ought to do something, then it must be the case that one can do it" (Pereboom 2006, 560). If one is fully determined by natural causality, however, it seems that one can never do otherwise; hence, it would be false to say that one ever ought to do otherwise.

Pereboom raises two objections against the proposal that being subject to ought judgments constitutes a practical reason to believe in transcendental freedom: First, there might be "'ought' judgments sufficient for morality that do not presuppose an 'ought implies can' principle" (Pereboom 2006, 561). These principles, like 'You ought not steal', might be able to "guide actions" by causally influencing "the selection of options for action" (ibid.), even if it turned out to be true that the person could not have complied with the judgment due to causal determinism. Second, independently of the truth of moral ought judgments, Pereboom submits that there could still be moral principles "about rightness and wrongness of actions" (Pereboom 2006, 561), such that "it is morally good/bad to do x/y" is true. For instance, even if a person were genetically determined to commit violent crimes, it would still be true that those crimes were morally wrong and that it would be morally wrong for him to commit them. According to Pereboom, these principles might be sufficient for "moral evaluation", "moral encouragement and admonition" (Pereboom 2006, 562).

If Pereboom's objections (especially the first one) were sound, this would be detrimental to Kant's practical justification. If a moral ought were possible without the presupposition of transcendental freedom, we could not postulate transcendental freedom on the basis of the consciousness of a moral ought. The claim that we are transcendentally free would lack the *practical necessity* that is a necessary feature of a postulate. However, while Pereboom's objections may seem compelling if one only considers Kant's account in the first *Critique*, they can be answered by drawing on Kant's account in the second *Critique*.

To answer Pereboom's first objection—that a moral ought principle can be action guiding without implying transcendental freedom and ought-implies-can—we need to consider the reciprocity thesis that Kant establishes in §§5 and 6 of the second *Critique* (a version of which he had previously argued for in the third section of the *Groundwork*). The reciprocity thesis states that if a will can be determined by an unconditional moral law, it must be transcendentally free, and vice versa: a transcendentally free will must be determinable by the mere lawgiving form of maxims. To be sure, the moral law itself is not an ought judgment. However, it presents itself in the form of an ought judgment—the categorical imperative—for beings such as humans, who are not purely rational but also sensible beings that do not comply inevitably with the moral law. If the categorical imperative (and with it all moral ought judgments) is the way that the moral law presents itself to us, and if the moral law is the law of a transcendentally free will, there is no room for unconditional moral ought judgments that are able to guide actions without presupposing transcendental freedom of the will. That is, to refute Kant's thesis that moral ought judgments presuppose a transcendentally free will, one would have to attack the reciprocity thesis, but Pereboom does not offer reasons for doing so.

To be sure, Pereboom is certainly right to the extent that not *all* conceptions of morality are undermined by the denial of transcendental freedom. One could be a utilitarian, for instance, and use the principle of maximizing utility to guide one's actions without thereby presupposing transcendental freedom. Pereboom's aspiration, however, is to show that *Kant's own* conception of morality can be upheld even if transcendental freedom is denied.[27] In the background of this aspiration is Pereboom's hope that "[r]ejecting the claim that we are morally responsible" will not "jeopardize moral principles and values" (Pereboom 2001, xix). Various passages provide evidence that Kant, by contrast, holds that there is an intimate connection between the kind of freedom that is presupposed by moral responsibility (or imputation) and that presupposed by the validity of moral principles. Recall two passages cited in Sect. 1: Kant holds that psychological freedom is not the kind of freedom "which must be put at the basis of all moral laws *and the imputation appropriate to them*" (Kant 1996b, 217; 5:96, my emphasis) and that without transcendental freedom "no moral law is possible and *no imputation in accordance with it*" (Kant 1996b, 217, 5:97, my emphasis). These formulations suggest that being subject to the moral law indeed presupposes transcendental freedom, just as moral imputation does. Judging from these passages, Kant's moral theory offers little promise for holding on to the validity of moral principles while giving up on transcendental freedom and moral imputation.

Pereboom's second objection against Kant's first practical consideration—that moral ought judgments presuppose transcendental freedom—rests on the idea that judgments about moral *goodness* are independent of judgments about what one morally ought to do. However, this is not how Kant describes the relationship between good and evil on the one hand and the moral law on the other in the section called "On the concept of an object of pure practical reason" in the second *Critique* (Kant 1998, 186; 5:57–58). He argues that we cannot conceive of moral good and evil independently of or prior to the moral law. This is what he calls the "paradox of method": "the concept of good and evil must not be determined before the moral law (for which, as it would seem, this concept would have to be made the basis) but only (as was done here) after it and by means of it" (Kant 1998, 190; 5:63). I cannot here do justice to this fundamental claim expressing Kant's view that moral laws are more fundamental than values. In a nutshell, Kant's view is that an action is good if and only if it is done in accordance with (and for the sake of) the moral law. Humans are not only rational but also sensible beings who are not inevitably determined by reason. Therefore, the moral law presents itself in the form of imperatives, that is, ought judgments. A holy will would act on the moral law inevitably; it would perform actions just because they are good. For human beings, the thought that an action is good is necessarily presented in the form of an ought judgment:

> All imperatives are expressed by an ought and indicate by this the relation of an objective law of reason to a will that by its subjective constitution is not necessarily determined by it (a necessitation). They say that to do or to omit something would be good, but they say it to a will that does not always do something just because it is represented to it that it would be good to do that thing. (Kant 1997, 24; 4:413)

Thus, to use Pereboom's own example, the principle "It is good to give to charity" amounts to the principle "You ought to give to charity" if its addressee is the human will who does not always do what is represented as good by reason. In sum, the dependency of judgments about moral goodness and badness on the moral law—and hence on what we, as rational and sensible beings, ought to do—expressed in what Kant calls the "paradox of method" grounds skepticism about Pereboom's suggestion that we might retain judgments about moral goodness and badness independently of moral ought judgments. It is at least difficult to see how one could do so on the basis of Kant's ethics, where ought judgments are more fundamental than values.

After discussing the implications of the moral "ought", Pereboom turns to what he takes to be Kant's second practical reason for affirming transcendental freedom: "if we lacked this kind of freedom our judgments of blameworthiness—and moral responsibility more generally—would turn out to be false" (Pereboom 2006, 562). Pereboom points to the passage on the "malicious lie" to illustrate that this is indeed Kant's view. In this passage, Kant claims that "even if one believes the action to be determined by these causes, one nonetheless blames the agent, [...] for one presupposes that [...] this deed could be regarded as entirely unconditioned in regard to the preceding state, as though with that act the agent had started a series of consequences entirely from himself" (Kant 1998, 544; A555/B583). Pereboom sums up: "The idea is that we have good practical reason to judge the liar blameworthy, and since blameworthiness requires transcendental freedom, we thereby have a good practical reason to believe that he is transcendentally free" (Pereboom 2006, 563).

Pereboom's argument against Kant can be summed up as follows: (1) Our practice of judging wrongdoers blameworthy presupposes transcendental freedom; (2) we do not have sufficient evidence to believe that we are transcendentally free; therefore, (3) our practice of judging wrongdoers blameworthy is not justified. If this reconstruction of the argument is correct, it does not object to the idea that we have a practical reason to believe in transcendental freedom. Pereboom is right that the *mere fact* that we judge the liar blameworthy hardly constitutes a good practical reason to ground a belief in freedom insofar as the judgment of blameworthiness could be false. If Kant were to treat the mere fact of blame as a practical reason for freedom, this would be circular: If we want to show that we can affirm that we are free because freedom is a necessary condition for moral responsibility, we cannot adduce moral responsibility as a reason for affirming freedom. This is not Kant's argument, however, and Pereboom rightly claims that, according to Kant, we have "*good practical reason* to judge the liar blameworthy" (Pereboom 2006, 563, my emphasis). But what is this practical reason? Pereboom does not appear to address this question. I will briefly provide an answer of my own and will take up Pereboom's objection to Kant's justification of a practice of blame in the following subsection.

On my reading, Kant cites his answer to the question of why we are *justified* in holding the liar blameworthy in the sentence following the quote. Here, Kant asserts that a judgment of blameworthiness is not just factual but indeed reasonable (it is "grounded on the law of reason") insofar as it is reasonable to assume that reason "could have and ought to have determined the conduct of the person to be other than it is". That is, the reasonableness of blame hinges on what Pereboom discussed as Kant's first practical reason: the existence of a moral ought judgment. In other words, blameworthiness presupposes that the person has violated a moral principle that is valid for her. The practical reason to judge a liar blameworthy is ultimately (and bracketing a complication that I will address shortly) that he is subject to the moral law. Being subject to the moral law, according to Kant, implies transcendental freedom of the will. Therefore, the fact that we legitimately judge people blameworthy when they violate moral principles does not constitute an additional practical reason to believe in their freedom over and above the fact that they are bound by moral principles.

The complication involved in holding others blameworthy for the practical reason that they are bound by the moral law is that the "fact of reason" only provides first-personal access to the validity of the moral law *for the person with consciousness* of the law. I cannot *know* whether another person, for example, the liar in Kant's example, also has this consciousness, such that I can infer his freedom from it. This seems to be why Christine Korsgaard says that the practice of holding others responsible occupies a "somewhat unstable position" (Korsgaard 1996, 174) in Kant's ethics. However, the close relationship between being subject to the moral law and being free in the sense required for it also holds in the case of other persons. This means that if we hold others to moral expectations in the sense of normatively expecting them to comply with the demands of the moral law, we must also presuppose their freedom. Normative expectation is a *forward-looking* attitude toward other people. It corresponds to the *backward-looking* attitude of judging them blameworthy for their failure to comply with these moral norms. On the basis of this picture, it seems possible to extend the application of Kant's notion of a postulate to the freedom of other persons: Even though we cannot prove their freedom on theoretical grounds, the assumption that they are free is necessarily bound up with the normative expectation that they will comply with the moral law—and therefore with moral practice as a whole.[28]

4.1   Does Kant's Justification of Transcendental Freedom Suffice to Legitimate Practices of Holding Each Other Responsible?

Let me now address Pereboom's objection that we do not have sufficient reason to hold each other responsible, in particular to express judgments of blameworthiness. As indicated above, I take this to be an objection not directly against the practical justification of freedom but against the view that Kant's justification of freedom suffices to legitimate the practice of holding each other blameworthy. Pereboom notes that the expressions of judgments of blameworthiness, such as expressing anger or punishing a criminal, are all "harmful to the offender" (Pereboom 2006, 563). One particularly striking example that Pereboom offers to illustrate Kant's view is that of the last murderer in a prison in Kant's imagined island society, which is about to dissolve (see Kant 1996a, 106; 6:333). Kant holds that the civil state cannot be dissolved before the last convicted murderer has been executed. In order for this harmful behavior to be justified, Pereboom contends, "one's justification [for one's belief in transcendental freedom] must meet a high epistemic or theoretical standard—much higher than the standard of consistency that Kant advocates" (Pereboom 2006, 564).

I agree with Pereboom that the practically justified belief in transcendental freedom does not suffice to legitimate all harmful practices of holding each other responsible. I disagree, however, that this is due to the "weakness" of Kant's practical justification in comparison with an evidential justification of freedom. Rather, transcendental freedom should be understood as a *necessary* condition for practices of holding each other responsible, according to Kant. As such, the assumption of transcendental freedom does not carry much weight in justifying particular aspects of these practices, notably the question of how harmful the expression of judgments of blameworthiness are or should be. To put it differently, even if one could satisfy Pereboom's demand for a stronger evidential justification of freedom, it would still have to be regarded as an open question whether one should sentence the last murderer in a dissolving state to death. Rather, the assumption of transcendental freedom has a mainly restrictive function: It is meant to restrict the effects of culpability to persons who are appropriate addressees in principle (rather, for instance, than blaming or punishing mentally handicapped or young children). Let me briefly sketch the limited role of our belief in transcendental freedom, first for the legal practice of punishment and second for moral imputation in everyday contexts.

In the passages on moral imputation from the introduction to the *Metaphysics of Morals*, Kant does not provide a concrete description of what a practice of imputation should look like beyond noting that the "*rightful* effect of culpability is *punishment*" (Kant 1996a, 19; 6:227). This claim provides a hint as to what punishment is according to Kant, namely an effect of imputation. It is not obvious, however, why Kant thinks that punishment is the legal effect of culpability. There is an ongoing debate about whether Kant views criminal law as justified on the basis of the idea of retribution or deterrence.[29] This is not the place to discuss the prospects of the different interpretations of Kant's justification of punishment, but it is helpful to note that the assumption of transcendental freedom alone does not decide the issue of whether, when and how criminals should be punished. The function of requiring culpability (i.e., imputation of the action and a negative evaluation of it) and thereby requiring transcendental freedom as a necessary condition for punishment is to prevent innocent people, or people who are mentally ill or too young, from being treated as mere means for the purpose of deterrence. I surmise that in order to fulfill this function (*restricting* harmful responses), Pereboom would not require a stronger evidential justification for our belief in transcendental freedom.

Leaving the legal sphere aside and focusing on the personal context, expressions of blame toward the offender might in principle take harmful forms, for example, expressions of strong anger or even hatred. Yet it is worth noting that Kant does not describe attitudes toward offenders as clearly harmful. Kant conceives of at least two duties of virtue that are tailored to a reaction to wrongdoers. Kant holds that it is a duty of virtue to "refrain from repaying another's enmity with hatred out of mere revenge" (Kant 1996a, 208; 6:461) and to remember that we are all in need of forgiveness (Kant 1996a, 208; 6:460).[30] Another duty of virtue refers to "generosity of interpretation": "It is, therefore, a duty of virtue … [to] throw the veil of benevolence over their faults, not merely by softening our judgments but also by keeping these judgments to ourselves" (Kant 1996a, 212; 6: 466). Here, Kant might be understood as criticizing "judgmental" attitudes, that is, being too ready to attribute fault or being too unaccepting of other's faults.[31] It is therefore possible, on a Kantian picture, to affirm that we are transcendentally free and morally responsible without thereby also affirming a harmful practice toward offenders. This seems to be systematically plausible: Instead of anger, for instance, judgments of blameworthiness could find expression in disappointment, a feeling accompanied by the thought that "you could have done better". A practical justification of transcendental freedom as a necessary condition for this kind of practice seems to be sufficient.

Finally, note that Pereboom's impression that we need to be in a better evidential situation to sufficiently justify our belief in transcendental freedom might suggest that Kant's practical justification is somehow epistemically or theoretically deficient. This is not the case, however. If Kant's argument is sound, the justification of transcendental freedom not only meets "standard[s] of consistency" and "credibility" (Pereboom 2006, 564) but cannot in principle be disproven (or confirmed) by any evidence to come. This means that the justification is as stable in time as any justification can be.

5   Conclusion

One aim of this contribution was to present Kant's practical justification of freedom; another was to bring Kant's account into contact with contemporary debates on freedom and moral responsibility. First, I showed that Kant's account of moral *imputation* captures central aspects of what is today referred to as moral *responsibility*. That an action can be morally imputed to a person implies that the person is regarded as its author and is a proper object of praise and blame (if the action is evaluated according to moral norms). I showed why Kant views transcendental freedom as a necessary condition for moral imputation: The capacity to determine an action by one's own reason (instead of being determined by natural causes) is meant to guarantee that the action is in one's control. Further, a transcendentally free agent can comply with an unconditional moral ought judgment. Second, I outlined Kant's account of how to reconcile natural determinism and transcendental freedom: In the solution to the third Antinomy, he argues for the logical possibility of an event's being at the same time naturally determined and transcendentally free. In the third part, I turned to Kant's practical justification of freedom. I focused on the account in the second *Critique*, where Kant argues that freedom must be postulated because it is a necessary, theoretically undecidable presupposition of the moral law. We can be aware that the moral law is valid for us through the fact of reason, and hence we must postulate freedom for ourselves. In the last part, I answered Derek Pereboom's objections against Kant's practical justification. The practical reasons for assuming freedom are stronger than Pereboom takes them to be and are intimately bound up with Kant's moral philosophy as a whole.[32]

Notes

1. Kant's works are cited using volume and page numbers (volume: page) of the standard Academy edition of Kant's writings (Berlin. 1900–), except for the *Critique of Pure Reason*. The latter is cited using the A- and B-editions (A/B).
2. As Peter van Inwagen points out, it was only with Harry Frankfurt's essay "Alternate Possibilities and Moral Responsibility" (Frankfurt 1969) that the concept of moral responsibility entered the discussion of free will (van Inwagen 2017, 215–216). Before, analytic philosophers always (tacitly) accepted the thesis that moral responsibility requires the existence of free will. Frankfurt's essay puts this thesis into question.
3. 'Responsibility' corresponds to the German *Verantwortung*. This is sometimes translated as 'accountability' (e.g., "being accountable to God", Kant 1996a, 190; 6: 439). 'Accountability', in turn, corresponds to the German *Zurechnungsfähigkeit* (cf., e.g., 6: 26). For a study of Kant's concept of imputation, see Blöser (2014).
4. This view of moral responsibility is widely shared. Even Peter van Inwagen, who considers the notion of moral responsibility to be unclear, sees an "intimate relation" between an agent's being to *blame* for a state of affairs and moral responsibility (van Inwagen 2017, 196).

5. For textual evidence, see Blöser (2015).

6. There are difficulties with integrating praise and praiseworthiness in Kant's ethics (see Blöser 2015 for discussion). Since these intricacies are irrelevant to the relationship between freedom and moral responsibility in general, however, I leave them aside and will focus on blame and blameworthiness.

7. I understand the expression "real ground" (in the German original, der "eigentliche Grund") as "central necessary condition". Kant also says that transcendental freedom constitutes "the real moment of the difficulties" regarding the question of freedom (Kant 1998, 533; A533/B561). The expression "real" ("eigentlich") seems to point to the fact that there are more (empirical) conditions and aspects to free choice, but it is the transcendental aspect—the necessary condition—that is of greatest interest since it prompts the problem of how to reconcile such freedom with natural causality.

8. See Blackburn 1996, 1980. Hume writes: "[L]iberty, by removing necessity, removes also causes, and is the very same thing with chance" (Hume 2000, 261–262).

9. One example of a contemporary reference to Hume's Fork (which does not make explicit its origins in Hume) can be found in Peter van Inwagen's "The Mystery of Metaphysical Freedom" (van Inwagen 1998). He sets up the problem by claiming that there is an argument for the incompatibility of freedom and determinism and for the incompatibility of freedom and indeterminism, but that one of them must be defective, on his view. His claim is that freedom remains a "mystery", since it is hard to see how to criticize one or both of the arguments.

10. Let me note one difficulty with determining the relationship between transcendental and practical freedom. On the one hand, Kant describes a close relationship between the two in the *Dialectic* (e.g., "the abolition of transcendental freedom would also simultaneously eliminate all practical freedom" (534, A534/B562); on the other hand, he divorces practical from transcendental freedom in the *Canon*, where he announces that he will set aside transcendental freedom in order to focus on practical freedom, which "can be proved through experience" (A802/B830). The tension between the two passages has troubled many interpreters—see (Schönecker et al. 2005) or Allison (1990, 54–70). Without aiming at a full explanation or resolution here, I assume that Kant is using two different (though not incompatible) notions of practical freedom, where

the notion in the *Canon* refers to the empirical appearance of the capacity to determine oneself by reason. It is necessary, however, to conceive of practical freedom as a species of transcendental freedom in order to see how it can ground moral responsibility, since only then can we assume that the person's will is the ultimate cause of the action.

11. For a more detailed presentation of both views and for passages and considerations that support each, see Blöser (2014, Chapter 2).

12. Defenders of the first interpretation include Henry Allison (Allison 1990), Christine Korsgaard (Korsgaard 1996), and Marcus Willaschek (Willaschek 1992).

13. The second interpretation is defended, for instance, by Jochen Bojanowski (Bojanowski 2006), Iuliana Vaida (Vaida 2014) and Stephen Engstrom (Engstrom 1993). One can hardly say that any one of the two interpretations has decisively more defenders than the other. Defenders of either interpretation concede that there are many scholars on the other side. Allison writes, for instance: "Contrary to many interpreters, I shall argue that Kant is there [in the *Critique of Pure Reason*, CB] concerned to provide a transcendental framework for a unified theory of agency, one that includes but is not limited to moral agency" (Allison 1990, 29). Vaida, who defends the second view, describes the first as the "received view" (Vaida 2014, 2).

14. As Karl Ameriks notes, Kant's notion of freedom as autonomy is a widely discussed issue, and much more needs to be said in order to fully grasp this "revolutionary proposal" (Ameriks 2019, 95).

15. Thus, Allen Wood's well-known characterization of Kant's project as an attempt to show the "compatibility of compatibilism and incompatibilism" is apt (Wood 1984, 74).

16. Pereboom describes Kant as a libertarian (Pereboom 2006, 538). Note, however, that there are important differences within the libertarian camp. Robert Kane's position, for instance, is incompatibilist because he believes that freedom is incompatible with natural determinism. Nevertheless, he believes that freedom is compatible with *probabilistic* causation, and that not all natural causation is deterministic. Kant does not take the possibility of probabilistic causation into account, however. Even if he had been aware of natural, probabilistic causality, this wouldn't have solved the problem for him. For Kant, the crucial point is that an action can be tracked back to the person's *reason*. Thanks to Marco

Hausmann for drawing attention to the differences between Kane's and Kant's positions.

17. For Kant's expression of this principle, see especially the *Religion*: "For, in spite of that fall, the command that we ought to become better human beings still resounds unabated in our souls; consequently, we must also be capable of it" (Kant 1996c, 66; 6:45; see also 6:65 and 6:68).

18. Note that Kant denies that there are strict psychological laws in the *Metaphysical Foundations of Natural Science* (see 4:471).

19. See Willaschek (1992, 31).

20. For more on "real" and "logical" possibility in Kant, also in earlier writings, see (Adams 1997, 818–819).

21. See also Allison (2013, 287).

22. See Allison (2013, 289–290) for a more detailed discussion of these worries.

23. See Willaschek (2010, 169) for this terminology.

24. For example, von Platz (2013) and Willaschek (2017).

25. Willaschek (2017) argues for this in detail.

26. Pereboom presents this argument in his book *Living Without Free Will* (2001, 141–152, 197–199) and in his article "Kant on Transcendental Freedom" (2006). I focus on the article since it is the later version of the argument and refer to the book only when necessary.

27. This interpretation of Pereboom's aspiration in the article is consistent with the position he defends in his book, where he argues that "the content of Kantian normative ethics" is consistent "with hard incompatibilism" (Pereboom 2001, 150), which is the view that the free will required for moral responsibility is incompatible with determinism and that we do not have it. This amounts to saying that Kant's ethics does not require transcendental freedom.

28. See also Korsgaard (1996, 208) for understanding the freedom of others as a postulate.

29. See, for example, Byrd and Hruschka (2010) for a rejection of the traditional view of Kant as a retributivist and on the importance of deterrence for the justification of criminal law in Kant.

30. For more on Kant's conception of forgiveness, see Blöser (2019).

31. See Watson (2012, 284) for these two forms of judgmentalism.

32. I would like to thank Guus Duindam and Marcus Willaschek, as well as the editors of this book, for helpful comments on earlier versions of this text.

References

Adams, Robert Merrihew. 1997. Things in Themselves. *Philosophy and Phenomenological Research* 57 (4): 801.

Allison, Henry E. 1990. *Kant's Theory of Freedom*. Cambridge; New York: Cambridge University Press.

Allison, Henry. 2013. Kant's Practical Justification of Freedom. In *Kant on Practical Justification. Interpretive Essays*, ed. Sorin Baiasu and Mark Timmons, 284–299. New York: Oxford University Press.

Ameriks, Karl. 2019. Kant on Freedom as Autonomy. In *Freiheit nach Kant. Tradition, Rezeption, Transformation, Aktualität*, ed. Sasa Josifovic and Jörg Noller, 95–116. Leiden: Brill.

Blackburn, Simon. 1996. Hume's Fork. In *Oxford Dictionary of Philosophy*. Oxford: Oxford University Press.

Blöser, Claudia. 2014. *Zurechnung bei Kant: zum Zusammenhang von Person und Handlung in Kants praktischer Philosophie*. In *Quellen und Studien zur Philosophie, Band 122*. Berlin; Boston: De Gruyter.

———. 2015. Degrees of Responsibility in Kant's Practical Philosophy. *Kantian Review* 20 (2): 183–209.

———. 2019. Human Fallibility and the Need for Forgiveness. *Philosophia* 47 (1): 1–19.

Bojanowski, Jochen. 2006. *Kants Theorie der Freiheit: Rekonstruktion und Rehabilitierung*. Berlin: De Gruyter.

Byrd, B. Sharon, and Joachim Hruschka. 2010. *Kant's Doctrine of Right: A Commentary*. Cambridge; New York: Cambridge University Press.

Engstrom, Stephen. 1993. Allison on Rational Agency. *Inquiry* 36 (4): 405–418.

Frankfurt, Harry. 1969. Alternate Possibilities and Moral Responsibility. *Journal of Philosophy* 66 (23): 829–839.

Hume, David. 2000. In *A Treatise of Human Nature*, ed. Fate Norton and Mary J. Norton. New York: Oxford University Press.

van Inwagen, Peter. 1983. *An Essay on Free Will*. Oxford: Clarendon Press.

———. 1998. The Mystery of Metaphysical Freedom. In *Metaphysics: The Big Questions*, ed. Peter van Inwagen and Dean W. Zimmermann, 365–374. Malden; Oxford: Blackwell.

———. 2017. *Thinking about Free Will*. Cambridge, New York: Cambridge University Press.

Kant, Immanuel. 1996a. *Metaphysics of Morals*. Edited and Translated by Mary Gregor. Cambridge: Cambridge University Press.

————. 1996b. Critique of Practical Reason. Translated by Mary Gregor. In Practical Philosophy, ed. Mary Gregor, 137–271. Cambridge: Cambridge University Press.

————. 1996c. Religion Within the Limits of Reason Alone. Translated by Allen Wood and George di Giovanni. Cambridge: Cambridge University Press.

————. 1997. Groundwork for the Metaphysics of Morals. Edited and Translated by Mary Gregor. Cambridge: Cambridge University Press.

————. 1998. Critique of Pure Reason. Edited and Translated Paul Guyer and Allen Wood. Cambridge: Cambridge University Press.

Korsgaard, Christine M. 1996. Creating the Kingdom of Ends. Cambridge; New York: Cambridge University Press.

Pereboom, Derk. 2001. Living Without Free Will. Cambridge Studies in Philosophy. Cambridge, UK; New York: Cambridge University Press.

————. 2006. Kant on Transcendental Freedom. Philosophy and Phenomenological Research 73 (3): 537–567.

von Platz, Jeppe. 2013. Freedom as Both Fact and Postulate. In Kant und die Philosophie in weltbürgerlicher Absicht. Akten des XI. Internationalen Kant-Kongresses, ed. Stefano Bacin, Alfredo Ferrarin, Claudio La Rocca, and Margit Ruffing, vol. 3, 531–543. Berlin; New York: Walter de Gruyter.

Schönecker, Dieter, Stefanie Buchenau, and Desmond Hogan. 2005. Kants Begriff transzendentaler und praktischer Freiheit: eine entwicklungsgeschichtliche Studie. Kantstudien 149. Berlin; New York: Walter de Gruyter.

Vaida, Iuliana Corina. 2014. The Problem of Agency and the Problem of Accountability in Kant's Moral Philosophy: Agency and Accountability in Kant's Philosophy. European Journal of Philosophy 22 (1): 110–137.

Watson, Gary. 2012. Standing in Judgment. In Blame: Its Nature and Norms, ed. D. Justin Coates and Neal A. Tognazzini, 282–302. Oxford: Oxford University Press.

Willaschek, Marcus. 1992. Praktische Vernunft: Handlungstheorie und Moralbegründung bei Kant. Stuttgart: Metzler.

————. 2010. The Primacy of Practical Reason and the Idea of a Practical Postulate. In Kant's Critique of Practical Reason. A Critical Guide, ed. Andrews Reath and Jens Timmermann, 168–196. Cambridge: Cambridge University Press.

————. 2017. Freedom as a Postulate. In Kant on Persons and Agency, ed. Eric Watkins, 102–119. Cambridge: Cambridge University Press.

Wood, Allen. 1984. Kant's Compatibilism. In Self and Nature in Kant's Philosophy, ed. Allen Wood, 57–101. Ithaca: Cornell University Press.

14

Does "Ought" Imply "Can"?

Peter van Inwagen

As my title implies, I am going to discuss the principle expressed by the well-known phrase, "*Ought* implies *can*"—the "*Ought* implies *can*" principle I will call it. The phrase "*Ought* implies *can*" is commonly associated with Kant, but, so far as I know, those are not his words—that is, their German equivalent (*Soll impliziert kann*) occurs nowhere in his writings. But he does in many places say things that are very much like "*Ought* implies *can*." Here, for example, is a well-known sentence from his *Die Religion innerhalb der Grenzen der bloßen Vernunft*: "*[D]ie Pflicht ... gebietet uns aber nichts, als was uns tunlich ist*" ("Duty commands nothing of us but what is doable for us"—or, a more idiomatic English sentence, "Duty commands us to do nothing but what we are able to do") (Kant 1793, 6:47).

I am, I say, going to discuss the "*Ought* implies *can*" principle. And yet I am going to say nothing about the meaning of "ought" and next to nothing about the meaning of "can." I will, however, remark that in this chapter I will generally use phrases of the form "A is able to X" rather than the corresponding phrases of the form "A can X"—for example, "Gertrude is able to speak English' rather than 'Gertrude can speak

P. van Inwagen (✉)
Department of Philosophy, University of Notre Dame, Notre Dame, IN, USA
e-mail: peter.vaninwagen.1@nd.edu

© The Author(s), under exclusive license to Springer Nature Switzerland AG 2021
M. Hausmann, J. Noller (eds.), *Free Will*,
https://doi.org/10.1007/978-3-030-61136-1_14

English" (I note parenthetically that the syntax of "Gertrude can speak English" is a peculiarity of English. One says *Gertrude kann Englisch sprechen*, not *Gertrude kann spricht Englisch*; one says *Gertrude peut parler anglais*, not *Gertrude peut parle anglais*).

I prefer "is able to" to "can" because the word "can" is radically ambiguous, and its ambiguities have been a source of much philosophical confusion. I don't mean to suggest that "is able to" is not also ambiguous, but its ambiguities are less serious and more easily dealt with than those of "can." I'll take just a moment to say something about the ambiguities of "is able to." Suppose the great pianist Grigory Sokolov is stranded on a desert island, and, as I believe is usually the case with desert islands, there's no piano on it. Is Sokolov *able* in that situation to play the Goldberg Variations? In one sense of the word, he is indeed able to play the Goldberg Variations—he has the piece in his fingers, as pianists say—and in another sense he is not. It is the latter sense of "able to," the sense in which Sokolov is *not* able to play the Goldberg Variations, that is the sense that is relevant to the "*Ought* implies *can*" principle. We must understand the phrase "able to X" in that sense if we are to translate Kant's *was uns tunlich ist* as "what we are able to do." Let us call this sense the Kantian sense of "able to X."

I begin the body of this chapter with some remarks that pertain to a philosophical problem that I'll call the problem of free will, although the phrase "free will" will not occur in these remarks. They are intended to make explicit the role that the "*Ought* implies *can*" principle plays in that problem. The word "able" will occur frequently in these remarks; it is everywhere to be understood in its Kantian sense. (I'll use the word "can" only in the phrase "*Ought* implies *can*." If I were being entirely consistent, I'd say instead "*Ought* implies *is able to*," but I'll continue to say "*Ought* implies *can*" out of respect for tradition.)

Now consider someone, anyone, who has done something, performed a certain act. Let's say that act was *determined* if, given the history of the world, the physical universe, up to that point, *and* the laws of nature, that person *had* to perform that act. Or, if I may use the technical jargon for expressing modal propositions that is favored by analytical philosophers, I could phrase the definition this way: that act was determined just in the case that in *every* possible world in which the past was the actual past and the laws of nature are the actual laws, that person performs that act. And if that act was not determined, we'll say that it was *undetermined*. That is, the act was undetermined if there is *some* possible world in which the past was the actual past and the laws of nature are the actual laws, and that person did not perform that act. Suppose, for example, that Alice told a lie to James at noon yesterday—told him, let's say, that his wife was seeing someone else, and told him that knowing it to be untrue. Alice's telling that lie at that moment was determined if, in *every* possible world in which everything was just as it actually was at every moment up to but not including noon yesterday, and in which the laws of nature are just as they actually are, she then told him that his wife was seeing someone else. And her act was undetermined if there are possible worlds in which everything was just as it actually was at every moment up to but not including noon yesterday, and in which the laws of nature are just as they actually are, she did *not* then tell him that his wife was seeing someone else.

Now there is a well-known philosophical argument that purports to show that if an act is determined, the person who performed that act was not able *not* to have performed that act, not able to have refrained from performing it, not able to have done anything else, not able to have acted otherwise. If that argument is, as philosophers say, *sound*—if its premises are true and if its conclusion follows logically from those premises—and if Alice's telling James that his wife was seeing someone else was determined, Alice was *unable* to refrain from telling James that lie: she simply wasn't able to do anything *but* tell him that lie about his wife. The usual label for that argument is the Consequence Argument—on which more in a moment.

All right, there's *that* argument, the Consequence Argument. But there's also a well-known philosophical argument that purports to show that if an act is *undetermined*, the person who performed that act was not able *not* to perform that act, not able to refrain from performing it, not able to have done anything else, not able to have done otherwise. If this second argument is sound, and if Alice's telling James that his wife was seeing someone else was *un*determined, Alice was unable to refrain from telling James that lie—she simply wasn't able at that moment to do anything else. The usual label for this second argument is the *Mind*

Argument—on which more in a moment. But I'll say now that it's not called the *Mind* Argument because it has anything to do with the mind; it's called that because it has appeared so often in the pages of the journal *Mind*. And perhaps I should also mention that the sense in which the conclusion of the *Mind* Argument implies that Alice was not able not to lie to James if her lying to James was undetermined is a rather subtle one. If Alice's lying to James was undetermined, then, of course, she *might not* have lied to James. But note that if an agent has performed a certain action but might not have, it does not follow that the agent was *able* not to have performed it. Suppose, for example, that Alice has tossed a coin and that the coin fell "heads" and that she had no choice about how the coin would fall: once tossed, the coin might have fallen "heads" and it might have fallen "tails" and there's no more to say about the outcome of the toss. Then Alice was unable to toss the coin so that it did not fall "heads"—and this despite the fact that it *might* not have fallen "heads" if she had tossed it.

Now Alice's act, her telling the lie to James, must either have been determined or have been undetermined. And, therefore, if the Consequence Argument and the *Mind* Argument are *both* sound, then Alice was not able to do anything other than tell James at noon yesterday that his wife was seeing someone else. And, of course, it isn't only the fictional Alice who's in that position: if both arguments are sound, *no one* is ever able to do anything other than what he or she in fact does.

Enter the "*Ought* implies *can*" principle. Most people believe that there have been occasions on which people have acted wrongly. Most people believe that there have been occasions on which it would be correct to say to someone, "You ought not to have done that" or "You should not have done that." But if the "*Ought* implies *can*" principle is correct, and if no one has ever been able to do anything but what he or she has in fact done, then such statements are always false. Consider lying Alice. Suppose a third party, Tom, says to her, "Alice, I've heard that you told James that his wife was seeing someone else. You should not have told him that. You *know* it isn't true." If both Tom's statement, "You should not have told him that" and the "*Ought* implies *can*" principle are true, then Alice *was* able not to tell James that his wife was seeing someone else. And if the Consequence Argument and the *Mind* Argument are both sound, she *wasn't* able not to tell James that his wife was seeing someone else:

The upshot of these considerations is that the following three theses:

> The Consequence Argument is sound
> The *Mind* Argument is sound
> The "*Ought* implies *can*" principle is true

together imply this thesis:

> There never has been an occasion on which someone did something that he or she ought not to have done.

I'll call this the Unacceptable Conclusion—for it obviously *is* unacceptable. There have been *lots* of occasions on which people have done things they ought not to have done—occasions on which people have acted wrongly. People have engaged in ethnic cleansing, owned slaves, bombed civilian populations, and sexually abused small children.

We might define "the problem of free will" this way: the problem of free will is the problem of finding out which of these three principles or premises or theses is false—which of these propositions that together imply the Unacceptable Conclusion is false.

If that is the problem of free will, there are four possible responses to the problem of free will. The most radical of them is *Moral Nihilism* (which is not a *solution* to the problem but, rather, a denial that it is a problem):

> The so-called Unacceptable Conclusion is not unacceptable at all; the widespread conviction that people have sometimes acted in ways in which they ought not to have acted is an illusion; the words "ought" and "should" correspond to nothing in the real world.

I will say nothing further about Moral Nihilism. Let us examine possible solutions to the problem. Here are two:

—There is a flaw (or more than one) in the Consequence Argument, and its conclusion is false
—There is a flaw (or more than one) in the *Mind* Argument and its conclusion is false.

Of course, a complete and satisfactory solution of either sort to the problem of free will would *identify* the flaw or flaws in the Consequence Argument—or, as it may be, the flaw or flaws in the *Mind* Argument.

Most philosophers who have addressed the problem of free will have attempted to solve it by finding flaws in either the Consequence Argument or the *Mind* Argument. I promised earlier to say more about the Consequence Argument and the *Mind* Argument, but, actually, all I'm going to say about them is this: many able philosophers have accepted one or the other. (And one or two very able philosophers have accepted both.) And that—being widely accepted by able philosophers—is the most a philosophical argument can hope for: for no philosophical argument of any, well, *consequence* is accepted by all philosophers, and few if any even by a substantial majority of philosophers. The reason I am not going to discuss either of these two important arguments is that my topic is the one remaining way of avoiding the Unacceptable Conclusion: by rejecting the "*Ought* implies *can*" principle.

Many philosophers, perhaps most philosophers, will say that it's not possible to reject the "*Ought* implies *can*" principle because it's an *analytic* truth—like "Being a bachelor implies being unmarried" or "Being a bishop implies being a priest." Here is a typical defense of its analyticity. "Look, consider the case of Alice and her lie to James. Suppose you confront her, and you say to her, 'Alice, you ought not to have lied to James'. And suppose Alice replies, 'But I wasn't *able* not to lie to James. In the circumstances in which I told the lie, I wasn't able to do anything else.' You may well not *believe* that statement, but if you believe it, you can't continue to affirm that Alice ought not to have lied to James. You can't say, 'Okay, Alice, I believe you—you *weren't* able not to lie to James. But so what? What's your point? Even if you weren't *able* to do anything else, you still *ought* to have done something else.'" Philosophers have been remarkably consistent in regarding the "*Ought* implies *can*" principle as an obvious truth. Although it is often ascribed to Kant, you can find appeals to it, or at least to very similar principles, in the Pelagian controversy of the fifth century. And I'm reasonably sure that if Pelagius had had available to him the concept of analyticity, he would have said that the principle was analytic. I am, moreover, aware of no philosopher who explicitly rejected the "*Ought* implies *can*" principle before the 1980s. Recently, however, the principle has come under attack by some practitioners of so-called experimental philosophy, or "X-phi."

The X-phi attack on the "*Ought* implies *can*" principle is based on a psychological study, the design and results of which were described in a 2016 article titled "Blame, Not Ability, Impacts Moral 'Ought' Judgments for Impossible Actions: Toward an Empirical Refutation of 'Ought' Implies 'Can'." (The article was published in a cognitive-science journal called *Cognition* (Chituc et al. (2016)). It is this study that is the main topic of this chapter.

The design and results of the study reported in "Blame, Not Ability" are extremely detailed and not easy to summarize. But summarize them I must, for I can't possibly present the study to you in all its detail. I do not want to be accused of presenting a tendentious summary of the study, so I will quote a long passage from a summary of the study that was published in the *New York Times* (also in 2016) by two of the four authors of "Blame, Not Ability." I ask you to forgive me for reading out a very long quotation from that article, but I think it is essential that I do so. I think it is essential that you hear a summary of "Blame, Not Ability" by its authors (two of its authors anyway) and not one provided by a hostile critic—for that is what I am. All right, get comfortable and prepare to listen to a very long quotation from the *Times* article.

[Consider this thought experiment]: Suppose that you and a friend are both up for the same job in another city. She interviewed last weekend, and your flight for the interview is this evening. Your car is in the shop, though, so your friend promises to drive you to the airport. But on the way, her car breaks down—the gas tank is leaking—so you miss your flight and don't get the job.

Would it make any sense to tell your friend, stranded at the side of the road, that she ought to drive you to the airport? The answer seems to be an obvious no (after all, she *can't* drive you), and most philosophers treat this as all the confirmation they need for the principle.

Suppose, however, that the situation is slightly different. What if your friend intentionally punctures her own gas tank to make sure that you miss the flight and she gets the job? In this case, it makes perfect sense to insist that your friend still has an obligation to drive you to the airport. In other words, we might indeed say that someone ought to do what she can't—if we're *blaming* her.

[We] decided to run [this thought experiment as a scientific one. We] presented hundreds of participants with stories like the one above and asked them questions about obligation, ability and blame. Did they think someone should keep a promise she made but couldn't keep? Was she even capable of keeping her promise? And how much was she to blame for what happened?

We found a consistent pattern, but not what most philosophers would expect. "Ought" judgments depended largely on concerns about blame, not ability. With stories like the one above, in which a friend intentionally sabotages you, 60 percent of our participants said that the obligation still held—your friend still ought to drive you to the airport. But with stories in which the inability to help was accidental, the obligation all but disappeared. Now, only 31 percent of our participants said your friend still ought to drive you … So who is right? The vast majority of philosophers, or our participants?

One possibility is that our participants were wrong, perhaps because their urge to blame impaired the accuracy of their moral judgments. To test this possibility, we stacked the deck in the favor of philosophical orthodoxy: We had the participants look at cases in which the urge to assign blame would be lowest—that is, only the cases in which the car accidentally broke down. Even still, we found no relationship between "ought" and "can." The only significant relationship was between "ought" and "blame."

This finding has an important implication: Even when we say that someone has no obligation to keep a promise (as with your friend whose car accidentally breaks down), it seems we're saying it *not* because she's unable to do it, but because we don't want to unfairly blame her for not keeping it. Again, concerns about blame, not about ability, dictate how we understand obligation (Chituc and Henne (2016)).

That was the quotation whose length I apologized for. Now I'm speaking in my own voice again.

I find the authors' interpretation of their results hard to follow at several points. I'll mention just one. Consider this statement, supposedly an "important implication" of those results:

> Even when we say that someone has no obligation to keep a promise (as with your friend whose car accidentally breaks down), it seems we're saying it *not* because she's unable to do it, but because we don't want to unfairly blame her for not keeping it (Chituc and Henne (2016)).

I feel compelled to ask, *Why* would "we" suppose that (in the case in which the driver did not deliberately puncture her fuel tank) it would be unfair to blame her for not keeping her promise? It seems obvious to me that it would be unfair for this reason and this reason alone: she was *unable* to keep it—that is, it would be unfair to blame her for not keeping her promise because she was unable to keep her promise.

Since I find their interpretation of the results of their experiment confusing, I'm not going to discuss that experiment. Instead, I'm going to propose another experiment designed to find out whether non-philosophers accept the "*Ought* implies *can*" principle. I will predict the results of my proposed experiment and interpret the results I anticipate.

I'll go on to consider a possible objection to my interpretation, and, finally, address the question, "But what would you say if the results turned out to be contrary to those you anticipate?"

All right, let's begin. Here's a little information that you will need to understand my proposed experiment.

There is a feature in the *New York Times Magazine* called "The Ethicist." The idea behind "The Ethicist" is this. Readers are invited to submit questions about concrete ethical problems to The Ethicist; a few of the more interesting of the submitted questions are published, along with answers to them, by the titular Ethicist—currently the philosopher Kwame Anthony Appiah. But since I am going to propose a thought-experiment—it's not one of those thought-experiments that it would not be possible actually to conduct; my thought-experiment hasn't been carried out, but it could be—that turns on an imaginary, and in my judgment bizarre, answer to an imaginary question submitted to The Ethicist, and since I do not want to imply that Professor Appiah or any other real person would answer my question in the bizarre way I shall imagine, I will pretend that the current Ethicist is one Saoirse Horowitz, who, I assure you, does not exist. (As far as I am able to determine from an online search, no one is named Saoirse Horowitz.)

That's the information you need. Now I will describe my thought-experiment. I imagine an empirical study. Participants in the study are to be asked the following question.

Suppose that someone has submitted the following question to The Ethicist:

My former wife and I were divorced when our daughter Mary was five. Since that time Mary has lived with her mother. I haven't seen as much of Mary as I'd like, but I've always loved her, and about ten years ago, I promised her mother that I would pay all Mary's college expenses. Mary is now a high-school senior and is applying to some very expensive colleges. She's a stellar student and will certainly be admitted to more than one of them. This puts me in a terrible quandary. Here's why. A few months before I made the promise, I had struck it rich as the result of a lucky break in the stock market. My ex-wife knew this and took it for granted that I'd be able to keep my promise to pay for Mary's college education. Because of my promise, my former wife didn't ask for any increase in child-support payments—she accepted my promise in lieu of increased child support—and she understandably did not try to put away any money to pay for Mary's education. But here's the problem: I lost all the money I'd made as quickly as I'd made it. And I had *already* lost it when I made the promise. At the time I made the promise, I was honestly convinced that I'd be able make a second fortune and so I wasn't worried about being able to keep the promise I'd made—after all, I had got rich once, and I was sure I could do it again. But it just hasn't happened. For years now, I've barely been able both to support myself and keep up with my legally mandated child-support payments. I don't need to be told I shouldn't have made the promise. But I did make it, and I don't know what to do. Can you help me? What's the right thing for me to do *now*, given the situation I've put myself in?

And suppose that Saoirse Horowitz's response was simply this:

You should keep your promise and pay all Mary's college expenses.

Was Saoirse's response a good response? If not, why not?

Those are the two questions to be put to the respondents in my proposed study—"Was Saoirse's response a good response?" and "If not, why not?" I contend that if this study were actually carried out, it would have the following result. Among those respondents who understood the question (there are techniques for discovering whether respondents in surveys of opinion have understood the questions that are put to them) all or almost all would answer, "No, her response was not a good one." I further contend that almost all the answers to the further question, "If not, why not?" would be some variant on, "But how is Mary's father supposed to *do* that? He doesn't have anywhere near enough money to pay for his daughter's education."

My colleague Walter Sinnott-Armstrong—one of the authors of "Blame, Not Ability"—has responded (in conversation) to an imaginary study similar to the one I have just proposed by contending that one should distinguish the "ought" or "should" of *moral advice* from the "ought" or "should" that figures in general moral principles (and, I would suppose, in the moral judgments one makes about particular cases by applying general moral principles). And he contended that the *ought* of "*Ought* implies *can*" is the "moral principles" *ought*, and that when Saoirse said, "You should keep your promise and pay all Mary's college expenses," the word "should" in this sentence was the "should" of moral advice.

If there is such a distinction, we must nevertheless keep it in mind that the advice the imaginary father was asking for was *moral* advice and not some other kind of advice: he wasn't asking what the most useful or most prudent thing to do was; he wasn't asking for *financial* advice; he was asking what the *right thing for him to do* was. (If you write to "The Ethicist" and ask for advice, moral advice is the kind of advice you're asking for.) All right, let's distinguish—verbally, at least—the "ought" or "should" that figures in moral advice and the "ought" or "should" that figures in moral principles and moral judgments. We'll do it this way. We'll reserve the word "ought" itself for the "ought" that figures in moral principles and judgments, and we'll use only the word "should" in statements that are supposed to be pieces of moral advice. After all, if a present-day Anglophone father went to someone for moral advice, he'd be much more likely to ask, "What should I do?" than "What ought I to do?" (An Oxford don of fifty years ago might have asked, "What ought I to do?" but a present-day speaker probably wouldn't.) All right: "ought" for moral principles like "One *ought* never to bear false witness against one's neighbor" and particular moral judgments like "Alice *ought* not to have told that vicious lie about James's wife," and "should" for moral advice: "What do you think the right thing for me to do would be?" "You *should* keep the promise you made."

Having made this distinction, can we agree at least that "*should*" implies "can"?—agree that if someone who is in some morally difficult situation comes to you for advice about what he or she should do in that situation (a moral, and not a prudential, "should"), you are required by the nature of the case (being asked for moral advice) to advise that person to do X only if you believe that he or she is *able* to do X. (If you think about it, that seems to be a feature of any kind of advice, moral or otherwise. "Where do you think I should take Alison for dinner?" "My advice is to take her to Auberge du Vieux Puits in Paris. Best restaurant in the world." "Are you serious? I was talking about tonight—and, anyway, I only have a couple of hundred dollars in my bank account." "Oh, I know you wouldn't be *able* to take her there, but that's still my advice: take her to Auberge du Vieux Puits.") And can we agree that everyone who understands the "*Should* implies *Can*" principle will accept it? I'm going to assume that the answer to this question is Yes.

I'm not willing to let matters rest there, however. I'm not willing to accept the alleged distinction between the moral "should" (used in giving moral advice) and the moral "ought" (used in stating general moral principles or in making moral judgments about particular situations). I hesitate between classifying the alleged distinction as elusive and classifying it as spurious. If this is a real distinction, I ask, what is its *basis*? What is it *grounded in*? Is it somehow related to the fact that giving advice is a second-person speech act and stating a general moral principle or making a moral judgment about a particular case is a third-person speech act? I don't see how that difference could be a difference that makes a difference, for any piece of moral advice is very tightly bound to the corresponding moral judgment. For example, "You should pay for your daughter's education" (addressed to the author of the letter to "The Ethicist") is very tightly bound to "The author of the letter ought to pay for his daughter's education" (addressed by the same speaker to the world at large).

Perhaps it isn't entirely clear what I mean by saying that "should" and "ought" are "tightly bound." I'll try to explain what I mean by telling another story involving The Ethicist. Let's suppose that Saoirse Horowitz is giving a public lecture about how she approaches the questions addressed to her as The Ethicist. She displays a short, pithy question by PowerPoint, and, when the audience has digested it, she displays her answer (which is to appear in next Sunday's *New York Times Magazine*):

> You should not inform Frank of the contents of Betty's e-mail. As you admit, you received the e-mail only because Betty carelessly hit the "reply to all" button. She obviously did not intend the message for you, and you have no right to pass its content on to anyone else, Frank included. You might be justified in doing so if the e-mail revealed that Frank faced some imminent danger that he could avoid if he had the information contained in the e-mail, but that is clearly not the case in this instance. And if that argument doesn't convince you, here's a second argument, a very simple one: if someone says something in an e-mail message, it doesn't follow that it's true.

Saoirse then asks the audience, "Am I right? What do you think? Which of these things is what the letter-writer ought to do? Tell Frank what she learned (or thinks she learned) from the e-mail that Betty mistakenly sent to her?—or not tell him?"

This question to the audience seems to make perfect sense. And in asking this question, Saoirse is asking her audience to make a third-person moral judgment. And she takes it for granted that her second-person moral advice ("*You* should not reveal the content of the e-mail") is correct if and only if the third-person moral judgment "*She* ought not to reveal the content of the e-mail" is correct.

It therefore does not seem that the supposed distinction between the "should" of advice and the "ought" of moral judgment can be explained in terms of or is based on the distinction between second- and third-person speech acts. And I am at a loss to discover what its basis is. I strongly suspect that the distinction is specious.

I can think of only one argument that purports to show that there is a difference between the "should" of moral advice and the "ought" of moral principles and judgments. Think back to the cases mentioned in the passage from the *Times* article by the two experimental philosophers that I read to you. Consider the version of the story of your friend's inability to drive you to the airport in which she herself is responsible for her inability—because she punctured her fuel tank. (Let's say that your friend's name is Susan.) Suppose that, having done this discreditable thing, Susan repents, and phones Saoirse (she happens to have Saoirse's number in her phone) and asks her a question along the same lines as the question the man who had promised to pay his daughter's college expenses asked her. Susan says, "I don't need to be told I shouldn't have sabotaged my car. I realize that now. But what should I do *now*, in this morally difficult situation in which I've placed myself?" I hope we're all agreed that it wouldn't be right for Saoirse to say, "You should drive your friend to the airport." But—and here's the argument I promised—*we*, later, looking back on this situation, can rightly say, "Susan ought to have driven her friend to the airport." And, therefore, there's a difference between the "ought" of third-person moral judgments and the "should" of moral advice.

In my view, that conclusion is unwarranted—although I don't dispute the statement that we, looking back on the events of the story, can rightly say, "Susan ought to have driven her friend to the airport." Consider this possibility. Suppose Saoirse really had responded to Susan's request for advice by telling her that she should drive her friend to the airport. If Saoirse did say that, she could then turn and say (not to Susan alone, but to the world at large), "What do think? Did I just give Susan the right moral advice? Was I right to tell her that she ought to drive her friend to the airport?" And someone who had overheard that response could correctly report it by saying, "Saoirse told Susan that she ought to drive her friend to the airport."

But, wait—if it wouldn't be right for Saoirse or anyone else to say at the time Susan made her phone call to Saoirse, "Susan ought to drive her friend to the airport," why it is it right for *us*, looking back on that situation when it is past, to say, "Susan ought to have driven her friend to the airport"? I answer that it wasn't right to say, at the time, "Susan ought to drive her friend to the airport" because she wasn't *then* able to drive her friend to the airport. And it is right for us to say, later, looking back on Susan's situation, to say, "Susan ought to have driven her friend to the airport" because we, at this point in time, can say truly, "Susan was able to drive her friend to the airport." Granted, when her fuel tank was empty, she wasn't *then* able to drive her friend to the airport, but that fact doesn't make our statement "Susan was able to drive her friend to the airport" false.

Susan *was* able to drive her friend to the airport because (or so everyone would assume) she was able not to have punctured her fuel tank. In other words, our statement "Susan was able to drive her friend to the airport" doesn't imply that she was able to drive her friend to the airport *when her fuel tank was empty* but only that she was able to do it *when she made her promise*.

Before leaving the topic of the supposed distinction between moral principles and moral advice, I offer some reflections on Kant's moral philosophy and its relation to this topic.

Let us remember that Kant maintained that one of the four questions addressed by philosophy was, "What should I do?" (*Was soll ich tun*). And, as every student of philosophy knows, he proposed a justly famous answer to that question, an answer he called "the Categorical Imperative."

I think it is instructive to look at the Categorical Imperative as a piece of moral advice. There is categorical advice—advice that does not depend on the contingent circumstances of the rational agent to whom it is addressed. And there is hypothetical advice, advice that does depend on the contingent circumstances of the rational agent to whom it is addressed, advice of the kind The Ethicist gives. The Categorical Imperative is put forward *both* as a general moral principle—although of course it is stated in the imperative, not the indicative, mood—and as an answer to the question, "What should I do?" In a very abstract sense, therefore, the

Categorical Imperative can be looked at as a piece of advice—as can any other moral principle.

I conclude, tentatively but with some confidence, that my opinion that the distinction between the "should" of moral advice and the "ought" of moral principles and judgments is spurious is shared by Kant.

I further conclude that if my proposed experiment were carried out, and if (as I anticipate) the subjects all or almost all responded by affirming some variant on "Saoirse's answer makes no sense—how can she tell the father to pay for Mary's education when she knows he's broke," this result would strongly support the thesis that most people accept—tacitly, at least—the "*Ought* implies *can*" principle.

But suppose I'm wrong. Suppose that one day my proposed experiment is actually carried out and that the result turns out to be the exact opposite of what I have predicted. Suppose, that is, that all or almost all the subjects say that "You should keep your promise and pay all your daughter's college expenses" *is* the right answer to the question the letter writer asked Saoirse. I'm not convinced that this experimental result would support any interesting or important philosophical thesis. I know of only one philosophical thesis of any consequence that this result might be supposed to imply:

> The meanings of the English words "ought" and "can" are such that the "*Ought* implies *can*" principle is not the logical or conceptual truth that Kantians and most other philosophers have supposed it to be. (And so, *mutatis mutandis*, for any other language—or at least any other language in which it is possible to express the "*Ought* implies *can*" principle.)

(Let's call this "the Conceptual Thesis.") I certainly don't think that either of the theses:

> Most people don't believe that (don't have the belief that) the "*Ought* implies *can*" principle is true
> Most people believe that the "*Ought* implies *can*" principle is false

is of any philosophical importance. After all, most people might be wrong. There are a lot of things most people are wrong about. (How many philosophers would regard a survey that showed that most people accepted the Argument from Design or that most people accepted Cartesian mind-body dualism or that most people believed that only the present was real as having important philosophical implications?) Neither the popular *New York Times* article nor the original empirical study seems to me to be very clear on this point. (If you read the former carefully, you will see that the authors think that the empirical data they have collected lend significant support to the conclusion that the "*Ought* implies *can*" principle is *false*.) In any case, whether the "*Ought* implies *can*" principle is true or false, the philosophers who have *regarded* it as true have supposed that it is an analytic truth—a proposition that one can see to be true simply by reflecting on the concepts expressed by the words "ought" and "can." A refutation of the Conceptual Thesis, therefore, would be of considerable philosophical importance. And this implies that the following proposition is of considerable philosophical importance:

> If the experiment van Inwagen has presented as a thought-experiment were actually conducted, and if most of the subjects did say (contrary to van Inwagen's expectations) that Saoirse's answer to the "college expenses" question was correct, this result would show that the Conceptual Thesis was right.

And the argument for this proposition would be—would *have* to be—the following, or at least some very similar argument:

> The meanings of the words of a language are established by the way speakers use them. The subjects of the experiment have judged that "You should keep your promise and pay all your daughter's college expenses" is the right answer to the question submitted to "The Ethicist." This answer reflects the way they use the words "should" and "can"—and, since they are an unbiased and statistically significant sample of competent speakers of English—, their usage *is* English usage. That is, they are using "should" and "can" in the senses these words actually have in the English language. But their judgment about that answer to the submitted question is inconsistent with the "*Ought* implies *can*" principle. And if the "*Ought* implies *can*" principle were a logical or conceptual truth, their judgment would therefore imply that they were using at least one of the words "should" and "can" incor-

rectly—which is something that, by definition, they cannot be doing. The case is exactly parallel to the following simple case. A statistically significant sample of competent speakers of English are asked whether a cat that had lost a leg would still be a cat—whether it would still be correct to call it a "cat". They all say Yes. Therefore, the proposition "All cats have four legs," even if it happens to be true, isn't a logical or conceptual truth.

In my view, this argument is mistaken. It is mistaken because the users of concepts—that is, the users of words, for words are the "handles" we have on concepts—don't always see all the logical consequences of the propositions in which those concepts figure. (I am happy to concede that this objection to the argument applies only in the case of relatively complex propositions—propositions considerably more complex than "All cats have four legs.")

My standard example of a case in which an argument of that sort fails involves the truth-values of so-called indicative conditionals. Well over 2000 years ago, the logician Philo of Megara, a student of Diodorus Cronus, affirmed a thesis that could be expressed in the jargon of the present day as "An indicative conditional is false if its antecedent is true and its consequent false—and true otherwise." Let's call this thesis Philonianism. One frequently sees arguments against Philonianism that proceed along these lines:

> If Philonianism is right, then any conditional with a false antecedent is true—since any conditional that has a false antecedent is a conditional that doesn't have both a true antecedent and a false consequent. Well, here's a conditional with a false antecedent:

> If Munich isn't in Germany, it's in Schleswig-Holstein.

> But it's absurd to say that that conditional is true. I mean, just ask a lot of competent speakers of English whether it's true (ones who know enough geography to know that Schleswig-Holstein is a part of Germany and that Munich is in Germany and is not in Schleswig-Holstein), and every single one of them will tell you that it isn't.

Now I don't know what the result of such a survey would actually be— *but* I expect it might very well exactly be what the fictional author of that argument has predicted. I *can* tell you that the English journalist Auberon

Waugh devoted several pages of his autobiography to jeering at the ridiculous things his tutors at Oxford had tried to get him to believe during his brief sojourn as an undergraduate in that university. One of the objects of his mockery was the thesis that every conditional with a false antecedent was true, which he thought was something that only an idiot could believe. I don't know what proportion of non-philosophers and non-logicians would agree with Waugh's judgment. But let's suppose that all of them *would* agree, every single one.

I maintain this: they'd all be *wrong*. I maintain that it *is* true that if Hillary Clinton is the current president of the U.S., then Angela Merkel is its vice president, and that it *is* true that if Munich is not in Germany, it's in Schleswig-Holstein. And I'll tell you why.

Take the latter statement. It can be *proved* that if Munich isn't in Germany, then it's in Schleswig-Holstein. And the proof is, as they say, not rocket science. It's a very simple proof with only one premise: "Munich is in Germany"—which I expect you'll all be willing to grant. And here it is:

1. Munich is in Germany

and therefore,

2. Either Munich is in Germany or it's in Schleswig-Holstein

and therefore,

3. If Munich isn't in Germany, it's in Schleswig-Holstein.

The validity of this reasoning cannot be denied. Obviously, "Either Munich is in Germany or Munich is in Schleswig-Holstein" follows logically from "Munich is Germany." And, just as obviously, "If Munich is not in Germany, then Munich is in Schleswig-Holstein" follows logically from "Either Munich is in Germany or Munich is in Schleswig-Holstein." If you deny that (3) does follow from (2), you should deny that "If Frieda wasn't born in Munich, she was born in Frankfurt" follows from "Frieda was born in either Munich or Frankfurt." That is, you should deny that if something is either A or B, and it isn't A, then it's B.

Therefore, if it is indeed the case that—in a carefully controlled X-phi setting—practically everyone would say that the conditional "If Munich is not in Germany, then Munich is in Schleswig-Holstein" was false, that fact would be of no philosophical interest. Of course, apart from its use as an example to illustrate a philosophical point, "If Munich is not in Germany, then Munich is in Schleswig-Holstein" is a totally uninteresting statement—if only because it's a statement that no one would ever *make*.

But a statement doesn't have to be interesting to be true and a statement can be true even if no one would ever make it. Consider, for example, the statements "There are more than thirty-two trees in the Amazonian rain-forest" and "Several Oxford colleges are not veterinary hospitals." Those are both truths, but they are uninteresting truths and it's pretty hard to imagine a conversation that starts, "Say, Frank, I've been meaning to tell you that there are more than thirty-two trees in the Amazonian rain forest" or "Frances, you should be aware that several Oxford colleges aren't veterinary hospitals." And the thesis that all conditionals with false antecedents are true doesn't imply that the conditional "If Munich is not in Germany, then Munich is in Schleswig-Holstein" is interesting. It only implies that it's true.

I maintain, therefore, that if you asked lots of people whether that conditional was true or false, and they all said it was false, that wouldn't prove anything about the meanings of the words "if" and "then"—for the simple reason that all those people would be wrong.

And that's precisely what I'd say if my proposed survey concerning the "*Ought* implies *can*" principle were conducted and (contrary to my expectations) all or almost all the respondents said that the right answer to the "college expenses" question was that the near-penniless father should pay all his daughter's college expenses—namely, that wouldn't prove anything because all the respondents would be wrong. (I hasten to add that I *don't* think that the very many of the respondents would in fact give that response. That is, I stand by my prediction that all or almost all the respondents to the survey would say, correctly, that "You should pay all her college expenses" was an obviously wrong answer to the father's question.)

I conclude, finally, that the "*Ought* implies *can*" principle is an analytical truth—or, at any rate, even if it isn't an analytical truth, the X-phi study that we have been examining lends no support to the thesis that it isn't. And, therefore, whatever the solution to the problem of free will is, there's no reason to suppose that it lies in the falsity of the "*Ought* implies *can*" principle.

References

Chituc, V., and P. Henne. 2016. The Data Against Kant. *The New York Times*, February 16. https://www.nytimes.com/2016/02/21/opinion/sunday/the-data-against-kant.html.

Chituc, V., P. Henne, W. Sinnott-Armstrong, and F. De Brigard. 2016. Blame, Not Ability, Impacts Moral 'Ought' Judgments for Impossible Actions: Toward an Empirical Refutation of 'ought' Implies 'can'. *Cognition* 150: 20–25.

Kant, I. 1793. *Die Religion innerhalb der Grenzen der bloßen Vernunft*. Königsberg: Friedrich Nicolovius. Citations of Kant's works refer to the volume and page number in the Academy Edition of Immanuel Kant, Gesammelte Schriften (Berlin: Walter de Gruyter and predecessors, 1900 sqq).

Name Index[1]

---

[1] Note: Page numbers followed by 'n' refer to notes.

Subject Index[1]

---

[1] Note: Page numbers followed by 'n' refer to notes.

© The Author(s), under exclusive license to Springer Nature Switzerland AG 2021   **337**
M. Hausmann, J. Noller (eds.), *Free Will*,
https://doi.org/10.1007/978-3-030-61136-1